INSIDE STALIN'S RUSSIA

THE DIARIES OF
READER BULLARD
1930-1934

INSIDE
STALIN'S RUSSIA

THE DIARIES OF
READER BULLARD
1930–1934

EDITED BY JULIAN AND MARGARET BULLARD

with a foreword by
DOUGLAS HURD

DAY BOOKS
OXFORDSHIRE

ISBN 0 953 22131 8

A catalogue record for this book is available from the British Library

This edition first published by Day Books, 2000
© Julian and Margaret Bullard, 2000
The moral right of the editors has been asserted

Printed in England by St Edmundsbury Press Ltd, Bury St Edmunds, Suffolk.
This publication is printed on acid-free paper

Day Books, 3 Park Street, Charlbury, Oxfordshire OX7 3PS, UK

CONTENTS

ACKNOWLEDGEMENTS

The editors would like to express their gratitude for help and encouragement received from many sources, and in particular to Douglas Hurd for his Foreword; to Gill Bennett and her team of historians at the Foreign Office; to Hugo Brunner; to Richard Davies, librarian at the Brotherton Library, University of Leeds; to E.C. Hodgkin, editor of two volumes of RWB's letters; to Geoff and Kathy Murrell for help with historical notes and many points of contemporary detail; to Sylvia Platt with her scrupulous eye for detail; to Antonia Bullard, who helped us surmount the first obstacle by cracking the code; to the scholars and librarians of All Souls and St Antony's College, Oxford, who were so generous with their advice; to those who discovered the fate of Pyotr Andreyevich Kulagin; and finally to our publisher Edward Fenton for the enormous trouble he has taken to improve notes, spot inconsistencies and inaccuracies, and for his excellent advice at all times.

ILLUSTRATIONS

Front cover (based on a 1928 poster by Vladimir and Georgii Stenberg, advertising the magazine *30 Dnei*): portrait of Stalin by I. Brodsky (1935) reproduced by permission of the Society for Co-Operation in Russian and Soviet Studies. Back cover: poster by G. Roze ('The Five-Year Plan is not Failing. Break the Paws of the Mischief-Makers and Meddlers!') reproduced by permission of the Victoria and Albert Museum.

1, 2. R.W. Bullard.

3. A page from the diary.

4. Moscow, Leningrad and surrounding area, c.1930. (Map drawn by Olive Pearson.)

5. William Strang. (Photograph reproduced by courtesy of the Foreign and Commonwealth Office.)

6. The Bullard family, October 1931.

7. Lady Muriel Paget, 1912. (National Portrait Gallery Archive; reproduced by courtesy of the Paget family.)

8. 'The "Freedom" of the Bourgeois Press.' (Reproduced by permission of the Victoria and Albert Museum.)

9. Poster for anti-slavery meeting. (Brotherton Library, University of Leeds; reproduced by courtesy of the Paget family.)

10. Sosnovka, the *dacha* built on the northern outskirts of Leningrad for the use of the Distressed British Subjects. (Brotherton Library, University of Leeds; reproduced by courtesy of the Paget family.)

11. George Bernard Shaw in the USSR, 1931. (Brotherton Library, University of Leeds; reproduced by courtesy of the Paget family.)

12. Group of unidentified Distressed British Subjects and Relief Association workers outside Sosnovka. (Brotherton Library, University of Leeds; reproduced by courtesy of the Paget family.)

13. Tehran, December 1943. Facing camera: Anthony Eden, Reader Bullard, Winston Churchill, Marshal Voroshilov and Josef Stalin.

14. Miss Daunt in old age. (Reproduced by courtesy of H.T. Daunt Esq.)

☆

FOREWORD

In 1961 the distinguished British diplomat Sir Reader Bullard wrote his memoirs under the title *The Camels Must Go*. As this inspired title suggests, Sir Reader devoted most of his recollections to his diplomatic career in the Middle East, during which he progressed upwards to end as Ambassador in Tehran. He did not pay great attention to those years in the early 1930s when he served as Consul General in Moscow and then in Leningrad. His son Julian (himself a distinguished diplomat with a sharp but kindly mind) has done right to rescue and publish Reader Bullard's diaries of that time.

Reader Bullard wrote in a laconic, almost abrupt style. The wit and the occasional emotion can be detected below the surface, but they are never allowed to break out into the open. Indeed, the very first paragraph—with its details about tinned herrings and Ryvita—could have come from one of Evelyn Waugh's travel stories of the same period.

This laid-back style is particularly suited to the business of exploring and experiencing the Soviet system. Bullard did not come to Moscow with any prejudice against that system, if anything the reverse; but his natural shrewdness prevented him from being deceived. There are no denunciations of the cruelty which he began to find around him, just the straightforward record of facts. 'In 1927 the Vladivostok Consul's office messenger said he expected to be put in prison for a few days but didn't anticipate anything worse. He was optimistic, for they shot him. His wife used to bring him clean linen and so on, and one day she was told she needn't bring him any more.' A few months after he heard this story, Bullard was invited to meet a highly distinguished British historian. 'Dined with Strang and the Tawneys last night,' he recorded. 'Very pleasant. Tawney rather surprised at the degree of repression he finds here, and wondering whether it is necessary.'

By then Bullard had realised that repression was not an add-on which could be abandoned, but the very foundation of the regime. At least Tawney realised that something was going astray. Most of the progressive

☆

visitors whom Bullard encountered still believed that they were seeing the future and that somehow it could be made to work. Later, in Leningrad, Bullard became closely acquainted with a local OGPU leader. The story of his rise and fall is itself a classic tale of how Stalin's system worked.

Julian Bullard has written an introduction to his father's diaries which sets the scene admirably, so that there is not much to add. The readiness of Anglo-Saxons to be deceived was not confined to the Soviet Union. I remember exactly the same phenomenon during my own first diplomatic posting in Peking between 1954 and 1956. The same kind of sympathetic visitors were whisked round the early show-pieces of the People's Republic of China. They emerged deeply impressed. They were indignant at even the slightest reservations which we might express out of our own experience when they dropped in for a nightcap at the British Embassy after a day interviewing reformed prostitutes, radiant peasants, and employers apparently longing to have their businesses stolen from them by the State. Many of us have reservations about modern journalism, believing that its habits make successful government in democratic countries more difficult; at the same time we must acknowledge that it has also become more difficult for tyrants and torturers to conceal what they are up to. It is not impossible to imagine a new dictator in Russia, but he would hardly be able to obliterate the truth and deceive the world in the manner so cogently described here by Bullard.

DOUGLAS HURD

INTRODUCTION

When R.W. Bullard stepped into the train at Liverpool Street station bound for Moscow in October 1930 he had a precise and definite objective in mind. He was attracted not principally by the pay-rise, nor the promotion, though both could only be welcome to a man of forty-four with a wife and four (later five) children at home in Oxford. There was also more to it than a change of scene after twenty years in the consular service in the Near and Middle East. Russia had long been a magnet for him. At Trebizond in 1910, his chief distraction had been to drink tea and talk French with the Russian vice-consul. His set of Chekhov (in Russian) was inscribed 'Jeddah 1924'. But this too did not represent the whole story. The move to Russia was his chance, and the only chance he was likely to get, to judge for himself the success or failure of the socialist experiment.

Today, after the passage of seventy years, and with the collapse of socialism in almost every country where it has been tried, it requires an effort of the imagination to understand the feelings of the British apologists for Russia in the 1920s and 30s. Capitalism, they argued, was visibly failing: the strikes and hunger marches were evidence of that. But in Russia a different mood prevailed. If some had had to suffer—the Tsar and his court, the rich peasantry, the officer class and the bourgeoisie—were not these precisely the people whose selfish and incompetent management had been the ruin of pre-war Russia and the cause of the Revolution?

In his book *Debts of Honour*, Michael Foot has written of that time: 'How deeply the Left craved to give the benefit of all the doubts to Moscow! No one who did not live through that period can appreciate how overwhelming that craving was.'[1] Margaret Cole also explained her feelings in her biography of her husband: 'We saw in Soviet Russia the

---

[1] Michael Foot, *Debts of Honour*. Davis Poynter, 1980.

★

negation of the immoralities of industrial capitalism and the system of private profit. We were eager to follow the gleam . . . . The hopes for what the makers of the Revolution set out to achieve compared with the dead hopelessness of breadlines and the dole were more than enough to outweigh doubts.'[2]

There is a note of idealism here which at the outset Bullard might have endorsed. Having started life a poor boy in the East End of London, with a makeshift education, he felt an instinctive sympathy with the Soviet experiment. But he found himself sickened by the miserable quality of life of the man in the street, and the lies and oppression on which the regime rested. In his diary, Reader Bullard paints life as it really was for most people; he describes the food shortages, the dishonesty and cruelty of officials, the abject living conditions, the forced labour, torture and imprisonment.

The official Soviet answer would have been that no price was too high to pay for speedy industrialisation and the collectivisation of agriculture; the Consul General, however, could not conceive of any goals which could possibly justify the application of such methods as he witnessed daily. It vexed him that so many of his visitors accepted the figures and explanations provided by their guides, and he never tired of trying to persuade them that the true picture might be other than it seemed. Yet if the Coles, like the Webbs and Bernard Shaw, proved incorrigible, there was at least the refreshing voice of Malcolm Muggeridge, then a young reporter and later a leader-writer on the *Manchester Guardian*, who did not accept the necessity of class-war or believe that the abolition of property, profit and religion and the fight against illiteracy justified either the hunger or the ruthlessness of a police-state.

Following the ARCOS raid in May 1927, when hostile printed material was found in the London office of the Soviet Foreign Trade Organisation, political relations were broken off and the trade agreement of 1924 suspended. After the change of government in Britain in 1929, diplomatic relations were restored, and a procedure was agreed for handling certain difficult matters such as fisheries and claims; while in a separate agreement all hostile propaganda was mutually abjured. It was a wary relationship, with little warmth on either side. Trade was small in total, with an imbalance in favour of the USSR. Bullard's responsibility for British interests brought him into contact with many of the foreigners employed in Russian industry at that time.

[2] Margaret Cole, *Life of G.D.H. Cole*: Macmillan, 1971.

☆

Visits from experts in turbines, fisheries, flax and paper were among the raw material from which he built up his judgements on food supplies, industrial output, health and, of particular concern in England, on whether the Russians were or were not using forced (or slave) labour, contrary to international agreements and possibly threatening jobs in this country. Bullard soon reached the conclusion that the conditions of life in logging enterprises north of Leningrad, for example, amounted to forced labour. As to the related charge of 'dumping', Bullard's view was that the question was meaningless since true costs existed nowhere in the Soviet economy.

Into this chilly Anglo-Soviet pool, on 11 March 1933, there dropped, like a heavy stone, the Russian seizure of the Moscow office of the Metropolitan-Vickers Company and the arrest of six members of its British staff, together with some of their Russian employees. The new government in London responded to the sentence of imprisonment on two of the engineers with a selective embargo on British imports from the Soviet Union, a measure repealed only when the condemned men were permitted to leave the country. The Metro-Vickers affair overhung the transaction of all other Anglo-Soviet business for several weeks. Bullard was intensely interested in what could have caused the engineers Thornton and MacDonald to plead guilty to the trumped-up charges made against them.

Six months after arriving in Moscow, nervous about the possibility of prying OGPU eyes and nervous of getting others into trouble, he had started to use a primitive home-made code. An example from 1 May 1931 reads: 'W- tot ma d so nt Red Sq. trz tome vt tw-o f 2½ rs aww st-g ltti t Army Commander adminstered t oath tot troops. tz m- tb impressive b tz solg a trz some repj ta tz merely boring.' Presumably he felt safer in Leningrad, for the code was not used after his transfer, except on 29 July 1931 to record his visit to the Hermitage with Sir Robert Witt, for reasons which the entry makes obvious. But on 22 April 1933, in the middle of the Metro-Vickers crisis, Bullard destroyed his duplicates of the diary, fearing that diplomatic relations between Moscow and London might be broken off and he might not have time enough to destroy all his papers.

A recurrent theme in the diary is the extent to which Russian Jews occupied senior posts in the Soviet system and exercised influence on policy and events. He was not the first to notice the prevalence of Jewish faces and names in positions of authority. Bertrand Russell had written to Lady Ottoline Morrell on 25 June 1920: 'Imagine yourself governed in every detail by a mixture of Sidney Webb and Rufus Isaacs, and you

★

will have a picture of modern Russia.'[3] The theme has been extensively researched and written about. Arkady Vaksberg comments: '1920–1934 was a period of State protection for Russian Jewry. Jews moved into leadership posts in all spheres of Party, Komsomol, State, union, economic and cultural life.'[4] This interested Bullard greatly, as is evident both in passing references and in the brief but cogent report which he sent to Moscow about minorities in the Leningrad area (p.160). He noticed that Jews were well established in the Communist Party hierarchy: the foreign minister and his wife were Jews, as were the two top men in the Leningrad Commissariat for Foreign Affairs and also the Party representatives in factories and Pioneer camps he visited. Mordechai Altshuler records that Jews were prominent in the secret police and in journalism.[5] Bullard noted that the journalists who reported on the Metro-Vickers trial, and the Intourist guides who worked for the OGPU, were all Jewish. The signatories who protested about sabotage had Jewish names. Not surprisingly perhaps he noticed that most concert-goers, musicians and the entire fur industry seemed to be Jewish. In the grain-growing areas, they were in charge of keeping the peasants in order. They seemed able to get more favourable treatment when they applied to emigrate. In fact what Bullard describes was a period when there was a window of relative tolerance for Jews in Russia. He observed that those who suffered most under the Soviet regime were Slav, and the survivors largely Semite. Since his sympathies were always for the underdog he resented this, but to deduce from his repeated mention of Jews that he was anti-Semitic would not be correct.[6]

A large part of a consul's life is made up of dealing with shipping, trade and the affairs of British subjects abroad, and at the end of June 1931 the office of consul general was transferred to Leningrad, the major centre of business for these matters. Another concern was the plight of the 'Distressed British Subjects' (DBSs),[7] of whom there were

[3] *The Autobiography of Bertrand Russell, vol. II, 1914–1944*: Allen and Unwin, 1968.
[4] Arkady Vaksberg, *Stalin against the Jews*, trans. Antonina W. Bouis: Knopf, 1994. See also Nora Levin, *The Jews in the Soviet Union since 1917*: New York University Press, 1988; and Z. Gitelman, *Jewish Nationality and Soviet Politics*: Princeton University Press, 1972.
[5] Mordechai Altshuler, *Distribution of the Jewish Population of the USSR*: Hebrew University of Jerusalem, Centre for Research and Documentation of East European Jewry, 1993.
[6] RWB's personal abhorrence of anti-Semitism is evidenced in his *Letters from Tehran*: I.B. Tauris, 1991, p.210.
[7] A category of British citizens abroad for whom the British government took limited responsibility.

☆

144 in Leningrad alone. To deal with the large numbers holding British passports, with little income and sometimes only a distant connection with this country, a charity had been set up called the British Subjects in Russia Relief Association, whose moving spirit was the remarkable Muriel Paget, born Lady Muriel Evelyn Vernon Finch-Hatton. In 1915, fired with enthusiasm by Professor Bernard Pares' description of conditions in Russia,[8] she had been instrumental in establishing a base hospital for other ranks in Grand Duke Dmitri's baroque palace on the Neva, and later she took charge of a field hospital, first near Kiev and then near Odessa. In his life of Lady Muriel, Wilfrid Blunt describes her method of working, which shows that Bullard was not alone in finding her difficult to work with: 'Lady Muriel knew nothing of Russia at first hand, and would not wait until she had felt the atmosphere of the place. She did not understand what could, and what could not, be done; she knew next to nothing about the inside running of a hospital, and could not understand what did, and what did not, lie within her sphere of action. And she could not bear opposition.'[9]

In 1924, after hearing of the plight of British subjects in Russia, she decided to do what she could to help. A grant of £100 per annum from the Treasury was supplemented by money that she begged from wealthy friends, and spent on sending food parcels to Russia. Dissatisfied with the results of this arrangement, Lady Muriel came out herself, bringing with her Miss Dorothea Daunt, a social worker who had worked in the Society of Friends' Famine Relief Mission to South Russia from 1922 to 1925.[10] Lady Muriel held that half the trouble with the DBSs was quite simply depression, and she made a point of sailing into dirty shared kitchen-quarters wearing impeccable Paris outfits, which she believed would brighten up these people's lives. A *dacha* which she called Sosnovka was built on 25 acres of land made available by the Soviet authorities, and later the Paget Relief Centre for British Subjects was opened in the Krasnaya Ulitsa, Leningrad, where a gramophone record of King George V's Christmas message was played to every newcomer.[11]

[8] Bernard Pares, *Day by Day with the Russian Army, 1914–15*: Constable, 1915.
[9] Wilfrid Blunt, *Lady Muriel*: Methuen, 1962.
[10] 'I cannot speak too highly of the admirable work that Miss Daunt has already begun to do,' Lady Muriel wrote home to her husband. 'She is full of resource, tact and knowledge of local traditions and at the same time has real affection for the Russians and human sympathy that inspires her with a desire to do everything that she can to help the Distressed British Subjects.' (This and all subsequent extracts from Lady Muriel's letters and diaries are taken from the Paget Collection, MS 1405, in the Leeds University Library Russian Archive.)
[11] Una Pope-Hennessy, *The Closed and Forbidden City*: Hutchinson, 1938.

Lady Muriel's obituary (*The Times*, 21 June 1938) described her 'tiny voice, high-pitched and sometimes scarcely audible, and a little chuckling laugh which possessed her whole frame'. Any civil servant would have been critical of her contempt for rules and regulations, and the Consul General in Leningrad was no exception, but she had nothing but praise and gratitude for his handling of affairs, and must she not often have helped to relieve a dull existence for him?

In Bullard's memoirs *The Camels Must Go*, published in 1961, his Russian experience was condensed into forty pages. The present selection from his diaries, though scarcely more than half the size of the original material, is on a scale which we hope will allow the reader to appreciate his acuity and his wit, his range of interests and depth of emotion.

JULIAN AND MARGARET BULLARD

FURTHER READING

Bullard RW. *The Camels Must Go*: Faber and Faber, 1961.

Bullard RW. *Letters from Tehran*, ed. Hodgkin E: I.B. Tauris, 1991.

Bullard RW. *Two Kings in Arabia*, ed. Hodgkin E: Garnett, 1993.

Conquest R. *The Great Terror: A Reassessment*: Oxford University Press, 1990.

Degras J, ed. *Soviet Documents on Foreign Policy, vol. II, 1925–32*: Oxford University Press, 1952.

Garros V et al., eds. *Intimacy and Terror: Soviet Diaries of the 1930s*: New Press, 1995.

Getty JA. *Origins of the Great Purges*: Cambridge University Press, 1985.

Hosking G. *A History of the Soviet Union*: Fontana, 1985.

Hughes M. *Inside the Enigma: British Officials in Russia 1900–1939*: Hambledon Press, 1997.

Martin K. *Low's Russian Sketchbook*: Gollancz, 1932.

Woodward EL, Butler RD'O. *Documents on British Foreign Policy 1919–1939, 2nd series, vol. VII*: HMSO, 1958.

☆

DIARIES
1930-1934

A CITY RUN TO SEED

MOSCOW, 1930

THE LATE 1920s had seen the beginnings of Stalin's worst excesses. The first Five-Year Plan, which called for forced collectivisation of agriculture and rapid industrialisation, had been introduced in 1928. The following year Stalin tightened his grip on power by expelling Trotsky and dismissing the leader of the Communist International, Nikolai Bukharin. He also called for a 'counter-offensive against the kulaks', and by March 1929 almost 60 per cent of peasant households had been forcibly collectivised with extreme brutality. The peasants responded with large-scale slaughter of cattle and horses, plunging the countryside into chaos. Stalin then sounded a partial retreat, criticising the 'excessive zeal' of local officials.

It was against this background that, after a thirty-month suspension, diplomatic relations between Great Britain and the Soviet Union were re-established in December 1929, and Sir Esmond Ovey was sent to Moscow as ambassador. In April 1930 a temporary Anglo-Soviet trade agreement was concluded. Suspicion between the two countries remained strong, however: and in the summer of 1930 there was renewed hardening of communist ideology, when the Sixteenth Communist Party Congress called for a long and determined struggle to complete the process of collectivisation.

31 Oct. Left Liverpool Street station 8.15 p.m., 29 October. Arrived Moscow two days later. Met by Pott, acting Consul General. Found that I must share a room at the Savoy Hotel with him. Living conditions are much better *for us* now than they were even two or three months ago. In the summer Pott was living on tinned herrings eaten with Ryvita in his bedroom.

2 Nov. Sunday. Pott is producing all kinds of good things out of tins for our meals. He cooks sausages etc. over an electric stove.

I walked through Red Square. Loudspeaker roaring at each corner and hardly anyone taking any notice. Went along river, Kremlin looking beautiful in sun. Saw our new Embassy—a fine building.[1]

Dined in Ambassador's rooms. His wife prefers to talk French. He prefers to talk all the time, so it doesn't matter. Tried *kvass*. Afterwards the Ambassador, Lady Ovey and the Strangs played beginners' bridge. Walker and I read.

5 Nov. The thirteenth anniversary of the October Revolution which occurred on 26 October 1917 (Old Style) is commemorated on the corresponding day New Style, viz. 7 November. The streets are being covered with red bunting and inscriptions, platforms and hoardings are being erected, the busts of Lenin, always numerous, are being multiplied, and in many windows are cardboard groups of the simple cartoon order. In one MacDonald, Briand[2] and other statesmen, very small, express surprise at the healthy size to which the USSR has grown in thirteen years. In another a small Tsar and his wife head a procession of people disappearing into a gulf—a capitalist, an official, a tsarist officer. Noticed a sign on a shop: 'No milk today.'

6 Nov. These partings with one's wife and children, one's spirits go up and down. The last week before one leaves home it is very bad. The journey keeps one busy, and the first few days after one arrives there is much to do and to think about. I'm now in the third stage, when I have time to think of what I have lost and of the fifteen years from now until I am sixty and can retire.

7 Nov. More cheerful today. The bag comes tomorrow, with Miriam's[3] first letter. By the way, why didn't I telegraph to her when I arrived? The first day my head was aching and I couldn't think straight, but I ought to have thought about it next day. The first confusion, which must have been great when the Embassy came back about a year ago, is diminishing. A question to consider is whether the Consul General ought not to be at Leningrad, where there is an independent post with more varied work.

[1] The new Embassy, on the Sofiiskaya Embankment, had once been the home of the Kharitonenko family, who had done well in the sugar trade. The British government paid £20,000 key money (purportedly to find accommodation for the former occupants), and a rent of £4500 a year for twenty years. This handsome building is still the British Embassy.

[2] At this time British prime minister and French foreign minister, respectively.

[3] Miriam (or 'M') was RWB's wife. Her father was A.L. Smith, master of Balliol 1916–24.

11 Nov. Newspapers have a fantastic story of an intervention plot in which the Poles, the French, and even the British are alleged to be concerned. T.E. Lawrence is dragged in. The revelations are suspected to be mainly an excuse for inability to carry out the Five-Year Plan.

12 Nov. A terrible show last night—an evening reception at 10.00 at the Italian Embassy to celebrate their King's birthday. At 3 a.m. the Ambassador and Lady Ovey stopped playing cards and left.[4] I was given a lift in Patons' car, and on way we bumped over an island and the car wouldn't go any farther. Luckily Ambassador's car came by and rescued us, but it was 4 o'clock before I got to bed.

Circular letter, 13 Nov. My first impression of Moscow was of a city run to seed. The pavements all need repair; here and there are great holes full, at the moment, of water. The roadways are all cobbled, with mud oozing up between the cobbles. The shop windows are usually dirty and often broken, and the fronts of all the buildings are shabby and dilapidated. There are a few new buildings, e.g. a fine post- and telegraph-office which has been built by a German firm, but there are not many of them.

When I arrived the city was busy with preparations for celebrating the thirteenth anniversary of the October Revolution. Having only just arrived I have no *carte d'identité*, so I did not go to the parade. A lot of planes were up, and a small dirigible balloon. I expected the streets to be much more crowded. We got to the office and back without difficulty. There were many red streamers across the streets, most of them with inscriptions relating to the Five-Year Plan. This is a scheme to increase industrial production to given targets in five years. The scheme has been modified by an announcement that it is to be carried out in four years, and by the dropping of three months as 'not counting'. The great slogan is: 'The Five-Year Plan in four years.' The same statements, slogans and figures appear in all the papers, are thrown on to all the screens before the films begin, are given in the form of lectures and news on the wireless, and are served up in speeches in factories and clubs.

I find that my Russian is adequate for conversation with the DBSs, customs officials, messengers and the like, but I have not yet had a chance to test it more severely. Except for the few officials whom we

---

[4] The official birthday of the monarch (in this case of King Victor Emmanuel III) is the occasion for a large party in embassies abroad. In those days an ambassador's staff were not permitted to leave before he did.

have to see on business, we have no chance to talk to Russians. The only thing I can do is to read, to go to the theatre now and then, and to listen to lectures and propaganda on the wireless. Today I read this in an article about a collective farm: 'They are agitating to have a crèche in the well-lighted and spacious house of the exiled priest.'

A little snow on the ground this morning—the first I have seen. By night it was nearly all gone. I have been able to buy a Russian wireless set (crystal) for about £1, and with a pair of earphones, which I got from an Englishman for £1.1.0, I can get all the Moscow stations. Heard a woman announcer (very clear) saying something about the production of bicycles, followed by a gramophone concert of Italian opera for the benefit of such workers as happen to be resting. There is no general day of rest here. Everyone has one day in five free but not necessarily the same day as his pals or his children.

When I see the queues of people waiting at the food and other shops every morning I feel that we are very fortunate; it must be cold work standing in queues this weather. Some of the windows are 'dressed', but a good deal of the stuff is dummy. I pass every day a confectioner's shop full of empty chocolate-boxes, and a provision shop which I thought well stocked until I saw that the butter was yellow paper and Dutch cheeses painted wood.

22 Nov. Lady Muriel Paget[5] arrived to see about DBSs. I dined with her at Grand Hotel. She lent me G.B. Stern's *Mosaic* and I read in bed and again this morning from 6.00 to 8.00. Went to anti-religious museum, which is housed in a church—a strange mixture. Greek Orthodox icons, the skeletons of various saints, an ugly figure of a priest computing his winnings on an abacus, a model of an anti-Jewish pogrom, with priests carrying the cross round while the massacre goes on—realistic and dreadful. There were many exhibits which seemed irrelevant—merely anti-imperial. One dreadful case contained photographs of men with the organ of generation amputated and women with their breasts cut off.

24 Nov. Several inches of snow, but the men already at work with wooden shovels pushing it into the road. Wore my fur coat. Wish I had a fur cap and my snow-boots.

Went to see the few DBSs in Moscow with Lady Muriel, Lady Ovey

---

[5] Lady Muriel Paget had set up the British Subjects in Russia Relief Association (see p.7).

and Miss Daunt, a social worker whom Lady M has brought out to look after the DBSs in Leningrad.

Robinsons. Mr R, a blind jockey aged about sixty-five; as a 'social parasite', is 'third category'[6] for food. Wife a brave, cheerful woman. One child—a boy of twenty-five who is deaf and dumb and imbecile. The Relief Fund gives them 50 roubles per month and occasional gifts of clothes. Oil stove burning with a wretched stew on it. No wood for heating. Lady M gave Mrs Robinson 40 roubles for fuel. No food in house but a little black bread and a scrap of a loaf of sugar.

Mrs Stock. British but speaks only Russian and German. Lives with daughter. Mrs S thin as a skeleton. In great pain, and doctor says she cannot last more than two or three weeks. Daughter's husband can rarely keep a job because of bourgeois origin. Daughter and boys cover crayons with paper and make rough boxes for them to earn a living. At prices paid, a pretty poor living.

25 Nov. Visited Miss Redgate with Lady Ovey, Lady Muriel and Miss Daunt. Gave her half of a one-pound tin of cocoa milk, the other half was sent to Mrs Stock. Miss Redgate, aged eighty-one. Remembers no English but 'Sank you' and 'Gentle Jesus, meek and mild, look upon a—' there she stops. Full of courage, and unwilling to ask for anything.

Had difficulty in getting home because of organised demonstrations to demand the punishment of the men who are being tried today on charge of organising sabotage and foreign intervention. There must have been miles of processions, with bands and banners. I saw companies of Red soldiers marching. All the banners in the same strain—'We demand justice against . . . , etc.' One huge placard was standing in road outside Opera: 'Let us strengthen the sword of the dictatorship of the proletariat—the OGPU.' As the OGPU is already empowered to shoot without trial and has exercised the privilege on many people who were accused of hoarding small change, they would appear to need very little support.

Lady Muriel took me to see *Squaring the Circle* at the Little Stage Theatre, a dependency of the Government Artistic Theatre—light yet sympathetic comedy. Snowing hard when we came out.

---

[6] Food entitlement was by categories. The first category consisted of members of the Soviet government, Communist Party and Red Army, as well as manual workers. Employees of Soviet institutions, students, professors, teachers, doctors and intellectual workers were in the second category. The third category comprised members of the bourgeoisie, the unemployed and the elderly ('social parasites').

☆

26 Nov. Lady Muriel left for Leningrad. She is a kind steam-roller, but I prefer not to be in her track. She has a scheme for building at Leningrad, on a site at Dyetskoye (formerly Tsarskoye) Syelo[7] which she hopes the Soviet Government will lend us for forty years, an almshouse to accommodate all such DBSs as can be persuaded to live in it. It will be appallingly expensive, if it is built, but no one knows what it would cost—least of all Lady M. I wrote for skates yesterday. The others have been skating for several days on the flooded tennis-court.

Sledges have taken the place of carriages.

27 Nov. Went to Thanksgiving dinner with Chamberlin, American correspondent of *Manchester Guardian*. Other three guests all Americans—Deuss (Hearst Agency), Junius Wood (*Chicago Daily News*), Smith (General Motors). It appears that the way to get things done is to put a complaint in a press message: the complaint is cut out but the grievance is remedied, e.g. correspondents used to have to wire as interviews summaries of statements which were simply handed to them by the Narkomindel janitor, but this was stopped when Wood ended with a message 'The statement was as usual handed to us by the office boy'—though that part was cut out by the censor.

None of the journalists think there's much in this hysterical tale about the eight accused. Several Russians had suggested to Smith that Ramzin,[8] whose long confession is the basis of the trial, was an *agent provocateur*. Walton, who has been to the trial every day, says the chief feature is the complete indifference of the accused—though that might be because the certainty of death is better than life without hope.

Went with Walton to hear the trial of the eight 'wreckers' and 'organisers of intervention'. It is being held in an enormous building which was formerly the Nobles' Club[9] or meeting-place. The great hall packed with people. The accused sitting in a box, nearly all with headphones on, microphones in front of President of Court, Public

---

[7] The Imperial village, Tsarskoye Syelo, had been renamed 'Children's Village' after the Revolution.

[8] L.K. Ramzin (1887–1948) had been closely connected with Lenin's electrification strategy. In 1930 he was arrested with many other prominent Soviet scientists and the economist Kondratiev, all of whom confessed to being agents of foreign powers. This was the first public confession by prominent Party members and caused widespread consternation. It later became known that Ramzin had agreed to denounce his fellow scientists in return for a total amnesty for himself. (See Arkady Vaksberg, *The Persecutor and the Prey*: Weidenfeld and Nicolson, 1990.)

[9] The Nobles' Club was renamed 'The Hall of Columns' after the Revolution and used for show trials. It is now the House of Unions.

Prosecutor Krylenko,[10] and the accused or the witness who is being examined. The accused appeared to be uncommon calm. Soldiers with fixed bayonets all over the place. A considerable crowd outside, for the feelings of the people have been cleverly worked on. There were at least eight searchlights in the hall. The first day they were flashed on the accused so that photographs could be taken. Walton says they all sat up and put their collars and ties straight. A loudspeaker near us reported what the speaker was saying, but even Walton could not follow all that was said. Krylenko seemed to be trying to get the witness to incriminate himself. A disagreeable feature of the business was that in the corridor just outside the courtroom was a bookstall full of propaganda against the 'wreckers' etc. and with inscriptions to the same effect. Of course the Bolsheviks think our legal system and professions of a desire for fair play are all bourgeois humbug.

It was a good jest when the accused were asked whether they had been well-treated while under detention. All said they had, and one man said he had put on weight. At this implied compliment to the Lubyanka[11] as a health resort, the whole audience—carefully picked as it is—laughed so loud and so long that the proceedings were interrupted for a considerable time.

1 Dec. Drew my first salary on Consul General's pay. Total salary and allowances at present £1950 per annum. Todd, probationary Vice-Consul, arrived early today with wife and large dog, also furniture for my immense new offices, suggesting in their relation to the small amount of work I do the proportions of stellar space to the earth.

2 Dec. The 'wreckers' trial drags on. No one can make out the truth, though no one accepts it at its face value. It is a revolting show if they intend to execute the accused—the searchlights, the loudspeakers, the judges and the Public Prosecutor smoking cigarettes, the two judges taken from the workshop bench to sit on the judicial, the propaganda. The Narkomindel are denying all knowledge of the Ambassador's protest made on 30 November on orders from the Foreign Secretary. Why should those accused roll out all these confessions and mutual

[10] R.H. Bruce Lockhart described Nikolai Krylenko as 'the most repulsive type I came across in all my connections with the Bolsheviks' (*Memoirs of a British Agent*: Putnam, 1932). Disliked by Stalin for personal reasons, Krylenko was shot without trial in 1938. (David King, *The Commissar Vanishes*: Canongate Books, 1997.)
[11] Lubyanka no. 7 was the headquarters of the secret police (OGPU) and a prison. Before the Revolution it had contained the offices of an insurance company.

accusations so glibly and at such length? Have they been promised their lives, or at least that their relations will not be tortured or exiled or made *lishentsy*, i.e. not only deprived of all political rights but of all right to get food and clothes etc. except in the open market. In the old days the Russian revolutionaries rarely confessed.

3 Dec. When relations with the USSR were broken off in 1927 the Vladivostok Consul's office messenger said he expected to be put in prison for a few days but didn't anticipate anything worse. He was optimistic, for they shot him. His wife used to bring him clean linen and so on, and one day she was told she needn't bring him any more.

4 Dec. Ambassador has made three protests this week about the trial of the wreckers, because of our alleged connection.

Dr Bell, a BS born in Russia, lectures at Leningrad University. Recently the director informed him his lectures were contrary to Marxian economics and hinted in plain language that he must alter his talks, i.e. make out the situation is more favourable—or be sacked. He is refusing. If he were a Russian what would he do?

Last night the hotel restaurant band woke me with a particularly loud *morceau* at 1.45 a.m. Feeling wakeful I made myself some cocoa and then read for an hour. I am re-reading *Anna Karenina* (in Russian). To read *Anna Karenina* now, in Moscow, gives one an almost eerie feeling. The world in which Kitty and Anna and Vronsky moved has completely disappeared; there are no longer in Moscow any people like them; and to read of them in the town where they lived makes one feel that there is a more real world behind the one which we see here every day but have almost no contact with.

5 Dec. I am forty-five today. I have invited our mess to come and celebrate the fifteenth anniversary of my retirement—*par anticipation*. I fitted up a praying-wheel. It is clear that large numbers of people here are hypnotised by words and phrases which they only half-understand and I suggest that it would save a lot of trouble if they had the words and phrases written in a cylinder and twirled it round, as the Lama-ites do. I made one out of a cocoa tin, with a choice selection of stock phrases on it, and hung it in the middle of the room, from the lamp. Had the Patons and the Strangs to a birthday supper. I produced a soup, sausages and beans, and fruit, and afterwards we went to the Patons' rooms and had lots of tea. I enjoyed the evening. Nice people, all of them.

☆

6 Dec. Sentence on the eight 'wreckers' is to be given tonight. Crowds were lining up to go in as I went home.

8 Dec. Sentence was given at 2.30 a.m. Everyone had to stand while a long considered judgment was read. Five of the eight are to be shot and three got ten years. Walton says that when the sentence was read out the audience clapped as at a play—many standing on tiptoe and clapping with their hands above their heads so that it might be seen that they were doing their bit. A revolting sight.

Circular letter, December. If you have read what *The Times* said about the trial of the eight men accused of conspiring with foreign powers to wreck the industries of the Soviet State and bring about foreign intervention and the overthrow of the Soviet regime, there isn't much to add. The eight accused all told a tale that fitted in well with the Soviet Government's policy, in that it provided an excuse for the great shortage of food and manufactured goods and turned the anger of the people against certain foreign countries. But the Russian people are incredibly ignorant: all the news they get comes from one source, and no foreign newspapers come in to counteract it. There is no doubt their feelings were successfully worked up against the 'wreckers'.

I am sorry that all the stuff I write tends to be against the Soviet regime. There must be many thousands of people in factories and elsewhere who would fight for the present regime to prevent a return of the old or perhaps the advent of any other, and many who get a moral satisfaction out of the belief that they are showing the world the way to a better life, but one doesn't see them. What one does see is the way in which the regime is run—the unscrupulous deception, the unrelenting despotism, and above all the cruelty.

9 Dec. The sentences on the 'wreckers' have been reduced: the five are not to be shot but to have ten years, the others to have eight years instead of ten. This makes the 'plant' more obvious than ever. What humbug it all is!

The Ambassador has sent to FO my suggestion that the consular posts at Moscow and Leningrad should be swapped before they get dug in too deeply.

I hear that Lady Muriel is complaining to the FO about Keane. She wanted to complain to me but I wouldn't listen. I said he was doubtless busy, but she said he did nothing but walk up and down his room all day. The reply to this, which I couldn't very well give, was that when

★

Lady M is about all you can do is walk about and wait until she has gone.

11 Dec. Strang rapped at my door and asked me if I would like to go and chat with him and his wife 'if I was lonely'. I said I was never lonely but would very much like to chat with them. Strang is one of the best officials and most likeable men I have met. We talked for a couple of hours.

The only two Mission employees who were not taken on by the Norwegians after the break in relations in 1927 were Surkov, the Embassy messenger and second chauffeur, and a woman doorkeeper called Vera Rublatt. Vera Rublatt spent three years in Siberia. Surkov was sent to the dreaded camp in the Solovetskiye Islands.

18 Dec. Walker went to the one music-hall last night. He says one turn was a long monologue full of hits at the present regime, e.g. 'The peasants are wondering which they had better do: start their winter sowing or fill up the Government questionnaire (78 pages containing 253 questions) about the winter sowing.'

21 Dec. The bag brought a pair of new skates which I have had screwed on to a pair of old boots. I went on the ice for the first time since 1914 (at Erzerum). I only fell over twice, but I can't recover the one simple trick I had learned—the outside edge on the right foot.

The Chef de Protocol of the Diplomatic Corps is one Florinsky. It is said that his father was shot by the Reds and he never raised a finger. Asked how he could work with Bolsheviks after this, Florinsky is said to have asked if one's father was run over by a tram should one cease to ride on trams?

A few evenings ago I went up to talk to Pott, and thinking that I might overlap his dessert I put a slab of chocolate (with almonds and raisins) into my pocket. I found Walker there and two Russian ballet-dancers. Pott and Walker danced with them to the sound of a gramophone, but I'm not sure that I wasn't the feature of the evening, for I produced my chocolate, and the girls fell on it like dogs on a bone.

Last night Walker gave a party and invited the two ballet girls. The two girls greeted me with cries of 'the chocolate grandpa!' so if I had had any illusions about my value to the party they would have been dispelled.

25 Dec. Christmas Day. I opened my two parcels—one a cake from M, the other books.

Yesterday I took Pott to call on Mr and Mrs Chamberlin. She gave us tea with real lemon in it (the lemon a Christmas present, I gather) and lemon cheesecakes made with some stuff flavoured with Eiffel Tower lemonade powder. Chamberlin says that the high-water mark of plenty, cheapness and variety in food was 1926–27, just before Lenin's New Economic Policy was rescinded. He and his wife found a great falling off when they went on tour this year. They carried sugar and tea with them, and if they stood anyone a glass of tea with sugar in it, it was hailed as a great treat.

26 Dec. We were all invited to Christmas dinner at the Embassy. Walker, Pott and I walked there through a perfect frosty night—a slight powdering of snow on the ground. The Red Square even a sight to dream on. The Kremlin and the 'Pineapple' church at the far end, picked out lightly in snow, were unbelievably lovely. But I pitied the sentries, for all their long sheepskin coats.

The dinner was much more nearly a success than such mixed dinners usually are. All the staff were there—typists and all. Much of the success must be attributed to Lady Ovey who, for all her French blood and her previous marriage to a Mexican, is the most successful British ambassador's or minister's wife that I have seen. She is simple in manner, kind and sincere. Part of the success was doubtless due to the wine. The Ambassador was in good humour, pleased with his Embassy and ready to show off its beauties. He is justifiably happy in the wonderful view of the Kremlin that he gets from his front windows. I was Father Christmas in my Gilgit dressing-gown with bits of cotton wool stuck on my face with government paste.

27 Dec. Very cold, about 42°F of frost, *and* a wind. I skated for about fifteen minutes, but couldn't stand more. We are having more windows puttied up.

☆

RIGHT DEVIATIONISTS AND LEFT DISTORTIONISTS

MOSCOW, 1931

IN FEBRUARY 1931 *Stalin made a famous speech demanding no slackening of the pace. Old Russia, he said, had been repeatedly beaten because of her backwardness, and was fifty or a hundred years behind the advanced countries. 'We must close this gap in ten years,' he declared, 'or we shall be crushed.' In the following month, foreshadowing the show trials to come, former Mensheviks—including the Party historian Sukhanov and the economist Groman—were sentenced to long terms of imprisonment for allegedly setting up a counter-revolutionary organisation.*

3 Jan. Typing annual returns most of the day. HMG are enquiring about the cost of foodstuffs here. Prices of uncontrolled goods are fantastically high. Figures presumably wanted in connection with accusations of dumping. For myself I don't believe the Bolsheviks know what anything costs. They take from the farmer all they can squeeze out of him, paying him partly in goods, partly in money, partly in promises (they don't call what they take 'taxation'), and sell as much as they can, where they can, at the best price they can get. There's no question of any particular item 'paying'. The whole thing 'pays' if they can stagger on, keep the system from collapsing, carry out a specious portion of the Five-Year Plan, and pay for propaganda.

5 Jan. Went with Walker, Walton and Roubiniu, a clever, mild Jew from the Commissariat for Foreign Affairs, to the AMO motor-works—the Soviet factory where cars and lorries are made and bodies fitted to imported Ford chassis. Some of the processes we saw seemed very primitive, and nowhere did we notice any great activity. We saw the good side of the Soviet method: the daily newspaper apparently run by the workers—the 'factory newspaper', i.e. a board with contributions by the workers stuck on it—and an enormous dining-room full of small tables, where, we were told, the workers could get a three-course lunch for just under twopence.

9 Jan. For some time there have been no lemons for our tea, and someone suggested that we should get scurvy and our teeth would drop out. I urged that if that happened it should be kept secret from the FO lest they cut down our allowances on the ground that we were saving money on dentistry.

10 Jan. Yesterday I saw Kataev, the author of that entertaining play *Squaring the Circle* and of a book translated into English as *The Embezzlers*. He wanted to make a declaration that two persons—one an American journalist, the other a Russian educated in America—had made the authorised translation of his play. I believe that Mrs Litvinov, a Hampstead Jewess, made one translation.[1] What will happen to Kataev if her translation is not used?

21 Jan. Albert Coates has arrived to conduct at the Opera for several weeks.[2] He seemed to be out to make the best of Soviet Russia and was praising to the artistes things like the Soviet hydroelectric schemes—which he hadn't seen.

There is a new slogan: 'The Sanitary Minimum.' There are bills about: 'Pioneers! Be scouts of the Sanitary Minimum.'

The *Daily Worker* reads just like a Bolshevik paper. I wonder whether it really believes all it writes. It says that the stories of forced labour in Russian timber camps are all lies.[3] The *Moscow News* prints an alleged interview with an American named Vallon, who is said to have worked in timber camps for twelve years or so and never to have seen any forced labour or indeed any but ideal conditions. Contrasting evidence comes from the Savoy Hotel manager who borrowed Walker's *Times* and was much interested in the articles on forced labour in timber camps. He said it was much worse than *The Times* depicted it.

---

[1] The English novelist and journalist Ivy Low was married to the diplomat Maxim Maximovich Litvinov (see below).
[2] Albert Coates (1882–1953), English composer and conductor, born in St Petersburg. He had been the chief conductor at the Imperial Opera House before the Revolution.
[3] The use of forced labour would constitute a breach of international law (see p.5).

Circular letter, 25 Jan. This has not been a bad winter for snow, but even so the town and the snow seem to be engaged in a continual struggle. The tenants, or their *dvorniks*, have to clear the pavements of fresh snow by 8 a.m. The snow is swept into the road, and from there it is eventually taken away in sledges. Then snow is carried from the roadway onto the pavement where it is trodden in by the feet of pedestrians, and frozen, and this forms a dangerous sheet of ice which has to be chipped off and swept into the roadway and carted off. Finally the roofs have to be cleared. This is a specialist's job. The experts hurl the snow down on to the pavements, and from there it is swept into the roadway for the sledges to take away. And so on.

31 Jan. Junius Wood, the Chicago journalist, is a great character. Perhaps the fact that his headquarters are in Berlin and that he only comes here for a few months at a time gives him greater liberty than a journalist who lives here, but even so . . . . Mrs Litvinov invited him to tea, but he said he had found that no Russian would ever accept his hospitality, so he must decline. Envelopes addressed in English often have the address written on them by the Post Office, often in green ink. Wood found a smear of this green ink on a letter of his when he opened the envelope. He drew a circle round the smear and gave the letter to the postal authorities with the inscription: 'Sack this man. He is careless.' He drafted a telegram for his paper. 'It is reported on good authority that Ramzin is again lecturing at the University, that Fyodotov would have been lecturing at the University if he had not died of shock, in prison, on hearing that he was not going to be shot, and that X would also have been teaching in the University if he had not hanged himself in prison with his underclothes.' The censor rang him up and said that the telegram could not be sent: it wasn't correct. The three men were in their cells, and all quite well. So Wood wrote out another telegram more or less in these words. 'It is not true, as White Guard wreckers maintain, that Ramzin (wording as before) . . . underclothes.' The censor then rang up and said the telegram could not be sent. Wood said: 'But it's what you told me!' 'Well,' said the censor, 'we must make enquiries.' They are still making enquiries. The reports that Ramzin has been released and is working again, that Fyodotov died in prison, and that the other man managed to hang himself in prison, are persistent and probably correct.

2 Feb. Had a visit from the Norwegian Consul at Archangel. He was interesting on labour used in loading timber. As to the man who wrote to *Manchester Guardian* and said he was nine months there and saw no forced labour, Consul said even if he didn't *see* it, he must have known it was there. Often no guards, but the men are under collective responsibility. If one escapes, all are for it. Consul often goes on board Norwegian ships, and frequently seizes a chance to speak to any Russian on board, e.g. the man working the winch. Man often says he is a prisoner. It is suggestive that the moment the United States laid an embargo on Soviet timber all prisoners were at once taken off the work of loading timber and replaced by Comsomoltsy.

Lady Muriel is evidently quite unable to understand a balance sheet. I have had to write to explain to her that the figure you see at the bottom of each side is not the balance in hand.

A week ago I had a rum visitor. He said he was the Red Commandant of some unit at Voronezh. Did I know, he asked, why Trotsky was deported? I said I had read Trotsky's autobiography in England, but I didn't see what it had to do with me, as politics weren't my business. He said he was surprised to find me afraid. I said it wasn't a question of fear: we didn't interfere in Soviet politics, and he was running some risk of being seen to enter the Consulate General. He scoffed at this: he had a brother in the Red Army in Moscow and had nothing to fear. The Poles had listened to his tale: why wouldn't *we*? However, I refused to listen, and he went away. Now was he mad? Or an *agent provocateur*? Or a malcontent hoping for support? If an *agent provocateur*, as one would expect, why expect us to have any sympathy with Trotsky?

Simmonds (Commercial Secretary) tells me that about a year ago, soon after the Embassy was established, a man came and wanted to see the Labour Party representative. It was explained to him that the Embassy represented the British Government and not any particular party, but he insisted that there must be a Labour Party man there as distinct from Government representatives. In the Soviet Embassy in London there are presumably representatives of the Communist Party and the OGPU who are independent of the Ambassador.

Circular letter, 17 Feb. The only personal news is that in a few months the Consulate General is to be transferred to Leningrad and that I am to go with it. The work will be more interesting, and the country round too, and there is good bathing in the summer.

There are signs that foreign exchange is very short at present. The Soviet Government are terminating the contracts of a number of foreign technical experts whose pay is partly in roubles and partly in foreign currency. They are trying to get Germans who will accept contracts in roubles.

★

23 Feb. Junius Wood came in for some income-tax formality. He said he got hold of three very interesting numbers of the *Northern Pravda*. One contained a notice giving a clear warning to *kulaks* that they would be shot if they ever spoke about forced labour. He got two telegrams away to USA but the Narkomindel borrowed the two later papers from him because they were so interesting—and now they 'can't find them'.

The Kondratiev group were to have been tried.[4] They had all made 'confessions', but they have all repudiated the confessions, and the Prosecution have got to start all over again—many arrests being made, and people being sent into exile. One woman has heard nothing of her husband for six months and the OGPU won't tell her whether he is alive or dead, here or elsewhere.

New dodge for getting money. OGPU send for a man who is suspected of having savings in gold or foreign currency. They ask him ever so politely to subscribe to—say the new zeppelin. If he says he can't, they say perhaps he would like to think it over for a bit and come back in a few hours. He is shown into a room where there are probably other people also thinking it over and given a stool to sit on. If he nods off to sleep he gets a poke in the back from the butt of a rifle. 'This is a waiting-room: you can't sleep here.' One man held out three days, one eight. When victim decides to subscribe, OGPU still polite: 'Thank you so much. Knew you'd agree in the end that it was the right thing to do.'

25 Feb. Went to Leningrad to see Keane. Leningrad is a much finer city than Moscow (apart from the Kremlin, which is unique), and the Consulate is on the famous Nevsky Prospekt, a wide street which looks at least two miles long, but the size of the buildings only seemed to throw up the shabbiness of the people. It was snowing all the time too, and everything and everybody looked wretched. I found my colleague living in a good flat warmed chiefly by open wood-fires which must cost the eyes in his head, and furnished almost entirely with bits of furniture left by British subjects who have left the country and dumped their possessions at the Consulate. The unfortunate Vice-Consul and his wife have nothing for a bed but a borrowed divan which they extend to the required length by supporting the pillows on three office chairs. These pampered officials!

---

[4] N.D. Kondratiev (1892–1938), economist who championed agricultural development and financial stability. He had been arrested in 1930, and despite appearing as a key witness in the Menshevik trial of 1931, was sentenced to eight years' imprisonment in 1932. He was executed abruptly in 1938.

28 Feb. Miriam writes: 'Giles produced his own composition the other day. Unluckily it has got lost. I did mean to keep it for you. He and Matt had been playing at schools and Giles asked for a pencil and paper and sat down and wrote: "WI IS THE TAPON BECOS SUNBODD AS LEFTITTON"—an exact account of one of his crimes lately.' Quite good, I think; Giles is four and a half.

1 March. Spent a day with official, mess and private accounts. I have much less in hand than I hoped to have—just enough, perhaps to buy kitchen stuff and crockery and stores for Leningrad.

5 March. Last night Ambassador gave a dinner for Coates. I dined with Strang, whose wife was of the Embassy party, and we went in afterwards. Coates played some of his own compositions—two waltzes rather good. Then the Ambassador's niece, Miss Ovey, who is an actress, was asked to recite, and she and Greenway did the prison scene in *Hassan*, with Strang and me coming in as minor characters at the end. I have never seen the play and I found it terribly moving. Miss Ovey has a good voice, knew most of the part, and played with intensity, and Greenway read well too—though perhaps a little too violently. Coates composed a running accompaniment.

7 March. Touching letter from Wardropper, a DBS living in the Urals, about the parcel of clothes sent from Leningrad. You can see the wretched family standing round the parcel and their 'joy' as his wife takes out 'thing after thing.' Despatch of food parcels from Leningrad to DBSs in my district delayed because in all Leningrad no string, wrapping-paper or sacking (parcels have to be sewn up in sacking or some other material, for the post) could be bought. The recipients of parcels are being asked to post back the wrapping!

8 March. Am being appointed Consul General from 2 November last. Relieved, as I thought they might postpone appointment until I went to Leningrad, to save money.

Last week Simmonds travelled from Berlin by same train as the Ambassador's niece. The train was crowded and not only was there no reserved first-class berth for Simmonds, but he had to share a second-class sleeping-compartment with Miss Ovey—small and with no washing arrangements except those in the lavatory at end of carriage. The Ambassador refused to protest to the Commissariat for Foreign Affairs. He ought to get his salary from the Soviet Government, not

☆

from HMG. I had heard that he wouldn't listen to anything against the
Soviet Government, but I had not seen that myself until this week, when
I discussed with him the question of the exchange. He was annoyed with
the Foreign Office for 'doing him out of' various sums at various times
and for being rigid about the official rate of exchange, and was
proposing to ask for a large increase in his allowances, but he seemed to
feel no annoyance at all that the Soviet Government should be charging
us for roubles at 9.4 to the pound while admitting in various official
transactions that they were worth less.[5] All the clerical staff live on cheap
roubles. Greenway wanted to borrow a bank chit from me in order to
pretend that roubles he had won at bridge were roubles bought with
sterling at the State Bank. And it is annoying to remember, every time
you pay for something in roubles, that your foreign colleagues are
paying one-seventh for the same thing.

Chamberlin told me that the *kulak* is now considered the national
enemy, and as an object of abuse and contempt in newspaper articles
and caricatures he overshadows even the imperialist powers themselves.
He estimates 500,000 *kulaks* carried away last year. Only half sent to
north, owing to lack of transport. Rest dumped in steppe with almost
no tools, and neighbouring villages punished if they gave the poor
wretches food. Cholerton says Ahrens of Press Bureau admits 150,000
kulaks removed, but the game is to represent them as settlers building up
a new life in the north, being unable to go home for fear of the people
in 'the new collectivised farms'.

22 March. Skated probably for the last time. There is a tremendous thaw
on. Gave our maid Paulina some clothes from England. She was quite
overwhelmed—shoes fitted, cardigan had a stripe, etc. Later she had to
bring it all out to show Mrs Paton.

27 March. Here's a piece of typical cant. It is from a speech of Yakoviev,
Narkom (Agriculture): 'The poor and middle peasant who still hesitates
about joining the collective farm is confronted with the question: with
the *kulak* or with the collective farm? The *kulaks* are waging a fight
against the collective farms which (will) lead to their liquidation as a
class. It is the business of the individual poor or middle peasant farmer
to decide as to which will benefit him most. There can be no doubt
about his eventual choice, and day by day the facts are pointing to the
ultimate triumph of collectivisation.'

[5] The black-market exchange rate was about 50 roubles to the pound.

Chamberlin and his wife came back yesterday from their attempt to visit timber camps. The OGPU wouldn't allow them to see any penal camps and wouldn't see them. All the way up they saw cattle-trucks of prisoners at every big station—five or ten or twelve. There is evidence that there was a clean-up a week or two before Molotov[6] made the speech in which he invited diplomats and newspaper correspondents to go and see for themselves.

2 April. Simmonds and I dined with Chamberlins last night. Also there: Deuss and his wife. Deuss (Hearst Agency) has been down in the South with Cholerton (*News Chronicle*). Gives a gloomy picture. Crimea starving, but coast worse, except health resorts. There is bread but almost nothing else, and on coast ration is very very low. Sugar, 100 grams a month. No tea, but wine and vodka. Same everywhere. On railway to Odessa the second track has been torn up to repair the first, so only single line with loops at stations. One of the Crimean representatives on the TSIK protested at the last meeting at the starvation of the Crimea. He has been thrown out. Coming back they could only get places on train by seeing stationmaster or OGPU and claiming to be 'foreign delegates.'

Lady Muriel, having been foiled in her attempt to build a £20,000 house near Leningrad, proposes to send out a five-bedroom wooden villa to be erected. It would be paid for by the Charity Commissioners out of a fund they have, but it would have to be maintained by the Relief Association and if their funds failed I suppose HMG would be asked to maintain it. It is meant for Miss Daunt, the excellent social worker who certainly needs somewhere to live, for an English nurse (to be paid for partially by a British firm), and for four 'special cases'. The special cases would lose the rooms they at present occupy and would never get them back if the villa ceased to be maintained. I foresee that I shall have trouble about this. The Ambassador is writing to Lady M to discourage the despatch of the villa. But it won't be any good. She has no sense of business, and she is determined to have a building which she can call by her name.

7 April. Chamberlin made out a long telegram to the *Christian Science*

---

[6] V.M. Molotov (born Skryabin, 1890–1986), student agitator, Bolshevik and founder of the Party newspaper *Pravda*; prime minister 1930–39, foreign minister 1939–49 and 1953–56. RWB subsequently met him at the Tehran conference in 1943, and was surprised to discover his love of American films. (See *Letters from Tehran*: I.B. Tauris, 1991.)

Monitor in which he said, among other things, that he could not say anything about conditions in the penal camps as he was refused admission to them. He took this to the censor's department in the Commissariat for Foreign Affairs, and they considered it for three-quarters of an hour. Then they said that he ought to have applied to them and they would have had him admitted. In that case, he said, he would go straight back. But they did not 'implement' their offer; they however let his telegram go.

9 April. In yesterday's paper it was announced that in the Middle Volga region twenty-eight *kulaks* had been sentenced for impeding grain collections: six to be shot, twenty-two to be imprisoned for two to ten years. Molotov made a long speech recently with references to foreign policy and he said, with regard to the 'forced labour' campaign, that the foreign diplomatic representatives and the foreign correspondents possessed the power of locomotion: why didn't they go and see? The *Moscow News* published an interview with a Chicago journalist, Wales, which said there was no forced labour, but I learned that (1) Wales does not know a word of Russian, (2) he was taken around by an official interpreter, (3) there were signs that Archangel had been cleaned up, (4) he did write some strictures about treatment of *kulaks* which the *Moscow News* didn't print.

13 April. Yesterday was Russian Easter. The churches all crammed. Our servants made a great occasion of the feast—and produced a cake and a mound of sour cream with a cross and X.B. (initials of the words 'Christ is risen') on it.

15 April. Turkish Consul revealed to me yesterday the ingenious method by which the Turkish Embassy circumvent the official rouble exchange rate. The *tovarishchi* are curious to know how they get their roubles, and sometimes ask, whereupon the Turks reply that they don't spend any money in the country! The British Embassy must be the only mission that buys from the State Bank, not a bean does the State Bank get out of the Italians, the Germans and of course the Persians, Greeks, the Japanese, etc.

Mr and Mrs Imer came in last night. He is as contemptuous as ever of the part of the Five-Year Plan that he knows. He is adviser to the engineer in charge of 'rationalisation', who was appointed to the job six months after coming out of college. The so-called engineers, who are all very young, are always exposing their gross ignorance by asking

☆

questions that no engineer needs even to look up.

Last night I picked up a concert on the wireless. Russian airs by soloists, choruses and balalaika orchestra. Before each item the announcer asked the hearers to write down the name of the composer and the piece etc. One of the questions was: 'Of what class was the composer a representative?'

Strang told me the Embassy are dodging the exchange with official Soviet connivance over the cost of a tennis-court. It will cost at least 5000 roubles, which to buy at the State Bank would cost over £530, but the OGPU sporting-club Dynamo have undertaken to do it in return for a motor-mower and a motor-roller (I think) which will cost about £120!

18 April. Dined with Strang and the Tawneys[7] last night. Very pleasant. Tawney rather surprised at the degree of repression he finds here, and wondering whether it is necessary. He had made the acquaintance by correspondence of Riyazanov, head of the Marx and Engels Institute in Moscow and a noted Marxist writer, and he thought it would be a good thing to have his letters addressed 'c/o Riyazanov' against his arrival here on his way home from China. This is a good jest. Riyazanov lost his job and was put in prison two or three months ago for being a right deviationist or something the Party didn't like; there are no letters waiting for Tawney (they are probably in Riyazanov's file in the OGPU), and Tawney is probably regarded with the greatest suspicion.

Giles reports in a letter: 'gRaaSS ToRTuS is derd.'

23 April. Went to Chamberlin's yesterday after dinner. Also there: Tawneys, Deusses and Cholerton. Tawney trying to keep his head under the fire of anti-Soviet statements. Tawney asked whether there was not at least equality in the USSR, but no one present would admit this. They gave all sorts of examples, e.g. in the munitions factories people work much longer hours than seven or even eight. Chamberlins last year stayed with the president of a *kolkhoz.* It was the only place throughout the tour where they got decent food: but host dressed in rags and implied that he could not afford to look better-off than the others, and when his wife wanted to buy something special she got someone else to get it for her.

---

[7] Professor R.H. Tawney (1880–1962), professor of economic history at the University of London from 1931 to 1949, and author of *Religion and the Rise of Capitalism* (John Murray, 1936). He had married Annette Beveridge in 1909.

All seemed to think that the men at the top were quite cynical in their indifference to equality. Mrs Deuss saw Voroshilov, Minister of War, pass in a fine car. Her chauffeur sneered: 'Yes, he's got four cars'— specifying them. 'No bourgeois ever had four cars, but he can have four because it's the workers' money he is spending.' Molotov has a lovely country place. The lower floor is a museum; he has all the upper. Once a week he takes Speransky, the best women's doctor, in his high-powered car to see his family—as a matter of routine. The ordinary person waits hours in a queue to see a doctor. Speransky sometimes has to leave a lecture to go and see Stalin's baby. When asked why he didn't call in Rosenberg, Stalin said: 'Oh, he's a Jew.'[8]

Mrs Chamberlin found out that at the rest-home for Foreign Affairs officials the food allowance was 10 roubles per day, whereas the allowance in the maternity home for mothers with babies is one-twentieth of that sum. She was recommended to a certain tailor as the best (his brother is a successful tailor in Paris). She went to his place but he was at the Kremlin fitting Mrs Molotov. As a private tailor he had no food-card, neither had his wife, and she had just paid 9 roubles for a kilo of sugar.

Cholerton spoke of Schaeffer, a very capable German journalist (*Berliner Tageblatt*) who was refused leave to return because he knew too much and had criticised the USSR. The Russian girl who read the Russian papers for him every morning was given five years in exile for espionage, and a Russian (who had been at college with him in Germany and used to visit him sometimes) ten years in a penal camp.

Cholerton's wife's relatives are having a hard time. She is Russian. The sister and sister's husband were imprisoned charged with espionage for Cholerton, and eventually she was made minus twelve for five years,[9] and he was condemned to five years in a penal camp. The husband is a fanatical communist, to such an extent that Cholerton, who only saw him a few times out of politeness, found it wise not to argue with him. The husband's brother is high up in the Kremlin and eventually got the sentences commuted: the husband and wife are to go to Novosibirsk for three years, where he has been given a job. But now a cousin of Mrs Cholerton's has been arrested, and they can get no exact news of him, though they heard a rumour that he is to have ten years' penal camp.

[8] G.N. Speransky (1873–1969), paediatrician. Stalin's fear of Jewish doctors was to culminate in his invention of the so-called 'Doctors' Plot' in 1952.
[9] A less severe punishment than imprisonment was banishment from a specific number of the USSR's largest cities (in this case twelve) for a specific length of time. (See David Dallin and Boris I. Nicolaevsky, *Forced Labor in Soviet Russia*: Hollis and Carter, 1948.)

★

Mrs Cholerton's sister's experiences in prison were interesting, if rather unlike those of mere murderers who get ten years in the model prison which is shown to foreigners. She seems to be a courageous woman and managed to prevent one disgracefully overcrowded cell from having a lot more women thrust in by starting a hunger strike. She was made a 'monitor', and by her persistence she obtained permission for the women in her cell, on her guarantee, to go out to the lavatory so that they might discontinue the use of the open commode in the middle of the cell. All the cells were verminous; in one they were so crowded that they all had to lie on their sides, wedged tightly together.

One of the exhibits produced against the husband was an allegedly important map which he was said to have taken to give his mother to pass on to Mrs Cholerton and to have lost. He recognised it as a map of a battle from a common military textbook. But the OGPU just dropped that 'proof' in a bored way and went on with something else. It is evidently just as much a daily business now, this inventing of crimes against the State, as the ordinary work of the Vine Street policeman is dealing with drunk-and-disorderly cases. Cholerton described the 'shock-workers' in the factories as blacklegs, undercutting the current wage. Tawney described the forcible collectivisation of agriculture as the Soviet version of the Enclosure Acts.

27 April. Gave a dinner last night: Strang, the Tawneys and Duranty, an Englishman who represents the *New York Times*. Cholerton invited but apparently forgot. We had an interesting discussion. Strang's attitude rather that of the sincere liberal, mine that of a man who sympathised with the nominal aims of socialists but was disillusioned by its experiments in this country. Tawney, though appalled at the lack of freedom, finds some good things here: (1) there is a *plan*, whereas no other country knows what to do; (2) the people who run the show are keen and enthusiastic whereas the leaders in England are sceptical and the businessmen no longer believe in the 'system'; (3) the people are as well-clothed and look as well-fed as people in a manufacturing town in Lancashire. Duranty is a supporter of the Soviet regime, and as he says the readers of his paper are always attacking him he must be supposed to be sincere, though I could not reconcile some of his opinions (e.g. about the absence of religious persecution) with some of the facts he himself gave.

We all agreed that class distinctions are painfully strong in England. Tawney saw it particularly during the War, when he was a private and, later, a sergeant. He found, for instance, that his word was doubted by

☆

his officers as a matter of course. It annoyed him that a friend of his who was an officer in the same battalion couldn't talk to him, though a French officer will sit and drink with a private, and of course our Dominion troops do the same. Mrs Tawney found it too. The family income stopped and she had to apply for a separation allowance, and she was met with great rudeness and arrogance and dilatoriness, and finally Tawney had to threaten to have the matter brought up in Parliament if his wife was not attended to, and the matter was settled at once.

We all agreed that the boarding public-school was on the whole a curse. I suggested that only the reduction of big incomes would bring about their abolition, and Tawney agreed.

Circular letter, 28 April. In speeches for consumption abroad the Soviet leaders speak of little but the success of the Five-Year Plan. This week there have been two articles about the defects in the Giant tractor factory at Stalingrad. In the Nadyezhda ('Hope') factory, 97% of their produce had to be rejected. It appears to be easier to cut timber, pump oil and grow grain than to carry out the more delicate manufacturing processes—e.g. the casting of good steel. The common opinion of foreign observers is that the Russian experiment is being financed out of the country's enormous natural resources, oil, timber, furs, platinum, etc. Given the incredibly low standard of living which the Russian people seem prepared to accept and able to keep alive on, the manufacturing experiments can go on for a long time. Some things, big rather than difficult, like the hydroelectric dam, the Dnyeprstroy, are successful enough, but I imagine that any country with a huge river, that did not pay its debts and used the money to hire American engineers, could carry out a similar scheme.

1 May. Went to the May Day ceremony in the Red Square. There was a march past that lasted for 2½ hours and when they were standing all together the Army Commander administered the oath to the troops. It was meant to be impressive but it was so long and there was some repetition that was merely boring. It was as long as the 119th Psalm and not so well-written.

8 May. I met a fine old Englishman named Otten. His daughter and another woman have been taking turns to go to the prison every day to see whether their husbands' names were on the list of those who were to be sent away—the only information given out by the authorities. A few days ago she found her husband's name on the list, and in accordance with the established practice she went to the prison next day with a parcel of clothing etc. for him. This was the first news she had had of him since his arrest last October. Since then she has been allowed to see him every ten days. She was allowed to shout to him across a wide passage, through two gratings, with many other prisoners and their relatives conversing in the same way at the same time. He told her that in December he was called up and asked one question, 'Do you admit that you have been guilty of sabotage?' When he said very emphatically 'No,' he was sent back to prison. No further attention was paid to him or to the many other textile engineers in the same prison, who had all had a similar experience. They then began to wonder whether it would not be better to plead guilty of sabotage rather than to remain in prison for an indefinite period, and one of them volunteered to try it on. He confessed that he had been guilty of sabotage; the authorities were extremely nice about it, provided him with a confession already written out in detail, and when he signed it sentenced him to five years in an isolation camp—commuted to work in another factory at his own job. The others all sang like birds and got similar sentences, five to ten years. Otten's son-in-law was asked where he would like to work. Moscow? No, he didn't like Moscow. The Urals then? Yes, he didn't mind the Urals. So he is off to a flax factory in the Urals for a five-year term, reduced by half as long again as he has been some years in a penal labour camp.

23 May. For the third week in succession there are no vegetables except potatoes and beetroot at the grocery shop where we buy food. But Moscow is much better off for food than the provinces, even a short distance away.

Today I heard from an Englishwoman about a Russian who is imprisoned on a charge of sabotage. Recently his wife was allowed to see him for a short time. The husband said he had been left for a month in a cell so dark that he couldn't see his own hand—then he was put in a cold cell where he nearly died of cold, and after in a cell so hot that he fainted with heat—the account agrees exactly with one given in a Russian paper published in Berlin of the way in which the OGPU extract confessions from their victims.

The Russian papers are beginning to say that the workers want another loan. I suspect that they want another loan as much as the sons of Mrs Pardiggle wanted to give up their pocket-money to get kissed.[10]

---

[10] In *Bleak House*, Mrs Pardiggle diverts her sons' pocket-money for the benefit of the Tockahoopo Indians and other good causes. For forced loans, see pp. 43 and 55.

The Russian papers claim that wages are rising. But they are not rising as fast as prices. In the last fortnight petroleum has gone up 50% in price and postal rates 50% or more.

3 June. It is the King's birthday but we are having no celebration because the Ambassador has lost so much money on the exchange that he can't afford to give a party. To make more room in the Kremlin they have blown up one church and they are blowing up another.

11 June. I have been going through all the letters M has written since I left home and picking out the parts about the children I cannot bear to burn. Here is one bit: 'Julie is very comic. The other morning I went in to him early—he was yelling out with a nightmare. JULIAN: I dreamed a tiger was coming after me to eat me. MUMMY: But there're no tigers in this country, Julie. JULIAN: Yes, but I was in *their* country!'

Circular letter, 15 June. I have invented a slogan for the country: instead of the old '*dostat I perestat*' ('overtake and surpass'), '*otstat I otstabat*' ('to fall behind and to stay behind'). One gets so tired of their slogans. A recent one is 'self-criticism'. You don't see many signs of self-criticism as a rule. I heard the night before last on the radio: 'Comrades, what is self-criticism? Self-criticism must be directed against the class enemy, the opportunist, those elements which are opposed to our policy . . . .'

This country is a paradise for parrots. Every speech sounds like every other: '. . . liquidation of the *kulak* on the basis of intensive collectivisation . . . real Bolshevist fashion . . . Bolshevist tempo . . . shock brigade tactics . . . as Marx said . . . as Engels said in 1856 . . . Lenin . . . our comrade Stalin . . . sabotage . . . foreign interventionists.' I have never heard a speech that seemed to have been composed by a human being for human beings. I used to wonder whether the people themselves do not get sick of this propaganda, and recently I had one proof that they do. I went to see a play about the socialisation of the fishing industry. When it was due to start a typical communist with a black blouse and high Russian boots began a political speech. Soon the audience began to clap. The speaker at first looked flattered, but then he realised that the applause was a sign of boredom and not enthusiasm and he yelled at the audience that they ought to listen to 'the truth'. Finally the speaker had to retreat in a fury.

15 June. For the last year or two great efforts have been made to stamp out the self-employed worker. Taxation was made very heavy, and recently these workers were deprived of their food-cards, which meant, at best, semi-starvation. The authorities have now discovered that there was no one to do many necessary jobs, and they published a decree reducing the taxation, but blaming 'right deviationists and left distortionists' for the regrettable state of affairs. It may be presumed that they will do as they did with the NEP men, asking them to work so long as they need them and then crushing them again. With a great flourish today the papers announced a reduction in the taxing of small home-workers.

The commercial secretaries of all the embassies and legations have been planning a tour to several of the important industrial centres in the east about which the Soviet Government have been boasting. They were to have started today, but at the last moment they have been refused permission.

I move to Leningrad a fortnight today—29 June. I am glad to be going to Leningrad if only to see the treasures of the Hermitage before they reorganise it on Bolshevik lines, as the recent arrest of a large number of the curators suggests they intend to do. It may be they want to put in people who will close their eyes when treasures are sold. Truth and frankness are not qualities on which the Russian communists pride themselves. Their object, as they repeat daily, is to 'build socialism', and the end justifies the means. The art treasures must be a great temptation to them when they are in such desperate need of foreign currency, and they don't value the art of the pre-revolutionary age. Art and literature must be 'proletarian' and must all point the same way as the programme of the Party. The result is that films and plays get duller and duller. There is no country in the world with more material for plays and novels, and yet there is no country where the scope of writers is so strictly limited.

★

A NEW CIVILISATION?

LENINGRAD, 1931

STALIN'S CALL FOR *industrialisation at the beginning of 1931 was followed by sweeping changes to the agricultural economy as well, and a fresh wave of forcible collectivisation. As conditions worsened, however, Bullard's own fortunes took a turn for the better. 'Leningrad made a very good impression,' he wrote a month after his transfer from Moscow. 'Fewer slogans, and the streets not less well-paved than before the War, and certainly better than the capital. Two months ago the facades of houses looked very dirty and dilapidated, but an intensive campaign of cleaning, painting and plastering is going on. Moscow is a grubby provincial town with narrow streets full of people at all hours of the day, but Leningrad is laid out on a plan with wide streets and wide pavements, and walking is a pleasure.' One indication of how much more relaxed he felt is that he abruptly suspended his use of code.*

9 July. I have called on all my colleagues—German, Swede, Dane, Finn, Pole, Latvian, Norwegian, Italian, Estonian and on the local representative of the Commissariat for Foreign Affairs, Weinstein, the man whose note was returned on the instigation of Lord Curzon and who was degraded to Leningrad.[1] Keane hated Weinstein. I don't think he is so bad, nor does Cave, who has no reason to love Bolsheviks. Weinstein is cross-eyed and talks English with a vile American twist. He has an assistant, Orlov-Ermak, who must be very near the inner council, for he speaks with authority. The department concerned said it would

---

[1] Lord Curzon was foreign secretary in March/April 1923 when the British government sought to dissuade the Soviet authorities from carrying out death sentences on a group of Catholic clergymen. Weinstein, head of the Anglo-American department of Narkomindel, responded using language which caused the chargé d'affaires in Moscow, Robert Hodgson, to refuse to accept his reply.

take a month to transfer a telephone from one room to another, but he telephoned to them, said this 'tempo' would not do, and told them he was promising the Vice-Consul that the work would be done in two days.

My two vice-consuls are Todd and Cave. Cave is a man of fifty who was born in this country and has spent most of his life here. He was with our 'interventionists' in Siberia, and at one time, after General Dieterichs had investigated the 'execution' of the Russian royal family, he was for a fortnight in charge of a suitcase containing the remains of those unhappy people—a finger, buttons, bits of charred corset, etc.

Miss Daunt met the director of the night sanatorium, a large yellow stone building situated on the Malaya Neva, Pyesochnaya Embankment, and he invited her to see his place. She took me with her and also an Englishwoman, Mrs Eccles, and an Anglo-Russian, Mrs Hay.

The sanatorium occupies what was formerly a handsome private house. The director found it deserted and half-ruined in 1923 (the time of the famine and the typhus epidemic), and repaired it with the voluntary aid of workers from the factories. The patients are all consumptive. They continue to work at their ordinary occupations, but live in the sanatorium at night. They pay nothing. They are taken in batches of fifty at a time for six weeks, men and women alternately. The wards are big, light and airy. The place was comfortably clean and the people in charge gave the impression of being keen on their job and proud of it. Each district of the city now has a night sanatorium.

It was a warm summer evening and the patients were allowed to wander in the garden. Two were sitting on the sunny side of a bush with their dresses pulled down over their shoulders so as to expose as much of their backs as possible to the sun. Except for the inevitable wireless-loudspeaker blaring to an empty sitting-room I saw no signs of propaganda—no slogans, not even a bust of Lenin. All members of the staff seemed friendly to each other and not afraid to talk.

Next door was a big garden with scores of little children standing or playing about. I asked the doctor who they were and he said '*bezprizorny*', i.e. waifs and strays, most of them the offspring of 'free marriages', i.e. unions which people don't trouble to register. 'Such people simply throw the children away,' he said.

Miss Prachte, a German artist I met in Moscow, hurt her head and the German doctor who examined her thought the skull was fractured. He telephoned for an ambulance which came at once (the 'first-aid' service seems to be good both in Moscow and in Leningrad) and Miss P

★

was taken to hospital, Mrs Chamberlin accompanying her. At the hospital they waited forty minutes before any attention at all was paid to them, and then, although the diagnosis was fractured skull, a form had to be filled up in which the most important questions related to Miss P's class origin—was she a 'worker' in Germany, did she belong to a trade union, and so on. Medical attention is provided according to class origin rather than to the gravity of the malady.

Navashin and sixteen others have been turned out of their labs and fifteen years of experiments wasted. He has been put in charge of research work on the soya bean. He hasn't yet got a passport to go to England to work in a laboratory where he was offered a job, and he daren't show any eagerness to go. An American woman of Russian origin, a research worker, is working on the gum cells, and she finds that her work is expected to prove some communist hypothesis. She attended the meetings of the Science Congress in Moscow and said they were robbed of all scientific value by the manner in which every speaker dragged in the Party line. She tried not to be influenced by the reaction she is suffering from her former enthusiasm, but after making all allowances she felt that the speakers were men repeating a lesson. I went with her to visit the plant-breeding institute. The work they do is interesting, but more interesting is the 'Red' assistant director, Kovalyov. He is called 'Doctor', but he is obviously simply a Bolshevik politician put in to keep the Party line. He explained the institute to us in elementary language, with gentle corrections now and then from a man who had studied in England and America and knew something about his job. We saw some men who spoke English—all mad keen to talk, poor things. Next day was a day off but the assistant director volunteered to take us to see the plant-breeding station at Dyetskoye Syelo. He wanted to take his girl for a joyride. He introduced us to Karpechenko and Pissarev, who showed us round. Karpechenko plays about with chromosomes, and has made a hybrid cabbage-mustard plant. He is trying to make a fertile hybrid. Experiments are also being carried out to test the effect of extending the length of the day by artificial sunlight. Hybridisation being tried everywhere. One kind of flax being bred for strong stem which enables it to be cut by machinery; another for its large content of linseed oil. They have a wheat which will ripen as far north as the Arctic Circle. Hybrid oat doing well. It has been named 'Bolshevik'.

Norman Bentwich and his wife came out on a Workers' Travel Association tour, £25 for twenty-one days, including return passage in a Soviet boat. At Moscow they were allowed to leave the party and go to

☆

the Crimea to see the Jewish colonies.[2] These are the result of co-operation between the Soviet authorities, who want to outdo Palestine, and an American society. The moving spirit is an American Jew named Rosen who, Bentwich says, is a wonderful organiser: they wanted him for Palestine but he preferred to stay in the Crimea. The colonies are doing pretty well, but not so well the last two years, on account of the horrible squeezing out of grain by the authorities. The result has been that keen Jews—the type who were being converted into capable farmers in three years—now find the factories more attractive: regular pay, and the rations in the town are better. The Jews talked to him eagerly about Palestine, and when he said Palestine was better, they said, with truth, that at least the authorities don't allow pogroms in Russia now. (One reply to this is that the OGPU pogrom is going on all the time but that the Jews don't mind it because it is directed against a social class from which they were almost entirely excluded. Also it is run largely by Jews, or at least, Jews figure largely in the present ruling class.) Bentwich found food very short indeed. They were taken about by a plump Jew named Michael; wherever he went the best food was produced for him.

Bentwich had missed seeing the Public Prosecutor in Moscow, but he saw the one in Leningrad. The PP's office is under the supervision of the workers in a factory, to see that the working-class mentality is retained. Bentwich was impressed by the simplicity and speed of the proceedings in the courts. But I must see for myself how they are conducted.

A French doctor who was dining at the Embassy said he had been to the biggest hospital in Moscow and seen the doctor in charge. He asked about the casualty ward and they told him it was divided into two sections: accidents and suicides. Q: 'How many accidents a day?' A: 'So many.' Q: 'How many suicides?' A: 'We are not allowed to say.'

The master of a British ship wrote to the Consulate and said he was a stoker short and could not sail until the place was filled. Cave, not thinking, asked the Sovtorgflot man with whom he deals whether the Soviet Government could find a stoker. He roared with laughter and said that thousands of men from ex-generals down would apply for a

[2] Norman Bentwich (1883–1971) was attorney-general of Palestine from 1920 to 1931 and professor of international relations at Jerusalem University. In 1924 Stalin had set up two organisations, Komzet (Committee on Land for Working Jews) and Ozet (Society for Land for Working Jews), and Jews from the Ukraine and Byelorussia were encouraged to move to collective farms in the Crimea. Blagoveschensk, a collective in Birobidzhan (Siberia), was designated as an autonomous Jewish entity to be an alternative to Palestine.

stoker's job in a ship due to leave Russia but did not suppose that one of them could get permission to leave.

Weinstein has offered to take me to see the sights. I told him that I wanted to see everything, not only factories but also schools, courts, hospitals, etc.

The German Consul General has left for a visit to Archangel and if possible Murmansk. He says that Germans and Finns of Russian nationality—*kulaks*—have been sent to the apatite deposits near Murmansk where they live in bad conditions and work in water.

Dr Bell says there is much typhoid about. He had twenty-three new cases today. Mrs Eccles saw a murder from her window. Some men had a fight and one fell down. He sat up, whereupon another held him down while a third went and collected a big stone and bashed his head in. An engineer who had been buying some provisions dined with the Bells, and he left at 9.00 because he said he wouldn't get home with his load if he left it until later.

Miss Clyman, a Canadian woman journalist who spent some days in Leningrad, said that what struck her most was the military preparations, e.g. the interval at the opera was filled with a lecture about gas warfare and appeals to be prepared for it—Mrs Eccles said the same thing. She lived opposite a barracks, where she saw boys and girls of sixteen to eighteen being drilled in a very business-like way by regular NCOs. I have myself seen such boys and girls marching through the Moscow streets with rifles and fixed bayonets. Miss Daunt says that a maroon went up one day and all the police put on gas-masks and the people were ordered to go home quickly as 'a new gas was being tried'. She met a sailor who said: 'You wait till we go to war with you. You don't know what sort of gas we've got.'

19 July. The Soviet authorities are exporting a lot of plywood to America. The local manager of Exportlyes makes a declaration that no forced labour has been used, and the declaration comes to us for legalisation of the signatures of the Leningrad Agency for Foreign Affairs. What would be the position of a manager who refused to make such a declaration?

We rang up the State Bank to ask them to do something for us. The manager of the foreign department said he was very sorry, but he couldn't: he and all his staff were just going out to weed the vegetable fields. Thousands of people go out as 'volunteers' on their free day, but this is not sufficient: the employees of the various institutions are being sent out to help.

☆

Miss Daunt wanted to get hold of the Lutheran pastor to bury a DBS. No one would admit knowing where he lived. Finally a woman of English origin, who overheard her talking about it, told her that the pastor lived over the British Consulate! The pastor did not dare to see her, nor will he recognise her if he meets her in the street. It is difficult to find out the condition of the clergy and the churches. The cathedral opposite—the Kazan—is open: it rings a bell (rarely) and services are held, and I even saw the priests on the steps in full robes holding a funeral service. But the great cathedral of St Isaac is an anti-religious museum; some churches are closed and the tower of the Dutch Reformed church is being pulled down and the building turned into some sort of club. The general weapon against religion now is taxation. The authorities levy taxes they know cannot be paid and then seize the church in satisfaction of the debt. But communists still make merry on their name days—possibly because this provides an excuse for drinking!

The new loan which the workmen 'asked for' is being raised according to plan. All workers and employees (and indeed everybody) are expected to promise to put a month's pay into the loan, and instalments are deducted from their pay. Mrs Bell and her son both refused to 'invest' more than half a month's pay in the loan. The son has been 'black-boarded' at his factory. Of course, they are British subjects, but the son says that a few others in his factory have also refused. (How many refuse and why don't more refuse?)

Dr Bell has two jobs because 'you can't live on one'. He gets 165 roubles as water expert, and 125 roubles as doctor in a hospital, from which he gets home at 11 p.m. or after. His wife is also a doctor. The son is an engineer and a little boy of eight is at school. All four have different 'days off': their fifth days never coincide. There is also a girl of eighteen who 'finished middle school' (i.e. left high school) last year but is doing nothing because, not being of proletarian origin, she can't get into a university.

There are many cases of typhoid here; Dr Bell now speaks of some forty-five to sixty fresh cases a day, but the authorities will neither publish statistics nor allow any to be published. The nearest they have got is to warn the public against drinking unboiled water from the taps.

E.A. Lie, the Norwegian engineer, is just back from Siberia with his wife. They went to see her father, who has been in exile there for two years and has another year to serve. He went to Tomsk and then down the Ob to the Narym region. There he saw a camp of about 6000 *kulaks*. There are others thereabouts containing as many as 25,000. Of 6000, a thousand died within a month. The wives and children are there too—

☆

those that have not succumbed to the bad conditions. The *kulaks* are allowed to cultivate (they are given spades, but not much else) and to cut timber, but not to fish or hunt. A form of punishment is to be made to spend a night in the woods, where the persecution from mosquitoes is terrible. The members of the OGPU in charge are themselves in exile and presumably trying to rehabilitate themselves by their efficiency.

The people he saw along the Ob were full of complaints. They say that the Government demand (the 'norm') in fish, berries and everything else is so huge that it is useless hoping to produce that amount and something over for yourself, and if you produce a lot the Government raise the norm. The only thing to do is to limit your output and give up as little as you can. They have forgotten what butter looks like, though the area used to produce great quantities. Some of the regulations are incredibly foolish. For instance, in a sparsely populated area a man will be supposed to deliver a small quantity of milk to a centre 20 kilometres away. Presumably the peasants manage to secrete a little of their produce. Lie said that if he gave a peasant a cigarette or two, milk or something else would be given in return.

21 July. Miss Daunt, who is on good terms with the Red Cross people, was invited by them to see a camp which they run for Pioneers, and she took me with her yesterday. We had an hour in the train and I stood all the time, both ways. No Russian ever gets up to let a woman sit down, even an old woman or a woman with a baby. You have to be careful in offering your seat to a woman, lest some man slip into it. The camp we saw is for children who are not well—undernourished in many cases, I suspect. The children come for a month and then another lot take their place—160 at a time, all the year round. This fine weather they are only in their rooms for an afternoon rest and at night. The rest of the time they are in the open air. They gave us lunch—cabbage soup, coarse meat with carrot and potato chopped up—not very appetising, but not bad, and a water ice which was perhaps put on for our visit.

The children looked well and the dormitories were light, airy and clean. All the children are Pioneers. They are taught that the Party is above everything and (according to Radek)[3] they despise a teacher (and presumably a parent) if he is not a member of the Party. There are four

---

[3] Real name Karl Bernhardovich Sobelsohn (1885–1939), assistant commissar for foreign affairs. He was also a brilliant propagandist, his virtuoso articles appearing in *Izvestia* under the pseudonym of Viator. He was imprisoned in 1936 and was murdered by a fellow prisoner.

such organisations. The tiny children—corresponding to our Wolf Cubs and Brownies—are called Octobrists, after the month in which the Bolshevik Revolution occurred. Then come the Pioneers, boys and girls of ten to fifteen. Then the League of Communist Youth, which takes the young men and women past the age of twenty-one. Last of all there is the Communist Party. I have not yet heard whether there are any camps for those who are simply children and not Pioneers. I found it rather shocking to find a political camp supported by the Red Cross, but in Soviet Russia everything is subordinated to the Communist Party.

The camp occupies several *dachas*, i.e. Russian country villas, and the land between and around them. The food is simple and the children wear clothing belonging to the camp. One of the staff apologised for its condition. It was sketchy and ragged in many cases, but adequate for a summer life out of doors. In the reading-room was a pile of Soviet newspapers (chaffy diet even for grown-ups), and over the door was an inscription: 'We Pioneers protest against the murder of the eight young negroes.' When Lady Astor saw this a few days later she was furious, and asked the people in charge what they would think if we put up inscriptions in Boy Scout camps: 'We protest against the shooting of their political opponents by the Bolsheviks.'[4] On the wall was a mysterious card with five or six little test-tubes fastened to it. On examining the wording on the card (printed, and therefore presumably one of many) I found that the tubes contained substances which are supposed to smell like certain poison-gases, the names of which were printed under the respective tubes. The child takes the cork out of a tube, sniffs, and thus learns to recognise the associated poison-gas. I suppose he is also taught what to do to avoid danger from the gas. The whole day was devoted to such 'anti-war' training. Each day is devoted to one of a number of subjects. One day is Literary Day; on another day the camp fraternises with the Red Army and soldiers come from some barracks to see the camp and talk to the children; yet another day is devoted to collective farm study, and the workers from the collective farm near by come to the camp.

I got the impression that the doctors and the housekeeper (a most efficient man) got much satisfaction from seeing the children happy and

---

[4] Nancy Astor (1879–1964) was the first woman to sit in the House of Commons, having been elected MP for Plymouth after her husband succeeded to the peerage in 1919. The inscription at the Pioneer camp was referring to the 'Scottsboro boys' case. In April 1931, eight young black men in Alabama had been sentenced to the electric chair for attacking two white girls. Following appeals to the US Supreme Court, the State of Alabama dropped the case against four of the accused in 1936; the others were given varying terms of imprisonment.

improving in health without troubling much about politics, but the 'cultural' work of the camp is all in the hands of a very young Jew who is very much the Party man. He had all the catch words of the Party propaganda. Pinned on the wall, to serve as subjects of discussion, were Stalin's latest speech and extracts from the Soviet press about the crisis in Europe. It is evident that the children are stuffed with propaganda the whole time.

24 July. I have had many visitors. Miss Clyman and Cholerton. Gave Miss Clyman the Todds' room. Cholerton was promised a room at October Hotel but at 12.30 a.m. was offered a bed in a dormitory with ten Russians, so he came back and slept on my sofa. G.B. Shaw, the Astors and Lord Lothian (Philip Kerr) arrived.[5] Lord Astor came and talked for an hour.

25 July. Miss Clyman had a talk with Shaw (which she used for an 'exclusive interview' article for the *Express*). He wanted to see a church and the anti-religious museum and the people in charge of him wouldn't take him, so she suggested that I should capture him for an hour or two. At 3.30 Cave and I took him to see the Kazan Cathedral ('not very interesting') and then over to St Isaac's Cathedral (anti-religious museum). Shaw was interested. His two chief comments were that it was just the sort of stuff that used to be written and said against the priests at the Reformation and that he was glad to see the anti-religious propaganda tailing off into propaganda on behalf of the Five-Year Plan. Lady Astor discovered us at the museum. She indicated to the guide—a rather clever-looking woman—that she disapproved of the museum and believed in God, and she made the sign of the cross over the woman. The woman said 'I don't believe' and laughed. It is curious that the Astors had not noticed that the people appointed to look after them were all Jews—Litvinov, Lunacharsky,[6] Bloch (in charge of hotel and

[5] Lord Lothian (1882–1940) had been private secretary to Lloyd George from 1916 to 1921. Shaw (1856–1950), a lifelong socialist, had taken every opportunity to speak out in support of the communist experiment, but had never visited Russia until invited by Lord Astor to join his party. His article 'Touring in Russia', which appeared in *Nash's Magazine* in January and February 1932, undoubtedly had much influence, although his book *The Rationalization of Russia* (ed. Geduld HM: Indiana University Press) did not appear until 1964. (Michael Holroyd, *Bernard Shaw, vol. III, The Lure of Fantasy, 1918–1950*: Chatto and Windus, 1991.)

[6] Maxim Maximovich Litvinov (1876–1951) had been appointed representative of the new Soviet government in London after the Revolution; after the arrest of R.H. Bruce Lockhart in Moscow, Litvinov was arrested in retaliation, and was subsequently

transport arrangements) and the woman guide. Shaw came back with us. He said he didn't take tea but he had two cups, and he talked for an hour and told us a lot about Russia. He seemed very 'contrairy' and just waved away anything that did not fit in with his preconceptions: e.g. there were some photos of the big sabotage trial in the museum. I made some disparaging remark about the trial and Shaw grew quite indignant and said: 'But they confessed.' I replied, 'Yes, one of them confessed that he lunched with Colonel Lawrence at the Savoy in London on a date when we know he was in India,' but Shaw waved the argument away. Then I told him about the propaganda which is pumped into the children, e.g. at the Pioneer camps. He said that was the same in England where children at the church schools are taught the Apostles' Creed—as likely as not by people who don't believe it themselves. I said there is this difference. That when English children grow up they can meet people with other beliefs and read books etc. of opposing tendencies, whereas in this country there is no alternative to communist propaganda, but he waved that away too.

At tea Shaw said how much he despises parliamentary government as we have it in England and spoke in admiration of Mussolini and of the Soviet system. He said our parliament was devised to obstruct first the King, then the Lords, and later the rich middle classes, and now it can't do anything but obstruct. He said the Soviet authorities were beginning to admit that you couldn't take the child of any peasant and make a professional man of him. He himself never learned to read: he *knew* how to because he 'came of that sort of stock'. I said that so far the Soviet authorities had merely admitted that they could not do without trained engineers, and that for them to admit that they were mistaken in claiming that environment was everything and heredity nothing would be a long step to take. 'Oh,' he said, 'they will take it, they'll have to.'

Miss Clyman will be able to make many good points in her article. Shaw said to her, half-laughing: 'Don't write the truth, that is worse than speaking the truth.' She asked: 'But won't you tell the truth when you get back?' He said: 'But that is very difficult, they have been so kind.' Shaw told a good story about sitting to Rodin for his bust. A French lady who came on a visit, not knowing whether she could communicate with Shaw, asked Rodin whether Shaw spoke French well. Rodin was a very exact man who would not deviate from the truth even to make a compliment and he replied: '*Mr Shaw ne parle pas bien le français, mais il le parle avec une telle violence qu'il s'impose.*'

In Moscow at a birthday party which the Soviet authorities gave him, Shaw made a speech of effusive praise of the Soviet system. Sir Robert Witt[7] heard Shaw at lunch telling the Astors he was rather sorry he had to speak as he did.

Later—Saturday evening—I dined with the Astor–Shaw party at the Europa. Mrs Litvinov was on my right, Lady Astor the other side. They sparred a bit. Lord Astor and his son tried to discourage her afterwards from disputing with the *tovs* and telling them that some of the things they have are not new: we have had similar things in England for 500 years, and so on, but I said I thought it was a good thing that someone should tell them the truth: if their mouths were closed by the Soviet hospitality the Soviet Government's purpose would have been attained. Lord Lothian came round for an hour before dinner and had a long talk. Quiet but interesting. Speaking of the German crisis he said that the bankers run Europe, not because they are plotting against the public good but because they are in daily touch with each other by telephone and can come to an agreement quickly whereas the statesmen are sparring at each other and take a long time to come to an agreement— if they ever succeed at all.

26 July. I went to the Hermitage for an hour or two with Cholerton and Miss Clyman. Coming home behind a building near the Palace, Miss Clyman spotted some pigs through a window in a half-basement. I have seen them again since.

A party of English doctors and scientists passed through—mostly much impressed by what they had seen, and as they had been taken to all the show-places and nothing else this is perhaps not remarkable. They were shown the Metchnikov Hospital and found it better-equipped than English hospitals, but some of the party went out on their own and went into the first hospital they came to (in the Nevsky): the doctors were taken by surprise but received them politely, but the visitors found the equipment lamentably inadequate.

The iron balcony on a house opposite the Grand Hotel has been taken down and the hand-rails on the steps removed and replaced by

[7] Sir Robert Witt (1872–1952) was founder and president of the National Art Collections Fund (NACF), and trustee of the National Gallery and the Tate. His colleague Alec Martin (1884–1971; see below) had joined Christie's at the age of thirteen, upon assurance that he might rise 'to be one of the porters', and went on to become managing director. (*NACF Review*, 1971.)

wood. The metal is badly needed. There are some things such as saucepans and other articles of household use which are not sold but can only be got in exchange for old metal.

On Monday after lunch I started out with Miss Clyman for the islands. Our tram broke down half-way, so we caught a battered carriage and drove back to a park and there had tea out of our thermos and sat for an hour. Sandys[8] (Third Secretary at Berlin) and a friend named Fuller came to dinner. I saw Miss Clyman off by the 11.30 train to Moscow and then went with Sandys and Fuller to see whether it was true, as alleged by an English doctor, that homeless children in rags could be seen sleeping all around the Warsaw Station. We saw none, though we saw the usual number of drunks. Perhaps we were a little early—12.30. I think the doctor was there about 2 a.m.

29 July. I was at the Hermitage yesterday and had occasion to go to the office. There was a notice posted up saying: 'The weeding season has been extended five days during which period the Hermitage must furnish a hundred men' (? men days). The appearance of those appointed and those who volunteer is categorically obligatory (*strogo obyazatel'no*). Yesterday the Red Cross doctors were not working. They had to go out cutting turf for the Leningrad power-plants.

My purpose in going to the Hermitage office was to assist Sir Robert Witt and Alec Martin who wanted to know whether (as they heard) the Soviet Government are selling any more pictures. A number of valuable ones have been sold: e.g. Mellon, the US Secretary to the Treasury, has bought four, though he denies it. Witt and Martin had seen in Moscow a man high up in the antiquities department and he had given them the names of two of his opposite numbers in Leningrad. Witt said they were scoundrelly looking fellows. They at first denied that any pictures had been sold and when Witt told them what was sold and to whom, they said that was at a time when the Soviet Government wanted money: now they had no need of money. It was no good arguing however with these two picture experts. Witt fancies a big Tiepolo—'Cleopatra and Court'—but Martin says (truly) that it has no depth.

This afternoon I went with Miss Daunt to see Mrs Yates, an old DBS who is dying of cancer. The Yateses owned many factories; now she is destitute. She has an adopted daughter who teaches in evening classes

---

[8] Duncan Sandys (1908–1987) was in the diplomatic service from 1930 to 1935. He later served as a member of parliament (1939–45), becoming a cabinet minster before being given a life peerage.

for workers. The *only* reading book is about 'constructing socialism'—life of Stalin, 'sabotage', Soviet industries, etc. Came back in a tram which was so crowded that I couldn't get out in time and was carried past my stopping-place.

Martin, now a partner in Christie's, told me he used to sweep the floors there. When he was fifteen he worked in Paris as a waiter for four months to learn French, and spent his holidays for thirty years in picture galleries. He was in the Hermitage when one of the officials they saw with me the other day passed by. Martin smiled and bowed but the official hurried on without taking any notice. We had all remarked how harassed he looked, as though he might be jockeyed out of his job at any moment.

A few days ago an old lady, a Russian of over sixty, came in crying. Her son is in England and wants her to go and live with him and HMG have authorised grant of a visa, but the Soviet Government won't let her go. Evidently there are lots of applications to go abroad which are refused.

A tractor expert and a big American farmer have been over the main grain area in the south. Much seed sown far too late. It was painful to see how good American agricultural machinery was being misused: it is used up in one year instead of lasting for five. As to locally made tractors: at one place a hundred were expected, fifty arrived, thirty wouldn't run at all, and of the remaining only three were running at the end of the first day. The manager was not interested in anything except a giant roller which he had had constructed. He was anxious that the American should see it roll, so he had it hitched to a Soviet tractor, which at once petered out. An American tractor moved it all right, but the driver leaned round to speak to someone and the roller ran into the tractor and did a thousand dollars' worth of damage. The director was quite pleased. 'Stout fellow!' he said. 'That' (to the Americans) 'will show you which is better, your tractor or my roller.' The American farmer saw the grain-trust people when he got back to Moscow and talked to them for three hours, and told them how bad things were. 'We know,' they said, 'but what can we do!'

31 July. Lady Muriel Paget arrived this morning. Also, by air, a friend of hers, Miss Goldman.[9] We were joined at tea by a Mr Metcalfe, a

___

[9] Emma Goldman (1869–1940) was a leading figure in Anarchist International; she had first been sent to Russia against her will, having been deported there by the USA in 1919. She felt no affinity for the country—unlike Lady Muriel, who wrote upon her

businessman who is touring Russia. Much of what he says is more sensible than the anti-Russian stuff one reads in most English newspapers, but I don't trust him. He was praising the port of Leningrad, and the excellent arrangements for loading timber.

3 Aug. Four captains in today. I asked them how the work at the port compared with the work in England. They were all scornful, and said the men here couldn't do half as much as the men in England—partly through lack of skill, but partly, they thought, through unwillingness to exert themselves.

Miss Daunt came across a case where a doctor got tired of his wife, went out, and came back with a bill of divorcement and a new wife. The law provides that a divorced wife or husband cannot be ejected, and as the first wife couldn't find anywhere else to live, she stayed on with the husband and his new wife. This is the second case I have heard of. The other was at Moscow. The wife of one of the Embassy porters fell off a train and lost a leg, whereupon the husband divorced her and brought home another wife to the old room.

Lady Muriel has brought a Ford van for DBS work. On 1 August she and I and Miss Goldman and Martin went out to the islands. A beautiful place. Lots of people bathing—none in the nude, but some of the women with bathing-drawers and nothing else but wisps of stuff over the nipples. They were quite unconcerned. One woman of about thirty-five who was drying herself as I passed a few feet from her was polishing a pair of enormous breasts which were apparently as hard as the calf of a man's leg.

Circular letter, 4 Aug. Going in a tram is torture. A few days ago I was returning to the office at about half-past four, when the first workers were going home. The tram was packed so tight that when we reached my destination I was unable to get out. I managed to hop off while the tram was getting up steam, and then a policeman blew his whistle and wanted to fine me for getting off a vehicle in motion.

I have an immense flat to live in. The position is excellent (26 Nevsky Prospekt): we look out in front on a garden between the curved wings of the Kazan Cathedral; at the side we appear to look out mainly on a lady who on sunny days sits on her window-sill baring her back to the

return to the USSR on this occasion: 'The feeling of being back in Russia is quite indescribable to anyone who has lived there and has left a part of themselves behind and comes back to find it again.'

☆

waist. The huge premises easily accommodate myself and two vice-consuls (one married). My flat is exactly opposite the Greek portico in the middle of the cathedral. In the foreground is a statue of Barclay de Tolly balanced on the left by the statue of Kutuzov. They it was who, with the help of the Russian climate and of whoever it was gave the order for the burning of Moscow, brought about the defeat of Napoleon in 1812.

For over a week I have been busy unpacking, rearranging rooms, sorting out and reading up the files. A large corridorful of cases is packed with all kinds of junk. There was a mass of dusty stationery left behind when the Embassy left after the Revolution, cases and cases of archives going back to the earliest years of the 19th century, boxes of books belonging to a defunct English club, bound volumes of *Punch*, a billiard-table in bits with twenty cues, rusty fenders, a broken weighing-machine, curtain-poles without brackets and brackets without poles, tin trunks full of waste-paper and old photographs, and so on.

The Russians must be a remarkable people, physically. By our standard they are underfed and improperly fed, but they manage—at least in the summer—to look well. I have come to the conclusion that our rules of diet do not apply to a people who are the survivors of centuries of hard living. Foreigners who come in contact with Russian workers, e.g. masters of ships and engineers in factories, say that they cannot do the hardest physical work well because they are underfed, but for ordinary purposes they do very well.

5 Aug. Spent a couple of hours at the courts (16 Fontanka). All the time in the same court—civil and criminal cases. Court consists of a president and two assessors, who are supposed to keep him in touch with working-class principles. The president and the assessors sit at a table, and as the parties, witnesses, etc. stand, they are higher than the bench. The witnesses, accused, etc. stand so close to the judges' table that the proceedings can be carried on in ordinary tones, which makes it difficult for a foreigner to follow what is going on. The court withdrew to discuss two of the cases, but usually the decision was given after a little whispering by the president to each of the assessors behind his hand. All the cases were simple ones—child maintenance, disorderly conduct, threatening behaviour—and dealt with summarily: nothing was written down except the judgment, which was brief. The accused did not seem at all intimidated and justice seemed to be swift and pretty reasonable. Before deciding however, as Bernard Shaw would have done, that Soviet justice is better than English, it is well to remember that all cases which

☆

are considered by the OGPU to affect the security of the State (e.g. saving up too many small coins) are dealt with in secret by men who may execute at once without trial. I noticed that in a criminal case the accused was always asked whether Party or non-Party, and education.

13 Aug. I went with Lady Muriel and Miss Goldman to visit the 'Red October' works in Leningrad—formerly the Renault motor-car factory. Four thousand employees, of whom some 40% are women. It is being extended, and will eventually employ about 10,000. We were conducted round by the manager, the technical manager, the editor of the works newspaper, and an interpreter. To these were soon added three men who seemed to find our company more interesting than a trade-union meeting, and one or two other persons. We were favoured because foreign visitors are not now being shown over factories as freely as before.

Unfortunately I know nothing about motorcycles, or my inspection might have had more useful results. The Soviet motorcycles we saw seemed very small and lightly made, and hardly fitted in with the manager's statement that they wanted to make a strong machine which would stand up to the bad Russian roads, for which, he said, the British BSA motorcycles were not strong enough.

We asked questions about trade unionism and were at once shown into a trade-union meeting. As is common in important propaganda work in this country, the president was an able young Jew. He was well-grounded in the Party patter and answered questions in set phrases, and was much put out if one of his less well-instructed companions interrupted—as they frequently did. It was interesting to learn from him what one knew already, that the chief duty of the trade unions is to serve as an intermediary between the Party and the workers. Their main business, put in its plainest form, is to find out what the Party machine wants and then to try to make the workers do it. According to the Communist newspaper, the Leningrad *Pravda*, of the day following our visit, the trade-union members in the 'Red October' factory are not doing their duty in this respect: 'Stalin's instructions' about payment strictly by results have not yet been fully carried out. The factory works the continuous five-day week, one fifth of the employees having the 1st, 6th, 11th, etc. of the month as a holiday, another fifth the 2nd, 7th, etc. and so on. Men doing particularly heavy work, e.g. casting and forging, have a six-hour instead of a seven-hour day, and get a month's holiday in the year instead of a fortnight. Workers get from one to three hours' technical instruction after their ordinary work.

☆

The works newspaper contains a complaint by a worker that lunch is sometimes not ready when his shift knocks off for the 45-minute interval, and that the food provided is far from adequate. Where, he asks bitterly, are those square meals there is so much talk about? The meals must be the less appetising from the use of a device to prevent the theft of cutlery which I understand is widely used in the factory dining-rooms. The only implement provided is a large iron spoon, rather bigger than a tablespoon. The diner takes a spoon on entering and has to deliver it up before he can leave.

All our party thought that many of the workers looked tired and underfed. If they really work for one to three hours after a seven-hour day they may well be tired. Many of the men and women we saw must have been out weeding on some of their free days to save the vegetable crop, and all of them were looking forward to 'Industrialisation Day'— an impressive name for staying at your bench and doing an ordinary day's work instead of having your fifth day off.

We saw no signs of frenzied activity—the boasted 'shock tempo'. Many benches were idle—for lack of workers. The manager told us two causes of low production: staying away from work, and causing stoppages of machinery and faulty work through inattention and carelessness. Behind him were many specimens of *brak* which had been produced in the factory, and, under lock and key with the names of the culprits attached, tools and pieces of material which had been stolen and recovered.

We were invited to attend a factory concert a few days later, at 4.30. We went at 5.00 and found a meeting in progress. We listened for over an hour to political speeches. We heard about 'the interventionists, unmasked by our OGPU'. There were several speakers. The audience talked all the time and took no notice. Perhaps they also avoid looking at the posters, which always depict the same heroic figures of 1905 and 1917, the same shirkers and drunkards, the same priests hindering the Plan and keeping children from school. It might pay the Soviet Government in industrial efficiency to allow workers to appoint a Lord of Misrule now and then. I chatted with the manager and the first speaker—a decent little man who if he made anything material out of the Party certainly did not make either clothing or boots or food. We heard the first part of the concert, entirely by members of the works staff. Very good. I noticed that the same roll of material—an ugly brown stuff with a large white check—had served to provide shirts for the announcer and several other men and a blouse for the lovely Amazon from the factory office.

☆

From a report to HM Ambassador in Moscow on conditions in the Leningrad Consular District, 18 Aug.[10] The 'mobilisation of financial resources', i.e. the collection of revenue under all heads, is stated to have been completely successful in the city of Leningrad, but most disappointing in the country districts, where, out of an estimated total of 7,339,000 roubles, only 2,893,000 roubles has been collected. Loan subscriptions went particularly badly, bringing in only 282,000 roubles out of an estimated 3,923,000 roubles.

Eighty-five thousand workers and 'employees' (i.e. clerks and the like) are stated to have failed to subscribe to the latest loan. Such information as can be got indicates that professional people and employees rarely or never dare to refuse to subscribe to the loans; that manual workers are occasionally more audacious; and that the country districts are failing to subscribe because they have not the money at their disposal.

From the low revenue returns it may be concluded that the rapid collectivisation has thrown the province into some confusion. The same deduction may perhaps be made from the fact that the city had to be called upon to furnish 'volunteers' (to the number eventually of over 400,000 men-days) to help to weed the collective vegetable gardens on their free days and even on days when they should have been doing their ordinary work. While this was going on, the collective farms were being told to furnish contingents of men and women to become workers in the city factories. A foreign observer, who has been round some of the country districts recently, says that the difficulty is not to get collective farm workers to come to the factories, but to keep enough of them behind to work the farms. The factory worker at least knows where he is: he has a more or less fixed wage and a food-card, and when there is any clothing to be sold he gets the first choice. The collective farm worker knows nothing except that he is to get a given share of whatever the Government decides, at the end of the season, to leave for the workers to divide, and that hitherto the country districts have had great difficulty in procuring clothes and such small luxuries as tea or sugar. The Novgorod area has been without salt for two months.

20 Aug. Off on leave today. At the last moment heard of a most unfortunate incident: the chief engineer of a British ship has been shot dead by a sentry—for, it is alleged, failing to answer a challenge.

---

[10] The full text of this, and all of RWB's other reports to HM Ambassador in Moscow, can be seen at the Public Record Office in London.

☆

At the end of his ten weeks' leave in England, RWB returned on a Soviet ship.

11 Nov. The Baltic was sunny, the wind was behind us and it was not cold. The bath never worked but we were better off than the third-class passengers, who all slept with their beds almost touching, men, women and children together, down below. One man hung up a sheet to conceal his family from the public gaze, but another cursed him for his pride. It is better to avoid any action that can be called bourgeois.

I had my meals at a table for four; the others were an American engineer, his wife and a Scottish doctor. I was the only non-Jew. The American engineer is the only foreigner employed on a huge enterprise at Khibinogorsk, a new town near Murmansk, where an enormous deposit of a valuable phosphate called apatite has been discovered. The doctor was on a tour which would give him five days in Moscow. He hoped to be able to stay with a Soviet medical man to whom he had an introduction, but the ordinary Soviet doctor would tremble with fear of the OGPU if a foreigner wanted to stay with him. But as he is both enterprising and Jewish, he may be able to arrange something. Most of the passengers on the boat were Ukrainians who had gone to the United States when there was plenty of work to be got there. They will not find it easy to return to the United States should they be unable to get work or stand the bad food and conditions.

Also on board was a young English communist, with a degree in physics at King's College, London, who has a three-year contract with the Soviet Government to work on long-distance telephony. He said that there were great opportunities for development in that line in Russia—much better than England. Perhaps Russia gets credit for having been a century behind the times. The wife, a pretty, intelligent young woman, who expects to get tracing work in a draughtsman's office, sang 'The Red Flag' at Kiel with the others. They will not find living conditions very good for the husband has been foolish enough to sign a contract in roubles only. I fear they will find the difference between the propaganda and the reality shocking.

Also on board were a party of fifteen British workmen from a variety of factories and industries going to find out 'the truth' about Russia, with the aid of a Soviet interpreter and at the expense of the Soviet Government. I could have written their report for them. When we arrived at Leningrad, one of the Russian Jews waved a red flag and called for cheers for Soviet Russia and sang a song about the Red Army.

It has been a mild autumn in Russia. The windows have been stuck

☆

up for the winter, and with a very little heating we keep quite warm. Once the big tiled stoves have been lit, and the damper shut down, the stove keeps warm for two or three days.

On the morning of the 7th I had to attend the parade for the anniversary of the October Revolution. In the afternoon Weinstein gave an 'at-home' to the Consular Corps and a few officials who are let out for such purposes, notably a few members of the Academy. I met Samoilovich, Professor of Oriental Languages, and we talked Turkish together. He invited me to go and see the Academy.

My heavy stuff arrived yesterday—very welcome. The maids are delighted with their aprons, stockings and dress material. The gramophone was undamaged. I want to go very slow with it so as to keep the records unworn for visitors, and when I am alone to have music and propaganda on the wireless.

Cave is going to Finland on leave for three weeks. Poor Cave! Everything goes wrong with him. He lost his position in business, and his property, in the Revolution. While working in our consulate in Yokohama he lost his wife in the great earthquake and only just escaped with his own life. He suffers from asthma, and has the most painful coughing fits for about two hours every morning. He married his wife's sister—out of compassion. It seems she lives in Paris where she is consistently unfaithful to him, though he has not the means to collect evidence and secure a divorce. Meanwhile he has to keep her as well as his mother out of a very small salary as supernumerary vice-consul. About two months ago he began to spit blood. He has just had another attack, and although the doctor says that it is not tuberculosis it is difficult to see what else it is. And now, just as he is about to take a little holiday, he breaks out in a series of painful boils. Yet he is always cheerful and laughs at himself as having 'the devil's own luck!'

Dr Bell's daughter has just got into the university medical school through the influence of Cave with the authorities, after at first being refused admission because she was not of proletarian origin. She has first to do fifty days of theory, then fifty days working as a nurse, then another fifty days' theory and fifty days as an assistant doctor, before her final fifty days when she is in charge of ten beds under supervision. Pretty rapid progress. I had heard that the Soviets were turning peasants into doctors in three years. This is how it is done.

15 Nov. Still mild, but rainy. It gets dark so early I don't go out. The streets seem to be more crowded than they were. They may well be, for I hear that whereas the population of Leningrad was increasing at the

★

rate of 20,000 a month in the spring, during August and September it increased by 120,000. With this huge influx of people living accommodation is becoming more and more difficult to find. One of the two Leningrad papers has an article headed: 'Hundreds of specialists without a square metre of living room spend the night with acquaintances.' And goes on to say that one hundred of the employees at one factory have no home, that Engineer A lives with a family of five in a bathroom, Engineer B lives with three others in a dark, damp passage where each has 3½ square metres of space, Engineer C lives with his family of five and two strangers in a room of which the area is only 24 square metres, and so on. In the place Miss Kennell[11] lives, a married couple, two unmarried men and two unmarried women share one room. One would sympathise with them if they did not suppress all this in their foreign propaganda and hide it from their foreign visitors, to whom they show model dwellings.

The Leningrad *Pravda* recently printed an article in which they claimed that a Russian factory had made a 50,000 kilowatt dynamo in less time than Metro-Vickers could do it. This is the one British firm working in Russia. It supplies electrical machinery and equipment made in England, installs it, maintains it and teaches the Russians to make similar stuff. The head of Metro-Vickers told me that all the parts of this Russian dynamo that require strength or delicacy of workmanship were made in England and that although the dynamo was said to be finished in June, it is still not in working order. However the factory announces that it has 'fulfilled the Five-Year Plan', and six of the engineers have been given the order of Lenin. Of these six only two have any serious engineering knowledge. But if this kind of thing is going on all over the country, the standard of work cannot be very high and the standard of honesty not much higher.

I had Muir to dinner. He is a young working-class Scot with a good degree in chemistry at Edinburgh and a state scholarship enabling him to have eighteen months in Russia, studying soil chemistry. At first he had great difficulty in securing food and getting it cooked, but he managed to form a mess (called here a commune) and this has freed his mind for study. The other members of the mess include a communist woman factory-worker who is the only really fearless Russian Muir has met. Always criticising the communists for their selfishness, for using their position as communists to gain undue advantages, and for their complete failure to deal justly with the people. She disregarded the order

---

[11] Russian-born American writer whom RWB had met in Moscow.

☆

to parade on 1 May and 7 November. It has always been said that the Russian women have more backbone than the men. When the remnants of Wrangel's army were carried to Constantinople it was the women who opened restaurants and cafés and gave lessons in languages and music, while the men used to call on the British and French officers and ask what was to be done for them. Muir confirms that there is a great shortage of living room. He finds that the assistants in the co-operative stores here are as independent and unsympathetic 'as in the co-ops in Scotland'. In the institute where he works, there is a Party spy who ensures that the 'general line of the Party' is followed. Muir has had many arguments with him. Muir thinks that the people complain rather less than they did eighteen months ago. We all agree that some foodstuffs are easier to come by than a few months ago—fruit, for instance—though sold at very high prices. Each of the two summers he had been here Muir has been out on field-work for several months. In the Crimea he found food pretty short, but the Russian collective farms were better organised than the Tartar. Grapes were always to be had for the asking. But in general supplies were badly organised. One village had had no matches for two months, though they were on sale a few miles away. When the cart delivered the next month's supply of groceries there were still no matches. Muir said some scientists formerly hostile or indifferent to communism are beginning to support the system, though he couldn't say whether they were influenced by the desire for advancement or the fear of losing their employment. Muir was very critical of the system whereby the universities are supposed to be run by the students. In his institute the whole syllabus has been changed four times within a year—mainly at the dictation of the students, and the disorganisation was frightful.

Yesterday Dr Bell's son came to install the new wireless. It works wonderfully on the Leningrad station, and I got Moscow once, but I haven't been able to get any foreign stations. Last night I improved my Russian by listening to a lecture on work in a motor factory, followed by a concert by the Leningrad Philharmonic.

17 Nov. The Ford van came to take me to see the wooden house which the Relief Association are building on 25 acres of land near Dyetskoye Syelo with the aid of a grant from the charity commissioners. I had to certify that the work is well advanced.

I have asked the Society for Cultural Relations with Foreign Countries (VOKS) to arrange for me to see various typical institutions. The director suggested that I ought to understand the principles

☆

underlying the Soviet organisation and that I might like to attend some
lectures. I jumped at the chance as I do at any chance of coming in
contact with Russians. I think that the authorities must scent a possible
convert in me and that it is worth their while to make a good
impression. I don't mind what they think, so long as they enable me to
escape from the life of a fish in an aquarium.

20 Nov. Yesterday I went with my Swedish colleague to see the Oriental
Institute. We were taken round by three of the professors: Oldenberg,
who is the head of the institute, Samoilovich, in charge of the Central
Asian section, and a Tartar, Alimov, head of the Turkish section.
Oldenberg is a man of the old regime, indifferent to politics, but so
valuable as a world-renowned savant that he has managed to retain his
position. He showed us many ancient manuscripts which he had himself
found in Central Asia and rather froze the others out of the
conversation.

On the 18th I went to dinner with Tearle, manager of Metro-Vickers.
Two engineers from England were staying with him. After dinner we
went to the mess and saw all the fitters, erectors etc. who opened some
champagne in my honour. They are a good lot and I had a very
interesting evening. They complained that the younger workers have no
discipline and waste half their time in chat. I suggested that if you told
young people for long enough that they were the only free people in the
world, that the factories, and so on all belonged to them—all formulas
intended partly to win their support and partly to hide the fact that
fundamentally they are one of the least free peoples—they would
eventually want to act on it in some way or other. They act on it by
doing little work: a practice which the Government are now trying to
counteract by payment by results, by the distribution of prizes, and by
punishments of which all one hears is that so and so has been flung out
of the Party or that another (not a Party man) has been handed over to
the Control Commission, which may mean exile or worse.

22 Nov. An Englishman named Hirons, who has been here eighteen
months, came and stayed until nearly teatime. He represents the
General Electric Company who have a contract to supply plant and
advice. His tale does not differ from that of other engineers I have seen.
The mechanics are very poor. All are untruthful. There is much graft,
indeed little without it.

A Uruguayan mechanic, working for six months in the Putilov
tractor-works, came in for a transit visa. He has had enough of it here:

☆

poor food and little of it. Didn't think much of Soviet castings. When you tightened up a nut the thread came off.

A Miss Saunders and Miss Harrison came with letters of introduction. Thanks to them I saw things in the Hermitage which I had not seen before. Dr Waldhauer[12] showed us the early Greek gold-work. It is closely guarded and rarely shown to the public. Probably the public, being badly fed and clothed and having been taught that only utility counts, would want to know why all this gold was not sold. It is the most wonderful collection both for size and beauty. The most interesting exhibit is a large vase showing Scythian figures in relief. One man is having his wounded leg bound up, another a tooth pulled by a man who is a good deal calmer than the patient. Waldhauer said rather sadly that he wished foreign scholars would come to Leningrad. Professor Beazley[13] came in 1928, but no English scholar had been since. That kind of man must feel the isolation very much. We went back to his room, and on the table, half-consumed, was the meal which he had left to take us round—a cup of tea and a hunk of black bread without a plate. He is an old man and obviously very feeble.

A German-speaking assistant showed us some Watteaus and other pictures not shown to the public. She told us her salary was 100 roubles a month, about that of an unskilled workman, which she was occasionally able to supplement by writing articles. She was very indignant at the report that pictures by Rembrandt, Titian and Botticelli had been sold abroad to buy machinery. We were shown the studio for picture restoration. The man in charge talked rusty German and had a hungry face and the oldest overcoat I ever saw. The room was unheated and very cold.

Miss Saunders told me she was standing in a cinema queue when a boy of about sixteen spoke to her in English. His father had been employed in ARCOS in London before the 1927 raid and wanted to get back to England. Failing that he wanted desperately to have a pair of 'Oxford bags', which couldn't be got in Leningrad. Miss Saunders tried to console him by saying that no one in England wore Oxford bags now, and he replied that in that case they might hope to have them here soon,

[12] Oskar Waldhauer was keeper of classical antiquities at the Hermitage, and in 1927–8 (shortly before twelve of the staff were executed as spies) he briefly succeeded Troinitsky as acting director. Waldhauer is credited with having initiated a populist educational programme, with lectures for schoolchildren and workers. (Geraldine Norman, *The Hermitage*: Pimlico, 1999.)

[13] Professor Sir John Beazley (1885–1970), professor of classical archaeology at Oxford, 1925–56.

★

for Russia got all the foreign fashions when they had ceased to be the fashion.

Weinstein (nominally the Leningrad representative of the Commissariat for Foreign Affairs) is evidently a man of no importance, afraid to take any responsibility. The real force is his assistant, also Jewish in spite of his half-Russian half-Cossack name, Orlov-Ermak. He must be very well up in the Party for he can get things done and speaks with authority.

The first snow fell yesterday. The Vice-Consul's office, which is connected with mine by double doors, is heated by a tiled stove which warms my room a little too, but not much. At present when I am alone in the evening I put on my Gilgit robe and the sheepskin boots that M gave me and I'm thoroughly warm and comfortable—more comfortable than with a wood fire, which is a nuisance to keep up and never maintains a steady heat.

The Christmas presents I should really like to have would be some table salt, some cheap ash-trays (in a flat this size with visitors smoking in the office, the drawing-room and the dining-room, one can't have too many), and six to twelve coat-hooks with enough screws (and to spare) to put them up with.

Miss Kennell has returned from her trip to Siberia. She writes from Moscow: 'The trip had a most depressing and wearing effect. To return to a place coloured with romantic memories and find it a mudhole of buildings, with human beings sunk in their living standards to that of animals—people who, when I lived there, had a somewhat pastoral existence—I loathed it all. I can't become reconciled to the fact that the more they build the harder life becomes for the people. But there is no question that they are building—a most incongruous sight to see the big blast-furnaces, coke-ovens and power-plants rising and the people who are building them burrowing into the ground for shelter. I was ten days at Kuznetskstroy (the big coal-mining centre) and three days at my old home in Kemerovo—thirteen days there and eleven days on the road.' I hope she will come here on the way home.

28 Nov. I went out for an hour's walk. It was lovely—about 7°F below zero but dry underfoot and with a little sun still showing. The Neva was covered with small ice floes an inch or two thick—broken away during the day from indentations in the banks. Now it is a quarter past three and the sun is just disappearing behind the houses.

It is interesting to compare the Soviet reports published in the press with what is announced over the wireless. The newspapers are a permanent record, and go abroad, so they are more carefully worded. For instance, today's paper attributes short delivery of grain, flax etc. to the *kulaks*, grafters, etc. named so-and-so, but it is left to the wireless to name the people handed over to the Control Commission. Some years ago the Soviet Government declared that the death penalty had been abolished. A reservation was made in the case of offences that might be considered particularly harmful socially. This of course allowed the OGPU to go on as before shooting anyone whose face they didn't like, but it apparently also allowed the ordinary criminal courts to inflict the death sentence. Visitors to Moscow are shown a model prison with very agreeable murderers being imperceptibly reformed.

The Times of 24 November announces that with effect from 1 December most factories and establishments, other than public utility enterprises such as tramways, will have a six-day week with a common rest-day. In offices the 'continuous week' is hopeless. In theory there should never be a day when you can't get something done, but in practice you find that if the man you want is not away, someone he wants to consult is. I have heard that the working day is to be reduced from seven hours to 6½ to make up for the lengthening of the week. But it is always well to see what happens in practice. We may hear that 'the workers are voluntarily giving up the additional half-hour of rest'.

29 Nov. Mended about eight pairs of black socks. Ought to have waited until later. It is already lighter than when I was darning. The corridor in the wing and the unused rooms are very cold, and the servants go about muffled in shawls. The Office of Works have sent table-lamps but not any bulbs. I suppose they think that bulbs can be bought here as easily as at home.

Muir, the young soil chemist, has brought an invitation from the director of the soil institute for me to 'co-operate' with the institute in the compilation of a soil map of Arabia at the request of the International Society of Soil Science. I should like to help if I can in the interests of science and because it would bring me in touch with Russians who I should not otherwise meet. I must ask the Embassy, but I don't think they will object.

On Friday night I had the whole of Mussorgsky's opera *Khovanshchina*. I have never seen the Russian ballet, so the other day I walked to the Opera a mile or more away, and tried to buy a ticket, but there were no seats. There are not nearly enough theatres in Leningrad now that most of the population can afford to go to them. Only four, I think, and a music-hall and a circus.

☆

On Thursday the Woodheads and the Todds came to dinner. Woodhead is a specialist in the manufacture of paper, and has a red card such as is carried by members of the Communist Party, with which he can get a place on any train, however crowded. Some foreign specialists have a hard time at first, especially if they are not forewarned to take supplies with them. When travelling it is a good thing to take lots of soap and cigarettes. Woodhead bartered a chicken for a cake or two of soap and on one occasion got a chicken ready roasted for three packets of the worst Russian cigarettes. One engineer went to Siberia with his wife and for weeks had nowhere to sleep but a room which they shared with seven other men, and for the first fortnight they lived on a 13lb loaf of black bread and a few tins of sardines. The Woodheads had dreadful tales of the forcible collectivisation of farms. In one place the peasants were 'induced' to form a collective farm, but not liking the conditions went back to their village. The organisers of the farm stretched a heavy chain between two enormous tractors and dragged it through the walls of the hovels—'men, women and children inside,' says Mrs Woodhead. There is nothing inherently improbable in this story. The Government are determined to get large supplies of grain at all costs, and with the OGPU their chief instrument, having powers of life and death, anything may happen. Woodhead reckons that at the Paper Trust where he works there are 200 engineers and draughtsmen doing the work of ten American engineers.

Five o'clock, and I am about to embark on my usual evening programme—read (Russian, Latin and English) and listen to the wireless until about midnight, with about twenty minutes off for dinner, and two cups of tea at 9.30 to keep me awake. 'It must be so *interesting* to live abroad.' I think I had better go out for a stroll first, though it is quite dark and not very inviting.

30 Nov. I didn't after all spend my Sunday evening as I planned. I started out for a walk, but I saw people going into a shabby cinema to see an Armenian film and thought there might be some interesting pictures of Armenian life and customs. I went in and spent the equivalent of sixpence on a seat. The story was a conventional one, but to bring this into line with modern political and social theories, we were told at the end that this was Armenia sixty years ago, and modern Armenia was not like that—bourgeois love had been replaced by a deep biological theory—so that's all right.

6 Dec. I did not take any notice of my forty-sixth birthday yesterday beyond inviting Miss Daunt to come to dinner tonight. I hoped to have the new desk-lamps and furniture to celebrate the occasion, but although the boat has been in a week we haven't got it. Under the well of my desk, where it is colder than in the rest of the room, I have put a shallow wooden box with several layers of corrugated cardboard in the bottom—a good insulator. I have abandoned my office with its three enormous windows and open fireplace. The wood to heat it is too expensive. I had an inspiration. I will use the drawing-room as an office for the winter and the cost of heating it can be divided between me and HMG.

It is snowing today, but for the last few days we have had six hours of sun. Yesterday afternoon I walked along the Neva which is completely frozen, and although the temperature is 8°F (−24° of frost) the buildings protected me from the wind. All navigation on canals and rivers came to an end several days ago. The surface of the river freezes into little floes which for a time are swept away to sea. The floes then jam at the bridges, and those behind press down on those in front and pile up into hedges of points and spikes and needles. The surface of the river looks like a strange ice-garden.

The Times reports that all persons deprived of political and other rights are being turned out of Leningrad. Housing is a problem far beyond any ordinary solution. Huge blocks of rooms have been erected—for students, for factory workers, for people in general, but the influx of peasants is far greater than any building scheme can keep pace with. Dr Bell says that he recently saw a room occupied by five families in five beds. A plank stretched across the room served as a table for all five families. People sleep in the railway-stations, in trams, in the depots, in trains in the sidings—anywhere. In theory each person is supposed to have nine square metres, i.e. anything from a strip 40 foot by 10 yards to a square 10 foot by 10 foot, but many people have less. For anything up to the minimum you pay a fixed sum according to your income, but for every square metre over the minimum you pay three times as much.

I wish I saw Dr Bell more often, for he always has some interesting stories, though he is inclined to exaggerate. He has a friend, an engineer, who is employed on the construction of a huge building on the other bank of the Neva to house over 6000 people. It is being built almost entirely by prisoners who get a fixed wage of 10 roubles a month and some food. This friend needed a man with a particular technical skill, and as there was no one on the job with the necessary training, he told the chief (an OGPU man of course). '*Naidyom*,' ('We'll find one') said the chief. A week later the required man appeared, a prisoner. 'What are

★

you in for?' asked the engineer. 'I don't know,' said the man. 'They arrested me three days ago and here I am, and that's all I know about it.'

When Molotov made the speech in which he declared that no forced labour was employed on timber work, all forced labour had been cleared away from the ports of Archangel and Murmansk, where until that time it was seen by hundreds of foreigners. Some workers went to dig the White Sea–Baltic canal, but about 40,000 were sent to Siberia to work under the OGPU on a huge State farm.

An OGPU man offered to imprison a man for Miss Daunt a few days ago. It happened in this way. A Miss Brett was going to England on leave this summer and she offered to sub-let her room to Lady Muriel Paget for £25 to be paid in England. When Miss Daunt went to take possession of the room she found a man in occupation (Miss Brett's lover, it appears), who not only refused to give up the room but was exceedingly rude. Torgsin, who do a lot of business with Lady Muriel, knew about this, and the other day Kulagin, an OGPU man and manager of Torgsin, asked Miss Daunt whether she would like the man imprisoned, and if so for how long. She said he could hardly be imprisoned for that, and Kulagin laughed and said: 'Oh, we can soon get him for something else.' However, Miss Daunt refused the handsome offer. She also refused when the same man, Kulagin, after insisting on lending her his pocket-comb because her hair was disarranged, said: 'Did you leave a husband in England? Because I am alone at present.'

The recent announcement that prices in the 'free' shops were to be reduced by 30% would have been more welcome if the things people want to buy were available. There is no butter or sugar. There is a scheme by which you are supposed to be able to make certain of clothing if you pay for it in advance. Dr Bell paid in the early spring for a pair of shoes to be delivered not later than 1 August, but he hasn't got them yet.

Lady Muriel asked if Torgsin could be sure of finding in Russia all the material they need for the small house they are building for the Relief Association, and they said 'Yes.' Then they asked for locks, door-handles, etc. to be sent out from England. They have dug the well and they can't get a pump anywhere. Finally they were unable to find the glass for the windows. At last Kulagin heard that a shipload of glass was being sent off somewhere to be sold abroad and he rushed off to try to secure enough to glaze the windows in our house. I have not yet heard whether he got any.

7 Dec. I had a pleasant dinner with Miss Daunt last night. I gave the cook a bottle of English redcurrants and she made a two-decker tart that was very good. I shall try to get Miss Daunt to come in every Sunday because she gives herself no rest but works every evening up to eight or nine or even later, and a standing invitation may persuade her to take Sunday evening off and we can have some music. Last night she did not arrive until nearly 8.00 (dinner was fixed for 7.30) and she had come straight from work. She had spent much of the day at the Red Cross. There she found the assistant director crouched over the stove suffering from influenza and shivering with nothing but a sort of cotton coat over her thin dress. Miss Daunt asked whether she hadn't anything warmer, and she said no. Miss Daunt offered her a woollen jumper out of her Relief Association stock, but the woman said: 'I should be very glad if I could have it but that would be a shooting matter.' Miss Daunt did not know whether this would be for corruption, or for admitting to a foreigner that she needed warm clothing and could not get it in Russia.

Miss Daunt is dealing with a scheme which would make a British company, of which Lady Muriel would be a sort of honorary director, the clearing-house for remittances of money sent by people abroad for the purchase of food in Leningrad to be sent to relatives and friends in Russia. Miss Daunt explained to Kulagin that the senders would want some sort of guarantee that the recipients of the relief would not be penalised for their connection with people abroad. He was much hurt at these suspicions, and explained that the OGPU lived only for the general good. 'I,' he said, 'am the chief of the OGPU here. Do I look as though I could be guilty of such a thing?' Miss Daunt hastened to explain that she and Lady Muriel had complete confidence in the impartiality, goodness of heart and sense of justice of the authorities, it was merely a question of satisfying people abroad. She said that in fact the man looks as though he would murder his mother and not think twice about it.

Large numbers of *lishentsy* (deprived persons) have recently been turned out of Leningrad and moved to the country round about. In Leningrad they beg in the streets and keep alive somehow, but in the country there is nothing to be done.

Yesterday Dr Bell was called before the Public Prosecutor because over sixty people had fallen sick after eating in the dining-room of the factory to which he is the doctor. It was supposed he had been careless about some rat-poison which he had given the cook a few days before. However no phosphorus was found in the food and the trouble was due to the use of rotten meat. Two people have died and twelve others are dangerously ill.

☆

The six-day week for many factories and institutions has begun. The Foreign Affairs people now close on the 6th, 12th etc. of the month instead of the 5th, 10th etc. but they have to work half an hour longer. The only compensation for the six-day week is that forty-five minutes instead of thirty is now given for a factory lunch.

Cave is back. He has got rid of the boils and had his teeth seen to and there is no return of the blood from the lungs.

The Foreign Affairs people have told us that when we want to see a theatre or opera we only need to ring them up and tell them what we want the morning of the same day and they will arrange it.

There has been a revival of the mass arrests and shootings lately. Perhaps this is because the economic situation is bad and victims must be found. Transport is bad. Fuel is bad. The harvest seems to be very bad. I have heard of a second place in the country where swarms of *lishentsy* are arriving from Leningrad. There is little to eat in the country as it is, so that even if the local people wanted to feed the newcomers and were allowed to, they could not.

Owing to the slackness in foreign trade the authorities are desperate for *valuta*, i.e. foreign currency. A Canadian engineer who had a long contract to run is just being paid off; the Soviet Government say they cannot afford to go on paying him in foreign currency. Ericsson, the local representative of the Swedish telephone firm of that name, tells me that their long-standing contract will probably not be renewed since the Soviet 'trust' will not pay in foreign currency. He says that the Germans have sold enormous quantities of goods to Russia on credit and greatly fear that the Soviet Government will proclaim a moratorium on their debt. Lie, an optimist, has no fear, he thinks that the Soviet Government will do anything rather than default on their foreign debts, but he admits that things are bad, and says that, according to a Swedish communist he knows very well, Molotov, at a private meeting of important Bolsheviks, said 'Things can't go on like this.'

In spite of the boasts in the press it is difficult to point to any one thing that is a striking success. An enormous factory at Nizhniy Novgorod is eventually to turn out 140,000 Ford cars a year. That sounds very well, but any Soviet department or enterprise will strive to get a foreign rather than a Russian Ford. Torgsin are very anxious to buy the Relief Association's Ford van, and Kulagin told Miss Daunt that he wanted it because it was American and so much better than the Russian Ford.

The boasted achievements of the old Putilov works, which were said to have beaten Metro-Vickers all along the line in making turbines for

☆

electric generators, fall into their proper place when you read in the Soviet papers a month later that the same factory has failed lamentably in the provision of locomotive parts for the railways. They certainly haven't 'fulfilled the Plan', and much of what they have done isn't in the plan at all. Instead of axles they are furnishing piston-rods; instead of ball-bearings, axle-boxes, and so on. However, according to *Moscow News*, the British communist delegates who were on my boat find that everything here far exceeds even what they expected, believe that the Plan will be completed in four years, and propose to urge England to follow Russia's example. I remember R.H. Tawney, who knows many communists, said that unfortunately you can't believe a word they say. Being a communist seems to put a kink in the brain which can never be straightened out. I think that the reason is that they consider themselves to be at war with society and therefore entitled to use any weapon that comes to their hand.

15 Dec. Furniture arrived. The consignment was so large that three women have spent several hours just folding the wrapping-paper which we will save for parcels for the DBSs. Wrapping-paper cannot be bought here. Unfortunately there is a jagged tear in the upholstery of the settee on the edge of the seat where it cannot be hidden, but I have asked the Office of Works to send me a strip of the same stuff so that I can have two bands sewn over the edge, one over the tear and the other at the same distance from the other end. The dressing-table is the one weak spot. The top is screwed to the legs from underneath, and the least jerk is liable to tear the screws out by the roots. I have wedged it level, for our floors are uneven, and warned the servants not to move it when they sweep. We have sent a man with a written order with the consular seal to buy wooden planks from which to hang the curtains.

The Customs sent a man to examine the furniture. The first day he consumed some vodka, nearly half a bottle of whisky, and some odd drinks besides two square meals. He smacked his lips over some cold smoked fish and some pork. He said he had brought his wife and three children through very hard times in Leningrad towards the end of the War and after, though his old mother died of hunger. I said: 'Things are better now.' He thought a moment, and said: 'Things are better— because we are used to it.'

Lady Muriel told me the Prince of Wales was inspecting a hospital and said to a very attractive nurse: 'If I have an accident I hope that I shall have you for a nurse.' 'Sir,' said the nurse, 'that would require more than an accident, it would require a miracle. I am a maternity nurse.'

★

Miss Daunt, Pott and Cave came to dinner on Sunday. We played Beethoven's Third Symphony and began the Mozart Clarinet Quintet, but the gramophone was making a grinding noise which made me fear that the motor might go wrong so I stopped playing. Afterwards I moved it to the middle of the room where the floor was level and it went better.

The Arctic Society here gave a show last night to commemorate Amundsen's discovery of the South Pole twenty years ago. I thought that I ought to go. The best part was the music—Grieg quartets. After several speeches, we had a film in six parts of a Russian expedition in Novaya Zemlya.

It rather looks as though something has gone wrong with the Five-Year Plan. Imports exceed exports by a large amount and factories have been ordered to discharge superfluous labour. These superfluous workers must furnish between them a considerable body of unemployed, even allowing for the new factories, especially with the recent influx of peasants from the country. But the authorities do not admit that there is any unemployment—only surplus labour. And of course there is no unemployment benefit. There are one or two other signs of a slackening in the Plan or a change of direction but it is early to make up one's mind about them.

Miss Daunt is amusing about Kulagin, her OGPU man. He has insisted on giving her a pass for a special restaurant to which only people in authority like himself have access. It was a sort of Ritz before the war and is still the one place where really good food can always be got. The 'toiling masses' don't see the inside of it. Miss Daunt would rather go hungry than go to such a place. Kulagin told her he was head of OGPU in the south after the defeat of the Whites. If so he may easily have thousands of executions to his credit. Although nominally he is manager of Torgsin, rather akin in status to being manager of the Birmingham branch of Lipton's, he wears a large Mauser to assist him in the grocery business and he appears to have unlimited powers. His assistants run about like scared rabbits. To help Miss Daunt he arranged for an old woman of eighty to be taken into a home even though there is an order that no incurables can be taken. He rang up a suitable hospital and when they protested said: 'I, Kulagin, order you to do this.'

Miss Daunt had hardly time to get back here when the hospital rang to say the doctor in charge would be round with his car within the hour to fetch the old woman. Then again one of the DBSs wrote to Pott that his bread-card had been taken away because he was receiving food parcels from the Relief Association. Miss Daunt had only to mention the matter to Kulagin, for him to promise that within twelve hours the person responsible for taking away the bread-card would be severely punished. It reveals a queer conception of justice, and it also gives a glimpse into a curious hierarchy in which the manager of a shop in Leningrad can get an official in the Urals punished out of hand. It appears that the OGPU have men in all departments and enterprises, some of them in the most innocent positions.

I am trying to discover whether we are able to protect a boy of Russian parentage born in Canada who, after getting into trouble with the authorities, was put into the 'cold cell', where the prisoner rests on a plank not big enough to lie down on surrounded with running ice-cold water. He is sixteen.

16 Dec. I am beginning to wonder whether a public-school education is going to be the best preparation for the world into which our boys are growing up. The education in the narrowest sense at a good public school like Winchester is certainly far better than that which is to be had at the ordinary secondary school, but all the public schools have on them the curse which few of their boys escape—the curse of the belief that there is an impassable gulf between the public schools and other schools. Yet now that I have written this I wonder whether I am right? I am not conscious of a feeling that any of my colleagues mind whether I was at a public school or not. I was prickly enough about such points when I was at Cambridge.

Poor Cave is sitting opposite writing very carefully a long letter to his wife in Paris. It is a sad story. She lives in Paris and is always dunning him for more money. He owns a little wooden villa in Finland where she could live cheaply, but she refuses to leave Paris. He gets £650 a year and has no pension and no prospect and he has to support his old mother in Helsingfors. He is a wonderful man. He is not interesting, or well-read, or clever—except in dealing with Russians. He is plain, with a puffy face and asthmatic breathing, and apologetic manners, but he is most sincere and by far the most popular man here. The Russians will do almost anything for him, and all the other foreigners like him too. He is like the harmless, gentle people in some Russian books. A rare character. I wish he could get rid of his wife.

17 Dec. Heavy snow. Miss Kennell's train from Moscow was three hours late. She had a bad night for she had retreated into the corridor to escape her drunken fellow traveller, Richards, director of Metro-Vickers in England. He blew out the candle and locked the door in such a way that she had great difficulty in getting out into the corridor where she had to stay until the conductor could assure her that the man was asleep. She would not have had the same difficulty with a Russian. She had spent a few days in a half-collectivised village near Vladimir where she seems to have had a very interesting time. She found the village wretchedly hard-up for food and clothes. They had had no tea for a year, and tea means even more to the Russians than to the English. The peasants were selling off the last few things they had. Only about 10% had joined the collective farm, the others were suspicious and hostile. Miss Kennell told me of one man whose farm and everything he had had been taken away and who carried about with him a copy of the proclamation of 1917 in which Lenin promised the land to the peasants. He wanted to go to Moscow to recover his rights. Miss Kennell attended a three-hour meeting in which Party members tried to persuade the peasants to volunteer to pay a tax of 100% instead of 60%. There were murmurs of protest, and the vote was heavily against the increased tax. The chairman was livid, but went straight on with a proposal that every peasant should give up part of his land to grow fruit for the Government.

She visited a family called Costantinov. Mrs C is the widow of a very wealthy merchant. She has lost everything and shares one quarter of a room with her son of about twenty. Another quarter is occupied by a workman and his wife, and the remaining half by a communist and his wife. Mrs C is continually accused of having secret stores of money and jewels, and her water tax has been more than doubled. This may be to make her draw on the supposed hoard or drive her into the country to starve. Her sister, who came from an even wealthier family, was still living in part of an immense house of sixty rooms with some of the gorgeous furniture they owned. However these relations had completely given in, make no effort to repair anything, or clean anything, and seem to wallow in degradation and find some perverse pleasure in watching the disintegration of their former splendour.

Miss Kennell went first to Kuznetskstroy where huge iron- and steel-mills are springing up, where she was made comfortable by the many American engineers there. She saw large numbers of *kulaks* who had been exiled there from all parts of the country. Many of them have only tents to live in with their families, even through the Siberian winter, but some live in dug-outs. All the time there are 'covered wagons' bringing in peasants who have fled to the woods rather than join the collective farms. They are given a bit of ground and a spade and they make themselves a dug-out. On her way to Kemerovo, she managed to be allowed to spend the fourteen hours she had to wait with the local

OGPU, in the 'Red Corner' (the communist-atheist shrine) under a huge bust of Lenin and a picture showing people with their limbs eaten away by poison-gas. Her bed consisted of three chairs put against the stove. The last stage of the journey was in a fourth-class coach with wooden seats. She arrived at 4 a.m. in pouring rain and was met by a member of the village council and was allowed to sleep on a table in the office until the staff arrived. She found Kemerovo depressing and in many ways conditions were worse than before. A paradise for workers? *Some* workers! Though even the special OGPU restaurant at the junction could not produce much.

Our new Finnish maid, sister of Nusha who has been here for years, was summoned to the police-station and told she must spy on us for the OGPU. Cave and I agree that she must say she will report anything she sees and hears here. If she refuses she would be exiled at once, and even now the unfortunate father, a half-starved peasant, might be declared a *kulak* and sent up to the Arctic Circle to live in a tent at night and dig apatite all day. The girl has no education, speaks Russian badly, and as Cave says, could not understand us if we talked counter-revolution under her nose in Russian.

A Scottish mechanic came in to the Moscow Consulate in a state of hysteria with his wife in near collapse. They had been sleeping on the floor and undergoing other hardships, and all they wanted was to get away at once. The trust could have insisted that he fulfilled his contract, but perhaps they realised it doesn't pay to keep men so discontented. They have their fare to Warsaw whence they will have to be repatriated to England by the Consul. While Pott and Keane were dealing with this couple, who knew no Russian and couldn't even get a cab for themselves, another man with a wife and several children came in wanting to be repatriated. This man was an unemployed plate-layer who read an article by Bernard Shaw about Russia and sold up and started off via the Far East. From Harbin they went from one place to another in search of work. Finally after sleeping several nights in the railway-station, half-starved, and the woman and children ill, they came to the Moscow Consulate and asked to be sent home. Keane paid their fares out of his own pocket as far as Warsaw and wrote very strongly to the FO asking for something to be done to discourage people coming to Russia in search of work, or with unfavourable contracts.

—— *Dec.* This a great day. My 'emoluments' are reduced by £250 a year and the Finns inform us that the next mail from Finland will not reach here until 6 January. A packet came in just now but not a single thing

★

for me. I am telegraphing to M to post direct this week. A gap of three weeks at Christmas is a bit too much.

The FO have asked Keane and me what reductions we can make in staff and office expenses and local allowances. I have proposed a reduction of £100 in representation allowance and £150 in local allowance. This is quite generous to HMG, but during the War, when many of my colleagues were in financial straits, I happened to be in a post where saving was easy, so that I have reserves which other consular officers haven't.

HMG are looking everywhere to see how economies can be effected.[14] The messenger to Moscow is to be sent only every fortnight instead of every week, and I imagine the Embassy and Consulate staff will no longer be allowed to import so much stuff by bag. I wish I could effect some more economies here, but there isn't much that can be done. I am very careful of firewood, but however careful one is the amount used is enormous.

I have just written to the East India Club to resign—on financial grounds. I am sorry, for it brought me into contact with people outside my own service—in particular with men I knew in Iraq, but now that there is to be a cut in salaries and economies have to be made I could not be easy in my mind if I continued to remain a member. With the sub for the club servants' Christmas box it cost five guineas a year and I can find a better use for five guineas a year. It might go towards M's trip to Russia, which would be worth forty clubs.

Special anti-religious celebrations are being organised for Christmas. They are pulling down the chief cathedral in Moscow to make room for a Palace of the Soviets, and when it came to blowing up the dome they tried to have the explosion at the moment when the churches would be full. With their usual incompetence they didn't get the dynamite in time and the explosion happened the next day—but the spirit was willing enough.

I still haven't been to a play or a ballet or an opera in Leningrad. It wouldn't cost much, but it would cost something.

26 Dec. On Christmas Eve I visited the Institute for the Care of Mothers and Children with the Swedish Consul, Assersson. The enthusiastic

---

[14] In September 1931, under Ramsay MacDonald's first national government, the chancellor of the Exchequer, Lord Snowden, presented an emergency budget prescribing economies to the tune of £70 million. Salaries of all state employees were cut by 10%, and on 20 September Britain abandoned the gold standard.

Jewish woman doctor in charge, Mendeleva, seemed proud of its comprehensiveness: a maternity hospital, after-care department, orphanage, birth-control clinic, abortion clinic, hospital for tubercular children, research institute for experiments on animals, and so on. A building is shortly to be erected to supply 4000 children of the neighbourhood with a daily meal. The directress is very keen on mass feeding and evidently in agreement with the Party doctrine, that women must be got out of the home into industry. They are very proud of the labour legislation which prescribes that every woman worker shall have two months away from work, on full pay, before her confinement, and two after, but they despise the system which aims at making it unnecessary for a married woman to go out to work. She told us they never have a case of infection in the hospital. This is because they have a system of immunising all the other children in the ward by 'injecting them with a mixture of blood from forty different healthy people'. One professor is studying the action of the secretions in living animals. I hurried through the operating theatre where there was one dog under anaesthetic and another just going off.

That night I dined with the Woodheads, the paper specialist, at the Hotel Europa where they live. He says that the time wasted in discussion, or worse, in making orations under the impression that that is discussion, is incredible. The work done generally is very little. Grandiose schemes are always being brought to a halt because some essential point has been forgotten. For instance, a large number of houses of a standard American pattern were to be built in Kem', a dreadful place in the north where there is little at present but political prisoners. American experts came and the houses were nearly built, when they found that there was no tarred paper to put between the walls for insulation and waterproofing. Since they have no money to import tarred paper, they turned to Mr Woodhead for a project for *making* tarred paper, which may or may not be ready in two or three years. The fact is, it is far too difficult for people with so little experience as the Russians have, to co-ordinate so many diverse plans so as to have everything ready at the proper time and place.

Since Woodhead meets a large number of American engineers working in various parts of the USSR, he has some interesting tales. They had just seen a young American who had been out in the wilds prospecting for minerals for the Soviet Government and had lost over two stone in weight. He was working last near the border of Mongolia, hundreds of miles from a railway. Most of the time he lived on black bread and tea.

☆

On Christmas afternoon I walked about a mile and a half in the slush—it was thawing and the uneven streets were in a dreadful mess—to see the Metro-Vickers people. They had about fifteen guests, just getting up from a staggering meal, but they had tea and so did I. Afterwards Cave and I had a quiet evening with some music. I played one movement of the lovely Mozart Sonata no. 10. In the slow movement there is the phrase which appears in a hymn as:

How pleased and blest was I
To hear the people cry.

M. would recognise it and would remember it as one of the pieces we played at Addis Ababa with the gramophone in the passage when Godfrey was a day or two old. And that was Christmas Day.

27 Dec. I went with Assersson to an institute of dietetics and to the 'Prophylactorium of Labour'. We found the institute housed in an immense palace given by Nicholas II to a famous ballet-dancer.[15] In the garden, overlooking the street, is a little arbour which is famous as the place from which Lenin made his first speech, when the Germans smuggled him back into Russia.

The institute has drawn up two distinct diets, one for an excess of secretions, the other for a deficiency, and these diets are 'fed to' the workers in three big factories which formerly had the largest absenteeism. The director said the results were particularly encouraging. What do the poor people do when the special diet stops and they have to go back to what the ordinary man gets? Here as everywhere else in Russia they are concentrating on luxuries before people have necessities. We were shown a diagram claiming to represent the consumption of milk in Moscow, Leningrad, England and various other European countries. The consumption per head in Leningrad was represented as being slightly higher than in Moscow and less by an almost imperceptible fraction than in England. The ordinary person here gets no milk at all. Perhaps some goes to hospitals. Like half the figures published in the Soviet Union the figures are worthless.

The 'Prophylactorium of Labour' turned out to be a place where prostitutes are cured of VD (from which 95% of them are suffering) and trained to work. The woman in charge seemed to be a remarkable

[15] The palace was given by Nicholas II to his mistress Mathilde Kshesinskaya. In 1917 it briefly became Lenin's headquarters; it is now a waxworks museum.

character: very quiet, not, I should think, particularly well-educated, and not overflowing with propaganda. The girls seemed to like her very much. We asked how it was that in a country with, it was said, no unemployment, and no rich people to offer large bribes to corrupt youth, there could still be prostitutes. The directress said that the chief cause was the shortage of house room.

The girls make simple garments out of poor material, and the machining was not too good, but anything sells in this country. As we approached one ward where a number of girls were sitting about, talking or reading, the directress told us that these were all under treatment for VD in a bad form. I drew back. The directress assured me that there was no danger of infection. I explained that I had drawn back because I thought that our presence might perhaps embarrass the girls. She assured us that they wouldn't mind in the least, and she was right.

The last place we visited, a sort of night sanatorium for school-children, was in a large house formerly owned by the famous minister, Witte, who, it is said, was hated by Nicholas II for having told him that unless he made a revolution from the top there would be a revolution from below. Here weak or ailing children spend the time they are not at school.

I should have preferred to go without an interpreter, as I can get along quite well without, and talking direct is always less formal, but Assersson knows almost no Russian and I did not feel competent to translate for him. Our little interpreter Luknitsky, a Jew of Polish origin, talks remarkably good English. He told us he is not a Party member because for one thing there are things in the Party programme with which he does not agree and for another they wouldn't have him because his father was a merchant. I gathered his father was a pretty prosperous merchant in Archangel, but the son was so young when the Revolution came that he only just remembers a big flat which they had 'all to themselves'. He spoke to us about war expenditure and quoted a figure given by a Soviet financial authority, who said that the USSR spent only 8% of its total expenditure on armaments whereas other countries spent much more. I reminded Luknitsky that all sorts of things figure as Government expenditure in the USSR which are private expenditure in England, e.g. education, hospitals, factories and labour costs. Naturally with a budget constructed on those lines military expenditure would seem a small percentage of the whole. Luknitsky seemed much struck by this new light on Soviet statistics. It must be deadening for a good brain to live in this country where there is no free discussion. Here figures in accordance with 'the Party line' can only be repeated with approval. It is

★

not much use having a critical eye if you have to keep your criticisms to yourself.

30 Dec. There has been a round of dinners. Poor Cave not only has to go out to dinner with me tonight with the Bells, but he had to go to the Finns to lunch. We are proposing to walk but his asthma makes him a poor and slow walker. We ought to be able to get a tram back, at about midnight, which I suppose is when we shall escape. During the day the trams are quite impossible. Miss Daunt was so badly squeezed a few days ago that the doctor thought she might be seriously injured. Fortunately she is well again. Every day people have their clothes torn, their buttons pulled off, their gloves wrenched from their hands in the crowded trams. The Bells have just telephoned to speak to Miss Daunt. Their electric light has failed and the only candles are hers.

I have at last got the coal which I ordered from Torgsin three weeks ago. It won't be easy to handle as I have neither a scuttle nor a shovel nor a scoop. However I have a dustbin and a spare pail. I notice the maids use a saucer to remove the wood ashes from the grates and stoves.

Cave just back. He managed to get a broken-down carriage half-way home. The driver was just being arrested by a policeman for crossing on the wrong side of the road but Cave paid the small fine and the man was allowed to go. Fines from people who walk in the road, get off trams at the back etc. must bring in a useful sum.

The Bells' meal was excellently cooked, but the longest meal, I think, that I ever had. I soon lost count of the number of dishes. This is the Russian notion of hospitality, to overspend on entertaining.

☆

AMINE

☆

LENINGRAD, 1932

THE GREAT FAMINE *of 1932 was not a natural phenomenon but a direct result of the forced collectivisation. The authorities maintained a high level of State procurements and exports of grain, while peasants starved in the Ukraine and southern Russia. About five million families were deported during the collectivisation drive, and an estimated ten million people died. The death penalty was decreed for the theft of grain, and an internal passport was introduced as part of a series of measures to toughen labour discipline. In the summer a group of Party officials headed by the chief of propaganda, Ryutin, circulated a 'platform' which called for a relaxation of the pace of economic development, an end to authoritarianism in the Party and the readmission of expelled opposition leaders including Trotsky. It described Stalin as 'the evil genius of the Russian Revolution'. The Ryutin group were expelled from the Party following a Central Committee Plenum. Zinoviev and Kamenev, once Lenin's trusted comrades, were expelled for the second time for failing to report Ryutin's 'plot' to the authorities. In the course of the year, as the USSR sought to bolster its international position, non-aggression treaties were signed with France, Poland, Finland, Latvia and Estonia.*

1 Jan. This year I hope to see M for a visit in May but the boys not till next Christmas. Four months and a bit isn't so long.

4 Jan. We had a dinner party on 2 January. Just as the first guests were arriving the electric light failed, which perhaps accounted for the inadequacy of the service.

Yesterday (Sunday) Miss Daunt came for dinner and music as usual. We had the Mozart Clarinet Quintet and a Schubert duet played by Kreisler and Rachmaninov. I was shocked to learn that the Red Cross woman who accepted a woollen jumper from her has since disappeared

☆

and all that the other workers in the Red Cross say is that she is no longer employed there. I hope that the poor woman will get off with two or three years in exile.

5 Jan. Cave and I went to a dinner given by Platou, the Norwegian Consul, a well-known and popular merchant in Leningrad for the last twenty years. During the breach of relations between HMG and the Soviet Government, the Norwegians were in charge of our interests, and Platou was very kind to our Distressed British Subjects. He lives in the grandest style in a house which formerly belonged to a Swede. If you live on roubles from abroad you can buy beautiful furniture, plate, glass, china, carpets etc. in roubles in the second-hand shops—or rather you could. Platou bought at a good time. It is not known where all his money comes from, but Cave thinks that he either bought jewels and sold them abroad, or else he takes roubles from Soviet officials and credits them abroad with foreign currency. If a British Consul lived in that style the Embassy would want to know something about it. It seems to me legitimate to buy necessaries such as food in 'black' roubles, but I think it is rather indecent to cram a house with luxuries acquired in that way. However, I think all the diplomats and consuls except ours have bought antiques to take away and the French Ambassador who has just been transferred made a business of it, and the French official's standard of official honesty is pretty low.

7 Jan. It is Thursday and we haven't had a fire in the drawing-room since Sunday. But we must make a grand coal fire for our dinner party on the 9th, though I haven't got a proper shovel. I might sacrifice my flour-scoop. The coal brought up for our dinner party last week consisted mostly of dust which had been out in the snow, but I made balls of dust and snow—a freezing job, but very successful. Tovey, the engineer who has been supervising the building of the house for Lady Muriel's Relief Association, heard that I wanted a fire-shovel and he brought along a steel poker, tongs and shovel—a bit rusty—and a fender which he said his sister would be prepared to part with—for FIVE POUNDS. I did *not* buy them. I'd sooner put the coal on with my fingers until I can get a scoop from England.

A Russian-born Jewess came in the other day to see whether we could help her get back to Glasgow. Her brother wrote so favourably from Russia after her husband died that she came and brought the four children. She now finds that no one dare write anything else. She and her children sleep on the floor, only one child has any work, she has sold

☆

everything she has to keep the family alive. I will see what I can do but I am pretty sure the authorities will not let them go back to the UK.

A letter from Colenutt—a colleague in Germany. He gives a gloomy picture of Germany and represents even solid people as wondering whether it wouldn't be better to try Hitler.

A few days ago Waldhauer of the Hermitage sent word that he would like to come and see us, so we have invited him to dinner next week. I wonder why he has suddenly decided that he can afford to be bolder. The OGPU have not shut up shop. Miss Daunt's admirer, Kulagin, has more than once said that he was tired because he had been working at the OGPU up to midnight. They represent themselves as an important body engaged on the laudable task of preserving the Revolution for the proletariat. Kulagin seems to have had a moment of anxiety recently. He reduced the Torgsin prices for the Relief Association, on the reasonable ground that, although the pound had fallen on the exchanges, it still bought as much in England, where Torgsin makes its purchases. For this and other favours shown to the Relief Association he was taken to task, and for some time has had to have a spy listen to his conversations. However, after a few days he was radiant: he had triumphed over his enemies and was free to do what he liked. During the spy regime his watcher said that Kulagin was too English or something of the kind, and that he wasn't acting like a workman. Kulagin said, turning to Miss Daunt (and out loud): 'He wants my job, but he isn't going to have it.' Then to the spy he said: 'I have never claimed to be a workman, and I see no merit in being a workman, though much in doing one's work well, whatever it is.'

Kulagin must be a man of great influence. Miss Daunt says he always carries an enormous Mauser pistol with an inscription saying that it was given to him for his services as head of the OGPU in the south. So long as he lasts he is very useful to the Relief Association. Yesterday Miss Daunt wanted to send a British subject down to the south. He has been very ill and cannot stand in queues for days to buy a ticket. So she acted on Kulagin's offer to help her in any way and asked him for a ticket. Kulagin scribbled a couple of words on a piece of paper and told her that would secure a ticket. Miss Daunt replied that she would prefer the ticket itself. In an hour or so in came a girl with the ticket—supplied on credit. Kulagin is nominally manager of a grocery store. I wish I knew exactly what his position in the OGPU hierarchy was. Who is above him?

Mrs Woodhead told me that on the boat on which she travelled out she met a Russian called Alexander Jupitus, who had been employed by the Russians in ARCOS in London. He told Mrs Woodhead that they knew the raid was coming. Mrs Woodhead asked him to come and see her if he came to Leningrad again. He came. He was furious. Nothing to eat, nowhere to live, and his good pounds, converted at a swindling rate, had disappeared like water. He was off back to England.

12 Jan. Our dinner on the 9th went off quite well. The cook cooked the grub we bought from Torgsin excellently and the service effected by the two hired waiters was first-class. Our savage Finns were a little sulky at first, at the ridiculous thought that they had anything to learn from Russians, but when they saw the table laid and the napkins folded they saw reason, and Nusha went into my bedroom and looked through a clear spot in the coloured glass to see how the strangers waited at table.

Evidently the word has gone forth that selected Russians are to frequent European houses again, for last night there were Russians present at the German Consulate General for the first time, my hostess told me, for two years. The Germans used to have a reception every week or two at which there would be fifty or more Russians—musicians, artists, professors and the like, but this all stopped. The Russians present were Radlov, a professor of art and his wife, also an artist, and the wife of Alexei Tolstoy.[1] Mrs Radlov was full of questions about England and English books. She admires Aldous Huxley and is in the middle of *Antic Hay*, and someone has promised to lend her *Point Counter Point*.

The Chamberlins stayed only one night. The *Manchester Guardian* wanted some information about the alleged sale of the Hermitage pictures, but the Chamberlins couldn't find out anything. The underlings at the Hermitage trembled with terror if asked anything to do with the number of pictures in the place and referred them to an official who, in spite of the recommendations they had, sent out word that he hadn't one moment to spare for them.

The Soviet authorities boast that unemployment exists only in capitalist countries, but there is now a good deal here. No mention of it in the press but one factory I know of has discharged 1500, and the famous Putilov works 9000. Some of these surrounded the Chamberlins at the station offering to carry their luggage, and said that 14,000 had been discharged at Putilov on the grounds that they were overstaffed, but lack of money for raw materials seems to be at the back of it.

[1] Alexei N. Tolstoy (1882–1945), stormy petrel of Russian literature. Despite serving with the White Army he was honoured by the communists for his novels such as *Peter the Great* and *Bread*. His wife was Natalia Vasilevna. (See Isaiah Berlin, *Personal Impressions*, ed. Hardy H: Oxford University Press, 1982.)

Mrs Chamberlin sat next to Bernard Shaw at a dinner in Moscow, and she found him 'contrairy' to the last degree. He waved his hand at the excellent food and said 'Russia short of food? Look at this!' She told him about being unable to buy any milk at all for her child all winter. 'Nurse her yourself!' said Shaw. 'But my daughter's four years old.' 'Never mind,' said Shaw, 'Eskimos nurse their children until they are eighteen.'

Chamberlin told me a joke about Stalin: Jesus Christ came to visit Stalin, riding on an ass. They were deep in conversation when the ass began to bray. Jesus Christ started up to go out, but Stalin restrained him and asked why he was going. Jesus Christ said it was because the ass brayed. 'He must be hungry and must be given some food.' 'My dear chap,' said Stalin, 'why worry? I've got 160 million braying all the time, and I don't give them a damn thing!'

I am getting a tiger at staying up late. Last night we did not leave the Zechlins until after one and it was nearly two when I got to bed. At 8.30 this morning I was quite ready to get up. Poor Cave was less ready. He always smokes and drinks just a little more than he should and at meals he breathes like a broken pair of bellows. Greenway and Byron[2] arrive tomorrow. Byron is the great partisan of Byzantine art and a great opponent of representational art.

16 Jan. Byron went off to Novgorod, where there are some interesting old churches, at midnight, returning early on the 18th and leaving for Moscow the same night. I like him. He is interesting and often amusing. And he laughs at my jokes as though they amused him—an endearing characteristic.

17 Jan. The dinner yesterday went off pretty well. The Russians enjoyed the food and drink and they got quite gay. They also admired the gramophone very much. Mrs Orlov-Ermak, Mr Weinstein and the director of the port, Bronstein, stuck to the gramophone all the time, and as they went off at 11.30 there was no time to be dull.

Miss Daunt works very hard and life at the Bells, with whom she

[2] Robert Byron (1905–1941); traveller and writer. He recorded in his diary on 12 January 1932: 'The problem [is] the patent evilness of it all and yet one is mentally refreshed and really rather wishes their plan a success. Russians have cast off the idea of objective truth. One is refreshed because they have cast off so much of the falsities and extravagances of western life, but unfortunately the good qualities are being exploited by evil at the top . . . . OGPU rule country entirely.' (See also his *First Russia then Tibet*: Macmillan, 1933.)

lives, is not exciting. Russians come there pretty often, but she says the
talk is about nothing but food and how to get it. And recently life has
been unpleasant. Someone in the family has taken out a food-book in
her name, and been using it for some time. Cave says all Anglo-Russians
are untruthful and dishonest. We can't have Miss Daunt and the Relief
Association brought into disrepute.

The Ambassador used to have a teacher of Russian, Valentine
Petrovich, who the Embassy took for granted was a spy, but it was
supposed that he was otherwise a decent creature. Recently they have
discovered that he has been stealing cigarettes and gramophone records
from Greenway. Valentine Petrovich is in prison, nominally for theft,
but as Greenway says, really for having lost a job in which he was useful
to the OGPU. Greenway is being replaced by Vyvyan, a nephew of
Tawney. Tawney passed through Moscow the other day on his way back
from China. He sent word to me that I was not to think him as much
'sold' to the Bolsheviks as I had appeared to. I wish he would come here
for a few days. It is dull when we are thrown on our own resources.

18 Jan. Byron arrived at 6.30 a.m. We had some tea and both went to
bed again. He found quarters in the old Archbishop's Palace at
Novgorod, which is used as a rest-home for scientists. He managed to
get hold of a sleigh, and he was able to get into all the churches he
wanted to see except one where he had heard that there were pictures by
El Greco. Here they were met by a screaming maenad in a red head-
kerchief who pushed them out and barred the door. A bystander came
to Byron secretly and told him that the gold was being stripped off the
iconostasis and the authorities did not want the fact to be known.

Greenway went to bed and Byron and I discussed Russia. He
reported that even the Ambassador, who never seems disgusted or
horrified by anything the Russians do, seemed a little out of
countenance when he heard that happy crowds of workers in Sverdlovsk
were thronging the house where the royal family were put to death. It
was probably inevitable that the Tsar and Tsarina should be executed,
but a civilised race do not murder children.

Byron told me he had gone up to Oxford with enthusiasm for
history, which his experience at Merton had completely stifled. The
history school was regarded mainly as a memory test and he refused to
work on such lines, only got a third, and to show his contempt for the
system refused to take his degree. A good tutor should have brought out
the good stuff in him, for him to have done what he has in history and
Byzantine art before he is thirty. He told me that the election results in

☆

England were awkward for several of his friends who were having what they thought would be a trial run for hopeless constituencies and found themselves elected. Unfortunately they haven't either the time or the money to serve as MPs. He said enormous sums were lost in bets based on the atmosphere of complete pessimism prevailing at Lossiemouth the weekend before the election.[3]

Poor Waldhauer came to dinner last night. Last week I should not have said 'poor' but I find he is only forty-eight though he looks sixty. He is not Russian but a Balt. He despises the Russians for their docility, their moral cowardice and their treachery to each other. According to his account, his life work at the Hermitage has been destroyed. His library has been taken away for the sake of 'centralisation' and most of his former assistants are in exile on the dreadful island in the White Sea. It is difficult to teach ancient art to students who do not know whether 700 BC was before or after 400 BC. Most of all he feels the separation from his colleagues in other countries. He was very anxious that friendly messages should be sent to Beazley of Christ Church and to Fosdyke of the British Museum. Waldhauer says he feels fairly secure since, like Pavlov, he is well-known abroad. Also he has a female assistant who knows all the Party patter and puts some of it into everything he writes. That did not prevent his looking round every few minutes to make sure we were not being spied upon. He says he is not badly off materially, as he receives a pension as a professor in addition to his salary from the Hermitage. He enjoys a low controlled rent and a cheap midday meal at the Hermitage dining-room. He has known worse times. In 1919 the only fuel he had was some wood stolen from a fence near the Hermitage, and all the Hermitage staff fell upon a horse that died on the quay. He made soup out of his bit. In the famine of 1922, on the Volga, if you heard of someone who had died, unless you got there at once there wouldn't be half a body to bury, the rest would have been eaten.

The American journalist, Deuss, told me about the rescue of the two Italians, members of the Nobile expedition, by the icebreaker *Krassin*.[4] He says the Government were very secretive about it, probably out of

---

[3] The general election of 27 October 1931 had returned a National government, with Ramsay MacDonald remaining prime minister despite a large Conservative majority. Lossiemouth was MacDonald's birthplace and home.

[4] The airship *Italia*, carrying General Umberto Nobile's expedition to the North Pole, had crashed on an ice-floe off Spitzbergen on 25 May 1928. Two Italians, Mariani and Zappi, and a Swede, Malmgren, set out on foot in search of land. Malmgren was wounded, and collapsed after two weeks. After forty days Mariani and Zappi were rescued by the Russian icebreaker *Krassin*. A relief expedition was led by Roald Amundsen, but his aircraft also crashed and his body was never found.

☆

political consideration for Italy. He saw the doctor of the *Krassin*, who believed that one of the Italians, Zappi, had eaten some of Malmgren. His reasons were: that Zappi had eaten within twenty-four hours and there was no other food, that whereas Mariani was terribly weak and had to be carried on board, Zappi was pretty strong and walked on by himself, also Zappi had two sets of clothing on while Mariani had one; and finally that Mariani in his ravings (for he was off his head) seemed to fear only one thing—that Zappi would eat him before he was dead. Zappi was put in a kind of exile, but that might be because he did not cut a sufficiently Roman figure in abandoning Malmgren. Probably the truth would come out if the Italians and the USSR ever quarrelled.

22 Jan. Lenin died on 21 January eight years ago, but the 22nd is kept officially as the anniversary of his death, and we have had the flag flying at half-mast all day. I should fly the flag with greater pleasure if Lenin had died of something more agreeable than syphilis of the brain. He was a great man, though a fanatical brute and devoid of pity. There is no one of his calibre now.

I spoke to Dr Bell about the food-book incident. Miss Daunt has discovered that the matter was in the hands of the police. He affected astonishment and denied it, but I was pretty sure he was lying. According to the house committee, Mrs Bell applied for the document and the son signed for it and it had been regularly used by the Bells. The dishonesty and the lying to me are bad enough, but the really repulsive thing is that the Bells forced their maid to say she was responsible. Food is short and the recent investigation discovered that several thousand persons were using these unauthorised food-cards. There will be trouble for the Bells, particularly as they have already had a warning. As they are British subjects they might be required to leave the country. It is unfortunate from every point of view. British subjects have been guilty of fraud against their country, and against Miss Daunt, who has done them many kindnesses. Miss Daunt must find another place to live, and that is very difficult, and I lose the one point of contact I had with Russian life. This kind of thing is very common. The general standard of honesty, truth and loyalty is low. And yet we are expected to believe that an economic system requiring the highest ideals can grow in this soil.

The Board of Trade are trying to decide whether the amount of British shipping in Archangel necessitates the appointment of a consular officer. I don't know what to do. I fear that if Cave is sent to Archangel he will go to pieces at once. Cave has a weakness for whisky which he is keeping under at present and his health is pretty bad generally.

24 Jan. Sunday. Went to *William Tell* last night—the first performance since the War—perhaps the first performance ever given in Russia. The opera had been made to conform to 'the general line of the Party' and Arnaldo was made to part from Matilda for good, since the doctrines of the class-war do not admit that human affection can transcend social distinctions. Weinstein sat next to me; the Orlov-Ermaks were also there. He suggested taking me to a ballet soon. He was surprised to hear that I had never been to a ballet in Leningrad. I did not tell him that I hadn't been to a ballet in Moscow either—or anywhere else!

It is impossible for Miss Daunt to go on living with the Bells, but in this overcrowded city, where is she to find a room? I have been wondering whether she could be fitted into this large but inconvenient flat. The only possible arrangement would have to be made at the expense of the Todds, and Todd is not a cheerful sufferer. Just as he walks about with his hands in his pockets while his wife moves heavy furniture and packs his trunks, so he keeps his moral hands in his pockets when there are other people's interests to be studied.

The Soviet authorities have recently opened a swagger hotel called the Astoria with a restaurant and a jazz band going until 3 a.m. The Woodheads invited me to dinner there. He says the department which plans all the paper plant for the Soviet Union has not been allowed any *valuta* at all for this year. Later in the evening Lie came in. He sells paper machinery and is therefore well up in the same subject. He had just been to Moscow to try to get orders and had come back in a very pessimistic mood. He says there is no money at all. Paper is very short. The shops never wrap up goods. People take an old newspaper or a rag to wrap up fish or butter. There is a process for de-inking old printed matter to enable it to be reused, and the heads of Woodhead's department asked him to plan something in that line. He pointed out that every scrap of paper is used up in this country so that there is nothing left to de-ink.

After a week of thaw and rain, it froze last night and an inch or two of snow fell. It was lovely today and I went for a walk as far as the Neva.

A Russian workman told Lie a story which I should dismiss as merely fantastic if there was not plenty of evidence of the flight from the collectivisation of the farms to the towns. A man started out to visit his mother. When he arrived at the station, he found nobody. The station-master told him that he would see plenty of people if he waited for the train going the other way—i.e. back to Leningrad. He waited and soon an army of peasants appeared with carts. He asked one how much he

★

wanted to drive him to his village. 'Take the horse and drive yourself,' said the peasant. The peasants were all being forced to join a collective farm with their animals and they were just abandoning everything and fleeing to the town. Nevertheless the Leningrad paper says that the plan for grain collection has been more than fulfilled.

26 Jan. I think I have recorded how a lad of sixteen, known to us because he was born in Canada, was kept in the OGPU's 'cold room' in Moscow. Everyone knew about the cold room, but that was the first evidence we got at first hand. Similarly everyone knows about the 'hot room', but until today I had never got close to an actual case. We now have the tale of a sufferer by this form of torture, through his niece, Mrs Hay, who works for Miss Daunt. Mrs Hay is Russian-born, well-educated and trustworthy. She owes her name to a Scotch husband—now dead. Her uncle, an old man, formerly a lawyer, has just had twenty-six hours with the OGPU, his wife of seventy rather fewer. The Soviet Union is so desperate for foreign money they torture all persons suspected of having gold or precious stones or foreign money or of owning money or property abroad. This old man and his wife were put into a small room where there were about forty people packed close together. The OGPU add insult to injury by being very polite. After taking down the list of things the victim admits he possesses they say: 'Be so good as to step in here. Perhaps you will remember something else which you would like to give to your country.' Under the floor are pipes which keep the room at a high temperature and every now and then waves of hot air are pumped in from above. At night the OGPU took him out on account of his age, and showed him a latrine where they said he could sleep with his coat over the hole. Next day he was again confined in the hot room, though at one moment they took him to the back door for ten minutes to revive him. Eventually he was allowed to go either because they thought they had got everything out of him or because it was clear that he had had enough. On the whole he stood it fairly well, but his wife is in a state of collapse. The day after their release the old people had to take round the things they had declared. The OGPU were very polite, thanked them nicely and hoped they would not suffer any ill effects. Those who admitted to having property or money abroad were compelled to sign papers saying that they wished to give the money or property for the industrialisation of the country.

According to the local paper, Kazan Cathedral, the fine building opposite the Consulate, is being handed over to the Academy of Sciences for the establishment of an anti-religious museum. There is already an anti-religious museum in the Cathedral of St Isaac. Perhaps they just want to shut the cathedral and put a stop to the services and thought the museum plan the best excuse.

27 Jan. My Aunt Dorothy wants to contribute to Miriam's trip to Leningrad. We could then have the scullery done up. M says it needs it badly.

At the Opera the other night Mrs Radlov, to whom I talked at the German dinner a week or two before, was in the same row. She passed me in the interval and shook hands as unobtrusively as possible and said: 'I'm afraid to speak to you.' I was surprised she ventured to say as much as that. Tawney, to his annoyance, was cut in a hotel by a Soviet official he had seen on business that afternoon.

I'm afraid poor old Waldhauer is drinking himself to death. Miss Daunt has seen him in trams blind-drunk.

29 Jan. The authorities seem to be calling up men for the army and spreading the story that there is a danger of war. What the object is it is hard to say—perhaps to distract the attention of the public from the wretched conditions they live in, and from the discouraging news that there is to be a second Five-Year Plan—an announcement which naturally tends to make people think about the promises of what they were to have by the end of the first one.

31 Jan. Sunday. Last winter, in spite of the cold, I never once caught cold, but I've got a cold now. It is lovely today—frost and bright sunshine. I hear Miss Daunt has bronchitis. I must walk over and see how she is. Yesterday I sent her two tins of soup and a small tin of plums and some biscuits, because I thought the Bells were not looking after her very well, although they have made rather a good thing out of her. Apart from the frauds of which I have written, they have been buying on Miss Daunt's book quantities of stuff which they could not possibly use in the house. They have probably not found it difficult to sell the surplus.

The Relief Association's Armstrong-Siddeley has finally arrived—much trouble—mainly owing to the incredibly unbusinesslike methods of Lady Muriel.[5] She crammed the car full of parcels of clothing and did

---

[5] Lady Muriel wrote in her diary: 'A car is a greater necessity than ever here this year . . . . The Armstrong will pay all its expenses and the Ford lorry pays also for lighting, fencing and trees at the *dacha*. The two cars are both insured—in both cases the insurance allows for the killing of five people—presumably per annum.'

★

not mention them in the shipping documents. When I need a car I shall hire this one. It will cost less than any other form of transport, it will be certain, and the payments will help the Relief Fund.

I'm looking forward to going round in it with Miss Daunt to visit her dependants. I should like to see the conditions in which they live and hear what some of them have to say. If the trams had been normal trams I should have made a tour before, but I don't want to get my fur coat wrenched off my back.

This mild winter is a boon to the authorities in that their stock of fuel for heating private houses was quite inadequate for an ordinary winter. Lots of people have no fuel at all for heating, only for cooking. The latest slogan is: 'Turn Leningrad into a model city.' What is wanted is more trams or buses and more living room. They are building more storeys on crowded tenements and if they are really adding to the number of trams the effect is not noticeable. This is the opening paragraph of an article in the local newspaper: 'The correct solution of the bath-laundry problem plays an important role in the improvement of the cultural living conditions of the workers.'

3 Feb. Statement from the bank showing that there will be money for M's journey. Also letter from M asking what I think about an English doctor's favourable report on a large Russian maternity hospital, reported to have a mortality rate of two per thousand whereas in England it is four per thousand. I wonder which hospital is meant. The Russians are incredibly hardy and it is possible that the death-rate really is less than ours. It is possible that the statistics were faked. There is no person in authority, from Stalin down, who would not sign a hundred pages of false statistics and think nothing of it. The few people who care for truth haven't the courage to stand up for it, but most Russians don't care for truth at all, and the Bolsheviks laugh at it, as they do at our conception of justice, as bourgeois. The Bolsheviks believe in what they call 'proletarian truth', that is, any statement which for the moment advances the cause of the proletariat. Similarly they believe in 'proletarian justice', which means letting a murderer off lightly and shooting people for accumulating small change, and in general, giving all proletarians light sentences and all other people heavy ones.

The daughter of the porter at the place where Cave lived before the War came yesterday to ask for a cake of soap. She had just come out of a maternity hospital. She got her treatment in hospital free, and full pay from the factory for two months before and two months after her confinement, and she also received some clothes for the child. But she said that even with two salaries they had difficulty making ends meet. Last week her husband brought home only 65 roubles of his nominal salary of 175 roubles. There was a cut for the loan, then a huge cut for taxes, then 8 roubles entrance fee for the co-operative in addition to the monthly co-operative subscription. Then there was the usual political subscription. This month it was 2.5 roubles for MOPR, the society for assisting revolutionaries in foreign countries. Then there was the newspaper subscription. He has to pay for three newspapers, though he hardly ever sees one. No one dares to object.

Not only is the Soviet Government short of foreign currency, but there is evidence that it is also short of roubles. On 1 February the prices in the co-operatives were raised by 30% without notice, also demands for rent in advance were issued. Hitherto rent has been paid at the end of the month, and people have only just paid their rent for January. Moreover few had received their January pay, and some have not had their pay for December. Those who fail to pay the February rent in advance are threatened to be treated as counter-revolutionaries, which means the hot room, or exile, or death, or anything the OGPU like.

The official figures of the population of Leningrad give the increase for the first eleven months of 1931 as half a million. I heard another 100,000 flooded in, in December. Is the flood never to stop? There is no more demand for factory workers here than there was a few months ago.

Letter from the FO to say they have chopped £100 off the local allowance and £60 off the representation allowance. I have written to Mudie's lending-library to ask what their terms are. I have been wishing for a new book or two lately. My cold doesn't get any better. I go into an unheated room to get at the safe, pass through an unheated room to get to the dining room, and have meals in a room in which the stove is lit every three days or so.

We have had an Irish Catholic born in Londonderry in the office, one McMullin. When I was in Moscow, a year ago, I received a letter from him written from a place in Siberia. He said he had deserted from a British ship in August 1930 at a place which he calls Igahi about 120 miles up the mouth of the Yenisey, and wanted to go home, but the OGPU had taken his papers. Would I issue a passport to him and his wife? I told him to find his way to Leningrad where the Consulate has means for repatriating deserters. He says he was in the Naval Reserve, and third mechanic on a submarine called the *Rowanburn*. We gave him an emergency pass for the journey to England, and the OGPU gave him an exit visa valid only for a day and told him to get out at once. When he went to the International Sailors' Home to get his bag there seems to

★

have been some trouble, and he abandoned it. He seemed rather scared and anxious to get away. Our messenger saw the man to the station and showed him the train. The bag was found to contain, besides a few rags of clothing, about a hundred Russian silver coins and a silver coffee-pot. I suspect there is an unpleasant history behind this man's adventures in Russia.

A few days ago I went out with one of the Metro-Vickers engineers and Miss Daunt to see the house which is being built for the Relief Association. The Charity Commissioners have a sum of about £2500 subscribed during the War for certain purposes in Russia. They may not use it for general relief but they could let Lady Muriel have it if part was spent on the building and part on a car. Hence the unwanted house. It will be ruinous to run. She had better sell it before it eats up all the funds. The terms on which she receives the money do not compel her to keep the house once it is built.

From a report to HM Ambassador in Moscow, 8 Feb.[6] I am well aware that what strikes the attention of the foreigner is the unusual, and that the majority of the population here are probably unaffected by what appear to us intolerable burdens. Such a burden to us would be an increase of 25% or more, without warning, in the prices of all ordinary articles of food, at a moment when the time of plenty, which was to set in at the end of the Plan, should be in sight. Even before this increase the worker's budget had little if any margin, and foreign workers in receipt of Russian rates of pay are wondering how to make ends meet; but though I have heard one or two complaints from Russian sources on the same ground, I should hesitate to say that they represent a widespread feeling of discontent. The Russians lived through worse times in the early years after the War, and then there were few of the social services which many town-dwellers, if few of the peasants, enjoy at the present time. The temper of the Russian population is probably one of the strongest links in the chain on which the Soviet Government depends.

Finance. No complete statistics for this area have been published lately. It was announced that by 15 December 1931, with only a fortnight of the year to run, Leningrad Province had paid up only 69.7% of the estimated receipts, and 35 million roubles remained to be

[6] RWB's report on conditions in the Leningrad consular district was sent to Sir Edmund Ovey and transmitted on to the foreign secretary, Sir John Simon (1873–1954). As a lawyer, Simon was subsequently to share RWB's outrage at the Soviet action against Metro-Vickers, and strongly backed British counter-measures. (See his *Retrospect*: Hutchinson, 1952.)

collected. That there is an acute shortage of rouble currency is suggested by measures which have been taken within the last few days. On 1 February, without notice, prices in the co-operatives were raised 25% (in some cases more), and the rents for February were demanded in advance. Rents have hitherto been payable in arrears, and tenants had only just paid for January. The well-known lack of foreign currency is emphasised by the extraordinary measures by which the OGPU are trying to extract the last scraps of precious metal, down to silver spoons, from persons suspected of having any left, and by the inability of even the most important industries here to obtain authority to buy even essential requirements abroad this year.

Trade and industry. Much faith is placed in the Khibinogorsk apatite. The works are being extended and a much larger output is expected this year. If a Finnish agricultural chemist, who recently spent some months in this country, is to be believed, enormous quantities of this valuable fertiliser could be utilised in the USSR. He considers that even the rich grain areas of the Ukraine are only about three years from being worked out, owing to the extravagant way in which they had been used and to the lack of fertilisers. At Kandalaksha, near Khibinogorsk, a factory estimated to produce 40,000 tons of aluminium a year is to be begun in May. The raw material will presumably be nepheline, which is found with apatite, and is said to contain 20% of aluminium, though two experts I have met are a little sceptical about the possibility of obtaining such good results.

In 1931, 1,400,000 tons of peat were produced for the Leningrad power-stations. It is proposed to produce more than twice this quantity in 1932. As last year's supply was only obtained with difficulty by utilising the labour of thousands of people from other occupations on their free days, it is difficult to see how so large an increase can be effected, unless part of the now surplus population is employed on peat-cutting under some system of compulsion. There is some evidence that convict labour was employed on peat-cutting last year.

13 Feb. Last Saturday we went to dinner with the Finns. It was a heavy meal and I was so unwise as to admit that I used to waltz, and Mrs Keistinen, the wife of the Vice-Consul, made me dance a waltz with her. It wasn't at all bad. Mrs K dances very well, and the record was old-fashioned and slow.

The food parcels which the Relief Association distribute to destitute British subjects used to be done up in the Consulate. All parcels are supposed to be sewn up in canvas and the transport of the food to the

Consulate and of the parcels to the post-office was a great business. Also in warm weather it was not pleasant to have large stocks of cheese, bacon etc. in the Consulate. Consequently, when Torgsin offered to despatch the parcels themselves we were glad to accept the offer, though a little doubtful how it would work. It has worked very badly. A number of parcels have disappeared in the post. Foodstuffs are naturally tempting to half-starved employees, but Miss Daunt's parcels were never touched because they were marked with the consular seal.

We have been employing an upholsterer to repair some of the office furniture. He used to come in his spare time but now he comes every day. He explains that his factory is shut down owing to a shortage of raw material. Workers here are paid by the month, so in theory their pay should not be affected, but a meeting is summoned and it is proposed that they should volunteer to forego pay for the days they do not work and the proposal is passed *nem. con.* That is the way everything is managed.

14 Feb. I saw a considerable number of people standing in the street trying to sell things such as toothpicks, wretched calendars, a cigarette box, a pair of child's shoes etc. I hear that unemployed people will stand in queues for hours for the things of which there are limited stocks, material for clothes, for instance—and then stand in the street and sell them for a higher price. We looked in a shop that had a large queue outside it and found it was full of what the Russians call *brak,* i.e. throw-outs, goods not up to standard. Garments made up of materials of different shades, a saucepan with the tin coating hanging loose from the iron and torn like silver-paper on chocolate. After lunch I read *Middlemarch*, which I have been spinning out to make it last because I have so little fiction with me; then tea, and, because it was Sunday, biscuits. Now I am typing in the fading light.

The OGPU 'hot room' is talked about everywhere, and whereas 'to sit' means to be imprisoned by the OGPU, 'to stand' means to undergo the hot-room experience. The popular belief is that the enormous new place the OGPU are building contains various interesting chambers for torture. Not so far off they are starting on an enormous hotel for tourists. Miss Daunt was in Torgsin when one of the managers, apologising because all the chairs were taken, said that in these days it was as well to practise standing against the time when one couldn't do anything else. One of the managers at the harbour branch of Torgsin is 'standing' at the moment. He is supposed to have acquired foreign currency by selling shop goods for his own account.

The mother of the ballerina Pavlova is one of the many Russians who would like to leave and claim the property which Pavlova left in England, but she is not allowed to.

Nothing I hear about the old regime in Russia leads me to think that it was any better than this. That system was bad, not because of the system itself, but because it was run by Russians, and exactly the same thing may be said about the present system. Cave, who has lived here all his life, worked before the Revolution for an American submarine company. He was sent to do some business with a senior officer in the Russian Admiralty. Cave knew all about the tipping system, but on that day he had in his pocket only one note for 25 roubles and another for one rouble. Two pounds ten was too much, and he didn't like to offer two shillings, so he gave him nothing. The officer made it clear that he expected a tip, so Cave explained his predicament. 'Oh, the rouble will do,' said the officer, and pocketed it. Workers are not allowed to strike now, but they were not allowed to strike then. On one occasion some workers in Cave's company tried to strike, but the employers called in the police, who marched the strikers off to prison. A day or two later Cave was sent to give a present to the Chief of Police for his promptitude, and he found that official having a quiet cigar in his office with the leader of the strike, who was a secret-service man and an *agent provocateur*. With ancestors like that it is not surprising that the OGPU are what they are.

17 Feb. Went round to see the Woodheads last night. Woodhead has been here for two years making plans for paper-mills. He has helped his trust to remodel two existing mills, and that is all the result he has seen from his labours. He told me that conditions in the lumber camps are bad and he has seen a considerable number. Timber-cutting is very unpopular work and the peasants who don't run away from it adopt passive resistance and do as little work as possible. Last year a group of English timber merchants reported that conditions in the timber camps they visited were very good, but they had just been let off part of a contract with the Soviet Government which was becoming onerous, so they can hardly be considered unprejudiced observers.

I have just realised what little company there is here. In Moscow there were people like Strang and Walker to talk to, and one could always borrow a book and there were more visitors. Before I went on leave there were several visitors and I was pretty busy at the new job. But now I see a succession of years stretching before me with only the same company, and though it is true that I have plenty of old books, reading some new ones is something like talking to one's contemporaries.

19 Feb. Post just in from Moscow, bringing a letter from Walker. He says: 'We all enjoyed your last situation report immensely.' When I reply I shall say that I should think more of the report myself if it had *displeased* both the Ambassador and Walker. The Ambassador likes to make the best of everything here, while Walker can see no good in anything in the Soviet Union. Strang liked my first general report, and I thought that high praise, because he is a reasonable and an honest man.

According to Dr Bell there are about 1400 cases of typhus (spotted fever) in Leningrad at the moment and at least five hospitals are taking in only typhoid patients. It is not surprising that there should be typhus too in view of the overcrowding and the lack of adequate facilities for washing.

21 Feb. Yesterday I visited 'The Fourteenth Anniversary of the October Revolution School' with Assersson and our Soviet guide Luknitsky. The school has 2500 pupils on its books, but not all are present at the same time. Each quarter of the upper school has every fifth day off. The primary school works in two shifts, half in the morning, half in the afternoon, but they have a continuous week, so that although every child has one day in five away from school, the school is always at work. The headmistress said it was difficult to draw up the syllabus, and I can believe it. Great importance is attached to manual training, here called 'polytechnicalisation', the fitting of every child for a place in the industrial machine.

The primary-school headmistress complained that a complete change of programme had been ordered a few months ago. Formerly they had the 'complex' system: you took a question and treated it mathematically, historically, geographically, physically, biologically, and so on. Nothing was taught as a subject but only in relation to some matter of interest. Now the school is reverting to the old scheme under which the children have lessons in reading, geography, arithmetic, etc. not necessarily related to each other, though here and there the 'complex' system is retained.

The food in the dining-room did not smell or look appetising, but it is something that the children should get a meal in the middle of the day although three-quarters of them looked dreadfully white and pasty. Their clothing too was painfully inadequate—stockings with hardly any feet left.

A great treat last night—Tchaikovsky's *Queen of Spades*. Orlov-

★

Ermak invited us and we had seats in the director's box. Even at the Opera there is a shortage of everything that has to be imported. The German Vice-Consul, Pfleiderer, a great ballet-lover, has gained much kudos by bringing back with him from leave a supply of strings for various orchestral instruments. The one thing that they seem to find foreign currency for at present is electrical development. I hope that this will continue, for it puts money into the pocket of Metro-Vickers.

22 Feb. I visited the Tikhyeyeva kindergarten with Assersson and the interpreter Luknitsky. The entrance is filthy and smells of cats and defective sanitation but the school itself, which is on the first floor, is pretty clean. Most children come every day, but some have four days at school and one at home. The children were rehearsing for a show to celebrate the anniversary of the Red Army. The children looked perhaps a little better-fed than those in the previous school, but their clothes were just as wretched. The teachers' clothes were dreadful too.

25 Feb. Bolstaad, the Norwegian Consul at Archangel, told me that prisoners seem no longer to be employed in loading timber into the ships. He could not tell me about the camps, but he is inclined to think that prisoners are employed on auxiliary work such as building railways and canals and not tree-felling and transport of the timber. This means that the Soviet Government now have an answer to people who talk about slave-labour in the timber trade. Bolstaad said that in spite of Archangel being a great fishing-port, it is impossible to obtain fish there except illegally, as the whole catch has to be handed over to the authorities.

A letter from M yesterday. Matt is bent on spending 21/- on a bird book. I am glad his passion for birds is lasting so well, but we shall have to try to make him understand that people with our income think many times before spending 21/- on a book. I have wanted *The Oxford History of the United States* for years, but at 32/- it is ruled out. I found a good second-hand copy at the *Times* book club once, but even that was 16/- and I thought it too much. Then I much want the huge book on *The Science of Life* by Wells and Huxley, which appeared a year or two ago, but it costs a guinea so I'm not getting it. I am not sure that this abstention is altogether admirable. I am helping to starve authors worthy of support in order to buy for the boys a more expensive education than will be good for them. I will write to Matt suggesting that he should give a shilling of his guinea to the Friends' scheme for providing allotments for the unemployed. I would make it up to a

☆

pound. Perhaps money would mean more to him if he knew that a single man on unemployment pay has to live on 15/- a week.

Yesterday was the anniversary of the independence of Estonia, and the Estonian Consul General gave an afternoon show with a buffet groaning with food. Tonight we have to dine on board one of the Soviet steamers in the harbour. The man who brought the invitation had a draft of the menu with him. There are to be twelve kinds of hors d'œuvres. I find it indecent to give such spreads. The Soviet Government has now, I see, been forced to admit that there is something like a famine on the Volga and in some other grain districts, and that they have got to return about a million tons of the grain which they had squeezed out of the peasants. And not so very long ago they sacked and brought to trial a number of the leading officials in the Grain Trust for saying that the amount of grain demanded as the Government share could not be obtained.

28 Feb. At the dinner on the Soviet boat the consular corps was balanced by an equal number of 'Russians'. Ten of the sixteen were certainly Jews and two more probably. It is not surprising that the Jews of the world are on the whole in favour of the Soviet Government. In tsarist times the Jews had little scope, except in business, for their great abilities, and not even their lives and property were secure. No Jew would have been present at such a dinner as was given us, let alone ten or more out of sixteen. Among the ten were Bronstein, a very able and determined man who is head of the port; Weinstein, the Foreign Affairs representative here, a timid intellectual who goes in obvious fear of losing his job; Buchstein, Director of State Theatres, Opera, Ballet etc.; a young man not a day more than twenty-five years old who is head of the enormous business of timber export (he must have some influence behind him); the Director of Customs, Trianovsky, a huge dark man with tortured eyes, a terrible-looking creature—who has been put in charge of Torgsin at the port. All these seemed to know each other well and said 'thou' to each other. After dinner I talked to Krinkin, who used to be in the Foreign Affairs office here but is now studying to be a professor of philosophy. He was interesting as most Jews are.

I have seen four factories this week: soap, beer, margarine and boots and shoes. The soap factory I visited was the State Neva Stearine works, formerly a British company. The brewery was even less interesting. The margarine factory, built in 1930, was well-designed and clean. We were told that the margarine has 30% milk in it, and we certainly saw great troughs in which the milk was being made sour by bacteria. The workers

☆

looked more healthy than those in some factories. From margarine we went on to boots and shoes. The 'Quick Walk' factory here claims it is the largest in Europe. It turns out about 50,000 pairs of boots and shoes a day.

2 March. Borrowed Ethel Colburn Wayne's *Life of Lord Byron* from the wife of the Latvian Consul General and *Angel Pavement* from Metro-Vickers—the first books I have managed to borrow in Leningrad. Every man who comes out has to bring a book or two with him for the library. Unfortunately there was hardly a book I wanted to read.

4 March. Lady Muriel has a new and very objectionable iron in the fire. She proposes to form a company in England which would receive money from friends and relatives of people in Russia. Torgsin would dispatch parcels of goods to the value of the gifts and send back receipts from the recipients. The senders will regard Lady Muriel as guaranteeing that the addressees really get the goods and that they are not penalised. Unfortunately this will reveal to the OGPU that the addressees have connections abroad. Strang shares my opinion. Will Lady Muriel?

The railway court here is trying a certain Kairevich on a charge of trying to wreck the Soviet plans for the export of timber. Whereas in the preliminary investigations K revealed the whole story 'with tears and repentance', in court he went back on the 'confession' and said that he had made it in a mood of 'psychical depression'. To make it worse the others then withdrew their 'confessions' too. It has just come to light that K, after first joining the Bolsheviks, went over to the Whites in Kolchak's army—a fact he managed to conceal for years. I suppose he now sees that his life is forfeit in any case.

Nothing has come of the police investigation into the abuse of Miss Daunt's food-card, and this makes us the more uneasy. We have heard that Dr Bell was in with the OGPU, and the fact that the enquiry seems to have been stifled tends to confirm this. A German doctor here was in Murmansk some years ago when Dr Bell was in charge of hospital services. Dr Bell was accused (with justification) of embezzling large sums of money, but after an interview with the OGPU, the matter was dropped. Possibly that happened which frequently happens when a man in an important position puts himself in the wrong: no proceedings are taken, but he becomes an OGPU agent. We did not like to believe this, but Dr Bell certainly lied about the food-card, and other people working similar swindles were imprisoned, so it looks suspicious. It is regarded as absolutely normal to get a false doctor's certificate of ill-health if one

☆

wants time off for anything, just as the doctor who gives the certificate regards it as normal.

Miss Daunt went to the funeral of a DBS. Small children hung out of the windows of a building overlooking the cemetery and called the priest a fool and joined in the prayers with words of their own.

5 March. A book by Bessedovsky, formerly counsellor at the Soviet Embassy in Paris, has just appeared in English. It confirms what is generally known about the staffs of Soviet embassies and legations. The titular head may be a normal official, but the mission contains persons over whom he has no control. There is always a representative of the Party and always an OGPU man to spy on everyone and maintain discipline.

6 March. Sunday. *The Times Literary Supplement* has a review of *A History of Russia from the Earliest Times to the Rise of Commercial Capitalism* by Professor Pokrovsky. It says Professor Platonov, formerly President of the Academy of Sciences, and Professor Lyubavsky, formerly Rector of Moscow University, have been exiled.

Ericsson, the Swede whose company's contract has now been terminated, is staying on to collect about £40,000 due to them. He has collected a little, but he says that they have no *valuta*—and they haven't many roubles either. I see they are floating another internal loan.

Our guide Luknitsky told me that a prominent picture in the Hermitage about which I asked had been removed to be photographed. So I told him that that picture with many others had been sold and showed him the reproductions in the *Illustrated London News* of the most important pictures sold by them last year. He was quite upset.

The Soviet Government want to remove the centre of the fur trade from London and Leipzig to Russia. Last year they held an auction in Leningrad, and they repeated the experiment this year. The auction was held in Yiddish. The accompanying lunch was an excuse for the most revolting ostentation. The tables were loaded with complicated kickshaws, pâté de foie gras and the like, and with pyramids of butter two feet high. I was ashamed to sit at this feast with the hungry waiters and the hungry orchestra as spectators, though I was glad for the Intourist interpreters scattered among the guests. As often there was a remarkable display of Jews. At the top table were Bernstein, an American but born in Russia, Byelinki, head of the Soviet fur trust from Leipzig, an under-secretary for foreign trade, then the big dark man who runs Torgsin at the port, Trianovsky, Weinstein, Yanovsky, representative of the fur trust in Leningrad. Bronstein, the director of the port, was to have been on my right, but he could not come. Instead I had the Leningrad representative of the Soviet news agency TASS, also Jewish.

A week ago there were no eggs even in our co-operative. We got in touch with someone who keeps a few chickens and we were offered eggs either at a huge price or else in exchange for butter. We gave some butter for the eggs, and very good ones they were.

10 March. Waldhauer came to dinner. He was in very good form. His voice was much stronger and the drink he took had no effect on him, except to please him. He would like work in Germany or England, but he says he would come back, in spite of everything. He has been in the Hermitage for nearly thirty years, and he feels it is his duty to his subject and to the world of science and art to remain at his post. But he is pessimistic about the future of his department. Now there is the sale of pictures and other treasures, the heresy-hunting and the constant interference by ignorant fanatics whom he calls the Bandar Log.[7] What has saved the Hermitage is the fact that it is visited by so many distinguished foreigners.

11 March. I dined with the Woodheads at the Astoria, which violates all the original Bolshevik principles. You can't get in without a collar and tie. He is hoping to have the building of one machine at last. It is to make paper for wrapping and insulating electric cables, and they are hoping that the money can be squeezed out of the budget for electrical development, which seems to be the only thing there is *valuta* for. But about everything else he was very sceptical. A paper-plant in the Urals which was supposed to open in January 1931 has not yet been begun.

17 March. The boil on my foot is getting better but I can't get a boot on, so I have to stay indoors. Sir R. Hodgson, formerly British representative here, has a Russian wife whose relatives are still here. When relations were broken off her two brothers were at once exiled, and it was only after relations were resumed that they were released, both broken in health. Lady Hodgson's sister works at the big steel-works, the Putilov; she wants to leave, but may not until she finds a substitute to do her job.

A Lancashire man named Greenhalgh came to see me. He was engaged to advise the Russians on the spinning of the finer counts of cotton, but he has been here over six months without having much of

[7] The monkeys in Kipling's *Jungle Book* who mistook fine words for good deeds.

that to do. No Egyptian cotton is being bought and the cotton from south-central Russia is dirty, uneven, and of short staple. The 1860 machinery wouldn't still be working if it weren't English. No money for new machinery.

Bolstaad, the Norwegian Consul at Archangel, came to see me again. He has been in Murmansk and finds great changes since he was first there in 1913. Even in 1924 it was still a sort of wild-west town. Now it has roads and 40,000 inhabitants, but not enough houses. Bolstaad saw tents along the railway—tents in winter in that latitude! The authorities propose to electrify part of the railway, but at present the engines burn wood and the country is being rapidly deforested all along the railway and reverting to tundra. They have found in Norway that that is fatal; for once it has become tundra it remains frozen in summer and it can never grow trees again. Only about one quarter of the trawlers are working. The catch has to be handed over to the State factory and is sent to Leningrad either salted or in ice. The first care of the authorities is to keep Moscow and Leningrad as well supplied as possible. What they would consider badly supplied can hardly be imagined.

Kulagin, our OGPU friend and head of Torgsin, came in last night with Lady Muriel and Miss Daunt, and brought with him his prohibited records. He told Cave his father was a Georgian gipsy and he is certainly fond of singing. He sang—after first closing the door very carefully—a prohibited song, a lament for the death of some Russian students who were shot for anti-Soviet activities.[8] He professes to believe that the Five-Year Plan is being pushed much too fast, and to have quarrelled on this point with the big dark man I have referred to—Trianovsky, the Leningrad representative of the Commissariat for Foreign Trade. Kulagin is in charge of all Leningrad exports, and is therefore under Trianovsky. According to Kulagin, Trianovsky tells Moscow that the Plan can be realised, in which, says Kulagin, he is a fool. Kulagin wanted a job in the Soviet Trade Delegation in London, but Trianovsky defeated the project.

24 March. Pott arrived on the 19th and stayed for three days. I was still having to put compresses on my boil but fortunately the swelling

[8] Lady Muriel wrote in her diary: 'Kulagin is a very intelligent little man, typically Russian dual personality, very artistic, adoring music. We turned on the gramophone and he was very excited at hearing the beautiful voice of Varatinsky. He said that in 1917 he was in the Red Army when Varatinsky, in the White Eighth Army, was taken prisoner and condemned to death. His wife begged Kulagin to let him escape, which he did, but Kulagin got two weeks in prison.'

subsided and we were able to use Lady Muriel's tickets for *The Three Musketeers*. The chief point of going was to see Mme Lopokhova, the sister of Mrs Keynes, who was to dance.[9] She danced well and was a great favourite with the public. My foot was rather painful. The next evening I had another attack of fever, caused—as the one the week before must have been—by the poison which brought out the boils. It was not an ordinary boil. Small boils formed at perhaps twenty places where there were traces of the skin trouble which has annoyed me since Jeddah days. I spent the next day in bed and the next I kept my feet up as much as possible. The post from Finland contained no letter from M so I sent a telegram asking for news.

27 March. Sunday. Spent most of the morning hanging up two coat-racks. Then I read *The Times*. I don't know which is the more serious for England—the Irish situation, or the spirit of those who think the country is going to the dogs because some men no longer dress for the stalls.

Miss Daunt is back from Moscow—we shall hear about Lady Muriel's adventures there. She is quite, quite mad. She had the face to tell us that the OGPU had given her a guarantee that none of the Russians who received goods through Posilki Ltd would be molested for it and that orders had been given to all the local police to that effect.[10] She must know that such guarantees are worthless. My feet are normal again.

The *tovs* have given two shows this week to commemorate the Goethe centenary. I could not go to the first as I could not get a boot on. The one I went to yesterday was mostly speeches. The celebrated Bolshevik writer Bukharin spoke for an hour and three-quarters with the aid of four glasses of tea. He was followed by Lunacharsky, formerly Commissar for Education, and one of the best speakers in Russia. He went everywhere with Shaw, and Shaw spoke of him with great appreciation. His position was a little shaken when he was in Berlin, where his wife, a popular actress, attracted too much attention by the expensive jewellery she wore. Later she was playing at a theatre in Leningrad, and Lunacharsky used his authority as Commissar to detain the express train so that he and his wife could return to Moscow that night. For this he was 'unstuck'.

[9] Mrs Keynes (1892–1981), wife of the economist John Maynard Keynes, had been born Lydia Lopokhova. Her two brothers and her sister were also dancers. Their father had been an usher at the Imperial Theatre and their Scottish mother a housekeeper.
[10] See above, 4 March 1932.

28 March. A Canadian biologist named Mozley came to dinner tonight. He has permission to go to Siberia to study freshwater molluscs. He is staying with Professor Maximov, a physiologist, whose wife is also a scientist. His trip seems to be backed by Soviet scientists, so he is hopeful of bringing it to a successful conclusion. He reported that the Maximovs have to show an economic use for everything they do. The programme for each year is drawn up by a mixed committee of scientists and communists and every item has to be justified to the satisfaction of the communists.

Dr Bell says that many of the peasants who left their homes and came to the towns last year because there was nothing to eat and no fodder are going back because things are so bad here.

29 March. Yesterday I visited an educational 'combine' with about 3000 pupils. The purpose is to fit every scholar for industrial life. We watched a class having one of its first lessons in metal-work, learning to file in time with a metronome.

Strang wanted to visit Samarkand and Bokhara, but the *tovs* won't let them go. They don't like people going to the Tartar republics, where little trouble is taken to keep up the fiction that the 'autonomous republics' are free and willing members of the Soviet Union.

Good. Six books have arrived from the library in Reading to which I sent a subscription. The temptation to fall on the books is very strong. The six are: Sir S. Hoare's *The Fourth Seal* (on Russia just before the Revolution), a book about naval intelligence during the War, Compton Mackenzie on Gallipoli and Sisley Huddleston's favourably reviewed book on France, *Between the River and the Hills*, and two novels: *High Table* and a Basuto novel, *Chaka*.

Greenhalgh, the cotton expert from Lancashire, tells me that Mrs Morton, the wife of the man who accepted Lady Astor's offer and came out here with his family, is believed to be an OGPU spy.

5 April. 9 p.m. Completely demoralised by the books from the library— have read three in two days (one was Sunday).

An English workman called Derby came in today for advice. He is an expert in making micrometers and other measuring instruments. He answered an advertisement by ARCOS in an English newspaper and was taken on—without a contract. He is paid entirely in roubles. It was never explained to him that Russian roubles are worthless outside Russia. He earns fairly good pay and has saved quite a lot, but the balance is no good to him. Since Christmas his concession to send small sums to his elderly mother has been withdrawn. He wants to go home on leave, but it would mean landing in England without a penny in his pocket. A very decent fellow and I am sorry for him. The Passport Office have promised to explain the currency snag to intending emigrants to Russia. Derby has met many of the Russian-born Americans who have come here. They are flooding back almost as quickly as they came— usually with empty pockets. One man brought in $2000; declared it at the frontier, but when he tried to take out the $380 that was left, the authorities confiscated the lot.

I fear Lady Muriel will now come more often as she has taken a flat belonging to the Swedes as an office and accommodation for Miss Daunt.[11]

6 April. Assersson, Cave and I managed to get tickets on 30 March for a play, *Strakh* (*Fear*).[12] It was well we did, for it has now been taken off. It is not a great play, but it gives a good picture of present-day Russian life. The central figure, Borodin, was a physiologist, an elderly non-Party man who is director of a research institute. Proof of sabotage comes to light, and a member of the staff accuses the director, who is interrogated by the OGPU—of course in the kindest manner. Are the OGPU deceived? The OGPU are never deceived. No criminal ever escapes them, but no innocent person they interrogate is ever punished. In no time the informant is unmasked as the real criminal, and the old scientist returns to his post at the institute. Even more interesting was a secondary plot revolving round a man who is high up in the Party. He would never have been admitted to the Party at all if it had been known that his father had been a small landowner. So far as he knows the only person who is aware of his secret is a very old friend. He speaks to this friend of his guilty past and his dread lest it should be discovered. The conversation is overheard by his twelve-year-old daughter, who is a Young Pioneer. She gives him away to the OGPU and that is the end of papa. She is patted on the back and walks about with a self-satisfied smirk. I saw the play from a side gallery with a view of the whole audience. The sight of the ideal Soviet child did not seem to make them happy.

---

[11] In his biography of Lady Muriel, Wilfrid Blunt wrote that she had arranged to rent the second floor above the Swedish consulate in Krassnaya Ulitza for £20 a month. 'The flat is so spacious,' Lady Muriel wrote, 'that had it not been Swedish property, it would have been scheduled by the Government to house 150 people . . . . The luxuries include a Frigidaire, a Bechstein grand, comfortable sofas, armchair and electric light.'
[12] Play by A.N. Afinogenov (1904–1941). In *The Camels Must Go*, RWB described it as the most revealing play that he saw in Russia.

★

The staff at Metro-Vickers has been cut. I suppose the Soviet authorities do not want to pay the salaries (in *valuta*) of so many men. I had three of them to dinner the other night. They wanted to see whether a better effect could be produced by playing my gramophone records through the wireless. The experiment was not a success.

7 April. Yesterday was a good day. As soon as I had read M's letter I began to write her last-minute advice about the journey. Nearly finished when in came a telegram: 'MATTHEW SLIGHT WHOOPING-COUGH POSTPONING SAILING TILL THE 27TH.' Strange that I had not thought seriously of our plans being upset by illness. I have wired M: 'GRIEVED FOR YOU AND MATT. IF VISIT NOW VERY DIFFICULT CONSIDER GENERAL GOOD AND DON'T MIND ME.' I hope she will still be able to come and stay the four weeks. I have given Orlov-Ermak a list of the operas and ballets I should like M to see.

11 April. Miss Daunt was out in the car and a woman dashed across the road, as the Russians do, without looking round. The chauffeur is a very good driver and he was going slowly, so he was able to stop almost dead. The car just touched the woman, who fell down slowly like a dying peg-top. A crowd collected at once and began to shout 'Bourgeois!' and 'Foreigner!'—then a man in a leather coat appeared, told everyone the car was not to be touched, glared at the crowd, who slunk off (the woman had vanished), and so put an end to the incident. He was of course one of the ubiquitous OGPU agents and would probably have quashed the affair even if the car had been in the wrong. The hatred of foreigners is intelligible, since there are special shops where foreigners can buy what the ordinary Russian cannot. But why don't they attack the Government which makes this possible?

On the 9th Assersson and I visited the 'Red Weaver' woollen-mills. They were established long before the War by an English family named Thornton. I found them much better than most of the old factories I had seen in that the work-rooms were light and well-arranged and there were quarters for the work-people. We were shown over by two young engineers who were proud of their work without bragging. I brought our guide, Luknitsky, back to lunch. He is glad to be able to talk freely for once I think. He says most people are only interested in food and clothing. Even professional people will avoid politics and anything else that lies outside their immediate physical needs. You cannot criticise anything because it is dangerous, and even if it weren't it wouldn't be any good, for everything is done by a centralised committee which is

☆

unaffected by public criticism. The Russian press is uninteresting and misleading. You are told for months that everything is going well, and suddenly the alarm is beaten and you find that the country is threatened by famine, or that some important industry is in a very bad way.

12 April. Cave had a heart attack today. Dr Bell has given him an injection and some drops and told him he must get out into the fresh air every day (he hardly ever stirs out), and he mustn't smoke so much. Dr Bell said the Commissar from the Ministry of Health had been to see him about the six typhus cases and said: 'If you have an epidemic, Moscow will never forgive you.' Dr Bell reminded the Commissar that they had no sulphur for fumigation and that other disinfectants were useless against lice and even against bugs. He had sent fifty requests to Moscow for sulphur. 'Nevertheless,' said the Commissar, 'sulphur or no sulphur, Moscow will never forgive you if you have an epidemic.' The sulphur is taken by the military for munitions.

I think I recorded that some British engineers told me forty-one factories in Moscow had been put on to making munitions. Now comes Dr Bell's tale about the sulphur, and today an American called Bowers, who works in the tractor section of the Red Putilovets steel-works, told me that nine-tenths of the works is now producing war material. I asked him to lunch. He has been in the Putilovets foundry for three years. Like all the experts he says that the results the *tovs* brag about are often fictitious. Plant and machinery bought under the Five-Year Plan will be worth little by the time the Plan is over, they do no maintenance at all. He was asked to write an article on how to economise in their raw material, iron. He suggested that they look round the yards where there are not hundreds but thousands of tons of iron and steel. There is widespread overmanning. Half the time is wasted in conferences and arguments. The tractors that are turned out are often not fit to use.

Derby came to tea on the 11th. As he came from Lancashire I got the cook to make a huge apple-tart. It was served up hot and Derby had two chunks and several pieces of cake. He told me that last November the piecework rates in his factory were suddenly reduced by a third. He told me the workmen in his factory don't go to the meetings called by the factory committee, as they know that all the decisions have been arranged beforehand. Occasionally there is passive resistance to a decision. At one meeting it was decided that the factory should work on an off day and give the proceeds for the improvement of transport facilities, but the men simply didn't turn up. However, they *are* giving up two off-days for a factory memorial to Lenin. Derby has saved nearly

✩

2000 roubles but there is no way he can convert it into sterling. Cave mentioned Derby's case at the Foreign Affairs office the other day, and Orlov-Ermak suggested, very seriously, that he should buy caviare and sell it in England.

17 April. Still no news of when M is sailing. The Webbs[13] are coming to Russia for two months, and the DoT have written to say he would like to talk things over with me and Paton. One of the devices used by the Soviet Government to keep the people content is to pretend that conditions in other countries are far worse. Mrs Lie, the Russian wife of the Norwegian engineer, says that until she went abroad a few months ago, she was convinced that Europe was in a far worse state than Russia.

Kulagin told Miss Daunt that he had managed to rescue one of the Torgsin men from the OGPU. It had taken him five visits and he had had to bring the man home on a stretcher. Kulagin's words indicated that the man had been tortured and that he disapproved of such practices. He can't see that once you have an organisation that is above the law and can try in secret and execute in secret, the system is bound to extend.

The *tovs* are celebrating the fiftieth anniversary of the death of Charles Darwin. The papers are full of special articles. Here is an extract: 'We are not simply for Darwinism. We are for Darwinism remade by Marxism. For the bourgeoisie Darwinism is a theory in the past. For us it is a theory of action, it is militant materialism. Our slogan must be: 'Against anti-Darwinism in the struggle on two fronts—for the real remaking of Darwinism by Marxism.'

Supplies are very tight. Miss Daunt found Kulagin cursing two men for failing to produce flour. The town has been breadless for two days. Petrol for cars is short too. The Relief Association car had to get an order on the military petrol-store. Last night I saw long queues at a fish-shop and at a bakery. However the cross on the dome of the Kazan Cathedral has just been taken down, the huge gilt ball is to follow, and on 1 May a red flag will be flown in its place. Perhaps that will console the people for their empty bellies.

I have been several times to see Assersson. He is a well-read and well-informed man with an enviable library, old editions, modern editions in beautiful bindings and masses of pictures. I can always pass a pleasant hour with him. He told me of a Russian scientist he knows who went to

---

[13] Sidney Webb (1859–1947) and Beatrice Webb (1858–1943), social historians, reformers and economists. Their book *Soviet Communism: A New Civilization?* was published in 1935.

★

Poltawa in the Ukraine to give a series of lectures. He was offered a good fee, and promised a room with hot water to make his tea, but he was told to take with him all the food he will need for the period, including *bread*. This confirms the news from many sources that the Ukraine, which should be one of the granaries of the world, is starving. The agricultural expert attached to the German Embassy in Moscow says that the crop prospects in Western Siberia, the Ukraine, and the Middle and Lower Volga are very bad. Famine prevails over these areas, but doctors have been ordered to cease giving certificates that deaths are due to starvation.

The Germans who came here a year or two ago in such large numbers are going back again very discontented with conditions and completely disillusioned. It is supposed that the tales they have to tell have done much to counteract communist propaganda in Germany. We see quite a lot of Americans going back too. They come to us for transit visas.

Stewart, one of the Irish construction engineers, came to lunch on 30 April. He is working on a factory to produce cement blocks, but the building is hung up for lack of cement! His workers are peasants from the country who take care to do the minimum amount of work possible, complaining that however hard you work, the authorities leave you only just enough to keep alive—if that. He told me one of the official Moscow guides, showing a visitor the view from the top of a tall building, said: 'Feast your eyes on this scene, for you are looking at the future political capital of the world.'

The whole of the front of the Winter Palace is being covered by a huge wooden erection on which the usual picture of noble proletarians chasing wicked interventionists is gradually appearing. To mark the Orthodox Easter, which also falls on 1 May, two of the three Roman Catholic priests left have been arrested. They have also arrested the women who had been in the habit of sending parcels of food to the exiled Catholic bishop.

1 May. Bands are making a hideous din under my windows. It is just past midday; the military parade must be nearly over. The civilian procession is moving slowly along the Nevsky towards the Winter Palace Square. Last night the German Consul General gave a party: supper at 9 p.m., visit to a Russian church at 11.30, then back to an Easter meal, ending with cakes and a special Russian Easter cheesecake. The large church we went to was so crowded that the middle-aged widow of a German admiral nearly fainted, and the German Vice-Consul and I had to force our way out through the jam of fresh people trying to force their

☆

way in. We saw the priest heading a procession round the church. Off to Helsingfors to meet M this evening.

6 June. It is a month since M arrived. We went to Moscow intending to stay four days with the Strangs. We saw the Kremlin, the Red Square, Lenin's tomb and the gallery of French Impressionists. But that was the end of our sightseeing. On the 10th she fell ill with cystitis. We expected she would be well enough to travel back to Leningrad on the 15th, so I returned on the 13th, intending to come back and fetch her. Before I could start back I had a telegram saying she was not well enough to travel, so I decided to take some local leave in Moscow and returned with a supply of clothes for us both. It was a fortnight before she could be moved back to Leningrad. It would have been too sad for us not to be together when she had come out to see me for this short time, so I did the nursing—such as it was—and we had Walker's rooms as he was on leave. We had the usual difficulties about getting medicine.

The two weeks passed somehow. I read a great deal and did some translations for the Embassy to pass the time. I read aloud to M a good deal and didn't go out, for it meant asking someone to keep within call of M. One night I went with the Strangs to a performance of *Hamlet* and M had a wretched time. Lady Ovey's nurse was to keep watch and she knocked at the door every hour, but so quietly, in order not to disturb M if she should be asleep, that M had not heard. After that I didn't go out at night.

We had another disastrous delay when we left. We carried M from bed to the car and from the car to the station buffet. We were then told there had been a 'catastrophe'. After waiting nearly an hour, during which time M nearly collapsed with fatigue, we found that not only our train but also three expresses ahead of it were 'somewhere on the other side of Tula', i.e. four hours away from Moscow. There was nothing to do but return to the Embassy for another night. The next day M was terribly tired, and an hour before the train went it was evident that she was a little feverish, though we didn't dare to take her temperature. I was dreadfully anxious. I felt that if we sacrificed the second tickets and stayed on, M might be in Moscow for another week or more. All the time I stayed in Moscow I was using up my precious leave—*our* precious leave. If I didn't return, Cave, and after him the Todds, would not be able to take their long-planned leaves, and I didn't want to spoil their arrangements. I felt we ought to 'tip and run', and afterwards I was glad I had been so cruel, for although M was very tired when we started, she was better by the time we reached Leningrad.

☆

While M was with me an American engineer from Magnetogorsk came in for a visa and described conditions there. He told us of a typical deported *kulak* to whom he gave some bread and who asked whether he had any clothes to spare. He wore a long cloak and underneath had neither shirt nor trousers, only bits of rag wound round his legs—and this in a place where you get 29° below zero. He drew a sad picture of horses starved to death, and humans being buried anywhere like animals.

16 June. M got steadily better. The last week she was here we were able to take a few walks, and even go to the Hermitage to see the Scythian gold.

I gave a bed to Miss Clyman on her way to Murmansk and Archangel. She reports that recently there has been a great change for the worse in conditions in Moscow. There are now immense queues for everything. It is the custom for a serial number to be pencilled on the hand of everyone in the queue, so that there shall be no stealing of places. Miss Clyman saw the number 953 on a woman at the tail-end of a fish queue. In the new 'free' markets were only a few rotten potatoes for sale. No sugar to be had on the ration-card. The newspapers report that 'the insistent demands of the toilers' have not been rejected. The authorities have yielded to their request, and have agreed to issue another loan. Every person is expected to put a month's pay into it.

The Todds' cook was summoned to attend a meeting of domestic workers and they were all invited to give up a month's pay to the new loan. The meeting was an angry one. The non-Party servants said that when they got some food and clothing they would subscribe to the loan; the Party members said that *if* they subscribed to the loan they would— eventually—get food and clothing.

17 June. Miss Daunt looks such a skeleton. She is always overworked.

The Woodheads came in last night after dinner. Mrs Woodhead has been seeing a good deal of the Soviet violinist Soermus, about whom there have been many questions in the House of Commons in the last few years. He travels round England giving concerts and does not conceal his bitter detestation of things English. He gives lectures saying what a terrible state England, Germany and other countries are all in. Mrs Soermus is an attractive English pianist of twenty-seven (Soermus is fifty-two). She is horrified at the conditions here. Her previous visit was in 1925 when the New Economic Policy was at its height and there was plenty of everything. Soermus lives with his head in the clouds, giving away money when he has it with both hands. She is particularly worried as he is paid in roubles.

19 June. I was invited by Weinstein to visit an electric power-station. He asked me on the telephone whether I would bring my own car. I said no. He made no comment. When I reached the Foreign Affairs office at 8 a.m. yesterday I found that those consuls who had brought their own cars were expected to carry not only Weinstein and the Ermaks and two hangers-on, but also the consuls who hadn't cars. I did not wish to create an incident or I would have gone back home. Kechlin, the German Consul, a very good fellow, took me and the Italian Consul in his big car. Weinstein said that Volkhovstroy was three hours away. I took a half-pound slab of chocolate, for emergencies, but no food. It was fortunate that people who knew more about the distance than I did took some food, for we took *nine* hours, and what should have been lunch was eaten at 6.30 p.m. Weinstein had not troubled to take someone who knew the road, and we lost the way. We got off the made road and struggled along the edge of a canal for miles. In sliding down a bank our car hit a stone, which knocked a hole in the petrol-tank, and but for the fact that the Latvian Consul had been provided by his wife with a piece of soap, so that the leak could be stopped temporarily, we should have been stuck. It was a very hot day, the heat being hardly tempered by a slight shower which fell at about 4.00.

At Volkhovstroy there was a pleasant breeze blowing, and when we had washed and had a meal at the engineers' house we felt that there was little wrong with the expedition—except the prospect of the journey home. Weinstein was not at all abashed at his bad organisation. He contented himself with saying 'All's well that ends well,' and poking fun at those members of the party who had wanted to turn back half-way. I was one of these, for I was not convinced that we should ever get to our destination.

Being there, we visited the power-station built by Swedish engineers. It is a simple but fine building, and set at an acute angle with the right bank with a stone dam to keep the ice away from it in winter. The inside of the station is beautiful: high and long for its width, with white walls tiled with green up to the height of a man. The engineers said that Volkhovstroy could produce current at half a kopek a kilowatt hour as against 3–4 and 5–6 for current produced by burning peat and coal respectively. By the time we had finished having tea it was 10 p.m., but we did not start until 10.45 as the chauffeurs were still tinkering with our car. Our hosts assured us that we should be home, with the aid of a guide they lent us, in four hours, but no one believed them. In fact we took nearly seven. There were several punctures, and twice a car got bogged down and had to be dragged out. I got off at my door at 5.30 a.m. and got into bed at 6.00—just twenty-four hours from the time when I got up. Today I feel a little stiff but the Danish Consul who drove the whole way there and back himself suffered more than I did. We got one thing out of the trip: we saw a 'white night'. It was never darker than twilight and by 1 o'clock the east was already pink—very lovely.

21 June. Two ships' captains reported yesterday that they had had to send men to hospital. A bosun was injured and a second mate went off his head. One of the captains told me that his men seem to get plenty of roubles somewhere, possibly by smuggling in small articles and selling them. In Archangel a British seaman pulled out a ten-rouble note and was fined £4.

22 June. While M was here we made a new budget. I have made out a list of all the fixed payments which have to be met: that leaves £1120 for all expenses when income tax has been deducted.

I have just been reading the burial service at the funeral of the poor bosun. He was a fine strong man of only forty-four and leaves a widow and four children. These funerals abroad always seem doubly sad. Last night I went on board the ship to hold an inquiry into the cause of death. It was quite straightforward. The ship is carrying pit-props back to England, part of them as deck cargo. To enable the props to be piled up high, great wooden stanchions are lashed to the sides projecting a long way above the bulwarks. One of the stanchions fell down, striking the bosun on the head.

26 June. An Englishman named Westgarth has written an article in the *Express* poking fun at people like Shaw who live in expensive hotels for a few days and then know all about Russia. In an angry reply Shaw asserts that the Soviet Union is the only country where (a) wages are not falling and (b) prices are not rising. Even if both were true in the literal sense, everything depends on what you can buy at the co-operative which at the moment is little more than bread.

The newspapers report that the big factories have been ordered to start making more articles of common necessity to satisfy the needs of the people. The Karl Marx works, which makes textile machinery, is to produce pails, milk cans, funnels etc. Electrosila, which makes electrical switch gear, is to make sheep-shears, axes, chains for wells, iron protectors for boots, hinges, bolts and parts for harness. One is to open a workshop for mending kettles, another is to turn out 50,000 burners for Primus stoves this year, and a third to produce hinges, pitchforks, ploughshares and frying-pans. It is interesting to read the list of things which the wretched people of this country have had to do without for the last few years.

28 June. I was called to the telephone for a message from Moscow. After the usual false alarms and waiting and shouting and being cut off and told to hold on, I heard the voice of Walker saying that the Ambassador and Lady Ovey would arrive in Leningrad the day after tomorrow, and could I put them up? It is typical of the Ambassador to give so little notice. I said yes. I have sent Nusha a wire asking her to return and I am trying to find the excellent servant who waits at table when we have big dinners. I have telegraphed Cave in Helsingfors to ask him if he can to return on the 1st, and to bring some grub back, as there is very little here. Our co-op has no fruit at all and yesterday they gave us rancid butter for the second time in ten days. Miss Daunt says that no one except consuls have been getting potatoes lately, and ours have sometimes been black.

A clever-looking Scot from Australia came in today to register. He is a boiler-maker, originally from Dundee, and he thought he would like to see what was really going on in Russia. He found a job in the shipbuilding yards, but he says he doesn't think he can stand more than two months here. There is no serious work done, it is all talk and conferences, and no one will take any responsibility. The men grumble about the lack of food all the time and the conditions in the works dining-room are such that he put his head in once and fled.

Yesterday a Professor Richardson of Leeds University had lunch with me.[14] He is an economist and has come out for a month or two to study industrial relations. After only a couple of days he already inclines to the view that the trades unions have no say in working conditions, and no power to alter them or to protest against them.

Kulagin, the OGPU man, has been given a new job. He is now in charge of all the collective farms in the north. I met him in the street yesterday, and far from ignoring me, as any other Russian would, he called after me. He wants to take Miss Daunt and me out to see one of

---

[14] Professor J. Henry Richardson (1890–1970). A copy of his report on the Soviet Union can be found in Leeds University Library (Russian Archive, MS 800/13).

his farms. I should like to see one, and I should like to hear Kulagin talk about it.

3 July. Sunday. The Ambassador and Lady Ovey left last night. Their three-day visit was a great success. The weather cleared, and after seeing the Scythian treasures at the Hermitage we borrowed the car from Miss Daunt and bumped out to Peterhof, the palace of Catherine the Great. We were whisked in everywhere without waiting and without paying. In the evening the Ambassador and I sat up talking and watching the twilight on the cathedral opposite until midnight. He told me the story of how he got the legation in Mexico. He had stayed in England for years in order to be able to be near his first wife in an asylum, and so when he finally became counsellor at Rome, he was older than the average and was beginning to be pessimistic about his prospects. Then the Foreign Secretary, Sir Austen Chamberlain, offered him Guatemala. He was appalled at the prospect of spending five years there, but he replied that while he would have preferred a place of greater social and political interest, he placed himself unreservedly in the hands of Sir Austen. The Foreign Secretary was so much struck by this (as I should think it, strictly qualified) readiness that he gave him Mexico instead, much more important, much more agreeable socially, and with a perfect climate. Sir Austen later said to him that he had had so much trouble to fit men into posts, because so many made excuses on account of health or family affairs, that it was a great pleasure to find a diplomat who was willing to go anywhere.

On 1 July I sent them off to Dyetskoye Syelo to see the palace of the last Tsar, and on the way home Mrs Todd took them shopping. Lady Ovey bought some lovely pieces of old stuff and the Ambassador bought a large picture for the wall of the Embassy dining-room. We walked along the quay to see the former British Embassy;[15] the Oveys were pleased to see that it was much less impressive than the present Embassy in Moscow. On their last morning we drove out to the 'Arrow', the point of one of the famous islands. It was an exquisite day, and we stayed there so long there was little time for other sights, but we went to the Fortress of Peter and Paul. We saw where the tsars are buried, the prison where political prisoners used to be kept and also the little house where Peter the Great lived. While Lady Ovey went on another shopping expedition, I took Sir Esmond to the Hermitage again and Waldhauer showed us two newly opened Etrurian rooms.

[15] At that time the Krupskaya Institute of Political and Communist Education.

★

After dinner Kulagin came in to see Sir Esmond. In his new capacity he is largely responsible for the feeding of Leningrad, and he told the Ambassador with uncommon frankness that he did not know where to turn for food supplies. There was almost no meat, there was even a shortage of bread, and there were no fats at all. 'We don't believe,' he said, 'as the people in Moscow do, that all is well.' If he is to be believed, many subordinate officials send in favourable reports which they know to be untrue, because they have not the courage to report the facts, so that the Kremlin never really knows what the situation is. If this applies to local affairs, it applies even more accurately to foreign affairs, of which men like Stalin have no direct knowledge. It is believed, for instance, that the Soviet Ambassador in London has to go on stuffing Stalin with tales of approaching revolution in England and pretending that the *Daily Worker* is a very influential journal, etc. Sir Esmond was impressed with what Kulagin said. It was a novel experience for him to hear a man in a key position speaking so pessimistically about the future.

I liked the Ambassador better than I had before. He talks far too much, but he talks much better than he writes, and he struck me as more sincere than I had believed him to be.

4 July. A rare telephone call from Moscow today: Walker realises that he forgot to send on last week an important FO despatch asking for proposals for further reductions in consular salaries. The Treasury has found that we are all getting a more favourable rate for roubles than was expected and they expect a proportionate reduction in our pay. I originally offered to give up £250 and the Treasury took £160. I shall now offer to give up the other £90. It is always hard to consent to reductions but permission to get roubles elsewhere than at the State Bank meant an enormous increase in our salaries. I have calculated that until my pay goes up in November (by £50 gross, i.e. £38.10/- net), I shall have £420 a year for myself: living expenses, clothes, journey to England, champagne for guests, and everything. With economy it ought to be enough. If it were not for the obligation to entertain a certain amount it would be riches. One moment! I have forgotten that when I go on leave £50 is deducted from my representation allowance. Well, well! It will soon be November, and there will be a little extra coming in. It is quite clear to me that if this place was as expensive as an ordinary consulate general it would be out of the question for us to send all four boys to boarding-schools.

Kulagin has been to dinner and gone off, at 9.00, to work. He is President of the Leningrad Union of Co-Operatives. He said he works

☆

from 9.30 or 10.00 at night in his office and then takes work home and works until 2 a.m. and what with the volume of work, his health, and the worries—'No bread, no meat, queues, people stealing right and left'—he can't keep it up.

Everyone speaks of the lack of food. Assersson told me that a Swedish seaman, admitted to the seamen's hospital, was told he must have any food he wanted sent in because none could be provided. I paid our cabinet-maker with a pound of cheese and a pound of lard and he went off delighted.

Two old ladies who used to be British but are now Russian sent word to Miss Daunt on Sunday, begging her to go and see them. Until recently they had at least bread-cards, but these have now been taken away. They had one rouble in the house, and the authorities had just sent in a bill for rent for 1400 roubles on the ground that they had been undercharged for three years. I believe that they cannot be evicted without a decision of the court, but I don't know what sort of treatment ex-wealthy people get in the courts, which are supposed to decide cases according to their revolutionary conscience.

I have just read H.G. Wells' latest book *The Work, Wealth and Happiness of Mankind*. He thinks that the League of Nations has become purely political and diplomatic, and that perhaps more is to be hoped for from such non-political international bodies as the Bureau of Agriculture in Rome.

Yesterday's newspaper prints an interview with the Webbs, who have returned to Moscow after a 7000-kilometre tour in the USSR. According to the reporter, Webb said: 'We met with a hearty welcome and assistance everywhere and were able to see everything and everyone we wanted to see. We were particularly struck by four points: the Soviet Union is a country overflowing with hope and confidence—more so than any other country at the present time. Secondly, one feels tremendous energy not only in Government circles, but also among all the people one meets. Thirdly, in all places we were struck by the high degree of unity in aim and politics (in this respect the Soviet Government differs markedly from all other governments at the present time). Fourthly, we were struck by the enormous progress attained by the Soviet Union not only in the sphere of industry, but also in education and in all fundamental elements of culture. I cannot help feeling that the Soviet Union has not been affected by the consequences of the collapse of the capitalist system. The USSR is the only country in which production is growing quickly and unceasingly, and in which there is absolutely no unemployment. The secret of this lies in the fact that production is not organised for profit . . . .' Mrs Webb's comments on similar lines ended with: 'I also think that the Party ought to issue a decree against reddening the lips.'

9 July. I am having an exciting weekend. Last night I had Hugh Dalton, Under-Secretary for Foreign Affairs in the late Government, and Pethick-Lawrence, formerly Financial Secretary to the Treasury, to dinner. They have come to look at Soviet finance. This morning I have been talking for an hour to a Canadian KC. It was exciting to talk to people with brains and a knowledge of their subject—so exciting, in fact, that I slept very little last night. At about 10.00 they got up to go. As I found they were going for a walk I went with them, and finally left them at their hotel at midnight.

10 July. Sunday. The Webbs came to dinner last night—at least he came to dinner and she came to two pieces of toast and a glass of red wine. Nine out of ten tourists have their insides upset by the bad food, and Mrs Webb is one of the nine. They are no longer young (he is seventy-five and she is seventy-six), but mentally they are as vigorous as ever, and they must be pretty sound physically too, to have made so many long and exhausting journeys. They have not wasted their time, and with their knowledge, their long experience as trained investigators, the assistance they give each other, and the fact that they have an almost sacrosanct reputation because Lenin translated three of their books into Russian, they have had opportunities of seeing what the ordinary investigator would not see, although of course they were dependent on interpreters. Although they say that they were able to see what and whom they liked, it is evident that on the whole they have seen what everyone sees—the show-places—and I think they have been too prone to accept at their face value such statements as that in the Ukraine thirteen collective farms did badly last harvest because of bad management. The whole of the Ukraine is in a bad way for grain. They were interested mainly in the organisation of the State, the way the wheels go round, and they seem to have collected a great deal of information on that head. They are amused at many things—especially the repetition of shibboleths which it is manifest that most of the people don't understand. They wonder most at the efficiency of the Communist Party, which is the mainspring of everything and a most formidable engine. They stood by the opinions reported in yesterday's paper and I argued with Mrs Webb about their 'fourthly'. She stuck to her point that production for use and not for profit is necessary if

☆

unemployment is to be avoided, but she did admit that other factors here make it possible for practically all the labour there is to be employed, and also that you could not eliminate unemployment in England merely by organising for the consumer rather than the producer.

13 July. Naomi Mitchison rang up on Sunday.[16] I invited her to dinner. She is with Dalton and Pethick-Lawrence, but her special interest is archaeology. I told her which tram to catch, and kept an eye on the trams as they stopped in front of our house, but it was past 8.00 when I caught sight of an odd figure, looking in the wrong direction for our house. She was wearing a dress made from a Persian print, a felt hat, and a jacket made of some loosely woven white material, fuller in the lower part, which had pockets all round it like purses in a belt. She said it was her own invention. She is anxious to get away from the Intourist guides and see things for herself, and as she is going to be visiting archaeological digs she may manage it, but she knows little Russian and she will be pretty closely watched.

Platou, the Norwegian Consul, is at the port nearly every day, and says that almost nothing is being exported except timber, and that is being loaded very slowly because they are short of men. When a trainload of timber comes in, men are taken off the ships to unload the trains which have to be unloaded quickly because of the shortage of locomotives and rolling-stock. Rations are now so bad that men are running away to the country. Last year they were running away *from* the country. It is simply the human belief that somewhere else *must* be better.

A Russian woman who emigrated to Australia but returned here two years ago with her Russian husband and three children came to the office. She says food gets more and more difficult. There is almost no meat, no potatoes, and no milk, except in exchange for bread. She hears Russians complaining a lot, and even threatening what they would do if there were a war and rifles were dealt out to the reserves. But I doubt whether many people are bold enough to say such things, still less to do them. She is trying to get back to Australia, but the Soviet authorities won't give her permission. A friend of hers, a sailor, a naturalised Australian, came here to see how things are, but when he landed in

---

[16] Naomi Mitchison (1897–1999), tireless traveller and author. Her husband, Gilbert Richard Mitchison (1890–1970), was a Labour MP from 1945 to 1964 and subsequently a life peer.

★

Vladivostok his British passport was confiscated. He wants to return to Australia, but he daren't apply for permission to leave, because he is afraid of what they will do to him, and he daren't come to the Consulate for advice. I, on the other hand, dare not request the authorities to give me the passport, for fear of getting the man into trouble. I would like to be able to do something to help the man. Of all the objectionable things in this country the brutality of keeping people here who want to leave is the most objectionable.

18 July. A parcel of four books from the Ambassador: Lord Acton's lectures on modern history, and three books about Mexico, of which one is a new translation of Bernal Diaz. Has the Ambassador sent them as a gift or a loan? His letter says he is 'doing up a parcel of books for you'. One of the books I see was a present to him from a Mexican and taken together they are a costly return for three days' hospitality. I have already written to thank the Ambassador for the promised gift. If he meant them as a loan he should have expressed himself better.

Last night we had the Parhams to dinner. He represents an English firm that buys enormous quantities of wood-pulp for paper, a small steamer full of pulp every four days. He says the Canadian pulp cannot compete with the Russian which is uniform and not a mixture of various kinds of spruce. After they had gone, Cave and I went out for a breath of air. It was 11.30 and lamps were lighted, for the white nights are over. We walked down the second street from here and through the uncurtained windows you could see people in bed. The semi-basement had a line of beds in it about two feet apart. I must take the Naomi Mitchison sort of person past these places, as an antidote to the flats with plenty of room and full larders which they are shown by Intourist.

Yesterday I saw the Metro-Vickers people. All the engineers agree that the Five-Year Plan is slowing down. Tearle had found himself sitting next to the man who was responsible for choosing the type of motorcycle to be manufactured in the 'Red October' factory which I saw last year. He teased him about choosing a second-rate German machine to imitate instead of a good English machine. The man said he chose the machine with the frame which he thought they could most easily copy here with their equipment! The engine was a secondary matter. The next day there was a letter in the local paper signed by fifteen of the men engaged in the making of these cycles. They say that production has fallen to about seven cycles *a month,* and the factory has been given 'another task'. So much for the Five-Year Plan!

I had an interesting visitor yesterday, one R. Kirkpatrick, now retired from the Museum of Natural History at South Kensington. His hobby is meteorites. He is one of the few people who have made the journey that I made down the Tigris on a skin raft, from Diarbekir to Baghdad. He knew *Arabia Deserta* Doughty well and met Philby recently.[17] Philby's recent journey has established the fact that the supposed ruined city of Ubar is really a group of 'craters' such as are caused by the fall of meteorites. He believes that meteorites are of terrestrial origin, as he has found traces of organic life in them. If a body is flung from the earth at a speed of over six miles a second it will rise beyond the influence of the earth's attraction and will then circle the earth until, maybe, a conjunction of pulls from various sources brings it just so much nearer to the earth as to make it fall back. This he thinks is the origin of meteorites. He does not seem deterred by the fact that no scientist of importance has accepted his theory.

Now that country people are allowed to sell their surplus to the consumer, for the first time it is possible to buy food in the country. I have been wondering whether one year I could not take a villa on the sea within motoring distance of Leningrad and have M and the boys out for the summer holidays. I could borrow the car from the Relief Association. It is a project worth thinking about. Perhaps in a year or two I might buy a car myself.

20 July. A bad day in that the news about Ireland is depressing, but a good day in that there is a long letter from M.

Miss Daunt gave me a curious drink the other day. It tasted rather like ginger beer without the fizz, but it was a concoction made from a fungus, believed to have come originally from Japan and to be effective in preventing disease, particularly typhus. A piece of the fungus is kept in a liquid consisting of weak tea with sugar. Every day, after drinking the liquid, the tea left in the teapot, diluted with water and sugar, is fed to the fungus. The fungus has to be washed now and then and cut down when it grows too big for the vessel. It is more agreeable to take than the manner of its preparation would lead one to expect.

Lady Muriel threatens to come out again in ten days or so. At present she is abusing Miss Daunt and me and the FO all at once, everyone

---

[17] C.M. Doughty (1843–1926) had produced his seminal work on the Middle East, *Travels in Arabia Deserta*, in 1888. H. St J.B. Philby (1885–1960) was a diplomat and traveller. In September 1920 RWB wrote home from Baghdad: 'Philby is back as cantankerous as ever. I never met such a fellow. Any scheme that anyone else puts up he disagrees with. His great phrase is "I join issue with you," and he spends his whole life joining issue with someone.' The spy Kim Philby was his son by his first wife.

★

being out of step except herself. I wish she wasn't coming, for it is no use to explain figures to her.

24 July. Still sticky-hot. I shall soon be saying 'Four months to leave.' I aim to arrive in England on 17 December and return to Leningrad on 21 February. It will be pleasant to be at home for Christmas for once. We have never been all together for Christmas yet.

Kirkpatrick has been refused permission to visit the meteorite in Siberia. He wants, if he can, to save something from the wreck of his plans, by visiting a scientific station on Lake Baikal.

On Friday the Wilsons came with their letter of introduction from Robin Hodgkin.[18] He is in the Ministry of Transport and his sister is the secretary of the Oxford branch of the League of Nations Union. I had them to dinner and we talked for two or three hours. They would like to support the Russian experiment on idealistic and humane grounds, but I tried to convince them that it is being carried out by a band of ruthless people who have no use for idealism or for humanity as we understand it. Yet it is this ruthlessness which is the main cause of the success, for the experiment could not have lasted a year if those in power had not killed and exiled hundreds of thousands of people whom they knew or suspected to be opponents or potential opponents.

Late last night a Mrs Kemble arrived in some distress. She had come with two children of three and four to join her husband who has work at a furniture factory in Khalturino. Her husband did not meet her; her money, compulsorily changed into roubles, has gone. A hotel kept them for one night without payment but she has to leave today. Miss Daunt gave them a meal last night and I gave them two tins of Ideal milk and a tin of strawberries. I have wired to a man in the same factory whose name Mrs Kemble happened to know, to ask where the husband is.

A day or two ago I saw a young furrier who applied for a visa to enable him to go to England on his way to America. The new factory has 3000 hands, and they are building a second. They hope soon to be exporting prepared furs to the value of $15 million a year, which will put the English and American and German fur-traders out of business, since Russia has the best furs in the world and the labour is cheap. He seemed confident that the business will work well in the end; they can put up with hardship. Very often there is nothing to eat but black bread and salt but they don't mind. He was enthusiastic about the system and spoke

---

[18] Robert Howard Hodgkin (1877–1951), historian, brother-in-law of RWB, and provost of Queen's College, Oxford, 1937–46.

☆

about the OGPU as though it were just a necessary evil.

27 July. It is really hot now—over 90° in the drawing-room. Just back from a tiring but interesting day at Dyetskoye Syelo with the Strangs. Nothing could more clearly exhibit the limited and superstitious mind of the Tsarina than her bedroom which is *papered* with little icons; their private apartments swarm with private photographs, religious pictures and coloured postcards. Afterwards we went to the islands. People looked very brown and well, and some were rowing about in all sorts of costumes. Two buxom girls in one boat seemed to be wearing black brassières. I felt it was fortunate that the Alcibiades of Flecker's unpublished poem was not there:

> When Alcibiades
> Met naiades
> He would remove the bodices
> From those delightful goddesses.

Strang liked this and gave me in return:

> Diodorus Siculus
> Made himself ridiculous
> By saying thimbles
> Were phallic symbols.

28 July. Strang talked to people in the FO when he was in England and is confident there won't be any more cuts. If so we shall manage—unless prices in England rise very much.

31 July. Sunday. Miss Clyman's visit to the north has confirmed my opinion that a private person who speaks Russian and knows something about the country can get ten times as much information here as an official—a foreign woman even better than a man. Miss Clyman travelled with Miss Bennett, an American journalist who works on that rag, the *Moscow News*, and was commissioned to visit various new mining and hydroelectric schemes and other industrial places in the north. The whole of Karelia is under the OGPU. North of Petrozavodsk you have to apply to the OGPU before you can buy a railway ticket. In Karelia they travelled under the auspices of Karalyes (the contraction of the Russian name for Karelian Timber), which with Syeverlyes (Northern Timber) controls the whole timber industry in the North.

☆

Karalyes professed to be unable to give Miss Clyman any help in getting to Kem', the great convict station. The manager said that Karalyes had no branch there as the wood was poor and only good for local consumption, but the first thing she saw at Kem' was an immense five-storey building with 'Karalyes' on it in large letters. Karalyes claim to handle 90% of the timber in Karelia and to export 60%.

Miss Clyman observed that the whole of the area along the railway to Murmansk is the scene of a compulsory transfer of population such as occurred in Russia under the tsars. Miss Clyman found colonies of immigrant American and Canadian Finns who had been recruited on three-year contracts by the Finnish section of the Communist Party. They have food-books on Torgsin and seem to be content. Some of them even talked with enthusiasm of 'building socialism' and of not going back to Canada until a workers' republic had been established there. They live pretty isolated lives.

Miss Clyman tried to investigate the stories of forced labour denied by Molotov. The chauffeur who drove her to the station at Petrozavodsk told her that there were prisoners and *kulaks* employed in cutting timber up to the spring of 1931. He said that the real prison timber colony was in a district called Stary Latik, about 130 *versts* (138 kilometres) north of Leningrad, where there were about 200,000 of them, though many were moved up to work on the canal during the summer.

At Khibinogorsk Miss Clyman managed to meet the wife of a railway construction engineer, formerly a Miss Gordon, completely Russian in spite of her Scottish name, which probably goes back to some 17th- or 18th-century soldier of fortune. She said prisoners were never employed on timber work within about 200 kilometres of any large centre, but that if you took a horse, you could find prisoners at work in the forest at that distance. A year previously her husband, who was building a branch-line from Khibinogorsk, suddenly received orders to march all his 3000 prisoners twenty-four hours into the forest. He brought them back when the commission had left a few days later. Miss Clyman only managed to talk to this woman by telling her OGPU guides that she wanted to wash her hair, and she escaped. She found conditions here better than anywhere in the north: there was fish and the workers got bread, sugar and tea and there were even plenty of cigarettes. A procession was in progress to celebrate the fact that their subscriptions to the New Loan were 100% of estimate.

Miss Clyman was very keen to find out what she could about the workers on the canal which is to join the White Sea to Lake Onega. The canal runs beside the railway most of the way from a point 150 kilometres north of Petrozavodsk to the point where it reaches the White Sea. Miss Clyman saw thousands of men *and women* working on the canal, from Sigyeza northwards. She recognised Russians, Kirghiz, Tartars and Uzbeks. At first she thought they were troops as they wore a sort of uniform, but an OGPU courier on the train bragged about their having set the 'class enemy' to honest work, and said that there were 200,000 of them working on the canal. 'Look at them,' the courier said. 'No chance of sabotage now. With the exception of the chief engineer they are all prisoners.'

Many thousands of *kulaks* have been exiled to the north since the collectivisation of agriculture began. It is reckoned that at Khibinogorsk alone 32,000 out of a total population of 35,000 are *kulaks*, mostly from the Ukraine and the Nizhni-Novgorod area. They work on the mountain of apatite, the famous fertiliser, in conditions that must be appalling in winter. They live twenty or thirty families to a *tent* or three-ply wooden hut lined with tar paper to keep out the wind. She was told that during the first months after their arrival many hundreds died of exposure, typhus and smallpox.

An official at Khibinogorsk proudly showed Miss Clyman a crèche, but she pointed to the *kulak* children scrabbling about in the thick mud, and he admitted that the crèche was not for them, 'But,' he said, 'schools were being built for them.' Some of the huts are four kilometres from the nearest water, and there is no system of sanitation whatever. The whole of the area round the camps is in a filthy state.

Besides the prisoners on the canal and the *kulaks* working on the apatite deposits, there are in the port of Murmansk some 20,000 people called *ssylki* or exiles who live on the edge of Murmansk in an area called Ssylkigorod (Exiletown). They seem to be free, except that they may not leave the place.

There is one other category of non-free labour, viz. the prisoners in the huge convict station of Kem'. They are like convicts in other countries, completely secluded for long terms, sometimes for life. She gathered that 90% of the population of the Kem' district (said to be 50,000) worked in timber-cutting and logging in the winter. Two years ago things were bad, there were riots and shootings; but the authorities shot about eighty OGPU officials and now things were better.

I admire Miss Clyman's feat in gatecrashing Kem'. She not only managed to see Boyar, the Latvian OGPU man who runs Kem' and the terrible Solovetskiye Islands, but he gave her a wonderful dinner at the restaurant reserved only for top OGPU officials. Beyond extracting a verbal promise from her, which he seemed to think binding, that she would take no photographs, he did not interfere with her doings.

It is perhaps worth a separate paragraph to record that nowhere did Miss Clyman observe any signs of ill-treatment by the OGPU or hear any complaint on the subject. So far as she could judge their control was rather helpful and paternal. This seems the less curious when one recollects that once prisoners in Karelia are reduced to complete submission the problem for the OGPU is to obtain the maximum output from them which requires that they be supplied with a reasonable minimum of food and clothing.

4 Aug. Poor Cave has added another complication to his life. He has fallen in love. According to Cave she is willing to share his life anywhere and anyhow. She looks pleasant, but Cave has a faculty for getting into trouble, so I am suspicious. His present wife, who lives in Paris, told him after they were married that she had had forty-one lovers.

From a report to HM Ambassador in Moscow, 6 Aug. The Soviet regime is confronted by a crisis due to the growing food shortage, but although the crisis is serious, I venture to think that it is not mortal. In one respect the regime is stronger than it was six months ago; it has at last recognised that the experiment has been living on agriculture and has been providing inducements at the expense of agriculture for every class except the agricultural class itself. More and more workers have been brought into industry, and all of them have been receiving wages and privileges which, however inadequate from the western point of view, were greater than those enjoyed by the Soviet agricultural worker. The fantastic lengths to which this policy was driven is revealed in this fact that the former *kulaks* now exiled to the apatite mines of Khibinogorsk are congratulating themselves on having an assured livelihood, while the poor and 'middling' peasants for whose benefit they were driven out are known to them to be starving. It is difficult to believe that in a country where people are so easily satisfied, the agricultural population cannot be induced to grow as much as they grew under the wasteful system in vogue before the War. With the town population it seems to be enough to give them half-rations of food and clothing for the credit side of their life to take full effect—the extras in the way of short hours, holidays, medical facilities and other privileges, and the psychological stimulus due to the fact that no one in the country is obviously living without working, and that all work is represented with some reason as being done for the common good. It ought to be possible to do this for the agricultural population—though not without serious damage to the

Plan and a great diminution in the rate of industrial development.

The more inclined one becomes to believe in the material stability of the Soviet regime, the more dubious one becomes as to the quality of the human product, bred as it is in an atmosphere from which important ingredients, such as moral courage, seem to be absent.

There are indications that the 'tempo' of the Five-Year Plan is slowing down. Large reductions were made in foreign contracts which came up for renewal and capital programmes cut. The emphasis has been shifted almost entirely from primary products to articles of common use. Articles in the press are no longer about tractors, motor-cars and turbines, but about teapots, kettles and shoes. Peasants are now allowed to sell surplus foodstuffs on the open market, but the surpluses are not large and the grower does not want money but goods which at present are not to be had. The people were promised that by the end of the five-year period (i.e. by the end of 1932), the towns will have forgotten bread queues and there will be no lack of meat, vegetables, butter, eggs, boots and clothes. If every detail in this prophecy is reversed it gives a fair picture of present conditions. The queues are longer than ever. It is generally agreed that food supplies are less plentiful than at any time since the New Economic Policy was ended.[19]

7 Aug. Sunday. I shall be glad when this hot spell is over. It makes me sleep badly. The only thing I could find to read in the middle of the night was *The Lacquer Lady*. I am enjoying it as much as when I read it first. It mentions two Burmese names for dusk which are pleasing: 'Sky-shutting-in-time' and 'Brothers-would-not-know-each-other-time.'

Kemble turned up at last. His trust would not let him go to meet his family and he had no way of getting in touch with them. He is much dissatisfied with the living conditions, the food and the pay, and is taking his family back to England. He came out here full of sympathy for the Soviet regime. Ordinary workers, even Party members, were treated like mud. The new aristocracy, those who carry briefcases and take part in discussions, live privileged lives. He went to Moscow and complained to the trust that they were perpetrating a fraud on the workers of the world, and communists in western countries ought to be

[19] According to Miss Daunt's own report, 'Conditions are infinitely worse than they were even a few months ago—food gets scarcer every week. Even in the foreign shop on many days both bread and meat are unobtainable—sometimes no vegetables either. If things are so scarce for foreign currency it can easily be imagined how little can be found at the ordinary co-operatives.'

★

telling Moscow to treat its workers properly. 'They shook hands with me when I came in, but they didn't when I left.'

I had a visit last night from Jules Menken, head of the new business section of the London School of Economics and representing the *Economist*; Spicer, a journalist representing the *Week-End Review*; and the husband of Naomi Mitchison, a lawyer. Mitchison later introduced me to a rum-looking skeleton of a woman whom I afterwards discovered to be Margaret Cole, wife of G.D.H. Cole.[20] I liked Mitchison. He is a Labour candidate and an able and fair-minded man. Spicer seemed a bit disappointed when I said that in spite of the crisis I thought the Soviet Union would scramble through. It is so difficult to make even fair-minded people realise the difference between what the tourist sees and what goes on in the background.

8 Aug. I hope that the Kembles and Mr and Mrs Meade will leave tomorrow. Mr Meade was out of work and not liking to be dependent on his wife's salary, sold up and came to Leningrad. They were much influenced by reading glowing reports of the Soviet Union by a Quaker named Watts in an Australian paper. When they arrived they changed their money at the official rate of exchange, seven roubles to £1, only to discover that a more realistic rate would have been 100 roubles. Both of them managed to find work at the salary of 100 roubles a month, less various deductions, but the rent they were asked for their room was 200 roubles a month. They just didn't pay the rent, and lived on bread and cheese from the foreigners' shop. Then Meade got malaria and could get no quinine at any pharmacy in Moscow. One day they were nearly knocked down in Moscow by hundreds of people who had been waiting nine hours because it had been announced that some butter would be on sale—the stampede was frightening to watch. They had met some American tourists and told them about their experiences, but found it hard to persuade them that they were telling the truth. The Intourist guide had told them that the people waiting in queues outside shops were 'loafers who didn't want work'.

10 Aug. The Kembles and the Meades left on a Soviet boat. In spite of the law, the Meades were allowed to leave with £2 and the Kembles with a few shillings. I think the authorities were alarmed at the attitude of these workers, so different from the submissive Russians.

[20] See Margaret Cole's *Twelve Studies in Soviet Russia* (Gollancz, 1933) and her *Life of G.D.H. Cole* (Macmillan, 1971).

☆

11 Aug. Yesterday Hugh Dalton came in after a tour of about five weeks. He stayed to dinner and is coming to lunch. He has seen a lot despite being laid low with stomach upsets. He went to Sverdlovsk and Magnetogorsk and has seen some State farms, but he hasn't seen what is the key to the whole situation—the agricultural worker in the collective farm or working on his own.

16 Aug. Strang has sent me a report by a Canadian named Cairns, employed by the Empire Marketing Board, who has visited Russia on their behalf two or three years running. He visited Western Siberia, Kazakstan, various places along the Volga, the Ukraine, Crimea and Northern Caucasus. He is a farmer and studied agriculture at university. His reports are startling even to me. While going east on his first journey Cairns found at every station hundreds of peasants waiting for trains to take them, as they put it, 'wherever their eyes fall'. Conditions got progressively worse as he went south-east. The begging by children, women and men was 'simply amazing'. At Novosibirsk, capital of Western Siberia, the sight round the station was depressing: several hundred people, many asleep, many begging, many just sitting shivering in their rags. He quoted the very high prices for bread and clothing and the grotesque overmanning in the pig farm he visited. In 1925 the plains had been dotted thickly with cattle, but throughout his recent 116-kilometre drive he had not seen a single head of livestock. Thousands were travelling into Western China and Northern Siberia in search of food. At a place where they waited some hours for a train, Tatarskia, they had breakfast at the station buffet while little children stood round and begged for bread. Workers came in with slips of paper and were given soup, two small slices of black bread, a small piece of fish, and a glass of 'coffee'. As each worker finished there was a scramble of children and even some men and women for the soup plates to lick and the fish bones to eat. At another town a small boy was standing holding up his shirt and displaying thighs only about three or four inches thick. As Schiller, the Agricultural Attaché at the German Embassy, took a photograph of him, two women with tears streaming down their faces said: 'That is what is going to happen to all of us. Will you give that picture to the newspapers in America, so that they may send us food?'

Cairns' general impressions were that everywhere large areas formerly cultivated are now bare except for weeds, and that management everywhere is in the hands of administrators who want to show Moscow satisfactory figures and exaggerate the yield in order to be commended. Nearly everywhere the peasants in the collective farms are engaged in

☆

passive resistance. Here and there are apparently prosperous collective farms, usually near towns, containing a high proportion of communists, on which much money has been spent. Cairns is doubtful if mechanised farming can pay with the kind of labour available. The machines they have are badly made and badly designed. All tourists are taken to see a huge State farm Gigant, a show place, fully mechanised, yet last season 6000 workers had to be imported for the harvest. He is convinced that neither Gigant nor the model dairies and similar places pay their costs. They are hugely overstaffed. The workers seemed so desperate that they complain loudly whoever is present. Not even the presence of the OGPU restrained them. Cairns asks why, if everything is as successful as they are told, does all exposed film have to be handed to Intourist for development and none is allowed to be taken out of the country. The reports from the Crimea were best, from Ukraine the worst and the complaints the most angry and outspoken. In Kirghizia he found people eating horses that had died of starvation, and collecting grass to make soup. In one bazaar, wheatmeal was being sold at eighty times the price at which the Government is taking grain from the farms.

Cairns said at one institute he was asked to write in the visitors' book. Had he written what he thought, he would have put: 'In a country suffering from acute overpopulation in agriculture, I cannot understand your mania for agricultural mechanisation. Why do you let your horses die by the million and starve those you have left? Would it not be cheaper to grow hay and oats instead of exporting wheat and maintaining costly organisations abroad to sell it in order to buy huge foreign machines which you have not the expertise to use properly? Would it not be better to feed your peasants so they could work?'

In early April the *Economist* published a series of letters over the signature of Frank Wise, a Labour MP who is also paid £5000 a year to represent the Russian co-operatives in England. All the letters described how wisely and efficiently the Russians sold their grain compared with the Canadians and Americans. I see from Cairns' report that samples of meal which he bought at 2.9 roubles a kilo were a mixture of chaff, oat and other hulls, bran, straw, much fibre, a little flax and very little starch or other digestible nutrients.

Cairns also reported that a German American who was brought over to teach the Russians about the operation and care of railway locomotives was in despair. He said ten big US locomotives recently imported were all lying in the yards spoiled. Coal was saved by letting the steam drop from 17 to 8 atmospheres downhill or on the level, so that when it came to the upgrade, the engine could not pull the train;

☆

and the continual rapid expansion and contraction, due to the sudden changes of temperature, were ruinous to the engines.

At the State farm Gigant, the salaries were extremely low. Cairns went to five shops at a big village nearby to see what there was for sale. In the first empty shelves and many bottles of vodka, in the second a pile of cucumbers on the floor, in the third a liberal supply of cosmetics and some bread, in the fourth cosmetics, poor jewellery and six coats. In the last a large supply of vodka, white wine and a few vegetables. The one place where he considered that people looked at all happy was a big German agricultural concession called Drusag.

I will end with Cairns' account of a meeting he attended at the grain institute at Omsk. After a two-hour lecture on the Five-Year Plan, there was a discussion. 'I thought I would now hear their much talked-of self-criticism. But nothing of the kind. Man after man got up and criticised the speaker for being so pessimistic, and the second Five-Year Plan for not being based upon a higher tempo. A specialist from the grain mechanisation department said that the provision to increase the yield per hectare by 40% was too pessimistic, because it did not take into account the discoveries and improvements that were about to be made in farming. Other speakers thought that an increase of three to four times in the production of oil, electricity, coal etc. was too slow.'

19 Aug. Kirkpatrick was pleased with his trip to Baikal, or rather, having come so far and failed to see the site of the meteorite, he was glad to be able to see something of interest. He was put off the train at Irkutsk, and as there was no decent hotel, the geological institute gave him a bed in one of the labs for two days. Kirkpatrick came back unexpectedly to his room and found a Russian, whom he had met the previous day and who had offered to do anything he could do to help, rummaging among his books and papers in his luggage. The director of the biological institute at Baikal took Kirkpatrick back with him and he was put up for six days and they were very kind to him so far as their limited resources allowed. The food was monotonous and poor.

In Baikal, Kirkpatrick had come across two English carpenters who were making a boat with a young American. They had no previous experience of boats. Their meals at their common dining-room did not sound inviting, but they were all happy; they were communists, looking forward to the revolution in England and in America, but they did miss English books. I had lent Kirkpatrick Boswell's *Life of Johnson* and they read some of that with enjoyment and asked him to send them a copy and also a copy of *Lavengro*. I wish I could see these men. There must

☆

be some good stuff in them. I should like to lend them some books, but it would perhaps get them into trouble. I must set their contentment against the discontent of the other English people about whom I have written. But I can understand that an out-of-work carpenter might find satisfaction in building a boat on the shore of a great lake.

The Polish and Latvian Consuls invited me to join them on a trip to Novgorod on Saturday the 13th. The road would be considered wretchedly bad in England, but it is good for Russia and we got there in five hours (it is 125 miles), with a stop by the roadside for lunch. It began to rain while we were on the way, and it was dull for the rest of the day. We had a very good dinner from what we had brought with us and after the fatigues of the journey I soon fell asleep, but I was awoken almost at once with a terrific itching in my neck. I made a search and killed five bugs—a pleasant omen for the night. The cheap watch I had brought with me, so that I might not smash or lose my gold one, broke: the spring went with a great clang. I was glad when morning came. We spent two or three hours with Professor Prokofiev, who had sent word that he would show us round the antiquities. The best things are the church vessels in the cathedral and the icons in the art museum. We lost about an hour on the way back to Leningrad (lunch, two punctures, and a chat with some gypsies), but we got home at 8 o'clock.

21 Aug. Sunday. Cave thinks of little else but how long until it is time to telephone this woman in Helsingfors. 'Perhaps one day I will be able,' as he puts it in his Russian English, 'to arrange my life like other men.' Five or six years ago he took up with a young Estonian girl. He had no intention of marrying her, 'because she was of a different social class and had no conversation.' Last winter he found she had a lover, a chauffeur, even though she had been living on Cave's money. Cave much upset, but he expected an impossible fidelity. He said: 'I suppose my age is against me.' I had no reply to make to this. I don't think I should easily believe that a girl of twenty was in love with me, even though I am younger and less asthmatic than Cave. I hope Cave will sail into calmer waters soon. At present he lives with me and I let him pay one third of the cost of servants and local food and I charge him nothing for stores from England and very little for fuel.

25 Aug. It is about 20° colder than it was two weeks ago and it feels quite autumnal. The weather broke just too soon for the Soviet Spartakiad, the sports being held in Leningrad for teams from all parts of the Union. They take no part in the Olympic Games, on the ground that they are

★

capitalist games, but at present, of course, they could not spare the foreign exchange to enable competitors to go abroad. Yesterday hundreds of athletes from all the races in the Soviet Union marched through the streets. All this has its good side. Indeed, the work of the Soviet authorities for what they call *physkultur* is excellent.

Poor Miss Daunt is unwell again. She ought to go back to England but she feels she must stay as Lady Muriel is coming out soon, and if she isn't there Lady Muriel distributes money by the handful to all the undeserving sycophants among the DBSs. I go and see Miss Daunt every evening—it makes a good walk and I keep her supplied with books. She had a letter from Lady Muriel to say she had herself met the boat on which the Kembles and the Meades travelled to England, and sent them all down to her country place, Cranmore, to stay there for a month. Lady Muriel is the most curious combination of lavish kindness and unscrupulous brutality. She has a highly developed possessive instinct, and for anything that is hers—e.g. the Relief Organisation— she will commit any crime.

Rations for all foreigners, except consuls, have been cut down considerably. Miss Daunt is affected by this, and so is our messenger. I hear that the foreign engineers are going to make a protest, but I don't know that it will do any good. There just isn't the food to go round.[21]

26 Aug. The Moscow newspapers have just announced that parcels containing the following foodstuffs will no longer be accepted for posting in Moscow: grain, flour, bread, groats, peas, beans, maize, hemp and flax-seed containing oil. This means that Moscow people have been sending food parcels to relatives in the country, and even Moscow, the best-stocked place in the Soviet Union, has nothing to spare. I hope they won't apply the regulation to Leningrad, as we post food parcels here to DBSs in the country.

30 Aug. I think the Soviet Government, in order to get *valuta*, have brought in far more tourists than they can provide for properly. In particular the supply of trained guides is inadequate. People complain to me that their Hermitage guide knew nothing about pictures, many of

---

[21] 'Butter and other foodstuffs are being *exported* at the port,' Lady Muriel wrote in her diary. 'I have suggested I should buy foodstuffs directly for the DBSs and pay in £s. A friend of one of our workers thought a bit of meat she was cooking had an odd appearance and took it to the police who found it was human flesh. Tartars and Chinese are said to be culprits and are shot if caught dealing in human flesh.'

the pictures have no labels, and such labels as exist are often only in Russian.

A widespread illicit commerce in roubles has sprung up to meet the demand for a more equitable rate. Tourists are offered roubles by people in hotel lounges, in the streets and even by the hotel servants.

5 Sept. I never met a British officer who served in one of the 'White' armies in Archangel, Baku, Batum or Vladivostok during the 'Intervention' who had anything but contempt for the tsarist Russians. They drank, ran after women, idled, stole, sold the arms and equipment that we sent them, and moreover behaved towards the 'Red' enemy, their own men, and the potentially neutral public, as though their position had never been shaken. The latest to provide me with evidence about this is Macadam, who was here a few days ago. He was a sapper with the Archangel force, employed on lines of communication a good deal, riding up and down in a sleigh with a machine-gun. Late one night he came to a village, found quarters for the driver and then a house where he could stay himself. He had hardly sat down when he heard the sound of troops arriving. Having satisfied himself that they were 'Whites', he told the officers that there would be room for them in the same house, and food too. They followed him in and sat down. He hinted that there would be plenty of time for them to settle their men into quarters before the food was ready, but they took no notice of this. They sat on until dinner was ready, leaving their men to look after themselves. What wonder that their men faded away. It was a mad venture, and everyone except Winston Churchill must regret that we took part in it.[22]

Walker is here for a couple of days. Professor Waldhauer took us round the Scythian room in the Hermitage. The exhibits seem more remarkable each time I see them. The Tearles (Metro-Vickers) were to have come too, but were prevented by the death from typhoid of one of their engineers in Moscow.

Cave left for a month in Finland yesterday—much happier. He said that he couldn't afford a divorce at present. I contented myself by suggesting that it wasn't quite fair to the new love to be on with her before being off with the old. He proposes to have his villa in Finland put in order 'whatever it costs', and to instal the woman there. I hope that this will turn out all right.

---

[22] Churchill, who became minister of war early in 1919, argued strongly in Cabinet for a more active intervention to destabilise Bolshevik rule; however, he was virtually alone among western statesmen in believing that this was possible.

6 Sept. Butler, a young teacher from Dublin, came in. He has been engaged to teach in two institutions, and both have recommended his application for an extension of his visa, so he has hopes. He has had the good fortune to find quarters with a Russian named Archangelsky. A's mother occupies one room and Butler shares a room with Archangelsky. The flat itself is leased to a Russian army officer whose wife occupies the other two rooms. They all share the kitchen. The army wife and Archangelsky are on such bad terms that although they live in adjacent rooms they only converse on the telephone. In the usual Russian way they conduct their quarrel at the top of their voices, so their remarks can be heard quite clearly through the walls.

Sunday evening was spoiled by a dinner given in honour of a party of foreign geologists at the Astoria Hotel. It was half-past twelve when we got away. We sat through three speeches packed with communist propaganda. The dinner went on, the band went on playing, and the speakers barked louder and louder in their efforts to be heard. I sat between Weinstein and Bograchev, who is in charge of all construction work in Leningrad. He offered to show me some of the buildings they are putting up.

The Foreign Office have sent a telegram saying that Amery's son,[23] a twenty-year-old film producer, is talking of coming to Russia in order to marry an actress and that the relatives would be grateful for any unofficial assistance we might be able to give in dissuading him from his purpose!

8 Sept. The Winter Palace Square is being covered with asphalt. The work should be finished for the parade on 7 November. All the buildings round the Square are being painted in golden ochre except the Winter Palace, which in some lights looks almost salmon pink. They look very fine.

11 Sept. Sunday. Kulagin is back from his summer holiday in the south. He has had an operation and now wears a steel corset to support his spine. He and all the other men in his rest home each received free rail-fare, board and 1000 roubles. Unfortunately one of the other men had his suit and his 1000 roubles stolen, and Kulagin is of the opinion that

[23] John Amery (1912–1945) was the son of the politician L.S. Amery. He shared his father's anti-Bolshevik views, and during the Second World War he wrote and broadcast anti-Russian propaganda from Germany and Italy. After the war he was convicted of treason and executed on 19 December 1945; recently released MI5 files show that his brother Julian requested that the sentence be carried out.

they can only have been taken by one of the other inmates!

I hear Lord Marley[24] denied that Soviet figures could be falsified because 'think how ashamed the Soviet Government would be if their figures were proved to be false'.

I had Sir Percy Harris, Liberal MP for Mile End and a member of the LCC, and Dobbie Bateman from the War Office to dinner last night. I wish I had been able to see more of Harris. His replies to the questions he was asked in a school they visited surprised the listeners very much— especially his assertion that schooling is compulsory and free from five to fourteen. Everyone here is taught that the children of the workers in other countries are not educated. On a visit to the Peter and Paul Fortress, the chief prison under the tsarist regime, Harris asked the guide, with an air of innocent curiosity, how political prisoners were treated now, and she was surprised into admitting that they were sent to the north or to Turkestan.

One of the crimes against which the recent decree about shooting for theft was directed was stealing from trains. A British subject named Freshfield, who is a guard on a train, says that many people are being shot for this. There is no trial. There are OGPU men on all trains, and if anyone is found pilfering from the train he is shot at once. An American woman was travelling 'hard', lying on the seat fully clad at night, when a man came in and snatched some of her possessions. Her handbag, with a large sum in dollars, fell to the floor, and as she bent to recover it, he tore her sable coat from her back, leapt off the train and was gone in a moment.

13 Sept. Our messenger brought me a handbill which had been distributed to all the flats in his building. It orders each resident to collect six bottles, half a kilo of rags, half a kilo of bones, half a kilo of paper, three-quarters of a kilo of rubber, six kilos of old iron and one kilo of non-ferrous metal (brass, copper, etc.) and to hand them in. Quite impossible. Any scraps of old iron have been given in long ago. Paper is so short that the co-operatives give their customers fresh fish without paper. As for rubber—for a long time it has been impossible to buy a pair of galoshes unless you hand in an old pair.

On 11 September I visited Hansen, a Danish seaman in hospital. The poor man was trying to get into an overcrowded tram when it started and he fell off and the tram went over both his feet. The hospital amputated one foot but they hoped to save the other. Although he is a

---

[24] Formerly D.L. Aman (1884–1952), member of the Labour Party and Fabian Society.

Dane, he has lived in Hull most of his life and his family are British. He is only a year older than I, and has twin daughters of twenty-four. It is sad to see him crippled. He does not know that his second foot is in danger, and he cannot understand why he should have a headache and a temperature all the time.

15 Sept. The principal dramatic theatre, closed for six months for repair and renovation, was reopened tonight—a sad frost. Bubnov (one of Stalin's Old Guard and Commissar for Education) *read* a discourse which lasted for an hour and a half. An actor assured the Government that when the capitalist world attacked the Soviet Union, actors would be in the front rank of defence. There were speeches by delegates from the principal theatres. Poor old Karpinsky, aged eighty-six, President of the Academy of Sciences, read an inaudible speech. A telegram was read in which Bernard Shaw said how wonderful it was that this Russian theatre should have run for a hundred years: in England it was remarkable if a theatre ran for a hundred weeks. At 11.30 p.m. I ran away. The man in the cloakroom was much troubled by our leaving.

Lady Muriel is here. When she was last here she invited Mme Lopokhova, the sister of Mrs Keynes, and her mother to come to the hotel. She hinted that she had some clothes to give her. Lady Muriel exhibited the whole of her wardrobe to this poor actress, and Mme Lopokhova evidently expected something good, for she kept remarking to her mother that such and such a dress would just do for some part or other in her repertory. When the whole wardrobe had been examined Lady Muriel put everything away and gave Madame Lopokhova a hot-water bottle. I think there must have been some misunderstanding because Lady Muriel can be very generous.

18 Sept. Sunday. Lady Muriel's visit has not been unprofitable to me. She has lent me Charles Morgan's *The Fountain* and she has been scared into consenting to sell the house. It was the ingenious Kulagin who scared her. He visited the house with her and convinced her that the workmanship was unsound. Kulagin dangled before her eyes the prospect of using the price she gets for the house to build or lease a house nearer the centre of town, where Miss Daunt can live and a few old destitutes be taken in. I suppose Kulagin will be glad to get hold of the house cheaply. On the other hand he has a genuine liking and admiration for Miss Daunt, and knows that the house would have been a great expense to the Association, a great worry to Miss Daunt, and of little use to the destitute. I have said nothing to Lady Muriel about the

☆

house ever since it was built, for I know how obstinate opposition makes her. I did not even applaud when she told me of her intention to sell. She spoke as though she had never opposed the sale, and without the slightest embarrassment. Her mind was already full of the scheme for buying or building another house.[25]

She is sad because the family house in Somerset, Cranmore, has been sold, but she gets much satisfaction out of her many schemes (including kitchens in Shoreditch), and out of her children. She pressed Todd and me to go to dinner last night. Knowing what great difficulty Miss Daunt has in getting food even for herself, we refused, but said we would go in afterwards. We arrived at 8.45 to find a table laid for eight: they had not had dinner. She had collected Kulagin and his fifteen-year-old daughter, and a young German artist. After dinner three more guests arrived: two English scientists, here for a conference, and their Russian colleague. One of the Englishmen was Professor Bragg, Professor of Physics at Manchester.[26] They said good work is being done here and on a huge scale. They have enormous resources and do not count the cost. The best men were as good as the best in England or Germany. The young scientists, many of them Jews, were encouraged by the prospect of being put in charge of one of the newly opened institutes. At dinner Kulagin asked about the position of Jews in England and expressed amazement that they suffered under no disabilities. Even though Russians seem always to have been ruled by someone else—the Tartars, the Baltic Germans, and so on—it would be a mistake to conclude that they acquiesce willingly in their present subordination to a class that consists so largely of Jews. There is little sign of the fusion of Russians and Jews. Jews seem to remain in company with each other.

Kulagin brought with him his gramophone (a portable HMV which I think Lady Muriel brought in for him)[27] and his Russian records,

[25] Lady Muriel's diary records her visit to the *dacha*, which she decided to call Sosnovka: 'On close inspection found doors and windows will not close when opened nor open when closed; water only at night; cesspool lined with wood; side of water-tank fell out; wall more like concertinas, veneers crinkled, holes in roof. Electric light paid for but not installed. The lavatory a metre-length board in which are cut two small holes the size of tea-plates three inches apart.' However, the *dacha* was put in order and was not sold.
[26] Lawrence Bragg (1890–1971) had already won the Nobel prize for physics for his work on x-rays and crystallography.
[27] Lady Muriel recorded in her diary: 'Received following telegram in Helsingfors from Miss Daunt: "IF POSSIBLE BRING PATHEPHONE AND FOXTROT AND CHARLESTON RECORDS, ALSO RECORDS BY VARATINSKY." No Pathephone being procurable in Helsingfors, I bought His Master's Voice, which was incomparably the best . . . . I imagine that it must be needed to pave some stony way. Next telegram asked for an elastic stocking—presumably for use after the foxtrot.'

including the prohibited ones. He rang up a friend who is a fine singer and tried to get him to come round and sing, but although he gave him formal guarantees that he had nothing to fear, the man was afraid to come.

21 Sept. Last night Tearle showed me a copy of the *Daily Express* containing one of Miss Clyman's articles on her visit to Kem'. There was nothing much in it, but the authorities don't like people who know too much about the north, and when in today's Russian paper I saw a paragraph headed 'Expulsion of a slanderous correspondent' I knew at once that it was Miss Clyman. The report says that she is being deported for systematically spreading news about the USSR which is grossly insulting in form and which she knew to be untruthful and slanderous. I think that the evil she lived amongst, and the contrast between the reality as she saw it and the sickening humbug of the official propaganda, drove her into continuous opposition. I hope that the *Daily Express* will find her a job elsewhere.

I shall not easily find a better Russian teacher than Mrs Diedrichs. She knows about six languages and is familiar with the history and literature of those countries as well. I asked whether she could safely give me lessons, and she said she had served as a guide for Intourist for seven years without getting into trouble, and that in any case she and her husband had long ago decided that 'the blow would fall some day' and had become fatalistic about it. Meanwhile she seems to get great pleasure out of books. She writes verse and is also writing a historical novel about Spain. She gets plenty of translating work. I shall pay her partly in kind by giving her a meal now and then. She has promised to lend me some of her huge collection of books and she wishes to borrow some of mine.

22 Sept. I have been looking at some specimen Soviet school-books. *We Work and Struggle*, for children of seven to fourteen, contains this paragraph: 'In America and England, children work for twelve and fifteen hours a day in factories and mines. Their work is hard and they hate it. They have no time to read, they have no time to think even. Work from morning till night—go home to sleep—and the next day work again from morning till night.'

26 Sept. On Saturday I saw the Danish seaman again. He thinks that he is getting on well, though he admits that he still has headaches, but the doctor told me afterwards that it was very doubtful whether the second foot could be saved.

☆

Miss Clyman was brought back from Tiflis under escort. She was allowed forty-eight hours to pack.

A ship's captain tells me that the dockers will sell roubles to the crew at twopence each. The official rate is three shillings! All the tourists seem to be able to get cheap roubles now.

Mrs Lort Phillips and Miss Marley returned from their tour a few days ago, after the usual adventures. First their luggage failed to arrive where they were going and they had to spend five days without a change of clothes. On the Volga boat they were eaten by bugs and other insects and laid low by sickness; finally they left their passports at Kharkov. The hotel took them for registration and always said 'tomorrow' when they asked for them back. Finally in a hurried departure they forgot to collect them. They had been travelling for forty-six hours in a train which went at about ten miles an hour and spent forty minutes at each station. They were much relieved to find I could give them emergency documents to travel on. They had a bath and some breakfast and managed to get exit visas just in time.

A large commission which includes the two leading communists in Leningrad, and is apparently supported by troops, is starting off to compel the peasants to deliver more grain. Kulagin was ordered to go, but he was reluctant to embark on the brutal task of trying to make people produce grain which he knew they hadn't got, and he pleaded ill-health due to his spinal injury. He was congratulating himself that he had escaped, when he got peremptory orders to go to a district in the Caucasus that he knows well and to collect some fantastic quantity of grain. He knows that it cannot produce anything like this quantity, and he has to shoot people who don't produce what they are ordered to produce. He was in tears about it. He will probably come to a bad end. When he was in charge of the OGPU in the south after the Civil War the problem must have presented itself to him as a simple one. You just had to 'save the Revolution', and the shootings and imprisonment could easily be justified to your conscience. It is different now. But if he fails to carry out orders ruthlessly he is a lost man. There are plenty of men who will shoot if he doesn't, and he may lose his job and his position in the Party.

2 Oct. Sunday. Ten weeks tomorrow I shall be starting on leave. For a week I believed that I might be transferred to Baghdad. However the job—whatever it is—has gone to someone else. Scott[28] is very apologetic

[28] Sir David Scott (1887–1986), head of personnel at the Foreign Office.

and trusts that he did not raise false hopes. It was inevitably exciting to think that I might be going to an interesting post with greater responsibilities than I have here, but now that the matter is settled I can console myself that for climate, finances and leave I am better off in Leningrad.

Sour grapes? Not altogether. I was worrying a good deal, wondering what we should do if the job were really given to me. Finally I decided that it would be worthwhile spending some of our capital for a few years as the job at Baghdad would stake out something of a claim for the job I should like to end my career with—Jeddah.

We shall be quite a party for dinner tomorrow. Cave will be back. Miss Biggs, the Board of Education inspector, will be here; she is going to spend three days in Leningrad with me. I am also inviting Miss Power from the Ministry of Labour, and John Cliff from the Transport and General Workers Union, both members of the Whitley Commission on labour conditions in India, who are coming to collect information for a comparison between conditions here and in India. Dalton has sent me a letter recommending them and also the other member of their party, Sir Victor Sassoon.[29]

Kulagin has gone off to the Caucasus, leaving his daughter in Miss Daunt's care—not in her house, but under her supervision. It is strange what a moral ascendancy Miss Daunt has established over this man. I think he has some respect for me too—perhaps because I refused to allow Mrs Todd to smuggle in gramophone records from Finland for him. Lady Muriel bought a lot of records for him in Helsingfors, but being followed about by suspicious persons, she lost her nerve at the station and thrust the packet of records into Mrs Todd's arms telling her to bring them. Lady Muriel has no moral sense at all.

Miss Daunt asked Kulagin to find out whether the authorities had anything against her, as she has been having an increasing number of problems. Kulagin reported that they had nothing whatever against Miss Daunt, but that there had been trouble about Lady Muriel and Mr Lie, which had, however, now blown over. He would not say what the trouble was. Miss Daunt thinks this relates to a plan to buy and smuggle out of the country and sell a valuable carpet. Lady Muriel was to put up the money and she and Lie were to go halves in the proceeds. Miss Daunt told Lady Muriel that she was unlikely to get the carpet past the

[29] The banker Sir Victor Sassoon (1881–1961) was a member of the legislative assembly of India. The economic historian Beryl Power (1891–1974) kept an account of her Russian journey which is now in the archives of Girton College, Cambridge.

☆

customs. Lady Muriel then took fright. It is possible that the authorities discovered the plot.

5 Oct. Miss Daunt brought the Russian girl round whom we invited to tea when M was here and who did not come. It turned out she had gone to Sukhum on holiday. She told us how she caught malaria and what lots of fruit there was, and then she said casually: 'Bread was very dear—six roubles a kilo. But when Stalin came over from the place where he was staying they reduced the price to two roubles. He went round the bazaar asking the prices!' I have often speculated whether the people in the Kremlin are told the truth by their subordinates, and this affords an interesting piece of evidence. It makes it even more absurd that foreigners should hope to arrive at the truth by looking at what the Soviet authorities show them.

There was a thin layer of snow on the ground this morning. I have managed to buy some coal for roubles and this makes it so cheap that a fire costs very little.

The Danish seaman has had to have the second foot amputated. He is much cast down. His wife writes very sensibly and courageously. Poor man. He is a big strong man in the prime of life, and he takes it hard. I took him cigarettes and chocolate and a few oranges, but the doctor asked Miss Daunt if we could send him butter and eggs every two days—not large quantities at a time as 'he might not get them'! I had not liked to suggest sending food, as I thought the foreign seamen's hospital would not like it. Yesterday I sent the man a bottle of Horlicks, a tin of cocoa and a tablet of Lux soap. Mrs Todd has gone every day with tea in a thermos and some cooked dishes. Miss Daunt also goes to see him, but she has no food to give away, poor thing.

6 Oct. Last night the Sassoon–Power party came to dinner again, with Cliff, a silent north-countryman, Secretary of the Transport Workers Union. They were keenly interested in the contrast between what goes on here and what they have heard in England. In the anti-religious museum they criticised so many of the exhibits that the guide got quite exhausted writing the criticisms in the suggestion book: e.g. Sassoon assured her that King George did not dress in mauve, nor did rich men each have a wardrobe of a hundred suits! As for a picture of 'unemployed in Hackney, London', this was recognised by Miss Power as a scene in New York.

12 Oct. Two months today I ought to be going on leave! They are cleaning our windows and sealing them up for the winter. I find the coal I bought for roubles is much inferior to what I got for pounds at Torgsin last year. In my open grate it burns very sullenly like a heap of red-hot stones.

I am reading a life of Metternich and this morning I came across a comment which might apply to Soviet Russia. A liberal Austrian, writing of Austria under Metternich, put in his diary: 'Austria asks of the human spirit that it make a eunuch of itself. If it does so, then it is permitted all freedom.'

The drawing-room is going to look very pleasant soon. Miss Daunt has undertaken to supervise the making of the lampshade, and that will remove the greatest blot on the room. I have cut the piece of Indian stuff M sent into two pieces, and they are to be sewn together to make a wall-hanging.

Miss Daunt was sent some money to be spent at Torgsin on behalf of a woman known to be at Kem', one of the places which Miss Clyman visited. She was not in prison, but she was not allowed to leave Kem'. But the Red Cross told Miss Daunt that the woman had been cut off from communication with the outside world 'owing to the indiscretion of a foreign journalist who had since been deported'.

Butler has secured an extension of his visa for another month. He meets some Russians who manage to be astonishingly well-read in English literature in spite of the acute shortage of books. He even found one who knew much more about contemporary English poetry than he did. They borrow from each other, and a single book will travel all over Leningrad. One of the advantages of Soviet conditions is that people find how much they can do with small resources, whether of food, clothing or books.

I get consulted about a wide range of subjects. Miss Goyer, a young Yorkshire woman, who is doing research here for a year in the physics lab of a famous scientist named Yoffe, wants to know how she can get out her winter underclothes from England. I arranged for the Todds to bring them when they return from leave. Miss Goyer is a vegetarian and lives mainly on bread and jam and apples. She has a bed in a dormitory with five other girls, all scientific workers here for a short time. From her description we judge that where she lives was formerly the palace of the Grand Duke Vladimir, an uncle of the last Tsar. She seems contented and laughs at the difficulties, although they include standing for an hour in a tram morning and evening. The shortage of the most common necessities in the lab is acute. They can't even get notebooks or paper, still less common things she needed such as black paper or a magnet. I gave her a shilling exercise-book I happened to have and she was delighted. She said no one would believe that there was free universal education in other countries, and she found it impossible to make anyone believe that her sister went through university without costing their father anything. They can't bear to think that any other country has been before them in anything.

The papers have been boasting about covering the Winter Palace Square with asphalt. Unfortunately, the moment it was finished it began to sink here and there, and it is now full of puddles.

14 Oct. The Ambassadorial party arrived yesterday. The Hugessens were easy visitors and I quite enjoyed having them here, though I settled into my bedroom again with pleasure when they had gone. The Ambassador was in great form. He is pleased with himself and the world. I should not care to be on his staff and have to see him often, as he repeats himself frequently, and much of his conversation is self-confident proposals for the solution of the many problems of Russia. He repeated to me a saying of the former American Ambassador in Mexico: 'We judge ourselves by our ideals, whereas other people judge us by our actions.' Sir Esmond tried to draw the deduction that all nations are very much alike, and in particular that we should not act as though the Bolsheviks were any worse than ourselves. I agreed that we should not allow anger at the Russians' treatment of each other, or even their underhand behaviour to us, to make us bad-tempered or discourteous in our dealings with them, but I think as individuals English people are far more honest and trustworthy than Russians, and that any proposals put up by the Soviet Government should be considered in the light of this fact. The fact is that Sir Esmond is morally lazy and the dishonesty of the Soviet leaders does not disgust him.

One morning when the Hugessens were here I was making for my bath at 7.30 thinking deeply about something when I was startled by the sight of two heads raised from two pillows and looking at me with surprise. I had taken the usual route through my bedroom, forgetting that I had lent it to my guests. They took it as a good joke.

18 Oct. The injured seaman is getting on well and is in good spirits. His ship is back and his shipmates pay him a visit now and then. They wanted to bring him some English newspapers, but the port police took the papers away.

Last night I went to see the Woodheads after dinner. They don't like to ask me to dinner now as food has been cut down in quantity as well as quality, and I know prices have gone up enormously. He is just back from a visit of inspection to a pulp- and paper-mill at Lala in the Urals, which ought to have started to operate over eighteen months ago. The concern is deeply in debt, its employees are owed two months' pay, and the railways refuse to deliver any more goods until their bill for 500,000 roubles is settled.

19 Oct. I reckon that if there are no more cuts and the income tax remains as it is I shall have £420 left in 1932 after meeting all the fixed charges and paying tax. If things remain exactly as they are, I can keep myself and pay for clothes and a journey to England every year. It won't leave a great margin, but I could probably find the money for M to come to Leningrad by a cheap route.

The barber has just been. Like everyone else he is finding it difficult to get food. I don't like to have a starving man working for me, so I gave him a pound of lard instead of the six roubles which he usually charges. He was delighted. He scraped the paint off the tin, so that its English origin could not be seen.

Waldhauer came to dinner last night. His brother in Riga has sent him some butter. The Berlin Museum people have invited him to go there to work, expenses paid, but the proposal has been twice rejected by the authorities. He hopes to get there in the end. I talked to him about the change in educational policy of which there have been indications in the press recently. Formerly students were admitted to institutions of higher education because they were Young Communists or were of proletarian origin, not because they were fit to profit by the instruction. This has led to much criticism. Waldhauer attributes the change to Bubnov, an active Bolshevik who was one of the leaders of the October Revolution and is now Commissar for Education. Two young men, it is said, applied to be received in some college, and the application fell into the hands of Bubnov. Finding it full of gross mistakes in spelling and grammar and composition, he ordered the applicants to begin again in the lowest class of the workers' college where they came from and ordered all the staff of the Rabfak to be dismissed. The new director of the Leningrad Museum of Art reorganised the museum so as to make it illustrate the class struggle and he was sent to prison for seven months on a charge of 'wrecking' the museum. Waldhauer said that in his evidence he described the policy as 'pure sabotage' but withdrew the word as perhaps too strong, but the Public Prosecutor said: 'No, no, it is just, the word.' Waldhauer said there is 'witting sabotage' and 'unwitting' sabotage, and (this with a wink) that 'in the case of unwitting sabotage you also get at the man who appointed a fool to a responsible post'.

22 Oct. The Kazan Cathedral—a cathedral no longer—is being got ready for 7 November. The text in gilt letters is being scraped off the architrave. Yesterday I could just read 'Blessed . . . in the name of the Lord'; today the inscription has quite disappeared.

When I was out for a walk yesterday I ran into Mozley—the Canadian I saw in the spring when he was on his way to Siberia to study freshwater molluscs. He would have liked to come to see me, but his Russian friends had taken alarm and begged him not to go to the Consulate again. I should have liked to hear something about his experiences, but I thought it better not to talk to him too long, so we separated.

In future, for the lowest category of persons, to which all our destitutes belong, the quantity of potatoes that can be bought at the co-operatives is to be limited to 2½ kilos per person per month. Yesterday there was no meat and no fish—even for foreign consuls.

Kirkpatrick sent me the *Contemporary Review* containing a good article by Bernard Pares on 'English news from Soviet Russia.'[30] He holds that the first requirement for a person who wants to get a correct view of things here is to learn Russian, since many things which run counter to the Soviet Government's propaganda abroad can be found in the Soviet press. He begged Julian Huxley to learn Russian before publishing his book about Soviet Russia, but Huxley said it was already in the press!

24 Oct. Seven weeks today. I had just set off for bed last night when Lena came to say that an Englishman wanted to see me. It was Butler come to say that he had no home! He has been sharing a room with Archangelsky, but a frightful quarrel had driven him out and he could not get a room in a hotel even for one night. I gave him my spare room and this morning he has gone to close with a Polish family who have offered him a room which he can only get to by going through their kitchen and dining-room—which is where all the family sleep at the moment.

---

[30] Bernard Pares (1867–1945), professor of Russian history at Liverpool University and elsewhere, had been attached to the Russian Army from 1914 to 1917 and to the British Embassy in Petrograd in 1917. (See *My Russian Memoirs*: Cape, 1931; *Russia Admits a Critic*: Nelson, 1936.)

Yesterday for the first time for many months we had co-operative bread because the cook had not been able to make our bread as usual. It was a bad colour, soggy and contained grit that grated the teeth. However, there is always a little more food available as 1 May and 7 November approach, and there are promises in the paper that extra supplies of provisions will soon be distributed.

26 Oct. Orlov-Ermak says there is to be a banquet on 7 November—either this is a special show for the fifteenth anniversary of the Revolution, or else they think that if they feed us well we shall no longer believe the evidence of our eyes and ears as to the food shortage. A pleasant dinner on Monday: Butler (who had moved in with the Poles), Mr Woodhead, Miss Goyer, and Moore, a journalist with the *Daily Telegraph*. He told me he met a Russian in a train on the way here who had thousands of roubles and sold a lot to Moore at a hundred to the pound (the official rate being under seven). Moore made Moscow his centre and sallied out to the places he wanted to visit well supplied with food, and returned to replenish his supplies and have a good wash before the next visit. He saw the famous German farm mentioned in Cairns' report. The manager said that he could not entertain them at his house, as he would like to do, but must billet them some distance away where they would be less in evidence, since the authorities did not like to see foreign journalists as they all wrote in their papers how wretched the Soviet farms looked in comparison with the German concession. The farm is doing well and the Soviet authorities are negotiating with the management to hand it over to a neighbouring State farm of some 10,000 hectares. This is of enormous importance. Two or three weeks ago an unexpected notice appeared in the press saying that the Party had expelled thirty prominent members, among them Zinoviev and Kamenev, both well-known Jews, closely identified with Lenin in the early stages of the Revolution. They had been expelled for proposing that State and collective farms should be dissolved, and consideration given to granting concessions to capitalists. Since then everyone has been watching for signs that this policy was to be adopted (though not admitted), for on more than one occasion Stalin has got rid of his rivals by declaring their proposals to be 'bourgeois' or 'capitalistic' or 'right opportunist' or 'left deviationist', and has then adopted those proposals and declared them to be in strict accordance with the 'general line of the Party'. This is what he did with Trotsky.

The soap which I gave to Miss Goyer was stolen a day or two later, with her only watch. They were on the table by her bed in the room she

☆

shares with seven other women. There is much stealing and pocket-picking going on besides the stealing in the factories which the authorities try to put down by shooting. Miss Goyer reluctantly admits that they get very little to eat. She asked me to come and see the ex-palace where she lives. I should like to go, but I told her it would do her no good. We can no longer get eggs or chickens from the village people except in exchange for butter. We hadn't enough butter in the house to buy chickens for our last dinner-party.

27 Oct. The three maids report that all their clothes are falling to pieces and have put in an enormous list of things they want—at least enormous for this place where material is so short. There is not a yard of any material to be had.

Soermus, the Soviet violinist who visits England and combines his concerts with propaganda, is in some difficulty with his passport. Under the latest regulations, when a Soviet citizen returns from abroad his passport is taken from him, and if he wants to go abroad again he must apply for a new passport, and before it is granted he has to pass first a *chistka,* or purge, to find out exactly where the applicant has been and what he has done, and then an examination by a trio of communists. Mrs Soermus says her husband lives with his head in a musical cloud and notices nothing.

Woodhead has returned from another visit to the paper-mill. Two OGPU men who travelled part of the way with him had chickens and all sorts of things in their luggage. 'The new bourgeoisie!' one of them said to Woodhead. The mill, which ought to have begun operating two years ago, began in September and is making five tons of paper a day instead of forty-five tons. Woodhead attended an eight-hour meeting of about thirty men, only two of whom were engineers, the others were 'Red' directors, workmen etc. Woodhead refused to take any part in the discussion, which he described as worthless. To engage in the discussion would have been to admit that all these untrained people had a right to give an opinion on highly technical questions.

30 Oct. Sunday. All the foreign embassies and legations in Moscow have received a notice from Torgsin saying that in future they must pay for their purchases of food in foreign currency. I suppose that this policy is one of the first proposals of Sokolnikov ('Brilliant'), the former Soviet Ambassador in London, who was brought back to study the financial situation. This will not matter so much so long as we are still allowed to import provisions without payment of customs duty, we need then buy

☆

only fresh vegetables, fruit (if there is any), butter and sometimes meat. It will be easy to provide for ourselves, but we must provide for our servants too. We cannot leave them to exist on black bread and a few potatoes with a little sugar and salt fish when there is any. The pinch will come in clothes for the maids. Prices on the open market are fantastically high. I have a good stock of stores in hand, and I shall send off an order for stores to last six months. I did not want to lay out so much money just now, but it can't be helped. Cave is naturally worried. As usual he is overdrawn—to such an extent that he is down to smoking only twenty-five (Russian) cigarettes a day.

31 Oct. Six weeks today! Of the list of clothing that the maids wanted, they were able to buy one pair of stockings and a winter coat. The stuff is wretched. Lena came in, purple in the face with excitement. The coat reaches to her feet and the sleeves hide her hands, but she says that it can be altered. Anyhow, she was so excited that she had no sleep that night, and she made us a long speech of thanks and apologies.

Miss Daunt hires out her van to Torgsin when it is not needed, and the other day the chauffeur told her casually that he had been carrying things from the Hermitage to Torgsin. It was known that the authorities were selling art treasures in Berlin—mainly drawings, but it looks as though they are also supplying Torgsin shops. This is not surprising with *valuta* so short. I noticed when we visited the principal church in Novgorod cases packed and addressed to Leningrad.

The scare about Torgsin led me to examine the household accounts, which I had hitherto left to Cave, as he says he loves looking after the kitchen. He told me that the cook was very economical. To my annoyance I found he had taken no interest whatever in quantities and did not know that a kilo of butter a day for five people was excessive, also four kilos of lump sugar a week and three or four kilos of granulated sugar. I am not surprised to hear from Miss Daunt that when Nusha went home last week she had a bag with her that she could hardly lift. I am annoyed not at the cost, which is small, but because we have been demoralising the maids by our carelessness and encouraging them to waste and to steal for their relatives.

2 Nov. Just back from my evening walk: sharp to the right and straight ahead past the Tsar's stables to the Neva, along the Neva to the Summer Garden (almost deserted), and back through the garden past the Church of the Resurrection—that ugly imitation of the 'Pineapple' church in Moscow. On the way I began to type in my mind some pages of my still unwritten memoirs. I found myself half-crying at the recollection of the night when I came home and found that I was one of the successful candidates in the Levant Consular Service exam and realised that although it was a triumph for me, for my mother and father it was the beginning of the end, for it meant my going abroad in two years.

5 Nov. I am not looking forward to standing for four hours next Monday to see the procession. The weather is wretched but unlikely to be so bad as to justify us in staying away. The rehearsals are going on all the time—marching and drilling and singing, but no outward sign that nearly everyone except the police and the armed forces is hungry. The Government keep people quiet partly by means of the OGPU, and partly by filling the papers with news of the downfall of society in all other countries except Italy, whom they never criticise. The unemployed demonstrations in London have been meat and drink to them. There have been pictures of police striking men with their truncheons and riding them down with their horses. The papers have much about the Dnyeprstroy power-station, but the factories that are to use the current are not ready, and the unused capital is lying idle while heavy interest has to be paid on the advances from America. It is the same everywhere. Fox saw some beautiful electrical machinery supplied by Metro-Vickers lying idle because the rest of the installation wasn't ready. But about the natural resources of the country there is no doubt. Immense deposits of coal and iron have been discovered in the north. They say that the White Sea Canal is nearly finished—they do not say that those employed on it are all prisoners.

The London solicitor for Sovtorgflot (the Soviet shipping organisation) has been trying to get information for several cases due to come up before the English courts. Previously he not only felt that the Soviet experiment would succeed but that the people running it had a moral purpose which sustained them and took the place of religion. This time he finds the feeling changed: everywhere there is disillusion. Even the keenest communists are unable to defend the differentiation of people into haves and have-nots which has come about with payment by results. The puritanical spirit which enabled people to do without luxuries and to be proud of doing without has entirely disappeared. Most astounding of all is that whereas formerly jazz music and western dancing were forbidden as western vices, now several very expensive hotels provide not only jazz music but also well-dressed and painted women as dancing partners—and very possibly for other purposes too.

☆

R.W. Bullard. 'Stocky and somewhat below middle height, he gave an immediate impression of dependability and rock-like solidity. A square face and jaw, a craggy intellectual forehead, deep sunk eyes, a direct gaze which could melt into benevolence or humour, and a wonderfully modulated melodious voice made him a notable figure in any gathering.' (*The Times*, 27 May 1976.)

Reader Bullard (above), and
(left) a page from his diary.

Moscow, Leningrad and surrounding area, c.1930.

William Strang.

Miriam Bullard in
October 1931 with,
from left to right,
Giles (aged five),
Godfrey (aged two),
Julian (aged three) and
Matthew (aged nine).

Lady Muriel Paget; studio
photograph by Alexander
Bassano, 1912.

'The "Freedom" of the Bourgeois
Press.' Poster by Kukruiniksui,
1931. Corrupt journalists from
four different newspapers
(*Vorwärts*, the *Daily Mail*,
Le Matin and *Rule*) are shown
accusing the Soviet Union of,
respectively, oppressing religion,
using forced labour, dumping, and
expanding their empire by terror.

SLAVERY IN RUSSIA.

Opening of

INTERNATIONAL CAMPAIGN

against

BRUTALITIES IN
SOVIET PRISON CAMPS.

"CHEAP TIMBER."

[Drawn by G. D. Armour and reproduced
by permission of "The Morning Post."]

MASS MEETING

at the

ROYAL ALBERT HALL

Poster for mass meeting at the Royal Albert Hall, London, organised by the Trade Defence Union, 6 March 1931. The committee included the Duke of Atholl, Lord Melchett and Sir Edward Hilton Young, MP.

Sosnovka, the *dacha* built on the northern outskirts of Leningrad for the use of the Distressed British Subjects. Lady Muriel's initial plans, first for an architect-designed house and later for the importation of a prefabricated wooden house, were finally rejected in favour of this building constructed by the department store Torgsin.

George Bernard Shaw; snapshot taken by Lady Muriel during Shaw's visit to the Soviet Union in the summer of 1931.

Group of unidentified Distressed British Subjects and Relief Association workers outside Sosnovka.

Tehran, December 1943. Facing camera, from left to right: Anthony Eden, Reader Bullard, Winston Churchill, Marshal Voroshilov and Josef Stalin.

Miss Daunt in old age. All earlier photographs of her are believed to have been lost in a fire at her ancestral home, Kilcascan Castle.

8 Nov. It was a cold, raw day yesterday, but there was one consolation: the official parade was scheduled to last only two hours instead of the usual four. I noticed that the horses were all half-starved. Three tanks broke down in the square and had to be towed off under the eyes of the army commander and the foreign visitors. It was perhaps sabotage which caused a failure of current in an essential letter of an illuminated slogan, whereby 'Forward to new victories!' read 'Forward to new dinners!' I wish that the Soviet Government had a shorter official song and that they would not play it so often. It is no joke to keep your hat off while the 'International' is being played in the open with a cold wind blowing. I noticed that most of the hundreds of Soviet citizens in the next block of seats had their cloth caps firmly on their heads, so I put my hat on again and never moved it after that, however much they played the 'International'. I am not called upon to be more Bolshevik than the Bolsheviks.

16 Nov. The Torgsin business raises so many problems on which we ought to have a joint policy that the Ambassador suggested I should pay a short visit to Moscow. I was put up by the Ambassador and looked after by his valet. On the first evening he couldn't find my dress collars, but as I couldn't find them either, having left them in Leningrad, it wasn't his fault. Lady Ovey is very kind and sensible and did not mind my not being able to dress for dinner. No one else in the Embassy had a collar big enough for my neck. I really must carry out my plan to stick inside the lid of my suitcase a list of the things one needs for a short visit.

The Ambassador is a changed man. Only a month ago he was trying to persuade me that the Soviet officials were as honest as those in the United Kingdom, and now he is cursing them and in particular Litvinov, the Commissar for Foreign Affairs. Certainly L is a shameless liar and exceedingly insolent. I would like to know more about his early life. He is a Warsaw Jew and his proper name is Vallakh. He was in prison in England for a little while, but I think that was during the War on political grounds. He was sentenced to imprisonment in France for swindling before the War, when he was plotting revolution there. In order to raise funds a group of them forged Russian banknotes and Litvinov was caught trying to pass some of these. Of course Stalin in his young days raised revolutionary funds by what the Americans now call 'racketeering'.

Relations between HMG and the Soviet Government are not good at the moment. The Soviet authorities are furious at the denunciation of the trade agreement. A month or two ago they themselves denounced

☆

their trade agreement with Latvia, yet by the way they write you would think that no country had ever before taken advantage of the clause providing for abrogation after due notice. Then there is the Elias case.[31] The London police raided the headquarters of the organisation which ran the recent 'hunger' marches and say that they found a letter which Sidney Job Elias (a Jew of Russian origin) had written from Moscow to Wal Hannington. This letter (written in consultation with the International Trade Union in Moscow) may be taken by a jury to be an incitement to cause disorder, and if he is convicted there will be more feeling in England against the Soviets. Finally *Izvestia*, the official organ of the Soviet Government, published an amazing report accusing the British Government of sending agents to Russia to look for evidence of the involvement of the Comintern with unemployment unrest in Great Britain. A question has been tabled in Parliament and Sir John Simon has telegraphed to Sir Esmond for the facts. The Ambassador gave the most important points from the report with comments to say that it was the usual stuff and need not be taken too seriously. He is furious and with some reason. He has always been against exaggerating the wild reports about the Comintern.

17 Nov. Yesterday Miss Daunt was tipped off by a helpful man in Torgsin that she would do well to see Weinstein about the Relief Association's Ford van, which Torgsin has been in the habit of hiring, paying for it in the roubles with which Miss Daunt pays allowances to the DBSs. Fortunately Miss Daunt is on good terms with Mr Weinstein, thanks to a dinner to which I invited them both last winter, when Weinstein, mellow with wine and music, said to her that if he saw her committing a serious breach of the law he would warn her. This made a good opening for Miss Daunt, since she was able to reproach him for *not* warning her about the van. It was evident that he had the case at his fingertips, although he pretended to know nothing about its being used for hire. For the moment the van is not to be used except for carrying the Association's own goods. Lady Muriel, who arrives a week hence, will be furious and will accuse us all of mismanaging things. Unfortunately

---

[31] Frequent demonstrations and clashes with the police in various parts of England had resulted in the decision to raid the headquarters of the National Unemployed Workers Movement, and the arrest of Elias, its chairman, on 1 November 1932. In court, the prosecution produced letters that Elias had written from Moscow to his deputy, urging him to greater efforts in 'distributing leaflets, organising street meetings and keeping the agitation going.' The letters were said to have been sent on the orders of Profintern, a section of the Third International charged with control of the unemployed.

☆

this time she is bringing Mrs Maynard Keynes with her and proposing
to put her up at the flat. This will annoy the authorities, who reckon to
get *valuta* at the hotels from foreign visitors. Lady Muriel is probably
expecting to find plenty of roubles in the till, earned by the van, but she
won't find enough for the allowances for next month.

Foreigners who were at first enthusiastic or at any rate favourable
observers of the Russian scene are becoming increasingly disillusioned. I
have already spoken about the Ambassador. One day he remarked that
probably a couple of million people would die of hunger this winter but
that the authorities wouldn't mind that. He would not have said that a
year ago, nor would he have let anyone else say it without criticism.
Duranty, an Englishman by birth, who represents the *New York Times*
and is considered the leading English-language journalist in Moscow
(this year he received the Pulitzer Prize for journalism), has always put
the most favourable interpretation on the Five-Year Plan and everything
else. He asked a group of communists: 'What are you going to do? Coal
is unsatisfactory, iron is unsatisfactory, etc. etc. What are you going to
do about it? *My* reputation is at stake.' This is as true as it is funny. If he
now has to damp down the enthusiasm which he has himself raised it
will be difficult for him.[32]

Chamberlin is going on leave, and the *Manchester Guardian* have sent
out a young man named Muggeridge[33] to act for him. He was almost a
communist (he is the son of a former Labour MP), but Strang says that
in a very short time he has faded to a mild pink.

The English papers report the death of Stalin's wife. The official cause
of death is given as appendicitis, but the best information says that she
committed suicide. The body lay in state—not in the Kremlin—but in
a public place, exactly, according to Cholerton, like that of a monarch.
She is said to have shot herself, but Cholerton saw no sign of a wound.
Cholerton also managed to see the tremendous funeral procession but
he was turned away from the cemetery as was the German Chargé
d'Affaires. Cholerton was not allowed by the press department to
telegraph that suicide was suggested.

19 Nov. Since the cancellation of the trade agreement my newspapers

[32] In his 1944 book *USSR: The Story of Soviet Russia* (Hamish Hamilton), Walter
Duranty said that he would have taken a different line in the 1930s if he had known all
that he learned later. However, Robert Conquest suggests that the OGPU was
blackmailing him on sexual grounds, and forcing him to take a consistently pro-
communist line. (*Reflections on a Ravaged Century*: Murray, 1999; see also 7 April 1934.)
[33] See Malcolm Muggeridge's *Winter in Moscow* (Eyre and Spottiswoode, 1934).

have been arriving five or six days late. The OGPU have taken to opening Woodhead's copy and delaying delivering mine until they have finished with Woodhead's.

A new decree has been published. In future a worker who absents himself without proper cause even for one day may be discharged and deprived of his food- and goods-cards. Previously a worker could only be discharged for being absent for three consecutive days in one month, but this has apparently had the effect of encouraging people to stay away from work.

20 Nov. A telegram from Lady Muriel to say she will arrive tomorrow. I must lend Miss Daunt my camp-bed as Lady Muriel is bringing Mrs Keynes.

I have heard that my Russian teacher is back from her summer holiday but is afraid to come here on account of the fuss the Soviet papers are making about England. Even if she had come I should have asked her to stay away for the present. To send the wretched woman to Siberia for three or four years is just the kind of revenge the Soviet authorities would be likely to think appropriate for our denunciation of the trade agreement and the discovery of the letter of Mr Elias.

A young Englishman named Wild came in a few days ago. His firm deals in rubber and tea, and he has been sent out to inspect the plywood which they are buying for boxes. He has only been here about three weeks, but he has learnt already that Russians are incompetent, procrastinating and shamelessly untruthful. He has to reject about 30% of the plywood offered.

On Friday I had tea with the Tearles. He told me Metro-Vickers are negotiating a new agreement. The Soviet authorities try to put the screw on by pretending that the denunciation of the trade agreement prevents their giving such good terms, but Tearle does not seem to be alarmed. He says that Metro-Vickers are too closely bound up with the electrical industry here. The Soviet authorities seem to appreciate the work done by Metro-Vickers, and often say that of all the foreigners the British give the squarest deal. Tearle had just had to send a man to examine a huge German turbine, made by the biggest turbine-works in the world, that was giving trouble. As a sign of confidence in his firm it was pleasant.

21 Nov. I hope to leave in three weeks. Today I saw a man named Boyd, a director of Metro-Vickers and also of various firms that make railway-wagons. He calculates that the Soviet railways need to buy from abroad about 55,000 railway-wagons a year for several years. Only they have no

☆

money to pay for them. The question of the balance of trade with Soviet Russia is very difficult. It is true that we buy £30 million worth of goods a year and pay cash, and that Russia buys £10 million worth almost all on credit. If we kept the cash due on timber purchases against money owed, Soviet Russia could not pay the instalments due on credits obtained from Germany—and Germany could not repay money borrowed from England. In order to make some such arrangement it is necessary to tide over the two-year period during which goods already ordered by Russia have to be paid for, and Boyd thinks that the only way to do that, is by some sort of loan. Boyd thought the Russians were trying to put pressure on him with regard to the denunciation of the trade agreement.

Called to the telephone by the captain of a British vessel which has just arrived. One of the crew met with an accident in harbour and died before he could be got to hospital. I shall have to go on board to hold an enquiry, and to arrange about the funeral.

23 Nov. Went to the harbour and found a captain willing to take home the man who has lost his feet and a suspected cancer case. The law authorises me to *instruct* the captain to carry distressed British seamen, but whenever there is time and opportunity I like to consult the convenience of the master. I tried to find the ship on which the accident happened, but it was past 5.00 and very dark when I got as near to it as a car could go, so I postponed my visit till today. It was well that I did so, for it was not too easy to find even in daylight. For about three-quarters of a mile I had to make my way along a tramline with no path on either side. It is a sad business making these enquiries, and this one was particularly sad, first because the man was only twenty-seven and leaves a young wife and a child of four, and secondly because the accident was due to the breaking of a gangway which, if it had been fit for its work, would not have broken if ten men, let alone one, stood on it. The poor fellow had to remain on board without medical help for four hours. The harbour was frozen so it was impossible to send a boat ashore and the distress signal for a doctor was not seen.

27 Nov. This afternoon we buried the poor seaman who was killed through falling down the hold. The captain and three members of the crew came and Lady Muriel and Miss Daunt and I. Tomorrow I must write to the widow.

We were told yesterday that from 1 January there are to be no food-cards for second-category people. They will have to buy everything in the open market—or rather they will have to starve, since they will not be able to afford open-market prices. Class two includes among other groups all clerical labour, many of the doctors, and married women who do not work.

It was madness for Lady Muriel to bring Mrs Keynes with her and let her stay at the Relief Association's flat, particularly just at this moment when the Soviet authorities are inventing fantastic accusations against us. I showed what I thought of it by refusing to go to the flat so long as Mrs Keynes was there. Lady Muriel spent an afternoon at Mrs Keynes' mother's place and met all the family: Lopokhova and two brothers both connected with the ballet. She said they had lots of food from the OGPU shop, which bears out Cave's information that Lopokhova is an OGPU agent. Lady Muriel can't see anyone without inviting them to a meal, and she invited seven people from the party to come to dinner last night. Miss Daunt was nearly crying at the waste of money, but fortunately Kulagin returned in time to knock the project on the head. He scolded Lady Muriel quite fiercely first for being so unwise as to make a display of food when food is short, and secondly for having anything to do with Russians, and finally for having brought Mrs Keynes with her. Lady Muriel was really scared, but all Miss Daunt could do was to put Lady Muriel to bed at once and telephone to Mrs Keynes' mother that Lady Muriel was ill and that the party was off for that reason. Lady Muriel is for the moment a little subdued, but in a day or two she will be as confident as ever that she alone is competent to run not only the Relief Association, but also the British Empire.

Kulagin is back from 'grain collection' in the south. Miss Daunt begged him not to tell her about it, and particularly not to mention figures, lest the information should get out from some other quarter and she be accused of spreading it. He told her he slept all the time with two revolvers under his pillow. They collected some grain, but not what was required, and to those who did not pay up the worst happened. It was dreadful. There is to be a big conference here to consider the situation, which is very bad. Kulagin said that he would like to see me, but I refused to go to the flat to meet him. I thought it better to wait until he asks to come here.

Nothing but horrors this week. Yesterday a huge Finn came in for a visa for Canada. He had been working in Karelia on timber-felling and cutting. His wife had died of typhoid fever a week ago and he seemed quite stunned. He had two children with him—a little girl of about three and a baby of eighteen months. They sat on chairs in the waiting-room without stirring. But for all my sympathy I could not give them a

★

Canadian visa, as the man had no permit to return, and no birth certificates to prove that his children were born in Canada. I could only advise him to go back to Finland and apply to the Canadian High Commissioner in London, whose address I gave him. They looked so forlorn as they went out—the baby being carried and the little girl holding on to her father's coat, that I got out some biscuits and tried to tuck them into the little girl's hand. She turned round at my touch, and her face was streaming with tears though she wasn't making a sound.

Mrs Keynes went to Torgsin to spend five pounds for her relatives. She was horrified at the poorness of the goods and of the selection; she had been informed in England that Torgsin was like Harrods!

Lady Muriel called and talked for hours. She said that Karsavina,[34] who slaves away in London teaching incompetents to dance, said that she really must have either a regular job or a man. She had apparently asked several men, but without success. In the days when I saw her dance, before the War, she would hardly have had to ask twice. Paul Dukes has divorced his Vanderbilt wife and is married (or not married) to a Russian dancer. Lord Rothermere keeps *three* Russian dancers—and so on. I suppose some of it is true.

Miss Daunt has been wearing a ring lately, and it appears that she is more or less engaged to an engineer who is at present in Colombia. I am shocked to learn from Lady Muriel that he is Russian. I suppose she met him during the famine. However, she is old enough to look after herself, and she knows as much about Russians and their weaknesses as most people.

Last night I was on my way to visit the Woodheads, and I passed an old woman who was standing against the wall holding out her hand for money. She looked old, but clean and neat, with a patient, kind face. I never give to beggars here, but after I had passed her I turned back and thrust a couple of roubles into her hand. A look of incredulous happiness came into her face, and before I could escape she had seized my hand and kissed it—not servilely, but almost reverently. I should have liked to ask her something about herself, but for her sake I said nothing.

30 Nov. I am trying to write one of my general reports, and finding it, as usual, difficult. One trouble is the mass of material that accumulates

[34] Tamara Karsavina (1885–1978), member of Diaghilev's Russian Ballet, 1909–29; president of the Licentiate Club of the Royal Academy of Dancing. In 1915 she had married H.J. Bruce, head of Chancery at the British Embassy in St Petersburg.

★

in four or five months.

We are having a great scramble this week to get the two sick seamen away to England. In an ordinary port it would be so easy, and here the simplest thing is complicated by suspicion and red tape. I hope that the two men will leave tomorrow on a ship going direct to Hull, but I want to get them out of hospital as soon as possible. The food is getting less and worse, and our household and Miss Daunt's have to supplement their diet considerably.[35]

After the funeral on Sunday, Lady Muriel took the captain and three of the crew back to the flat and gave them tea and supper. Kulagin came in in the evening, and they appear to have had a very interesting discussion. Kulagin is young and has never known anything but communism and atheism. He could not believe that the men were not all officers, he found them so intelligent and well-educated. Two were English, one Scot and one Irish. Kulagin thought that he would at least have an ally in the seaman from Eire, but he stood up for England against Russia. Kulagin was amazed to learn about conditions in our merchant marine, and what provision is made for the poor and unemployed in England. Some day I will tell him that I am of proletarian origin. That will be the knock-out blow!

I should much like to see Kulagin, but I think it better not to meet at present and he agrees. He is quite fearless, as a rule, and with some reason, for he is a man of great power. He gave a curious proof of this a few days ago. Miss Daunt had a job to do in the evening that needed the car, but she said that she could not use it as the lights were not working. Kulagin said that he would arrange that, and he went in the car with her, sitting in front beside the driver. Not a single policeman made a move to stop the car, though it is a serious offence to drive after dark without lights.

Kulagin is much depressed. In conversation with Miss Daunt and Lady Muriel he suggested that new ideas are needed, and that Stalin at once ejects anyone who wants to try new ideas. One day he said despondently: 'Perhaps the diehards will win after all.' There is no doubt that things are in a very bad way. The experiment has been living on agriculture, which was supposed to be a bottomless bag, and now there is little in the bag and peasants have been so brutally treated that it is not worth their while to fill the bag again.[36]

---

[35] Lady Muriel recorded in her diary that 'Mr Bullard's personal kindness and attention to these men, quite apart from his consular duties, is very touching.'
[36] Lady Muriel recorded her own impressions in her diary: 'I left behind a short velvet

From a report to HM Ambassador in Moscow, 5 Dec. I do not think that the tone of these notes is more gloomy than the mood of the population. Food supplies are not only more scanty than at any time since the famine, but they seem to diminish from week to week, and there is no prospect of any improvements. Further drastic restrictions are expected in January. The unusually wide extent of the typhus epidemic is a disturbing sign, suggesting as it does a general condition of dirt and lack of nourishment. When to these miseries is added, as is now being added, unemployment on a large scale without unemployment benefit or poor relief, all the elements of physical wretchedness are present. Nor is there a feeling of hope to sustain the people. The ordinary man is completely sceptical, and so far as can be learned, there is a feeling of disillusionment even among those who have hitherto been sustained by an almost religious enthusiasm. But these feelings do not appear to be accompanied by an expectation of great changes, though there is a general feeling that something must be done about agriculture in order, presumably, that industry may go on living on it instead of becoming self-supporting.

The two fundamental changes of the last eighteen months—the institution of payment by results and the grant of permission to the agricultural population to sell their surplus produce in the open market—are being followed by a third no less significant. Entrance to higher educational establishments is to be by examination and the courses are to be much longer and more severe.

A serious epidemic of typhus has been raging in Leningrad for some two weeks. Not only is no official information published on the subject, but stringent orders have been issued to conceal the epidemic as far as possible. At the worst moment there were some hundreds of fresh cases a day and four hospitals, one of them the huge Mechnikof hospital, a show-place for tourists, are dealing with typhus cases only. Among the prophylactic measures taken by the authorities may be mentioned: (a) a categorical denial by the representative of the Commissariat for Foreign

---

coat which Mrs Kulagin had admired and this, with the gramophone records, is all that is required to fully repay the really invaluable assistance that Kulagin never fails to give to our work. He warns us when we should be warned and gives us invaluable information (which has proved to be correct) and has been of great help in handling several difficult situations. Miss Daunt has a very good influence on Kulagin, she patches up family quarrels, commands his admiration and respect, and her transparent honesty and devotion to her work carried her through many troubles. But as Kulagin says: "In many respects, Miss Daunt, you are just a child." This is true—and appeals to the Russians.'

☆

Affairs that there is any typhus in the town; (b) the imprisonment of the port medical officer for allowing the epidemic to spread into the port area; (c) the publication of a report in the press that serious epidemics of cholera and the plague are raging in Madras. At this juncture it is pleasant to read this passage from Professor Julian Huxley's book *A Scientist among the Soviets*, published a few months ago: 'Typhus has almost disappeared.' I do not mind living in a town which has a typhus epidemic every year as much as I mind having that fact denied by the authorities, and to have that denial accepted at its face value by a well-known English scientist. At the present moment the doctors in Leningrad refer to typhus as 'disease, type 2', the authorities having decided that typhus is not typhus when it is in the Soviet Union.

These are some of the names which, it is stated, are gradually replacing the old Christian names: Freedom, Era, Dawn, Aurora, Starlet, Rome, October, Spartacus, Electrina, New World, Shock-Worker, Barricade.

Russsians (by race) make fun of themselves for letting Caucasians and Jews lead them by the nose, but I think it would be a mistake to believe that their feelings go no further than that. In this area of my consular district it is the Jewish minority which is prominent. At a dinner at which the consular corps was balanced by sixteen Soviet citizens, one of the latter was an Estonian, two were Letts, ten were Jews, and of the remaining three, all that could be said with certainty was that the burden of proving they were Russians should be on them. A Russian in a position of importance tells me that he recently had to read a report in a committee of twenty-five, of whom the others were all Jews; the only Russians present were himself and the man who carried round glasses of tea. It is probable that only the high proportion of non-Russians, particularly of Jews, in posts requiring organising ability keeps the complicated machine of administration moving, but the Russians do not admit that. There is a strong tendency to attribute all the defects of the present regime to the predominance of the Jews in positions of importance. These feelings are not laudable, but I am sure they are held by many Russians and that, if at any time there were to be a relaxation of control, they would not need the encouragement from above which they are said to have received during the tsarist regime to break out in violence against the Jews.

☆

THE METRO-VICKERS AFFAIR

LENINGRAD, 1933

HAVING SPENT CHRISTMAS *in England, Reader Bullard returned to the Soviet Union in February 1933. Two weeks later, four British employees of the engineering company Metro-Vickers were arrested in Moscow, together with twenty Russian erectors, chauffeurs, translators, bookkeepers and secretaries employed by the company. Two more British engineers were arrested later, and all were charged with spying, bribery and sabotage at six electric power-stations.*

A show trial in April led to strong British protests and a trade embargo which the Soviet Union initially reciprocated. At the end of June, however, Moscow backed down. The prisoners were released and the following month the trade embargoes were removed.

In November diplomatic relations were formally established with the USA, the last of the great powers to recognise the Soviet Union. At the end of December the foreign minister, Litvinov—in a speech unusually devoid of ideology—expressed Moscow's desire for international stability, peace and security. Meanwhile Stalin launched the second Five-Year Plan (1933–37) and called for the output of coal, oil, steel and iron to more than double.

23 Feb. I got back from eight weeks at home. It is sad to come away. The thermometer at the Hotel Europa shows 5°, i.e. 27° of frost. Cave had two attacks of angina complicated by asthma during my absence. Miss Daunt was up with him several nights. He is to go to a sanatorium in Finland for a month's cure, where he will get nothing to smoke and nothing to drink.

Last night Miss Daunt and Mr and Mrs Willis, a Canadian couple, came to dinner. He is an architect who designs factories but now he is leaving. After working first in Moscow, they were sent to Kiev. The Ukrainians like to assert their autonomous rights as far as they can, and Ukrainian engineers will even visit a foreigner. Although Kiev is in the middle of the famous Black Earth grain country, the place is starving, and bread in the market is 20 roubles a kilo. Later they were sent to Sverdlovsk in the Urals where conditions were even worse. He was given a room in a Russian flat. As this was a breach of his contract, he demanded the cancellation of the contract. The trust accept his right to do this and to a compensatory payment, but say they have no money to pay. It looks as though he will have to go home and make a claim through the Foreign Office.

Conditions seem to be rather worse than when I left. Even Torgsin is poorly stocked. Miss Daunt says they have no proper tea and the potatoes are small, frozen and gelatinous. Potatoes were formerly very good and very plentiful, but something seems to have gone wrong this season, as with grain, meat, milk and everything else.

The new passport decree seems to be causing great distress. The Bolsheviks used to curse the tsarist passport system as a mark of slavery, but now they apply it themselves in a diabolically severe form. It is part of the scheme to cut down the concentrations of population in the big towns. Leningrad is to be cut down by 800,000 people somehow. If your father was a bourgeois the passport is refused. This means that you lose your work and your food-card and you and your family must leave in ten days—for somewhere. If you don't leave, you are put on any train that happens to suit the authorities. The thousands who flooded in from the country in 1931 are now being discovered and forced out into the country again.

Once more there is evidence of a shortage of roubles. Waldhauer's wife borrowed money from Miss Daunt, as neither she nor her husband had been paid for January. Dr Bell has also had no pay for January, and he says the scientists at the Institute of Geology have not been paid for December.

Two weeks ago the father of Nusha and Lena was arrested by the OGPU and brought to Leningrad where he is in prison. I expect it is part of the new agricultural policy. A few chief men from a village are arrested and later released with the threat of what will happen if they don't produce grain in the required quantities.

All the consuls are going to get butter and meat and vegetables every week or ten days from a Finn who lives just over the border. It seems to be simple and very cheap, but the Finnish village from where we still get potatoes warn us that the supply is nearly gone.

☆

27 Feb. While I was in England I heard that Kulagin had been wounded in a fight with peasants in Siberia. This is what his wife was told by the authorities. After a while, however, she learned that he is in the OGPU prison in Leningrad. She is not allowed to see him or communicate with him or send him food, and she does not know what he is accused of or whether he is still alive or has been shot. To add to her anxieties she has no means of support as her husband's pay has stopped. No one is anxious to offer work to the wife of a disgraced OGPU man. Mrs Kulagin comes to Miss Daunt every day, and I suppose Miss Daunt gives her something to eat. I wonder what the cause of the arrest is. Perhaps Kulagin refused to be ruthless enough with the peasants in Siberia, or perhaps he was as indiscreet in other places as he was sometimes at Miss Daunt's. If he is alive I should like to know what he thinks of the OGPU now.

Last night Miss Daunt came round at 2 a.m. She had just had a telephone message from Mrs Hay's daughter. The girl had managed to slip away while the house was being searched by the OGPU. Miss Daunt told her to show her passport and tell the OGPU that Miss Daunt was going straight to the Consulate. This had the desired effect. The girl was let alone and her room was not searched. The Soviet authorities are going very careful with British subjects while the negotiations for the renewal of the trade agreement are going on.

We are living on butter borrowed from the Finnish Consulate and on tinned sardines, sausages, salmon and Symington's soups (very good, even the kitchen approve of them, and all Russians are connoisseurs of soup).

Lady Muriel asked the Red Cross if the DBS destitutes could receive medical treatment at the Soviet health centres, and offered to pay. The Red Cross said the destitute would be attended without charge. Then later the head of the Red Cross proposed to Miss Daunt that the Relief Association should pay the Red Cross $16,000 a year to look after our seventy-odd destitutes—nearly £5000 a year. Miss Daunt mentioned this to some person in authority and now the head of the Red Cross is chopping wood in Kem'.

The last time she was here Lady Muriel bought a stuffed bird from Torgsin and made poor Mrs Tearle take it to Finland for her. I must go and see Tearle, I hear he is the only man left at Metro-Vickers.

1 March. Nusha's father has been in prison for a month. She has been told his offence comes under two articles in the criminal code relating to crimes against the Soviet Government. Nusha and her sister take food

☆

to their father every five days but they don't see him. While I was away Nusha 'borrowed' 80 roubles from Cave and bought a sewing-machine after spending a day and a night in a queue in a temperature of about 0°F. Moreover it works. The wait in the queue doesn't seem anything out of the ordinary to her.

Mrs Kulagin was called up by the OGPU the other day for daring to say to a Russian friend on the telephone that she had stood six hours in a queue for kerosene.

Pott sent a piece of social news: Walker is engaged to Lady Mary Crichton Stuart. She is reputed to have lots of money, and that will suit Walker, who likes to be quite comfortable.

2 March. I have already settled back into the soothing routine of life here. Work fills the office hours; I go for a walk after tea and fill in the time until 7.30 with odd jobs. After dinner I read sometimes with the wireless on. One night we had the whole of *Aïda*, and last night there was a Bach concert. I am reading a German detective story and a novel by Hans Carossa, *Dr Gion*.

Poor Cave. Everything goes wrong with him. I don't want him retired for ill-health. He would be penniless, for he never has a bean at the end of the month. He posted a letter to his wife with a copy of the divorce decree, but he has now heard that the Vice-Consul at Helsingfors has been telling a great many people that his new girlfriend, Mrs Acker, is a prostitute. Similar stories were spread here by Mrs Lie, who was staying in the same hotel a few miles from Helsingfors where Mrs Acker was a waitress. She tried to make love to Cave. Having failed she swore to make him rue the day, as the first man who had ever refused her love! Cave is evidently a devastating fellow. I hope the scandal about this new woman will be cleared up.

5 March. Yesterday as I was coming back from my walk along the Nevsky, thinking how wretched many of the people looked, and in particular how dreadful and how numerous the beggars were, I heard a woman's voice on the loudspeakers singing that lovely lullaby of Mozart: '*Schlafe, mein Kindchen, schlaf ein.*'

Lady Muriel is learning physical exercises suitable for old women and proposes to teach them to the old dependants on the relief fund.

Three or four months ago Professor Waldhauer was made an honorary member of the Hellenic Society. Professor Beazley told me that the honour would have been conferred years ago, but the Council of the Society thought that it might perhaps get Waldhauer into trouble. As it

★

happens it has done him good. The Soviet Government, although they attack England more than any other country, seem to have respect for our good opinion. Waldhauer says that the honour came at the right moment, just when the authorities had realised that you couldn't make engineers and doctors and archaeologists out of every chance comer. A fanatical communist who was put into Waldhauer's department and reported against him a year ago as full of bourgeois ideas and anti-Marxist has been chucked out.

This indicates a significant change in Soviet policy. Waldhauer is better-off than he was, he has been made a member of a very select co-operative for men of science; there are only 120 members and he can get most things—when he has the money. His pay, like that of many people, is in arrears. He is dying to go to Berlin, but he still cannot get permission. He is in a dreadful state of nerves, starting violently when a piece of old furniture cracked, and asking more than once whether there might not be someone in the next room or a microphone in the chimney. He smoked all the time, even while he was having dinner. I played him the first movement of Bach's Suite for Flute and Strings, but he said he couldn't listen, it was too painful. He repeats that whatever their faults, the Bolsheviks have done more for the museums and for art and science than their predecessors. In former times the exhibits were arranged according to their *size*. There were men on the pay-roll of the Hermitage who only appeared once a month to draw their pay. The Hermitage is attached to the Winter Palace, but Waldhauer only saw the Tsar in the Hermitage once, and then he was drunk. If the authorities remain in their present mood, things should be better with the intellectual workers.

Waldhauer is not easy about his position under the new passport system. He has had enquiries from German students who want to come and study under him in the Hermitage and he in return would like to send one or two Russians to study in Berlin, but he does not dare to suggest it.

I had Tearle to dinner on Saturday 4th. The Metro-Vickers contract expired a year ago and the negotiations for its renewal are still going on. The pretext for the delay is that the trade agreement has not yet been renewed, but Tearle thinks that the Soviet Government is simply desperate for money and is holding out in the hope of getting better terms. The signs of shortage of money are evident. Metro-Vickers make steam-turbines, and train Russians to make them. Metro-Vickers superintend every step of the work done by the Russians to make certain that the turbines will work properly, but the job goes very slowly and

☆

there is a lot of waste. He reckons there are twelve 24,000-horsepower turbines lying about unused: they have been completed and shipped but never erected. At the present moment one of the Metro-Vickers men is erecting a turbine in the Urals. It was delivered some time ago and was left out in the snow. When the English engineer arrived he had to have much of it taken to pieces and rusted parts replaced.

Before I went on leave Dr Bell was working from about 8 a.m. until midnight. Like many other doctors he had been compelled to take a second post by the authorities. This is called a '*nagruzka*', i.e. an additional burden, and the burdened one gets half as much for the additional work as for his proper job. The great worry at present is typhoid.

9 March. Mrs Kulagin continues to come to Miss Daunt almost every evening. She still cannot find out what her husband was imprisoned for or whether he is alive or dead. A man in Torgsin who was helping her has been ordered to leave Leningrad in ten days.

11 March. Miss Wilson, an old DBS, died a few days ago and her Russian niece came to inform Miss Daunt. As she was ill-clad and cold, Miss Daunt kept her for about twenty minutes and gave her some tea and something to eat. Next day the woman was arrested, and when they searched her flat they told her that she had been 'consorting with foreigners'. As evidence they carried off a volume of Ruskin and a copy of *The School for Scandal*.

On the 8th the usual lavish banquet was given for the fur-buyers who had come for the auction. I sent Todd. An English Jew, Marcus Ariowitsch, came to see me. He wanted to make a declaration, to be countersigned by the Consulate, that his business belonged to him and not to a certain Russian who was only the manager. The poor Russian was in danger of being turned out of Leningrad on the grounds that he formerly owned this fur business. Marcus Ariowitsch was very gloomy. For the first time, he felt that the workmen were dissatisfied. Trade is not going well. He hears from Leipzig that the Soviet Government are meeting bills which have fallen due there for German goods delivered last year or the year before, by raising money against gold which is to be exported later in the year.

12 March. Sunday. It is typical of Soviet propaganda that Stalin should have announced in a recent speech that wages are to be increased by a given percentage this year.

☆

16 March. About midday last Sunday, Strang telephoned from Moscow to say that the Metro-Vickers place there had been searched and four of the British engineers, two Russian women secretaries and two Russian chauffeurs arrested. He asked me to find out if Tearle was all right. I thought I would not telephone Tearle to let the OGPU know I was going round to see him (all our telephone conversations are listened to), but while I was putting some papers away before starting off I had a telephone call from Tearle. He told me afterwards that he had been trying in vain to get a message through to me all the morning. The OGPU must have cut him off until they heard the Embassy talking to me about the case. I went round to see Tearle at once, taking Todd with me. All was quiet. The OGPU had come the night before and searched the place and carried off some papers (including all the letters Tearle has ever received from his wife), but they had not touched Tearle, and had even told him that there was nothing against him personally. I jumped to the conclusion that the Soviet Government have no *valuta* to renew the Metro-Vickers contract, or perhaps, to pay what they already owe the company, and rather than admit this they are inventing a political excuse for breaking off negotiations.

A day or two ago the papers reported that seventy men had been arrested on a charge of sabotaging the agricultural plan and trying to starve the people, and a few days later announced that thirty-five of them were to be shot and the rest deprived of liberty for eight or ten years. Now the OGPU have 'discovered' a similar plot in the electrical plant industry. This sort of thing always happens when times are bad. Lest people should blame the Government, a few scapegoats are selected. Fortunately we know from past experience that the foreigners will not be shot as many of the Russians will be. Still it is an anxious time for the arrested men and their families. Yesterday the local paper contained a resolution allegedly passed by some foreign engineers in support of the arrest of the four British engineers accused: 'We have heard with satisfaction that the OGPU have succeeded in unmasking saboteurs in the Soviet electrical industry. We call upon all foreign specialists in the Soviet Union to join hands with the Soviet proletariat in waging a merciless war against saboteurs of whatever kind.' The signatures are supposed to represent USA, Germany, Austria, Hungary and England. The names are nearly all Jewish.

23 March. On Sunday the Ambassador telephoned and instructed me to go to Moscow that night and take Miss Daunt with me. He did not say much except that things looked very bad, but next day he said he had

☆

thought the Soviet Government would push the matter to a breach of relations. I stayed two days in Moscow, and when I left the issue was still in doubt. The statement in the House of Commons that the negotiations for the renewal of the commercial agreement had been suspended, was expected to make the Soviet Government realise how serious the matter was. It is significant that for a week now the newspapers have made no reference to the arrested engineers. I hope that the fear of losing their best customer will compel the Soviet Government to find a solution which will in fact involve the release of the four engineers. They have allowed the Ambassador and the Consul to see them, and they have given them better food than the arrested Russians.

Thornton is on the verge of a breakdown. He is the manager of Metropolitan-Vickers with whom I travelled out when I came out first in 1930. He managed a factory here before the War and until the second revolution in 1917, when his workmen protected him from harm. For the last seven years they have been supplying, erecting and maintaining electric plant as far away as Baku and Irkutsk. He is the man the OGPU hate most. Monkhouse, against whom they did not pretend to have any serious evidence and who was released in two days, was questioned for about forty out of forty-eight hours, and when he was given five hours for sleep, the OGPU, in accordance with their usual practice, woke him up twice during that time. The four men are kept apart from each other, and when they saw the Ambassador and Rapp nothing relating to the case could be mentioned, though the Ambassador told one man that everyone in England knew about the matter. I saw Monkhouse. He is a steady, strong-minded man and had stood his imprisonment well, but the intensive questioning must have been very trying. He was treated like an ordinary prisoner and his braces and tie were taken away so that he should not commit suicide.

The Soviet Foreign Commissar, that horrible Litvinov, began by being very rude to the Ambassador and insisting that they could do just as they pleased with British subjects. He seems to have assumed that the Ambassador would not be backed up by his Government, but what the Ambassador said here was nothing to what the Under-Secretary said in London to Maisky, the Soviet Ambassador. Among other things, he said that we could not allow British subjects to be the victims of a stage trial.

It was pleasant to be in Moscow for a day or two. The Ambassador talked incessantly and gave me the impression of enjoying the limelight very much indeed. He is naively vain. His talkativeness must be a sore trial to Strang who has to listen to hours of repetition and then work half the night to make up for it. As soon as we arrived the Ambassador held a two-hour conference, though all that was said could have been disposed of in fifteen minutes. As we went out I said to Strang: 'I imagine that this is not the first conference that has been held this week.' He said in a weary tone: 'I have ceased to react to words.'

I saw Cholerton in Moscow and was delighted to hear that he has been appointed *Daily Telegraph* correspondent and can give up the worthless *News Chronicle*. The press censorship people hate Cholerton because he can't be flattered or bullied into whitewashing the Soviet Government. They have been longing for an excuse to get rid of him, but it will be more difficult now that he represents a big newspaper.

24 March. The dispute is as it was, neither side wanting to give in. The Ambassador has been talking to Sir John Simon about the measures which can be taken when the six months' notice about the trade agreement expires on 17 April.

At Cholerton's I met Muggeridge. Since he took over I have noticed that the *Guardian*'s reports have been much more outspoken and nearer the truth. The change has been noticed in England too. Muggeridge says that old Scott was a fine fellow and so was his son, who was drowned soon after becoming editor-in-chief, but their successors are poor stuff. Muggeridge visited the Kuban area, where troops are quartered on the peasants and where the Soviet Government admit they have weeded out whole villages to be sent into exile for inability to pay the grain demanded. The *Guardian* wrote to say that they could not print his comments as they would then be in bad company—i.e. with the out-and-out opponents of Soviet Russia. They have always tended to toady to Russia, and it is supposed that this is partly because most of the orders for turbines and machine tools have been going to Lancashire. I thought that the arrest of the four engineers would perhaps annoy them a little, but they have been very half-hearted about it. Muggeridge says that the Kuban was a most depressing sight. It is one of the great grain-growing areas, and it has been ruined. He saw nothing but listless, idle, starving peasants and well-fed troops on guard everywhere. What made it the more distressing was that whereas the peasants were a good type of Russian, rather like the Cossacks, the troops were Mongols, and those in charge, Jews. It is Kaganovich who was put in charge of the punitive operations.

26 March. The parcels which Torgsin said they had sent to our destitutes in Moscow and other places in February did not arrive, and Miss Daunt eventually found they were despatched over a fortnight after Torgsin said

☆

they had gone. She thinks Torgsin hadn't the provisions to send, but did not like to admit this to her. When she was in Moscow last week, she went to the headquarters of Torgsin to complain. She saw the assistant director. Miss Daunt ended by saying: 'It is difficult for people like you, who are well-fed, to realise the position of those who have no food at all.' The woman interpreter looked alarmed and stopped, but Miss Daunt asked her to continue, and the woman did so. The assistant director turned scarlet and said that of course it must be very dreadful and took notes furiously. When Miss Daunt went out, the interpreter, who followed her out of the room, said: 'That was good. When are you coming again?'

According to Cholerton and Muggeridge even the young enthusiasts who come out to work on that rag, the *Moscow News*, are drifting away now that they no longer have permission to buy at special shops. A number of the women are what is vulgarly known in journalistic circles as communists by injection, i.e. they have been supplied with handsome young communists to sleep with them. Muggeridge's wife is a niece of Mrs Sidney Webb, and she has shown her aunt his letters from Russia. She describes how after reading one of them, Mrs Webb walked up and down the room wringing her hands and saying: 'Old people become set in their opinions and perhaps I was deceived.' She *was* deceived. Muggeridge is amused because Sidney Webb published an article praising the Russian co-operative system as the finest institution in the world—about two days before the system was swept away with a stroke of the pen. Muggeridge promised to show me, but forgot, a letter sent to the *Manchester Guardian* a few weeks ago by Bernard Shaw and some others, saying that a dead set was being made against the Soviet Union by ill-intentioned people and protesting against it.

28 March. It appears that Kerensky[1] is broadcasting lectures on Russia from Prague every few days. The station is powerful and the efforts of the Soviet stations to jam it have not succeeded. Kerensky only says what they all know, about the queues and other miseries of life in Soviet Russia, but it gives the Russian great pleasure to hear such things mentioned.

30 March. From today's Russian paper it looks as though the dispute

[1] A.F. Kerensky (1881–1970), lawyer and socialist leader. Having supported the March 1917 Revolution he became prime minister the following July, but was ousted by the Bolsheviks after the October Revolution and fled the country.

☆

about the four engineers must lead to commercial reprisals by HMG. I don't yet know what measures are to be adopted. The Soviet Government are talking heroically, but in fact the fuss made in England has certainly protected the prisoners from the grosser forms of injustice. The Public Prosecutor will not now dare to put up the kind of case that has hitherto been thought good enough to secure the death or exile of Soviet citizens. I see that the charge of bribery has been added to that of sabotage. I daresay that the English engineers helped Russian friends with presents of clothes etc. It is possible that in order to show their disapproval HMG will withdraw the Ambassador from Moscow and give the Soviet Ambassador in London his passport, but this will only be a diplomatic gesture and will make no practical difference. Strang would be chargé d'affaires, and we should carry on as before. I hope that many of the Soviet organisations in London will be closed down. Why should the Soviet Government have its own tourist organisation in London, when English tourist organisations, fifty times as efficient, cannot work in Soviet Russia? Also I don't see why the Soviet Government should have a large organisation in England for selling its oil, when we are not allowed to sell anything in Russia. But I should like to see all Soviet imports into England controlled by an import board which would see that the Soviet Government either bought more from us or sold less, and that the Soviet Government did not wreck the market and ruin competitors who would otherwise buy from us, by cutting prices to uneconomic levels—at the expense of their starving population.

1 April. Beginning to get warmer, and very soon we can have all the windows opened—and cleaned. The maid's father was released after forty days in prison. Nusha is one of five sisters, stupid, obstinate, but full of courage and determination. She fought to get a pension for her crippled father, and she succeeded in getting 65 roubles a month. Not much, but better than nothing. The pension stopped while he was in prison, and Nusha is trying to get it renewed.

I gave the poor old woman who cleans our office two one-pound tins of dripping as well as her wage. She was pathetically grateful. Miss Daunt has an assistant, Miss Healy, who has a 'second-category' food-card, but even so, apart from a ration of meat for the First of May celebrations last year, is entitled to no meat at all. Others are even worse off.

The trial of the accused engineers, English and Russian, is announced to begin on 9 or 10 April. Perhaps the authorities want to get it over by 17 April, when the trade agreement comes to an end. We think that the

☆

whole affair is a dodge to enable the Soviet Government to delay or refuse payment to Metro-Vickers, to whom they owe about £1½ million, and this view is supported by recent exhortations in the press, calling upon the heads of industries to try to find defects in foreign goods and demand reductions. In his last interview with the Ambassador, Litvinov surpassed even his ordinary rudeness. He said that our methods might do in Mexico, but they couldn't be employed in Russia (a personal insult to the Ambassador, whose last post was Mexico). Moreover Litvinov had this published in the Soviet press at once. The FO have recalled the Ambassador for consultations.

The acting Norwegian Consul, Bolstaad, who spends most of the year at Archangel, told me a story. 'When there's bread in the towns and none in the country, that's a left deviation. When there's bread in the country and none in the towns, that's right opportunism. When there's no bread, either in the towns or in the country, that's the General Line of the Party. When there's bread both in the towns and in the country, that's accursed capitalism.'

4 April. Last night I had a Canadian to dinner, one Nevitt. He is—or was—a socialist, came here last summer and got a job as a wireless engineer to find out the truth about Russia. He had the good fortune to find a room to sleep with some nice Russians and has learnt a good deal of Russian. But he has quite definitely come to the conclusion that if socialism is ever to be established it won't be established by the Russians. He has had enough and is going home today.

Dr Bell has just been out to Izhora, a manufacturing centre a few miles away, on a sanitary inspection. He has a stomach ulcer and lives on gruel and toast, just as well as he said there was nothing to eat at Izhora. He was quite moved by the horrors of the passport system—some people are given only four days to clear out. The second-hand shops are filling up with things left by these poor people.

Lady Muriel saw Kagan at the Soviet Embassy in London and told him that she was postponing a visit she had intended to make to Leningrad on account of the tension of feeling. Kagan said that there was no need for this. Had not the Soviet authorities done everything they possibly could for Miss Daunt—even to arresting the head of the Red Cross who asked for $18,000 for giving medical treatment to the DBSs?

A considerable number of documents have passed through our Consulate in Moscow, in which Soviet citizens instruct English stockbrokers to sell their shares and remit the proceeds to the State Bank in Russia. We wonder how many of these documents were signed under pressure applied in the hot room. We can't do anything about it. Our sole business is to legalise the signatures on the documents.

6 April. I wish I was in Moscow, to hear the stories told by the three engineers who have been released on bail.

My Polish colleague told me it was being said that the Soviet Government realised they had made a mistake in putting on the front page of the newspapers reports of the ill-treatment of Jews and communists in Germany, as most of the population took them in the wrong spirit. In one district people were meeting in secret to read these reports and to applaud the Germans. This may be a little exaggerated, but I have heard from other sources too that many Russians feel less sympathy than the Soviet Government for the woes of the Jews in Germany.

The *Weekly Manchester Guardian* has a strong article on the terrible conditions in the Kuban area of North Caucasus—evidently by Muggeridge. I heard similar accounts from a British subject named Richter, whom I saw yesterday, who has been working in a factory in Armavir, living mainly on parcels from the Relief Association, his rations being a pound of bread a day and nothing else. According to him—and he broke down twice while telling his story—the whole population is starving. People die in the streets daily from hunger, and those who don't die have swollen faces and limbs and bodies—sure signs of famine. The day he left there were corpses at the station—one of them that of a woman whose face had been eaten by rats. Public order is so insecure that anyone lucky enough to own a cow or some pigs brings them into his living-room at night.

9 April. A few days ago Lydia Ivanovna, with whom I had a few Russian lessons last autumn, came to see us. She has a hard time, but it has not destroyed her sense of humour. She and her husband, an attendant in a museum, are certain that one or both will be arrested and exiled some time or other, but they feel it is useless to worry about it. In a way it adds a zest to life. They have separate living quarters, and when they meet, which is nearly every day, they say 'Still at liberty!' or something of the kind, and feel a double pleasure. A pupil gave her a knitted coat which she hung on the door of the common kitchen while she was cooking and forgot it. When she remembered a few moments later it was gone.

I had a long chat yesterday with Mrs Morton. Her husband, an iron-moulder, told her from the start that the Movement came before her or

☆

the children. He volunteered to distribute the *Sunday Worker*, which meant a full day's work, naturally with no pay, every Sunday starting at 3 a.m. and his wife and children were made to help as well. He was always bringing home communists down on their luck for his wife to feed, and since she was very often the only bread-winner in the family, she went on strike. Then Lady Astor offered to pay the expenses of any English communist who would agree to live in Russia for two years, and Morton accepted the offer. They were treated pretty well, but quite soon after they arrived Morton died. The Soviet Government gave her a pension of 150 roubles a month for the two children and a job in a factory. She does not know what to do. She would far rather live in England and she never wants to hear any political talk again, but her children have become half-Russianised. She has to work very long hours, and on her only free day she cleans the flat and does the washing. If women are slaves in capitalist countries she would like to know what they are in the Soviet Union.

Lady Muriel has had to go to Paris for medical treatment. Three years ago she had an operation for cancer, and now the doctors fear that the trouble is beginning again. When one is exasperated by her incompetence and dishonesty one forgets her courage. She is always full of spirit and interest in life.

I am encouraged to hear that England is humming with sympathy for the imprisoned engineers, though I shan't breathe securely until the trial is over. If any of the men have said something indiscreet, one does not know how it will be twisted by the court. E.F. Wise, who is naturally an enthusiastic supporter of Russia,[2] described the arrest of the engineers as a 'bloomer'.

On 12 April the Metro-Vickers trial opened in Moscow. On 13 April one of the accused engineers, MacDonald, speaking firmly and confidently, denied his previous admission of guilt. The public prosecutor then ordered a half-hour adjournment, after which MacDonald—speaking in a low toneless voice—reaffirmed his original confession. One of the Russian employees to have been arrested, a secretary named Kutuzova, gave evidence against her former colleagues.

15 April. I felt a little sad yesterday on reading about the evidence given by MacDonald against himself and some of his colleagues at the trial, for

---

[2] See p.130 above. Frank Wise, who had been economic adviser on foreign trade to Centrosoyuz since 1922, was to die later in the year.

☆

though I knew that the evidence was false at least as against the others, it was saddening to think that any pressure could make a man perjure himself so grossly. Fortunately for us the Soviet Government, in forcing the wretched woman Kutuzova to accuse the engineers of all sorts of crimes, overdid it, as they always do, and got her to 'confess' that the engineers received 50,000 roubles from the British Consulate in Moscow for distribution for espionage. As we know that this is false, it strengthens our belief that not only the rest of her evidence but that of the other Russian witnesses is false. Her evidence will be accepted by the ignorant here, even though they know all about the OGPU methods of extracting it, but I am quite happy about the affair now in my own mind.

Some representatives of Metro-Vickers have given presents to various Russian engineers. That would be very wrong at home, but in a semi-oriental country where the practice is common, and where men of influence who are not given presents might wreck one's work, it is a very different thing. But all the rest of the case is pure fake.

I try not to despise Russians who will confess anything when in the power of the OGPU, because I don't know how long I should hold out *if I were a Russian*. One's wife and children can be sent away without any charges having been brought, or one can be sent away oneself to cut wood in the north and live on bread and *kasha* for ten or twenty years. I don't see how the case will end, and yet I feel that so gross a fraud cannot in the long run succeed. As to MacDonald, I feel that he will never be allowed to leave Soviet Russia alive, for fear he should tell the truth.

One good thing has come out of this dreadful trial: at last some of the horrors of life in Russia are set forth officially by the British Government.

This afternoon the Polish Consul and his wife took me out for a run of thirty miles or so in their car. The object of our journey would be described by the Russians as economic espionage, since we went to cast an eye on the fields and see how the rye sown last autumn was coming up.

Tearle comes round every day to discuss the case and to have a little company. He is alone except for the servants, two of whom are OGPU agents, which is trying for him, but he bears it very well. One of the papers which the unfortunate Thornton wrote under pressure and later withdrew mentioned several members of the staff as having engaged in espionage, among them Tearle. Poor Tearle! We had him and Miss Daunt to dinner last night and they are coming again tonight.

★

Many Russians see the great improbability in the tale of the principal witness, the woman secretary Kutuzova. They are supposed to have plotted in her presence to destroy a turbine. So likely.

I wrote to Weinstein asking whether anything could be done about the loudspeaker next to the Consulate which blared all day from 6 a.m. to 12 p.m. and sometimes in the night too. We had peace for three days, and then the noise began again. They had just moved the loudspeaker across to the opposite corner, which was no improvement as it now faces the houses opposite and the echo increases the noise. So after suffering for a week I wrote again to Weinstein, appealing to him as a colleague and a musician to do something if he could. We have again had several days of quiet, and are hoping that the nuisance has stopped. I thought that perhaps they would be particularly correct in a matter of no importance at a time when they were besmirching our name by means of witnesses perjuring themselves under intolerable State pressure.

The night before last Tearle was subjected to 'provocation'. At 9 p.m. there was a ring at the door. A man in a sort of marine cap pushed in and asked for a secret interview on a matter of great importance. Tearle said he would have no secret interviews and that the man must go. The man produced what appeared to be a CID card and Tearle reluctantly let him in, but said he must call a witness. The man agreed, doubtfully, and Tearle called the housekeeper and told the man that everything he said would be reported to the Consul General at once. This seemed to deter him and he made up a lame story about having merely come to ask whether so-and-so was employed in Metro-Vickers, and left, promising to come the next day in office hours. Of course he did not come.[3] But Tearle is a very intelligent man, and a man of strong character, for all his youthful appearance, and he is dealing very well with a very difficult situation.

[3] In a letter to Strang dated 17 May 1933, RWB described what followed: 'Next day the CID telephoned Tearle assuring him that none of their men had been to his house. The assistant chief came round and said what had happened could not have been done by a CID man because their men never worked alone, and he authorised Tearle to arrest the man if he came back. Tearle, who is full of courage and enterprise, asked whether he might arrest him in the street, and the CID man said yes. A few days later Tearle saw the man in the Nevsky, and marched him to the Hotel Europa, though the man blew a police whistle which brought a policeman, and produced a CID pass. The man however went quietly, and told Tearle his chiefs had bungled. There had been some lack of co-ordination between the sixth (secret) section, where he was, and the second, where the assistant chief worked. The assistant chief came at once in answer to a telephone call, thanked Tearle, marched the man off and told Tearle he would be informed of the result. He has heard nothing since.'

☆

On 19 April, five of the six British engineers were found guilty. Thornton was sentenced to three years in prison and MacDonald to two years; Monkhouse, Cushny and de Nordwall were ordered to leave the country within a week. Only Gregory was acquitted for lack of evidence.

22 April. I have just destroyed all my carbon copies of this diary. I thought it just possible that the trial might lead to a breach of relations and I didn't want to have too many confidential papers to destroy in a short time.

The OGPU threaten to send Miss Daunt to prison unless she provides incriminating evidence about the Relief Association.

Yesterday I saw Lie. Speaking as an engineer, he says that the men who claimed to have committed sabotage at Zlatousk on MacDonald's orders could not possibly have done what they claim to have done. Tearle says that the people at the various works are all smiles, and talk as though all was well again, and the imprisonment of Thornton and MacDonald a matter of no moment. A high-up official in the OGPU said to an Englishwoman who has been many years in Russia: 'Your country is very powerful. You've won.' Nothing about the guilt or innocence of the accused, but merely an assumption that the whole affair was a trial of strength between the two governments.

Vincent, the Moscow Embassy archivist, wrote to say that his personal view is that MacDonald made his 'confession' to save the families of various Russian friends, and that he will never tell the truth about the matter for the same reason. What a horrible business it all is. Unfortunately the Soviet Union has so many friends in England, some misguided and ignorant and some cynical.

On 18 April *The Times* published a letter from Vladimir Vyacheslavovitch Tchernavin,[4] once a senior scientist at the Petrograd Agronomical Institute and from 1926 to 1930 in charge of the laboratories of the Northern Fisheries Trust at Murmansk, before he was arrested. This ran:

> In *Izvestia* of 24 March 1933 the Chief Prosecutor of USSR, Vyshinsky, said, apropos the arrest in Moscow of the Englishmen employed by the Metropolitan-Vickers Company, that in the USSR accused are not put to torture during an enquiry.
>
> I was in prison in Petersburg in 1930–31, accused of being a 'wrecker'. I affirm

---

[4] Tchernavin described his experiences in *I Speak for the Silent* (Hamish Hamilton, 1935).

☆

that the OGPU inquiry consisted solely in trying to obtain from the prisoners by means of moral and physical torture a confession of crimes they had not committed. In a cell measuring 75 square yards more than a hundred of the accused were kept. The cell was infested with bugs and lice. Food was insufficient, and the diet was such that almost all the prisoners were ill with scurvy. They were kept in these conditions from six months to two or more years awaiting their sentence. The investigating officer wanted me to sign a statement that 'I plead guilty to being a wrecker'. As I refused to do so, I was threatened, by way of 'bringing pressure to bear' upon me: (1) that I would be shot; (2) that my wife would be arrested and my son, a boy of twelve, would be sent to an institution for vagrant children; (3) that my wife would be kept in prison during the whole of the inquiry into my case; (4) that my wife would be sent to penal servitude; (5) that unless I signed the statement within three days I should be shot on the fourth day. Finally I was taken in the night as though to be shot.

In spite of this I did not sign the false statement. Then they did not cross-examine me any more, and sent me without trial to five years' penal servitude at the Solovetsky concentration camp, from where I escaped in August 1932.

26 April. Cave returned yesterday. He and two others were present at the trial every day and took it in turns to listen and take notes. Strang managed to see MacDonald and ask him without being overheard whether he was really guilty. MacDonald replied: 'Of course I am not guilty, but there is a reason for everything.' MacDonald had seen no one but OGPU men since his imprisonment and did not know what the other engineers were going to say, or that HMG were taking an interest in the case, or indeed anything essential. Moreover, he was made to plead first, so that he was already branded as guilty before he heard the others plead 'not guilty'. The second day he pleaded 'not guilty', and began to say he had admitted guilt under pressure, whereupon the presiding judge adjourned the court. The court reassembled after twenty minutes. MacDonald was brought in by the guards looking like death, and answered 'Yes' to every question put to him about his wrecking activities and so on. Cave said it was a dreadful sight. It is generally believed in Moscow that MacDonald had a Russian wife or mistress and that she is the lever by which the confession was extorted.

I have told my Russian teacher that it is impossible to have any more Russian lessons, since she may be arrested and asked to make confessions like those of Thornton's secretary, that she received money from me for spying, and so on. I am sorry, for she is a nice and interesting woman, and if I did not learn much Russian, I learned a lot about Russian literature, plays and so on. When I type this diary I always use worn

☆

carbon paper deliberately so that what I write won't show up on it. One is always liable to leave carbons lying about, and one might be carried off by an office cleaner or someone and shown to the OGPU.

A British captain has just been in. Under the retaliatory orders issued by the Soviet Government he has to pay port dues at six times the usual rates.

30 April. I go to the theatre with Pott quite frequently. It only costs a few pence and we can now get good seats by telephoning the theatre. Perhaps because people have less money. Not only were wages cut heavily in January, but salaries are always in arrears. Many people have not yet received their March pay. We took Tearle to see *Swan Lake*. Dudinskaya danced the swan and Ulanova the wicked rival.

The man who runs the hand-puppets, Eugene Demenni, is one of the few people here I should like to see more of if conditions were different. He is a pleasant, quiet man, very enthusiastic about his work, and he showed us all his figures and costumes. One of the plays they do is *Little Black Sambo*. Demenni worked the tiger for our benefit. It had dreadful claws made out of quill toothpicks. It was one of the worst days of the trial, but nothing could have been less offensive than Demenni's manner, and afterwards he returned to us by a roundabout channel the money we had paid for our tickets—as the only way in which he could show his sympathy.

7 May. The police superintendent of the quarter in which Tearle lives told him that they had just turned 15,000 homeless children out of Leningrad. Some of them they sent as far as 1000 *versts* (over 600 miles) away, but some of these had managed to get back. I have noticed many such children about this winter. Their reappearance is probably due to the starvation in the villages and to the eviction of so many people from the big towns.

The captains of two British ships chartered by the Soviet Government before the embargo came in to see me. The moment they docked emissaries came on board and tried to persuade all the crew to go to the Seamen's Club to protest against the British embargo. Two ordinary seamen and the Arab firemen went off with them in the hope of getting a free meal.

Pott was out walking the other day and suddenly a girl darted across the road and seized his arm. It was one of the ballet girls who used to be allowed to meet foreign diplomats in Moscow. She is married now and lives in Leningrad. She seemed very pleased to see him, and said she

★

would ring him up and arrange a meeting. Pott said she had better not in view of the recent arrest of the British engineers. The girl seemed to have hardly heard of the case and to attach little importance to it. Two or three days ago he met her as she was coming out of a shop and she gave him a startled glance and fled. To consort with a foreign consul at such a moment would be to invite exile or a bullet.

A lot of classical plays are on in the Leningrad theatres. At the moment four by Ostrovsky are being played. We saw one magnificently acted and are to see another tomorrow.

11 May. I shall begin to believe in Russia as a paradise when Russian citizens are allowed to leave the country when they like, and when it is not the ambition of every girl to marry a foreigner. A Russian girl came in today who has just married an American engineer and is delighted at the prospect of leaving the country.

We shall soon be a very small band. The Canadian, Thomas, is going for good. He says it is just possible that a few of their men will get another contract, but he is not hopeful. Tearle is going home 'for consultations', but before going he is to give notice to all the Soviet employees of Metro-Vickers in Leningrad. This is not surprising, as there has been no contract for the Leningrad part of the concern for a year, and the office was about to be shut up when the engineers were arrested.

13 May. Miss Daunt is growing vegetables in the garden of the house that Lady Muriel insisted on having built. She got seed-potatoes without much difficulty but to get onion-seed proved much harder. But the authorities always help her (because the Relief Association spend something like £1500 of good English money here every year), and Smolny, which is in Leningrad what the Kremlin is in Moscow, i.e. the centre of the Communist Party and the mainspring of everything, gave orders that she was to have what she needed. One of the managers of Torgsin went with her to the only place in Leningrad where onion-seed could be got. A long queue of people were waiting there, and they made a fuss when the guide pushed Miss Daunt towards the head of the queue. The director said that he had no seed, and that there was none in the Soviet Union except at Penza, hundreds of miles away, but when he heard the orders of Smolny he said he would do what he could. She asked for enough seed to raise 600 kilos of onions, i.e. enough to carry sixty old women through the winter.[5]

[5] Some seeds were evidently acquired, because Una Pope-Hennessy recorded: 'The really

Before Tearle goes home to report to his company, he went to see the director of the Boiler-Turbine Trust—the organisation with whom Metro-Vickers have their contract. The latter was much annoyed at the request of Ball, the engineer at Cheliabinsk, to be allowed to go home at once. This was the man they thought they could count on and they were going to put his name in for the order of Lenin, but when the firm sent round a circular saying that they did not want any man to stay in Russia against his will, he asked to leave at once. This is a blow to the comrades. They refuse to believe that the man wants to go because he does not want to work with Russians after their treatment of his colleagues. They claim that his decision is the result of a political move by the company, clearly working hand in glove with the British Government. Evidently the Trust are much worried about their turbines. The first ones were made in England and erected by Metro-Vickers, and they run well. The plan was that later some of the parts were to be made in Russia, and it is this which has led to the present difficulties. The designs were provided by Metro-Vickers, but the comrades as usual tried to improve on the foreign design and the thing won't work. The director admitted that they would probably have to remake the parts and follow the Metro-Vickers design. And then they imprison the Metro-Vickers men!

The press has been making a great shout about a 'Soviet' turbine which is being erected at Nevdubstroy, a power-station a few miles from Leningrad which is to burn local peat. They claim that only 5% of the parts were foreign-made (Tearle says 30%), and that it is a great success. The director made it clear yesterday that the machine was 'shaking itself to pieces'. MacDonald worked there for a while, and the director said he was wondering whether MacDonald could not be prosecuted for the failure! Rather than admit they can't yet make or erect a turbine, the Soviet Government prefer to allow the unfortunate MacDonald to be blamed. But this kind of thing goes on in all their industries. Only yesterday I read that one half of the turbine blades made by one of the works in Leningrad had to be scrapped.

Tearle heard at his works that this year the workers are expected to subscribe 1½ months' pay—on top of the recent cuts. The other night at the theatre, the names of the actors who had subscribed more than a month's pay were read out, and outside the theatre there was a huge sign saying that the theatre as a whole had subscribed 130% to the loan. Miss Daunt was in Torgsin when one of the staff was protesting very loudly

---

remarkable vegetable garden is producing carrots, beetroot, tomatoes, lettuces, beans, peas and potatoes.' (*The Closed and Forbidden City*. Hutchinson, 1938.)

☆

against being made to contribute 150 roubles. She said her salary had been reduced to 60 roubles a month and she could not possibly find the money. The manager put her down, still protesting, for 100 roubles— over 1½ months' pay.

Three of the chief engineers from the Boiler-Turbine Trust entertained Tearle to a farewell dinner (starting at 11 p.m. and going on until 3 a.m.) They gave him messages for his firm to say that they expected Metro-Vickers to send out men at their own expense to put right the Russian-made turbines that won't work! Extraordinary after the way the firm's engineers have been treated.

I hear stories of misery every day—families ordered to leave in ten days with nowhere to go. One asked the OGPU what they were to do: throw ourselves in the river? The man from the OGPU replied: 'That is your business.' Yet some English workman who came here on a May Day delegation and was put up to speak on the wireless, assured his hearers that this was the only country where the government was trying to put the Sermon on the Mount into practice. This sort of thing makes one despair. How the Kremlin must laugh.

18 May. It seems our domestic budget does not allow enough for ill-health.[6] We must go through the expenditure of the last three months to see whether the allowance has been exceeded on any head. It is fortunate too that I am at a cheap post. If the FO propose to move me I shall ask to stay where I am. There is no other post where I could live so cheaply. My salary has still to increase by a nominal £200 a year (actually about £150). One of the first things we must do is to join the Mutual Medical Insurance Society so that we can cover all or nearly all our medical expenditure by a lump sum payment every year. I hope we can scrape along until I come home in October. It seems very extravagant, when our finances are in this state, for me to have spent £4 on a carpet and a rug. It is only because my dining-room looked very bare and wretched, and because, with 'black' roubles at my disposal, they were so cheap. The carpet is not of first-class quality, but it is pleasing in colour, and so big that when the dining-table is extended for fourteen people they can still all be on the carpet.

I see an English gossip-writer praises Strang at the expense of the Ambassador. It is damaging in that it tends to support the unfounded contention of the Bolsheviks that the trouble about the engineers was

---

[6] RWB had just received a letter from home saying that two of his children had had to have operations for a mastoid infection.

☆

largely due to Sir E. Ovey's mishandling of the situation. Strang is a much better man than Ovey, but then he is a much better man than nine out of ten diplomats. The difficulty is that the equivalent of our foreign secretary, Litvinov, has no influence. It is Stalin and his gang who run the country, and Ovey used to try to get to them through men who he hoped had influence with them. Where Ovey was wrong was that his vanity led him to boast of his cleverness. Vanity is a dangerous quality to have in any oriental or semi-oriental country. I find this country very oriental in many ways. Their behaviour to Tearle suggests the East, where two men will call each other filthy names and then sit down and have curry and rice together five minutes later.

20 May. The Rapps are here for the weekend. I took them to the Hermitage. The big Tiepolo has gone from the Italian room—'The Wedding Feast of Cleopatra.'[7] In its place there is a very dull picture and not even a notice such as we saw in the blank spaces left by two Bouchers and one Claude Lorraine, to say that the picture had been removed for restoration. I think it has probably been sold. Sir Robert Witt would have liked to buy it for the National Gallery, but he thought the price (I think £70,000) was too high. In any case he had no authority to negotiate at the time.

I am sorry to hear that Muggeridge has left Moscow and that the *Manchester Guardian* has gone back to Chamberlin.

Rapp told me he saw an American who, after working for some time on the *Moscow News,* went down to the Kuban (the place in the North Caucasus which Muggeridge describes, where there is an agricultural commune run by Americans), and who told him that the Plan has to be carried out literally, however absurd its application may be. For instance, you have to have sown a given area by a given date, and if half the ground is a sea of mud you must still put the seed in.

We thought we ought to go and see a play about life in England: *Joy Street.* We came out at half-time finding it more than our digestions could stand. The first two scenes were in a London slum. There was a strike with the trade union leader 'betraying the workers', the police arrested the strike committee, a boy delivering washing is knocked down by a motor-car and discharged for soiling the washing, which included

[7] Sir Robert Witt was unable to negotiate a price acceptable to the National Gallery, and the Tiepolo went to Melbourne. Among the fifty or so other pictures sold at that time were Jan Van Eyck's 'Annunciation', Botticelli's 'Adoration of the Magi', and Rembrandt's 'Polish Nobleman' and 'Portrait of an Old Man'. (See Geraldine Norman, *The Hermitage*: Pimlico, 1999.)

★

Lady Salisbury's lace knickers. A girl is raped. There is much hypocritical
church-going. Bailiffs evict the washerwoman for being behind with the
rent . . . . We had had enough. The cloakroom attendant asked why we
were leaving. 'England isn't like that.' 'Ah,' he said, 'I know a little too.'

23 May. A few days ago Mrs Kulagin was called up by the Public
Prosecutor and told that she might send her husband some butter and
tea. This reassured her as to his safety, at least. Soon after she was again
called up and told that he was to be exiled for ten years to a place even
farther north than Solovki, and that she could see him the next day to
say goodbye and to give him some clean clothes and other necessaries to
take with him into exile. She went to the OGPU next day, with her
fifteen-year-old daughter. There were crowds of other people to see the
last of their relatives. One of the soldiers who were keeping them back
said: 'What are you pushing for? Do you think your man is the only
one? Wait till you see how many are going north tomorrow.' (The Public
Prosecutor had said something of the same kind to Mrs Kulagin.) She
picked out one of the soldiers who seemed a little more human than the
others and asked him about her husband. The man asked whether he
was category one, two or three, and she said she had been told one, and
he said: 'Then he is downstairs in the cellars.'

At last Mrs Kulagin and her daughter were taken in and Kulagin was
brought to them. He had a beard to his waist and nails an inch long, and
his face was a strange grey colour. She gave him the clean clothes and
took away the dirty ones, which she afterwards found crawling with lice.
He was not allowed to speak of the 'trial' or of his alleged offence. When
he said 'I am innocent,' the OGPU man stopped him at once. He
managed to make her understand two words: 'Torgsin—Pathephone',
which his wife understood as meaning that someone in Torgsin had
given information against him, and that he had been convicted for being
in possession of a small gramophone which Lady Muriel lent him. I
don't think she brought it out for him: he admired it, and as he had been
so helpful about the DBSs she lent it to him, though I don't suppose that
she would have asked for it back. The visit lasted half an hour. The
OGPU man let Kulagin kiss his daughter, but dragged him away before
he could say goodbye to his wife. He was to leave from the Moscow
station next day, and his wife stayed there from 3.00 in the afternoon
until 2.00 in the night in the hope of getting another glimpse of him.
Every few minutes an OGPU van like a Black Maria would drive up and
back up against a goods truck, the men inside would be hurriedly
transferred and the truck sealed up. Many trains were sent off and the

vans were still arriving at 2 a.m. It was very difficult to see the prisoners, and Mrs Kulagin's friend at last dragged her away. At the last moment it was stated that Kulagin was only to be sent to Solovki after all. Only!

Mrs Kulagin has been to a great friend of her husband's who is commandant of aviation here, and he advises her to do nothing at all at present, but to wait for several months and then go to Moscow and see what can be done. He tells her that Kulagin has been condemned by the OGPU collegium here (a triumvirate of which the president is known by the nickname 'the Bear'), and that it is useless to appeal to the OGPU chiefs in Moscow who are nominally superior to them, because in such cases they shoot the prisoner at once so that Moscow shall not interfere. The person to appeal to, he says, is Kalinin, a former peasant, who is nominal Head of the State as President of the All Union Central Executive Committee.

It is encouraging to hear from Rapp that the truth about MacDonald may yet come out. What happened at the trial in the interval when the judge suddenly suspended the sitting after MacDonald retracted his confession was that the OGPU threatened to shoot his old housekeeper if he did not maintain his confession. MacDonald said that they had not even kept their word to him, for the old woman was still in prison. So we hope that as soon as MacDonald gets out of the country—even if he has to serve the full two years—he will reveal the truth whatever the fate of the housekeeper and her two sons.

It is very unfortunate that out of the six accused four failed to defend their innocence as strongly as they could have done. Thornton was apparently bound by the fear that his relations with his woman secretary Kutuzova would reach the ears of his wife and be broadcast over the world. Monkhouse wanted to conciliate the court because he wished to remain in Russia, partly because he has here a very good position such as he could not get elsewhere with Metro-Vickers or any other firm, and partly because he has built a lovely house here and thinks the life perfect. Moreover the Public Prosecutor flattered him on being a gentleman and on his beautiful Russian. In point of fact none of them knew Russian well enough to afford to plead in Russian: they ought to have all insisted on having the whole of the proceedings in English. For instance, when Monkhouse was being accused of spying he denied it and said that he merely collected information within the limits of 'vozmozhnost'. He meant 'permissibility', or what was right and proper, but he said 'possibility', and so gave the impression that he collected any information he could get hold of. Finally de Nordwall had to think of his Russian wife. So it happened that only two of the six could speak

★

out. Had all six taken a strong stand the case must have collapsed: probably it would never have come into court at all. It is a national tragedy, and our only hope is that MacDonald will speak out when he gets home.

The Rapps had three days here and we went to Tsarskoye Syelo. We were looking at a portrait of the last Empress, painted when she was a young woman. Our guide was my former Russian teacher who whispered to us that a cousin of hers who exclaimed 'How lovely she must have been!' on looking at this same portrait, was imprisoned for three weeks and later exiled for five years.

29 May. I have felt very Monday-ish today after a four-day holiday in Moscow. I had lunch with the Patons one day and with Walton another, dined with the Rapps and went with the Strangs to dine with the Lithuanian Counsellor, Rabinavicius, and his wife—very nice people indeed—and to have tea with the Chamberlins. I saw Cholerton twice: he was in good form, though he misses Muggeridge.

A man of English descent, Wardropper, who lives in the Urals and gets parcels from the Relief Association, wrote in his last letter that two men had just been shot for stealing two *poods* (a *pood* is 36 lbs) of grain. One may have to steal or starve.

Pott and I went to see Miss Daunt and there we met Mrs Kulagin, whom I had never seen. I should think she is a sensible, decent woman—not badly educated either. She said it was a relief to be able to refer to her husband's fate. While the trial was pending she had to go on pretending that he was still in the Bashkir Republic, where he was sent last autumn. However, the strain has told. Not long after we left she fainted, and it was nearly an hour before she came round.

The German Agricultural Attaché, Herr Schiller, just back from a tour in the Kuban, describes terrible conditions there and reports stories of cannibalism as there are also from Tiflis, Samarkand and the Ukraine.

Two decent-looking Soviet youths came to the Consulate—a most unusual occurrence. They said they were carpenters, attending classes at a workers' college in the evenings. They whispered that they wanted to enquire what prospects they had of acquiring British nationality and being allowed to leave the USSR. Conditions and future outlook were so depressing that all they thought of was to escape—nothing to live for, no scope for initiative. We had to send the youths away, disappointed at the thought that neither we nor any other foreign country could remove them from Soviet tutelage, but at the same time rather thrilled to think that they had done so daring a thing as to visit a consulate, and a British consulate, on such an errand and at such a time.

There are still a few misguided Canadians and Americans coming to work in Karelia—mostly of Russian origin. A recent German tourist boat brought in 107 of them with mountains of trunks, bicycles, gramophones, all addressed to Petrozavodsk (in Karelia). They had all been unwilling to believe what they heard about the Soviet Union and some had even taken Soviet nationality.

31 May. It is good news that the insurance company have paid £46 in respect of the mastoid operation etc. If I had been able to foresee the extra expenditure I could have cut down the order for stores which I sent home about two months ago. But it is more economical to get stores in large quantities, and moreover it seemed likely that our privileges would be cut down. I shall have to get an overdraft at the end of the month, but we ought to be straight again in a month or two.

2 June. Dr Bell has been in. According to him the typhus epidemic was nearly mastered, and two of the four hospitals restored to their normal use, when the advent of spring brought a recrudescence of the trouble. He says typhus is raging all over European Russia, and is brought to Leningrad mainly by peasants who come here to buy *bread*. 40% of typhus patients die because their power of resistance has been lowered by underfeeding.

Dr Bell also told me that the British embargo is popular with the people, since there is now some butter in the rouble shops and also, something quite new, sugar to be had at 15 roubles a kilo. The OGPU sweep up anyone they find lying in the streets and take them to OGPU headquarters where they are left in corridors with other people passing backwards and forwards all the time. Dr Bell went to the Public Prosecutor, who is supposed to be able to give orders to the OGPU, and asked him to stop this practice. The PP hesitated and then said: 'That is difficult for me also. Perhaps you can think of another way.'

To our surprise the chauffeur of the Norwegian Consul, Platou, has been arrested. Platou seemed to be on very good terms with all the big men here. The chauffeur has been sentenced to three years in a timber camp and is accused of cursing the collectivisation policy in some village, which is counter-revolutionary activity.

The Moscow Art Theatre are coming here for a few weeks to perform *The Cherry Orchard* and a play which has been banned for some time, *The Days of the Turbin Family*. My Russian teacher asked if I could get her a ticket. Her husband is now librarian of the Russian Museum of

☆

Domestic Art. The work is not uninteresting, but it is miserably paid, and there is always the possibility of being turned out as a former bourgeois. He looks like what he was—an officer in the Guards—and people in trams or in the street sometimes say 'Gentleman!' when they see him, which is dangerous. He has twice been arrested for his looks, once in the Caucasus and once in Moscow, but so far he has escaped. He and his friends are always getting undesirable attention because they forget that it is no longer permissible to kiss ladies' hands or give up seats in trams to women.

Cave is writing to his Finnish lady, Mrs Acker, to come as soon as she can get a visa and they will get married. Poor old Cave! I hope the woman is all right.

5 June. On 2 June a letter came to me from the FO through the Soviet post, marked 'Personal and Confidential'. It was a great surprise to find that the Birthday Honours List was to contain my name in the list of CMGs. I cannot say that I am excited, though I remember that I was excited when I received letters with CIE after my name. I am inclined to think that it is a bad scheme to have the letters of one's decorations put after one's name. If, as I suspect, it is mainly for my reports from here, then it is unjustly bestowed. Many men would have written reports just as valuable. I will keep the letter from Sir John Simon in the envelope marked 'Butter' which I keep in the despatch box.

On the King's birthday we invited to dinner the only English people here besides ourselves—Miss Daunt and Miss Goyer. Miss G shares a room with a girl who is planning to visit the Caucasus this summer and is saving bread for the purpose. This girl dries it until it cannot be dried any more, in which condition she can take this with her as it will last for a long time. There is no bread to be got in the Caucasus. Some people send their bread ahead in parcels, but the post is slow as well as unsafe, so that most prefer to take a sack of bread with them.

Today an Englishman visited the Consulate who has been working for two years as a blacksmith in the Siberian coal-mines beyond the huge industrial centre of Kuznetskstroy, now called Leninsk. He said his quarters were not bad and the food was monotonous but sufficient. Under the new Five-Year Plan much projected work is being abandoned. The decree about discharge for idling or absence is being applied strictly—even to foreigners. Discharged men are told they can go to a collective farm, or to a new industry in e.g. Kamchatka. There is much typhus in Siberia also.

Yesterday (Sunday) Miss Daunt and I went to see how the house that

☆

Lady Muriel had built was getting on. It is in a pleasant quarter and we found a place in the sun sheltered from the piercing wind. It is sad to see the house, which I think is useless. Were it filled with DBSs they would soon start quarrelling and Miss Daunt would have to spend all her time looking after them, whereas now they look after themselves. Also if the old people left their rooms, and the house had to be shut for lack of funds, they would be homeless. Miss Daunt tells me that Lady Muriel has promised to give it to the Soviet Red Cross when she should have no further use for it. At present the house is fulfilling one humanitarian purpose. It constitutes the happiness of the watchman and his wife and 4½-year-old son. The wife works like a horse, even bringing earth a good distance in a sack on her back to improve the sandy soil in the garden. She keeps the house clean and looks after a dog and some rabbits and chickens and is planting vegetables in the garden and seems radiantly happy. Miss Daunt found them in Leningrad. They had a little hut and a bit of land but were squeezed out of it by the continual increase in taxes until at last they were forced to abandon it. The woman put up a nice meal, with drinkable tea and two sorts of cake made by herself. She had even woven the tablecloth herself—but that was before the Revolution. Now she told us, if you keep back any flax for your own use, you get ten years' imprisonment.

Luknitsky, the guide who used to take me and Assersson to factories, came to see me. He has been discharged and this means he has also lost his food-card. He thinks that an article hostile to the treatment of intellectuals here which Robert Byron wrote for the *Magazine of Architecture* was perhaps the last straw. He had been Byron's guide, but he was in bad odour before, and was always expecting to be discharged. He obtained a post of a guide on the strength of his English which is very good indeed, but he was often in trouble for giving tourists honest answers instead of relaying the party line. In December he found the Intourist guides were nearly starving. They had a meeting at which the assistant manager made a report full of figures of the usual kind, and Luknitsky was rash enough to describe the figures as unreal. Now the poor fellow is without a job. One of the worst things is that you cannot relieve your mind by talking to others. He is only twenty-five. I felt his fate could best be described in Kipps' words: 'Crawling up a drainpipe till you die.' I lent him some roubles to carry him on for a while and I will write to Byron who had the highest admiration for him. He may help.

Our twenty-six cases of stores have arrived. They contain among other things about a hundredweight of dried fruit, which we shall be

★

glad to see. It is dark and cold, but I must go for my usual walk before dinner.

9 June. Lovely summer weather at last. On days like this I should like a car so as to be able to get out into the country in the evening. The trams are impossibly overcrowded—not to mention the danger of picking up a typhus louse.

18 June. The Soviet Foreign Commissar has announced that there is no crisis in Soviet Russia and that no amount of foreign trade can disturb wages or prices here. It depends what one calls a crisis, but the measures taken during the last six or eight months might be considered in some countries as suggesting a crisis. And a country is usually considered hard up when it sells pictures from its public galleries. Our barber this morning could hardly speak for indignation about Litvinov's speech, which he had read in the Soviet press. He said: 'To think that there is no free newspaper in the country, where a man could write and say: "This is a base, bold-faced lie. You have lowered our wages by 40% and increased the prices of everything by 20% or 30%." But many people abroad will know no better than to accept Litvinov's lies.'

From a report to HM Ambassador in Moscow, 19 June. During the period 5 December–12 June several important measures have been effected by the Soviet Government: the passport system has been reintroduced, unemployment has been resumed, and wages have been reduced by about 30%. Yet so good is Soviet discipline that there is little outward sign of these measures. All statements that 'it can't last much longer' have to be heavily discounted, and in addition there is the incredible docility of the Russian character. Wherever one penetrates below the surface of Soviet life one finds that not even young people are always taken in by the State propaganda, and that they often guess pretty shrewdly that, however bad the conditions in capitalist countries, they cannot be much worse than they are here at present; but no outspoken comment to this effect is to be expected, still less any demand for change. One accepts this submissiveness as suitable to the descendants of the serfs of seventy years ago, but it seems a kind of *trahison des clercs* when it appears in men of learning. It is easy for us to be severe, forgetting what happens to those who fall out with the Soviet State.

The Metro-Vickers Company have an office in Leningrad, but at the time when the trouble began there was only one engineer here. The place was raided and papers were carried off, but the engineer was not arrested, though he appeared in the list of spies whose names were extorted from Mr Thornton. Possibly the OGPU thought that it would not be easy to get a confession out of this engineer, who is a strong-minded, honest, ready-witted man without any Soviet relatives or connexions. The Boiler-Turbine Trust, with whom Messrs Metro-Vickers work, are now sending messages of undying affection to Mr Richards, the director who a few weeks ago was pilloried at the trial as the chief spy. The ground for their affection is that their turbines are in such a desperate condition that they need help at once. Their ingenuous proposal is that Metro-Vickers should send men out at once to put all the turbines right—without charge. When reminded that Mr Richards had been accused of being a spy, they said that this was a matter of secondary importance—meaning, perhaps, that having served its purpose at the trial, the accusation no longer mattered. The Russian is always showing some fresh trait that one associates with the East. There are many small signs that the ordinary Soviet citizen does not share the official view of the trial, but regards it as staged like other trials of the same kind, and the affair in general as a trial of strength between two governments.

13 June. Miss Daunt and I took our tea into the country. Miss Daunt had brought Mrs Kulagin, who had just received a letter from her husband brought by a man who has just finished his five years' imprisonment. We found a little clearing in a wood—and spent several hours there, coming back just in time for dinner. It was rather hot. We should have chosen a more open place. Also I had provided a quart thermos of tea—not enough for three people.

Mrs K gets little pleasure enough these days. The day before Kulagin left for Solovki Miss Daunt and Mrs K looked for a wooden spoon for him to take with him. There were none in the ordinary shops, but they found some expensive wooden spoons on sale to foreigners in the antiquities department of Torgsin, some of them with the inscription: 'Greetings from Solovki.' Tourists would not know that Solovki was one of the most dreadful penal camps. K is at Kem' at present, though he is expecting to be sent north to Solovki soon. He is hoping that he may be so useful at Kem' that they may keep him. Solovki is on an island, very remote and with a bad climate. He begs his wife to go to Moscow to get his powerful friends to intercede, but she is afraid that if she does the local OGPU will have him shot to get him out of the way.

She hasn't found any work yet; no one is anxious to take on the wife of a political exile. She has fortunately a few good friends of her

☆

husband's who help her (notably the head of the aviation service here) but they have to be careful. The man who brought the letter also brought the news that Rakovsky is at Kem'. This is interesting. Rakovsky, who is a Bulgarian and was, I think, originally a doctor, was at one time dictator in the Ukraine, and later Soviet Ambassador in London. He fell into disgrace for backing Trotsky and disappeared. The authorities said he was serving as a doctor in some provincial post. Mrs K was told that one man is in prison for making a derogatory remark about Stalin. Standing in front of a portrait of Stalin and asked by his companion 'What do you make of that face?' he replied without thinking: 'The face of a sadist.' Miss Cicely Hamilton says Stalin has the face of a *faux bonhomme*. I think that is the best description of him.

Dr Bell says that the authorities have told doctors there is a plague in the Crimea and in the Caucasus but if asked they are to say there isn't! Some people are returning from the famous rest-houses in the Crimea etc. because of the food shortage.

I have borrowed a very interesting life of Fouché, by Stephan Zweig, from the German Vice-Consul. I find it quite easy reading. My German has come back quickly. But my Russian gets worse and worse, for lack of opportunity, and since the trial I don't want even to read Russian— except the newspapers, which I must.

A few days ago I had a visit from Mr Cook, a vinegar merchant from Leeds. He had brought with him a letter from the Mayor of Leeds addressed to the President of the Moscow Soviet, but whom he had been unable to see. I invited him to dinner, but it was painful to talk to such an innocent. He had just seen a factory dining-room, and naturally found it good. Better, he said, than anything in Leeds. Great ass! However, he did admit that it was hard to defend a government that would not allow old people to leave the country, and that it was rather cruel to deprive a man of his food-card when he lost his job. I urged him not to remain tied to the guides at Kiev, but to go about the streets by himself.

It was pleasant to see Miss Cicely Hamilton. She spent many hours wandering about by herself. She found the conditions at Kiev dreadful. In the Ukraine ragged homeless boys came and beat on the train doors and begged, many of them hanging on to the train in hopes of getting to somewhere where there might be food. In Kiev famished beggars lie everywhere in the streets. She had brought what food she could with her and gave away all she could spare. She had a nice young Jewish guide, but who would not say what the long queues were for. Miss Hamilton speaks some Russian and she asked. 'Bread.' Miss Hamilton intends to write an article in *Time and Tide*. I am glad because the general attitude of the paper is on the whole strongly pro-Soviet. Naomi Mitchison writes in it a good deal. I hear at a dinner party she advocated a revolution for England. Bernard Shaw had told her he had invested money abroad for his wife to live on in case there was a revolution. I am sure he has not invested in Soviet Russia.

I would like to devise a quite special punishment for people who induce others to come to Soviet Russia to live. We have two sad cases this week: the Glucksteins and the Andersons. Gluckstein is a tailor's presser from Glasgow, I should think a communist. His wife is a German Jewess who wants desperately to get back to England with her three children, but as they are all Soviet citizens they will not easily get permission to leave. There are endless difficulties about a room, about food-cards and everything else. While I am sorry for them, I am much more sorry for the other family in distress, the Andersons, who appealed for help yesterday.

Anderson, in spite of his name, was born in Latvia. He is a bosun and came to Russia in hopes of finding work after hearing enthusiastic tales from British communists. A brother in Novorossisk encouraged him to come, but he finds now that his brother is in as desperate a state as himself. He arrived with £3 in his pockets, expecting to be welcomed with open arms. His money is gone and he cannot get work. Yesterday he brought his family round for help. The wife is a decent woman. She cannot understand that she ceased to be British when she married.

We are all very sorry for the children who are delightful. The father has seen enough to realise that pretty girls of thirteen are in danger in Leningrad. Miss Daunt says bitterly that there are no girls in Leningrad. She exaggerates, but she has cause to speak bitterly, as she lives down a street where there is a sailors' club and she sees girls, who she thinks cannot be more than twelve, accosting sailors there. There is a law about the age of consent (sixteen, I think it is) but I don't know that much fuss is made about violations of this law. Perhaps the normal consequences of intercourse with young girls follow less frequently here—there is always abortion. Miss Hamilton found that the rule is that the same woman cannot have two operations for abortion within six months.

Miss Daunt has come to the rescue of the Andersons, paid the hotel bill and rescued the man's ring which the manager had taken charge of, and sent them all out to the villa for a few days, while the man looks for work. Seamen are needed, and a man good enough to be bosun on a British ship is good enough to be a first mate on a Soviet vessel.

These cases are the most painful that we have to deal with. I don't

☆

know how the Andersons will live. They are foolish enough to praise England and run down Russia. The more they do that the less anxious the Soviet authorities will be to let them go. We notice that in this respect Jews are apparently favoured. The Hrutzky family were eventually allowed to go to Australia, and today a Jewish woman came in who had received permission to go and live with her son in England. I suppose the authorities can usually count on the Jews being pro-Soviet. So perhaps the Glucksteins will get away.

My German colleague, who lived in Vladivostok for some years, says the Soviet authorities established an agricultural colony for Jews near Blagoveschensk, to be a counter-attraction to Palestine, and got Jews from Lithuania and Latvia to go there. It was not a great success.

20 June. There was a lovely picture of Oxford in *The Times* a few days ago. I have pinned it up on the wall of my office. My affection is due partly to the glamour which clung to the names of Oxford and Cambridge in the days when I never expected to see either of them.

Anderson, the seaman who came in earlier, has got a job running a deep-sea tug. His pay is 95 roubles a month: not enough to keep himself let alone his family, but all the seamen get coupons which enable them to buy at Torgsin. He has found many people dying of hunger in the streets.

What with the poor and insufficient food Miss Goyer is having difficulty in shaking off her attack of influenza. She feels she ought to have a few weeks in England before her planned trip to the Caucasus, with the fatigues and privations which that will involve. She must have lost two or three stone in weight since she arrived.

Last night we had Lie and an Englishman named Grover to dinner. Grover represents the great steel firm Beardmore's. In 1931–32 he spent six or eight months working as an engineer on the Grozny oil-fields. He and an American were supposed to act as general advisers to the whole field, but no one took any notice of what they advised. He told us that there are regular statistics showing that such and such an enterprise or factory has 'fulfilled the Plan by 120%' or whatever it is. Any time lost through lack of equipment (a common occurrence) was not counted: the percentage was only reckoned for the time the men were able to work. This might be fair to the men, but the figures were misleading as to the total output.

We were speaking of Kirov,[8] a brutal-looking demagogue who is the

---

[8] S.M. Kirov (1886–1934) rose to be a full member of the Leningrad politburo and

☆

Stalin of Leningrad, and Lie asked us whether we had seen the cap he always wore. It is a cheap cap which Lie bought in Finland and gave him. Lie is on such good terms with many people in high places that he must give them things more valuable than caps. I cannot believe that the help and protection he gets are given for nothing, and I should not be surprised to learn that some of the biggest men in Moscow had money put away in banks in Europe through the assistance of Lie. This is bribery of course, but it is probable that Lie could not do his work without it. Lie said that a few days before he had accidentally knocked down a boy in the street. Taking him to hospital he learnt that he was a waif from the Ukraine whose father was dead and whose mother had brought him to Leningrad and left him in the street, which is where he lived. Lie gave him 20 roubles and left him at the hospital. But next day, when he went to enquire, he was told the boy had run away. A policeman came to see Lie to make a report on the accident. Lie gave him 50 roubles and 25 cigarettes, and the man tore up the report and went away. A man must eat.

The barber came to cut our hair this morning, but at 10.30 Cave was still not equal to seeing him. He likes to have breakfast at noon on Sunday and to get up for tea. He says he won't be able to indulge this habit when he is married. His fiancée's habits are to get up early, take walks and cold baths, and she hates anyone smoking. She is expected sometime this week. Cave is as happy as a schoolboy and behaves as though he was one. Miss Daunt has lent him some furniture including an immense picture of David playing before Saul. He has two rooms, now that the Todds have gone, and he walks from one to the other feeling, apparently, like a new peer who has just inherited his father's acres.

22 June. Cave's fiancée is expected at 1 o'clock today. If the formalities are completed the marriage will take place tomorrow. Meanwhile he is a cat on hot bricks, fearful that something will happen to prevent the marriage. We will have a small evening reception after the wedding for the people Cave knows well. We shall have to ask Lie without his wife, as Mrs Lie is still telling the world that the future Mrs Cave was a prostitute.

Pavlova's mother is in the office, signing a power of attorney. She

---

effectively Communist Party leader in that city. He was assassinated on 1 December 1934.

☆

inherited property in England from her daughter, and a year ago she tried to get permission to go there, which was refused. The Soviet Government want the poor old thing to sell the property, bring the money over here—and give up most of it to the Government. I shall report the matter to the FO, but I don't know what they can do.

I wrote to Byron about his poor interpreter, Luknitsky. He is much distressed. I thought perhaps Byron was well off and could do something considerable to help him, but he sends a pound, regretting that he can't send more. He says he is overdrawn £500 and earns about £300 a year. I don't know how he manages to overdraw to that extent.

I invited Miss Daunt to come to *The Cherry Orchard* as she is going on leave next month. She has twice disappointed us. We hoped this time it would be all right. However at the end of the first act she felt ill and had to go home. The car had gone away to take Cave about ten yards to the dentist's, so I had to bring Miss Daunt to the Consulate which is easier to get at than her house. Even that took two trams and a lot of standing. Having deposited her here and given her brandy I went to her house, to find that the chauffeur had chosen that moment to put a new leaf in a spring. It was 11.15 before the car came for her, and by that time the play would be over, so I did not go back for the last act as I had thought of doing. However, I had seen *The Cherry Orchard* before, and tonight I am going to see the same cast in a play about the Civil War in the Ukraine.

Typhus is still rampant. Dr Bell found two cases on one of the boats coming in, but most cases come in by train from the south. The doctors propose that trains coming from Moscow should be stopped outside Leningrad and passengers examined and their clothing disinfected. This has not been adopted since it would then become known that there is typhus in the country.

24 June. I did not send Walker a present at the time of his marriage but today I saw a two-volume book of Russian tales with lots of old woodcuts and it seemed appropriate. I sent it with a letter in which I said I had been wondering whether I should not have bought something more expensive to win his powerful favour, or less expensive, to avoid the suspicion of bribery. But on the whole the cost (about half-a-crown) seemed about right. He reads Russian well and the pictures will amuse him.

Every post has brought a handful of congratulatory letters on the award of the CMG. Today I opened a letter from Sir R. Vansittart, Permanent Under-Secretary and probably next Ambassador to France:

☆

Dear Bullard, I always read your work with such appreciation that I feel I know you well enough to write and tell you how glad I am of the more than merited recognition that has come your way. Your knowledge and your judgement have been of the greatest value to us all, and—if I may say so—you possess the great gift of your own language. Your post has been a hard one, but I hope the knowledge that this is recognised will make it easier for you.

If anyone complimented me on my 'judgement' in an ordinary political post I just shouldn't pay any attention, but in regard to Russia I am neither a diehard nor a communist, and I sympathise with any attempt to better the lot of the poor and to equalise opportunities while continuing to hate the dishonesty and fraud connected with everything the Soviet Government do, and this perhaps enables me to give a better-balanced picture of things here than some men would. But I believe that my reports are liked largely because they are entertaining. Vansittart is himself a stylist, in French as well as in English, and that side of the work might appeal to him. It is scandalous that one should get so much credit for what is after all an excrescence on one's more important work. However . . . .

Mrs Strang tells me in confidence they are to leave Moscow in October, after being there three years. Everyone will be sorry. No one minded Sir Esmond leaving, but the departure of the Strangs is another story. I hope there will be a good counsellor to replace him.

Cave's Mrs Acker is an immense woman, and has to sit on the edge of chairs and sofas so as not to squeeze herself. It is a pity, when Cave is content with so little, that there should be so much of her. She may once have been handsome. She says '*Ja*' and '*Ja?*' and not much else, but she is calm and will be good for Cave's nerves. She hides his cigarettes and won't let him drink.

25 June. One of Miss Daunt's protégés is an Englishman called Clare. He came here about 1908 and taught English at the University for twenty years, but is now paralysed. His Russian wife looks after him, and the Relief Association provide a parcel of groceries every month. He has a son who is a *tekhnik*, i.e. half-way between a mechanic and an engineer, and goes to evening classes in the hope of getting a diploma as an engineer. At first he was told the diploma would be given after two years, then the course was extended to three years, and when the students had completed that they were told to do yet another year. In that this shows that education is being taken more seriously it is a good sign. Mrs Clare admired our office and says that it would not be

★

uncommon to find twenty-five people living in a room half this size (about 30 square metres).

I wonder how English workmen would like to be paid for the first half of the month on the 22nd and for the second half on the 6th of the following month. That is the arrangement here, and even that is only the theory. Usually wages are paid much later.

I had Mrs Diedrichs and Miss Daunt to tea. Mrs Diedrichs is in a very nervous state. She blames it on malnutrition. She apologised to her husband because they had no sugar and he scolded her for mentioning such a thing when things in the Ukraine, where he came from, were much worse. She is not fishing for sympathy because she won't accept any presents of food for fear of being arrested and searched on her way home.

Dr Bell is due to appear before the dread commission today. He seems not to be afraid—perhaps because he has a British passport. Five cases of typhus were found in a shipbuilding-yard at Izhora, which is under his supervision. In theory he should be punished by the commission for that. He says he proposes to tell them that if they are not satisfied with him they should not punish him but sack him and appoint someone else in his place. I later heard he got a lot of harsh words from the commission but no punishment and he still has his job.

26 June. Yesterday we married Cave off at the registry office. There was a large queue there but we were taken immediately through to the registrar—amid murmurs of the crowd. I felt uncomfortable, but Dr Bell, who was there as a witness, said that those opinions were all very well in England but you couldn't act like that here. We came back to lunch in my rooms and drank the Caves' health in champagne. I hope Cave will be happy, but I also hope that his wife will not grow any bigger—she is considerably stouter since she was here in the winter.

Pfleiderer, German Vice-Consul, is being transferred to Berlin. I congratulated him, but he is not happy. He said: 'I don't know my own people.' He is a Württemberger and dislikes Prussians. What is happening in Germany now is Prussianism carried to its logical extreme. I said it was a good sign that Herr Hitler had not interfered with the diplomatic service. But Pfleiderer said 'Not *yet.*' I'm sorry for him. He is an honest, cultured, reasonable young man.

On the 22nd I took Miss Goyer and Mrs Diedrichs to see *Dnyi Turbiny* (*The Days of the Turbin Family*), a play that was banned for some years, but has been put on again recently because, it is said, Stalin likes it. It is not a great play, but it is of poignant interest. It is set in the

Ukraine in 1918. Mrs Diedrichs was much moved. I offered to lend her the book on which the play is based, but when she saw it was published in Paris she did not dare to borrow it.

The prices at which Torgsin sell their goods in the port area to foreign seamen and visitors have always been so low as to be almost reasonable, while the town prices are outrageous. As a concession to the Relief Association, Miss Daunt has been allowed to buy her goods from the town shops at port prices—a valuable concession. She has now been told that in future town prices will be charged. After considering a while she gave the top officials a tremendous lecture: Torgsin had broken its word. The officials were apologetic but said it had been done on orders from the Government. Later they came and told her they were making an appeal and hoped to have good news for her in two days.

A Jewish Russian engineer naturalised in Canada calls every now and then to collect his pension for a slight war disability. He works in the 'Red October' factory, where they were going to make 40,000 motorcycles this year, but recently announced they were going to make a hundred a month for the rest of the year. He was gloomy and said it looked as though production might stop. He doubted they had made more than fifteen machines altogether. Those held responsible for the breakdown had been arrested.

2 July. The Andersons have not yet found a room. They are still in the Relief Association's villa, but they cannot stay there indefinitely.

I mentioned a young Englishman called Wild who is here looking at plywood. A good deal of plywood is still being exported because it was paid for before the embargo came into force. Wild asked me about the possibilities of a Russian girl getting permission to go to England to join her sister, and would it be different if she were married to an Englishman. Evidently he was thinking of marrying the girl. I told him she would probably get out eventually, but I warned him of the high proportion of failures in cases where Englishmen married Russian women.

MACDONALD AND THORNTON RELEASED! I have just read this in the Russian newspaper. It is a great triumph for the embargo policy and it shows how dependent on the English market the Soviet Government are. This should help us to get the best possible terms in the commercial treaty which is to be concluded. We shall now wait eagerly to see whether MacDonald speaks out when he gets to England. I hope the censor won't think fit to 'lose' that copy of *The Times*.

A week or two ago Litvinov was telling the *Manchester Guardian* that

☆

the prisoners' plea for mercy would not come before the Central Executive Committee until November, perhaps later, and that the imposition of the embargo prevented his asking them to consider it sooner.

Poor Luknitsky has been given the job of quartermaster on an icebreaker plying between Archangel and the Kara Sea and other places in Siberia. Beggars can't be choosers and Luknitsky was almost a beggar. He had been lent a restaurant card which entitled him to a meal a day but the food was so disgusting sometimes he could not eat it. However if he left it untouched someone else would come up and ask if they could have it. Anyhow, Luknitsky had one good meal before he left, for he plucked up courage to come to dinner with me. He enjoyed his meal, and I sent him away with a thick sweater, some cigarettes and a bottle of lemon crystals (to make the dirty ship's water palatable). I lent him 200 roubles and gave him the rouble equivalent of the £1 which Byron sent him. He was much touched.

As an instance of the red tape which strangles everything here I will record Luknitsky's struggles to retain his room while he is away. His job is only temporary so in principle he has the right to retain it. First he applied to the Zhakht, the committee in charge of accommodation. The Zhakht sent him to the Zhilotdyel, the living accommodation department of the district soviet. The Zhilotdyel told him to produce a certificate from his place of work. This took two days, since someone had to be found to draft the certificate, someone else to type it, two men to sign it and finally one to authorise it with a stamp. This he took to the Zhakht who gave him a further certificate. He then took both to the Zhilotdyel who filed them and gave him another certificate to take back to the Zhakht. At last he was given the certificate he wanted allowing him to keep his room.

4 July. A more interesting weekend than usual. I was at Miss Daunt's on Saturday and Mrs Kulagin came in. She had had another letter from her husband—by secret means. She was not able to tell us much, however, as she did not want anyone but Miss Daunt and myself to know. But she did tell us this: as inducements to 'confess' Kulagin was told that not only his wife but his fifteen-year-old daughter were also in prison, and that he himself would be shot unless he confessed. When he continued to protest his innocence he was starved for five months. He has wretched quarters which let in both wind and rain.

On Sunday Miss Daunt took me in the Relief Association's car to a place near Peterhof where the Russian girl Amelia has a tumbledown

☆

summer *dacha*. The parents made a trip to Sukhum in the Caucasus last summer. One day a local woman asked them if they were Russians. She blazed out at them: 'See what you Russians have brought us to. You don't let us grow even millet to eat. We have to grow tobacco and nothing else, and you take it from us at your own price and give us a little bread.'

Last night when I was making my usual round and was about to turn into the Summer Garden, I nearly fell over a little boy of about four. He was seated at the gate with a battered enamel cup held in the crook of his knee, and he had fallen asleep. I put a rouble into his mug but he didn't wake. I would have put in some notes but I was afraid someone would steal them. The boy is probably a waif. Last Sunday we passed two large institutions which are full of them. Most are supposed to be from the bands which were roaming about some years ago.

8 July. I have noticed people begging at the door of the Nevsky bread-shop in the last few weeks. This shop now has a notice inside saying that if anyone gives bread to a beggar both he and the beggar will be taken to the police-station. One shopper was wearing a hat. A few years ago it would have been considered rather bourgeois to wear any hat at all. *Some* women are wearing black underclothing.

An American came in having been working as an expert in animal husbandry in Voronezh for three years. His farm had 40,000 pigs and he had been able to reduce the death rate from 65% to 18%. He told me that general conditions in that part were pretty bad. He had seen whole families die of starvation. He spoke of cannibalism as not uncommon.

Miss Daunt invited me and Mrs Kulagin to go with her and Mrs Hay, one of her helpers, to visit Amelia and her family. I took two tins of bully beef and some butter. It was a wonderful day, very bright and clear but not hot. Mrs Kulagin has found a job. She told us the rest of the news in her husband's letter. She only saw him once, for the final interview, and then he was not allowed to speak of his arrest or his imprisonment or trial, or the charges against him. He never went on the second mission to collect grain after all. He received his orders and all arrangements were made for him—tickets bought, orders issued and so on, and his wife saw him off at the station. Forty minutes later he was arrested on the train, and brought straight back to Leningrad and put in the OGPU prison. Two or three days after his departure his wife received a telegram from Moscow, purporting to come from him, sending love to her and their daughter, and saying he was being sent to a different place. It is clear this was sent by the OGPU to cover his tracks.

☆

When no more news came Mrs Kulagin got very anxious, and went to the Party Committee, the OGPU and other places of influence—but it was two months before they told her he was in prison. His alleged crime was that he had been 'unethical as a communist in his relations with foreigners'. It seems that he was accused of having said in the presence of foreigners that when he was down collecting grain in the North Caucasus they had 'mass shootings' of communists. The Russian-speaking Englishman who was here today noticed in the hall of an institution he was visiting a sealed box with a notice saying that it was for communications about purging the Party, i.e. it was inviting spies and tale-bearers to report on their colleagues.

Mrs Diedrichs has had her food-book taken away. It has been decided that the Writers' Union she belongs to does not entitle its members to food-books.

10 July. Yesterday we went to Strelny to have a sight of the sea and to see Amelia and her family, but it wasn't a very successful day. Mrs Kulagin was feeling particularly downcast as she finds it exhausting pretending to all the others where she works that she has nothing on her mind, whereas Amelia talked all the time about nothing very much. However the air was fresher out there (it is stifling in town these days).

Mrs Kulagin told us that at her workplace they had recently been celebrating the anniversary of the constitution of the USSR. They had to listen to speeches from 5.00 to 8.00 after a long day's work. It was the usual slogans of the day, the chief of which is that by the end of the second Five-Year Plan the classless State must be established and all bourgeois elements eliminated. The meeting ended with a collection for a new aeroplane. The names of all those present were called out and the amounts they should give suggested. Mrs K got off with 10 roubles, but she has promised 300 roubles, one and a half month's pay. In view of her connection with a man who is in exile—a Party man too—she felt it necessary to win the approval of the political chiefs there. Her subscription to the loan will be put on the red board (slackers, people who refuse to subscribe as much as is expected etc. are posted on the black board). This should establish her position. The director has announced that Kulagin is a 'responsible worker' who has been sent on a *kommandirovka*, i.e. a mission, and that will keep speculation quiet for a while.

12 July. When Stalin's wife died last year it was believed she committed suicide, though no one could say why. The story that seems to be

☆

generally credited now is that Mrs Stalin was against the violent oppression of the country areas. At a meeting when Stalin railed against the opposition, someone sneered that he had opposition in his own home. After the meeting Stalin wrote out an order for his wife's arrest to show that there was no favouritism, and when the order was taken to his wife she managed to seize a pistol and shoot herself.

The *Telegraph* reports that Skrybin, a member of the Executive Committee of the Soviet Union, has shot himself. The official notice criticises him for committing many bourgeois nationalist mistakes and having shown pusillanimity in killing himself. Skrybin was a well-educated Ukrainian and well-thought-of there. It is believed that he rebelled against Moscow's policy which turned the great grain-growing areas into a land of starvation, and he may well have wanted to obtain for the Ukraine some form of autonomy which would prevent such exploitation in future. But he is dead—by his own hand or by that of the OGPU—and it is expected that the control of Moscow will only be tightened as a result. The nominal freedom of the component parts of the Soviet Union means nothing at all.

Miss Daunt meets many Soviet officials, many of them OGPU men. They are all very polite these days, and are expressing their satisfaction at the conclusion of the Metro-Vickers dispute. I think that the embargo hit them very hard. Miss Daunt makes no secret of her opinions, though she keeps them to herself unless challenged, but she deals these people some hard blows and they respect her—more than Mr Litvinov respected Sir E. Ovey, who at first was rather disgustingly pro-Soviet.

15 July. Freshfield, the British railway-guard, has developed tuberculosis and Miss Daunt arranged for him to spend a few months on a State farm just outside Leningrad. We went out to see him today. He is much better and very happy. He has made friends with the head of the office whom he helps with his accounts, and with the cook, who sees that he gets the best of whatever is going. The cook really is a cook, having been for nearly thirty years with the family of Prince Yusupov—one of the two men who killed Rasputin. The cook sent in glasses of milk and some black bread and a dish of macaroni to the dining-room set aside for managerial staff, technical workers and shock-workers. We gave him a box of twenty-five English cigarettes. Freshfield had asked the director beforehand whether we could see over the farm, but the director said that it would not be convenient as there was a slight *proryv* (i.e. a hitch in the plan). Their cabbages for instance, had failed for lack of early rain. That wasn't the fault of the farm, but it was their fault that during a

☆

heavy storm the workers forgot to open the rabbit-shed and fifty does got very wet and swelled up and died.

Poor Anderson has just had a haemorrhage which suggests tuberculosis. He looked strong enough when he arrived a month ago.

I see the lovely Tiepolo which I missed from the Hermitage, and which I found had been sold to Melbourne, is on show at South Kensington for a few weeks.

Lie tells me that three men were shot here recently for 'speculation'. They bought some silver spoons and sold them to Torgsin. With the proceeds they bought food at Torgsin and then sold the Torgsin food on the open market for more than they had originally paid for the spoons. This is an offence punishable with imprisonment under the criminal code, but then the OGPU are not obliged to take the criminal code into consideration.

Miss Daunt and I spent the afternoon in the country. The wife of the watchman at the Relief Association's villa has been given money to have a dress made for her. Her excitement is worth seeing. It seems she has never had a new dress in her life.

Two Americans came to dinner. Mrs Tweed had earlier been an enthusiastic supporter of the Soviet Government. She has been shown barrack-like tenements as though they were the last word in domestic architecture and visited a collective farm with fields full of weeds. She was amazed that so many prominent Americans were communists and pro-Russian—among them Elmer Rice the playwright and Waldo Frank who is I think a banker. Louis Segal spoke at some industrial welfare congress in England the other day and said that in this respect Soviet Russia would in a few years be ahead of the world. He is employed by the Soviet Government in London and does a lot of propaganda for them. I have read subtly pro-Soviet articles by him in the *Manchester Guardian*, with no indication that he was a Soviet employee.

16 July. Today I had a very pleasant day in the country. Professor Waldhauer and his wife invited Miss Daunt and me to visit them at Peterhof where they have rented a small villa. The path to the villas passes a collective farm. I never saw such fields before. They looked as though they had not been cultivated for years. At a distance the fields looked like rough pasture, but when you got near you saw, among the mass of green, lines of stunted vegetables. There are almost no vegetables to be had in Leningrad at present. The co-ops have no potatoes even. It is a pity that when they 'abolished' unemployment the Bolsheviks should also have abolished vegetables. I should like to read again Dr

Dillon's book on Soviet Russia.[9] He was here in 1926 or 1927, just at the end of the New Economic Policy, and from his description of the riches of fruit and vegetables in the Leningrad market you get a vision of a huge Dutch still-life.

I took the Waldhauers two tins of peas, a tin of ham, a pound of coffee and some cigarettes and a loaf of white bread. They had another visitor, a young woman doctor, Miss Brock, who like themselves is a German Russian. We walked to a hill about a mile away where there is a villa in the form of a Greek temple built by Alexander I for his second wife. We were able to go over it. The view was lovely. On the way we passed one of those ridiculous faked ruins such as were built in noblemen's parks in the 18th century. It was quite well faked, with four columns standing and others in various stages of demolition and two or three lying broken on the ground.

The doctor works in a clinic for nervous diseases, though her speciality is brain surgery. The difficulties due to lack of equipment and drugs are enormous. She has to drill each hole in the skull by hand, which seriously lengthens the time taken for the operation. There are no anaesthetics or almost none, and many drugs are lacking. She spoke of cannibalism in the Ukraine as a matter of course. In the old regime you could get anything you wanted by influence (*protektsiye*), but now everything goes *po znakomstvu* (by personal acquaintance).

Professor Waldhauer's watch was lying on the table in front of him. It is a good old watch, gold, and would formerly be described as a hunter, but the two flaps of the case, back and front, were sold to Torgsin to get money for necessaries, and recently Mrs Waldhauer broke the glass and naturally there is no watch-glass in Leningrad that will fit. He has still to get permission to accept the invitation of the Berlin Museum to work there. Waldhauer has dug up a passage in which Lenin said 'We shall never establish socialism unless we master bourgeois culture' and on this he based an article which he thinks did some good.

We returned to Leningrad at 11.00—in time to see a queue of about two hundred men and girls formed up to buy petroleum the next morning.

19 July. Miss Daunt went to fetch Mrs Waldhauer to take her out to the *dacha* in the car. After she had left the neighbours came rushing in to see who had been arrested—the normal explanation of the appearance of a motor-car at the door of a private house.

[9] *Russia Today and Yesterday*: Dent, 1929.

☆

The 'All Union' games here are called 'Spartakiad' after Spartacus who led the slave revolt. The one figure in Roman history that the Soviet citizen learns anything about is Spartacus.

Guinness, an Irishman who was in the other day, told me about two women who had come up from Krasnodar (North Caucasus) to try to buy food and gave a horrifying account of conditions in that area. 'Not a wheel moving in the town of Krasnodar' and cannibalism common. Similar reports have reached me from a British subject named Richter who lives there, and from the German Agricultural Attaché who went there not long ago.

25 July. A pleasant middle-aged Jewess from New York has just been in for a visa for England. She has just spent six weeks travelling in the Middle Volga region with her brother, an engineer. She said what lovely country it was, but she shuddered as she spoke of the famine there, and of the inability of the traveller to do more than relieve for a moment the misery of a few of the people.

MacDonald and Thornton have written an account of their experiences. MacDonald at first denied all accusations. Then he was shown a document somehow wrung from Thornton but never used in court—a list of all the Metro-Vickers men who were supposed to be spies. MacDonald thought: 'Well, if Thornton says we are spies he must have some good reason for it,' so he followed suit. Then a Russian friend of his, Gusyev, reeled off a rigmarole about having received bribes from MacDonald to commit sabotage. Then his old housekeeper was brought in, very dirty and miserable from long residence in prison, and he was told plainly that unless he 'confessed' things would go badly with her. So in desperation he made all sorts of admissions, feeling that he was bound to be convicted anyhow, and believing that all the other British engineers were pleading guilty too. When he appeared in court and the others all pleaded not guilty, he also said he was not guilty, and after some exchange of questions and answers with the Public Prosecutor, the court adjourned.

All our people noticed the great change in MacDonald when he was brought back by the OGPU twenty minutes later. He again pleaded guilty. I do hope this will be published, for even some reasonable people in England feel that there must have been something in the accusations, while the pro-Soviet people, and men like Stafford Cripps take the trial at its face value.[10]

---

[10] Stafford Cripps (1889–1952), Labour politician and nephew of Sidney Webb, was to serve as British ambassador to Moscow between 1940 and 1942.

☆

A Canadian history professor from Manitoba telephoned me on Sunday. On the way from Moscow he had had his suitcase stolen on the train. He was travelling 'hard', i.e. in a wooden coach with four sleeping-berths in each compartment, the compartments having no doors. He had placed his coat in his suitcase and tied the end of the sheet to the handle of the suitcase, but he woke to find the suitcase gone. I lent him a sports coat and he will post it to Oxford when he gets to London. Professor Lower had been to see Chamberlin and met a prominent communist there—a Bulgarian Jew—who raved against Muggeridge for his anti-Soviet articles. So far as I know, Muggeridge only said what everyone knows—that the Kuban and the Ukraine were starving, and that no foreign journalist can tell the truth about the Soviet Union if he wishes to remain in it. About a month ago I sent in one of my miscellaneous reports. It was rather longer than usual, partly because it was six months since I had sent the last. A few days ago I received the following letter from Oliphant, one of the two assistant under-secretaries of state. He says:

> I have for once spent a pleasant time this morning, reading your review of the situation at Leningrad for the last six months. When I say pleasant, I do not mean that it makes cheerful reading, but it really is very nicely done indeed, and like your previous one, I have marked it to go to the King, the Cabinet and the Dominions. And this last fact is my only excuse for writing this letter to you about your report. It is a trifle long.
>
> When I say this I do not mean it in any spirit of carping criticism, and when you wrote it you were of course unaware of the distribution which it would be receiving, but it gives such a clear account of the situation, and various members of the Cabinet were so struck by your last report, that I am sure they would wish to see this second one. And it is only in connection with the pressure of work and the amount of reading that our masters have to do, that I suggest that in your next report it will appeal to them even more if, without leaving out any of the jam, you reduce it a bit.
>
> I hope you keep fit in spite of all the wretched conditions around you.

I have replied that I think there was a good deal of dead wood in the last report—at least it contained stuff which I might have sent in a less official form. The report which Oliphant says some ministers liked *was* rather good.

29 July. I have just read the sad news in *The Times* that HMG do not propose to publish the statements by Thornton and MacDonald. I hope MacDonald will publish something on his own account. If no

☆

explanation of his 'confession' is ever given to the world, the field will be left to the book by Cummings, the *News Chronicle* man, who was the only representative of the English press at the trial free to write a book.[11] Chamberlin and Cholerton have to continue to live in Russia. Cummings is able, but knew little of Russia and took too much at its face. The lack of evidence as to what happened to MacDonald behind the scenes is hard on those who supported him in spite of everything.

One of the proudest boasts of Soviet Russia is that prostitution has been abolished. It is true that eighteen months ago I saw a home for prostitutes and quite recently Cicely Hamilton was shown over another, but—prostitution abolished? Yesterday the captain of a British ship said that that morning a seaman had come on board at 8.00 after being away all night. CAPTAIN: 'Where have you been?' SEAMAN: 'On shore sleeping with a woman.' CAPTAIN: 'Oh, I thought that was all done away with.' Then, knowing the man had no Soviet money: 'How did you pay her?' SEAMAN: 'I gave her my socks.'

The captain says that women hang about the International Seamen's Club and are easily picked up. The usual price is the seaman's shirt. The women do not dare to accept foreign money, the OGPU might ask where they got it.

Stalin and Molotov passed through Leningrad on their way to visit the new canal a week ago. Dr Bell had the task of preparing a small steamer to take them. It is no light responsibility to try to rid a steamer of all the creatures that collect in a Russian boat and make it fit for the greatest tyrant in the world to travel in. No breath of news about his arrival had got round. Only those officials were told who had to know, and the quay was heavily guarded by OGPU agents and troops. When the steamer moved off Molotov remained on deck but Stalin was nowhere to be seen. Stalin was expected to return on the 30th but on the 26th it was announced that he had left Leningrad for Moscow the night before, i.e. he was already back in Moscow before the news was published. This is a very odd way for a man to travel who is always called 'our great leader'. The night he left, the German Vice-Consul was seeing a friend off to Moscow. He noticed a special very strong coach attached to the train, and just as it was about to leave Stalin appeared with twenty OGPU men. The Vice-Consul said it was amazing to see the way the people behaved. Stalin passed within two or three yards of hundreds of people who obviously recognised him—as they could hardly fail to

[11] A.J. Cummings (1882–1957) was political editor of the *News Chronicle* from 1932 to 1955. His book *The Moscow Trial* was published by Gollancz in 1933.

recognise a man whose portrait is in every shop and office, but they all looked in blank silence.

1 Aug. Miss Daunt has had a typical letter from Lady Muriel. She is bringing out not only her son and daughter, but also a schoolfriend of the son's. They would all stay at the flat and Miss Daunt was to 'hire' beds and bedding from Torgsin (who don't deal in that sort of thing). Lady Muriel didn't know by which route they are coming, but when she knew she would telegraph and Miss Daunt would then send roubles to the frontier customs for them. I wonder what mad scheme she has this time.

I think bad conditions may be due in part to Russian incapacity and not to communism, just as the good things, e.g. the relative rarity of unemployment may be due to the undeveloped state of the country, its relatively small population, and its immense resources.

The ship's captain who spoke about the facility with which seamen pick up women near the port was in Siberia last year. A string of vessels is led from Archangel to the Kara Sea by a Soviet icebreaker, to fetch timber. It takes a long time to get there, but the ice is gone by the time they come back. They spent some time at Igolka, some hundreds of miles inland, shipping their cargo. His sole passenger, a London Jew, was the only person allowed to go on shore freely. He said that three of the leading officials at Igolka once invited him into a hut. They shut and locked the door and put up the shutters. He thought they were going to rob him, but all they wanted was to drink without being seen. Among other drinks they produced, he said, the best wine he had ever tasted.

I see in the *Manchester Guardian* that Mme Sokolnikov, wife of the former Soviet Ambassador in London, has written a book on England entitled *Confrontation*. Her husband's position does not prevent her from describing as liars and thieves and hypocrites the British statesmen with whom she used to exchange hospitality. She also has some strange pieces of information about social life: e.g. there are few girls of twenty in England without false teeth. It costs £1000 a year to keep a student at Oxford or Cambridge, and undergraduates live on a vegetarian diet. Lady patrons of hospitals make the patients kiss their hands.

4 Aug. The new acting Italian Vice-Consul, transferred from Kharkov, called and described conditions in the Ukraine. More grain has been grown this year, but getting in the harvest is a serious problem. He told me that Skrybin, the Ukrainian who committed suicide the other day, was the idol of the Party there until he began to defend the Ukraine

★

against the exploitation which was starving it to death. He was violently abused and told he must make the usual recantation at a Party meeting. He went to the meeting, asked for a few minutes to correct his speech, went into a side room, telephoned his wife to come for his body, and shot himself. At the funeral, abusive speeches were made in the presence of his wife and daughter.

5 Aug. I wrote to Scott privately, to tell him that I was anxious to be in England by a certain date.[12] In his reply he wrote: 'All right. I quite understand about your preferring to remain in Russia for a while but I hope you will promise to let me know as soon as you feel that you could do with a move. It would not necessarily be to a Levant post and it might well be nearer England. So let me know. I, *meinerseits*, will let you know if anything is proposed before it goes far enough to become a concrete proposal.'

Had a letter from Pott today. He likes the new First Secretary, Coote. (Coote was once appointed to Persia but could not go because the Legation wired hastily to say that 'coot' in Persian had so improper a meaning that no man with such a name could possibly live in Persia.) Strang is to be replaced by a first secretary named Charles, now in Stockholm.

Buckell, the Metro-Vickers engineer who is going to wind up the office here, has returned. I asked him about the fate of the Russian employees of the firm who were arrested at the same time as the English engineers. Kutuzova, the woman secretary who was one of the chief accused and chief witness against Thornton and the others, is working for the OGPU in the Lubyanka. One of the Moscow chauffeurs has been exiled—apparently for failing to provide evidence to fit in with the OGPU case. Tearle's chauffeur from here is still in prison. His wife was not allowed to send food to him, and we know, from Kulagin's case, that that means starvation to try to secure a confession. Two women typists have been exiled to Archangel for three years without trial. The authorities are always short of skilled workers such as typists in cold and badly fed places like Archangel.

Buckell has brought with him an old Englishman named Healey to help wind up affairs here. Healey is a fine old fellow who worked as an engineer in Russian cotton-mills for many years. He worked here after the Revolution too, and retired on a Soviet pension of 200 roubles. He says that he would go on working willingly, but could not stand the

[12] RWB's wife Miriam was expecting another child in mid-September.

★

conditions in which the Soviet engineers have to work—especially, I gathered, control by ignoramuses.

Miss Goyer came to dinner. She finds that the people she knows, mostly scientists, are disposed to believe the charges against the British engineers. This is in spite of the fact that several are distinctly hostile to the Soviet authorities and tell dreadful tales of what has happened to relatives and friends at the hands of the OGPU. They really believe that foreign countries are preparing to attack them, and consequently they accept that British engineers would commit sabotage as a preparation for intervention. If this is typical of the attitude of scientists, it is different from that of the engineers, who know too many of their fellows who have been arrested on similar charges to take the Metro-Vickers case seriously.

6 Aug. The American engineers who are leaving had an excellent Scottish woman as housekeeper, a Mrs Finke. We are going to ask her whether she thinks she could run our place. She would be useful as a check on our Finnish establishment. We like the Finns to take some grub with them when they go home, but there are too many Finns in our kitchen, and too much food goes out.

Scott's suggestion that I might possibly get a post in Europe (I don't count Russia as Europe) would have filled me with expectation and hope a few years ago, but whereas a year ago I should have thought Germany an attractive country to live in, I do not think I could bear Hitlerite Germany, and I should hardly like the children to be there during their holidays. The only post that sounds attractive is Strasbourg. It is a beautiful town in beautiful surroundings, and if the boys came there during their holidays they could pick up some French and German.

Lady Muriel is in the offing. As usual her advent is heralded by impossible demands. Yesterday a telegram came from Riga to say that she was going to Tallinn—at least it seems to mean that, but it may mean that she is coming from Tallinn today. Miss Daunt is going to meet the train on the off-chance. Her telegram says that the Paris medical examination was satisfactory. I hope that she really is better.

10 Aug. Where else in the world could this happen? This morning a Russian lady was shown in. She apologised, and begged I would not think ill of her. She had found an English banknote for £50 between the leaves of an old book. This is an enormous sum for Russia, and spent at Torgsin would keep her for a year in great comfort. But any money paid to Torgsin is exchanged for coupons which must be used within three

★

months, or else they lapse. Also she dared not take so large a sum to Torgsin or the State Bank as they would not believe she had found it and . . . . She had no need to fill in the picture. The OGPU would call her up at once. At best they would take two-thirds or more as a voluntary contribution to State funds, at worst they would exile her for having some undisclosed source of foreign income, or keep her 'standing' in the hope of making her disgorge more. She said she had been just looking at the note for three days wondering what could be done with this wealth, and she thought perhaps it might be possible for us to change it into smaller notes. I told her we could not have anything to do with it. I was sorry. The woman spoke English almost perfectly and was obviously of the kind that formerly had English governesses. I wonder who put the note there?

Lady Muriel came in this morning in a great state. Miss Daunt has just had a letter from the White Russian John ———, to whom she is half-engaged. It was written three weeks ago in New York and said that as he had not received any reply to his last six letters to her he was leaving at once for Moscow. I should not be surprised if he were a Soviet agent. Fortunately Miss Daunt has decided to break off the engagement.

Lady Muriel arrived with her daughter, Lady Glenconner, twenty-four hours before they were expected, having mistaken the day of the week. The daughter is young and pretty, and rather silly.

Waldhauer came to beg for some quinine and other medicines for a pupil of his who is being sent on a mission to Berghana. I was able to give him some quinine and phenacetin. Miss Daunt is providing pyrimidon and he had himself found some aspirin. Except for aspirin, which the comrades make (very badly), these drugs cannot be got here—except by the OGPU and the big Party people. I went home with Waldhauer and he invited me to have some tea. He said it was quite safe, but near his door we met a Russian woman who is seen at all the official parties—the daughter of the President of the Academy of Sciences. She talks half a dozen languages perfectly and most of the consuls invite her to their parties because she can talk to everyone. When she bowed to me, W said: 'A dangerous woman. Now I know what question will be asked me a fortnight hence.' He described his feelings when his chief at the Hermitage—a communist and something of a scoundrel, but not bad to him—produced a long report written by a woman in Moscow who was formerly one of his pupils, accusing him of all sorts of crimes, the penalty for each of which, as his chief pointed out, was death by shooting or at least ten years' exile. That has happened four times, with different informers.

☆

Waldhauer thinks he is safe now, but he is evidently watched all the time. Recently the OGPU asked him to come and see them, and they questioned him about a letter which he sent to the Berlin Museum. They had opened and read it. The letter was harmless, but they asked whether he had not perhaps sent a supplementary letter by the German consular courier. He got out of it somehow, though the suspicion was in fact correct. He had sent through the courier an explanation which he could not send through the post.

I had never been to the Waldhauer flat before. They are lucky to have two rooms and a kitchen, but it looked pitiful. I suppose that when Mrs Waldhauer is there the place is better-kept, but it could not be made to look nice. It needs painting and decorating, the furniture is old and dirty and shabby, and there is a conglomeration of stuff—everything piled on everything else. Poor Waldhauer does not notice such things, I think. He is lost in his work. I lent him *The Wandering Scholars*, and he was charmed with it, and we talked about books—and about the OGPU.

12 Aug. Lady Muriel has gone to the Estonian frontier in the Relief Association car to meet her son and his friend. I took her daughter, Lady Glenconner, out for a walk this afternoon, and to see the anti-religious museum. I had not intended to spend my Saturday afternoon in that way, but I repented when I heard that Lady Glenconner was unhappy. Lady Muriel has told Miss Daunt that Lord Glenconner is carrying on with another woman and is thinking of applying for a divorce.

Lord Chilston is coming to Moscow as Ambassador. Coote says he is a good man to work with.

Old Healey came today to fix up the billiard-table which Metro-Vickers are returning to the Consulate, and I kept him to lunch. He has four daughters married to Russians. He knows someone in the OGPU who tells him that relations are strained between Stalin and Kaganovich, who was until recently a protégé of Stalin's and, I believe, also his brother-in-law. Kaganovich is a Jew and a bitter enemy of a notorious anti-Semite Akulov, Public Prosecutor for the whole Soviet Union. The Public Prosecutor is responsible for sabotage, grain collection and other things held to be of State importance, and as he has a good deal of arbitrary power, it matters much to the Jews whether he is a Jew or not. Many of the smaller, assistant public prosecutors are Jews, but now the head prosecutor is not only a Gentile but also an anti-Semite.

How very complicated everything is in this land! Mrs Diedrichs managed to get a card for two or three weeks in a sanatorium, to begin on 1 August. She could not go until the 2nd as it was not until the 1st

★

that she could collect the small sum due to her from Intourist for acting as a guide during July. When she reached the sanatorium she was first scolded for not arriving on the 1st and then turned out because she had not got the required medical certificate. She returned to Moscow and spent two or three days getting several certificates to entitle her to appear before the medical board which could give her the final certificate. I saw her the evening before the board, and she was much cast down. The certificates she has say she has tuberculosis in both lungs. She wishes she had not refused my offer to give her butter instead of roubles for Russian lessons, but she was afraid she would be searched one day when leaving the Consulate, and she and her husband would be punished for letting me know they needed butter. I suppose she has managed to return to the sanatorium or I should have heard from her. She always rings up nominally to fix the time for the lesson, but really to let the authorities know she is coming, so that they cannot accuse her of paying secret visits to the Consulate.

A Yorkshire journalist came in as he was leaving for England in the afternoon and Intourist had taken his passport from him. I was able to give him an emergency pass. He had purchased coupons for his meals on the train from Rostov to Moscow, but the train attendants made him pay in roubles. When he complained to Intourist they took the coupons from him, leaving him with nothing to show that they had not been used. I advised him to apply to Intourist or the Embassy in London, and said that, while I deprecated the use of blackmail, he would find that they would pay him more quickly if they knew he was a journalist than if they didn't.

The police advised Miss Daunt to get a dog for the villa, as the forest near was full of people without passports. She got one but he proved useless as he was terrified of human beings. The OGPU came to the rescue and have lent her one of their best-trained dogs—'because it would be a pity if foreigners thought that Russia hadn't any good watchdogs!' They have tested the new dog by sending their trainers to climb over the fence at odd times clad in padded clothes. The dog has flown at the marauder and hung on to him like death.

Waldhauer came to Miss Daunt and sold her a vase for £1. I don't suppose she wanted it but bought it from compassion. The professor is always hard up. Last winter in Moscow he was promised 200 roubles for an article which he wrote at once, but he has not received the money. At about the same time he was offered 10 roubles each for a series of forty lectures which he gave, but when he put in for his 400 roubles, he was told that funds for that sort of thing were exhausted.

★

I was at first amazed to hear yesterday that there had been a successful strike in a local factory and as a result workmen formerly getting 300 roubles a month were now getting 280 roubles plus 20 roubles in 'gold' roubles valid at Torgsin. But there was no need to get excited and wonder what had happened to the Soviet Government. The paint factory in question is run by a German firm (one of the very few foreign concessions left), and Soviet workers may always strike against a foreign company.

Our barber came yesterday. While he was waiting the cook showed him with pride how the refrigerator turned itself off and on according to the internal temperature. He explained that you could also stop the motor by taking out the plug. He took out the plug, pushed it back, but the refrigerator now does not go. These clever Russians. They are like monkeys with machinery.

Lady Muriel talks about going to Moscow on the 17th. I'm sorry for the Embassy, but the misery must be shared out among us all.

Seventy thousand of the wretched people who worked on the canal have been given reductions of sentence. One wonders how many prisoners there were altogether if 70,000 are rewarded. Miss Clyman's information was 200,000 and that was confirmed by the Norwegian Consul at Archangel.

18 Aug. The daughter of the man who used to be watchman in Cave's former house (the woman I gave a cake of soap to once) came today to see him, and I had a talk with her. She says the State is taking much less from the country people this year. The aim is to get people to sow more. Will the Government still be able to get all the grain it wants? Will it still have enough to supply the towns with rye-bread? But it is a good sign that a reduction in the crushing burden of taxation has been made. I gave the woman another cake of Lux soap and a pound tin of lard.

Yesterday an American woman came in wanting a visa for England. She is a consulting psychologist for subnormal and abnormal children and has been studying here for a month. She found little original work being done in Russia. She got tired of being shown as original and rare things that in many other countries are common. She was particularly sceptical about the Soviet boasts that they have abolished prostitution, since the young men in her party had had plenty of offers from Russian women anxious to make a few dollars. She has given away seven or eight dresses, several pairs of shoes and eight cakes of soap.

The day after Waldhauer was here he had an attack in the train coming from Peterhof, and today he had another one here. The OGPU

☆

had let it be known they would be glad to put him away for ten years, which has increased his ordinary nervousness. He is also worried about money. Two days ago he produced a small silver cup which he said dated from the time of Nicholas I and begged me to find a buyer for it for £1 to spend at Torgsin. I cannot bear to see this eminent man in so wretched a state and needing money so badly (even though I know that he tries to soothe his nerves with vodka), so I have given him £1. I wish Naomi Mitchison, who wrote so airily about the position of the intellectual worker in the USSR, could see Waldhauer.

The Leningrad *Red Gazette* announces that the Alexander Palace at Dyetskoye Syelo and the Pavlovsk Palace at Pavlovsk (now called Clutsk after some hero of the Revolution) will become model houses of rest for the best shock-workers of Leningrad. Also reported in the newspaper is that the Winter Palace is to be completely restored with the aid of engravings in the Academy of Arts. The outside is to be painted yellow. Last year it was painted orange and it was claimed that this was the original colour, but it did not look well.

This autumn the authorities propose to experiment with rubber galoshes for horses to replace iron shoes. If we see fewer horses slipping and falling and being beaten to make them get up it will be a good thing.

There has been talk for years about bringing water to Leningrad from Lake Ladoga, and now the papers say that 50 million roubles have been set aside for the scheme and that work is to begin next year. By the end of 1937 the installation will supply 400,000 cubic metres a day, to increase to 850,000 cubic metres by the end of 1939.

Town workers were again drafted into the country to weed the fields this year. On one day there should have been 24,000 but only 9000 turned up.

Several of the men and women whose characters had been reformed by forced labour on the Baltic–White Sea Canal gave their experiences in the press. They seemed to wallow in confessions as Marmeladov does in *Crime and Punishment*. They were all common criminals. No political prisoners gave their experiences. The portraits of four of the leading heroes of the canal appeared in the press. They were all Jews: Yagoda (head of the OGPU and supplier of the labour), Franckel (his assistant, apparently an engineer), Berman (head of the local OGPU) and Firin (Berman's assistant).

I was just off to dine with Lady Muriel when a Commander Keogh, formerly US Navy and working for the US Secret Service, turned up looking for her. As he was obviously a great friend of hers I took him with me, to her great pleasure. He was a sort of 'observer' with Kolchak, and later with Denikin and Wrangel.[13] He said that the refusal of America to resume relations hitherto had been due not, as was supposed, to the State Department, but to the American Federation of Labor, which at one time lost millions of members through the admission of some violent communists to its ranks.

25 Aug. I have been sent an article on 'Peace' by Beverley Nichols from the *Daily Telegraph* of 4 August. Nichols says that were his sister attacked he would defend her while waiting for the policeman. In international affairs there is as yet no policeman. Would Nichols countenance the use of force for defence until the League of Nations force could act? The main difficulty is that peace suits certain nations and not others. Countries like Great Britain, the United States, France and Russia could not hope to gain anything from a war; these countries are pretty consistently for peace in these days. On the other side you have countries like Germany, Italy and Japan, which openly intend to secure additions of territory, if necessary by armed action. It is hypocrisy to pretend that in desiring peace we are not doing what suits us better than it suits Germany. I am not in favour of giving back territory to Germany in the hope of keeping her quiet (I am sure that it would not keep her quiet). I am in favour of working for a world in which all the land and its resources, and the emigration and immigration of people will be controlled by some central power. This is evidently a long way off.

26 Aug. Commander Keogh has been talking to some prominent communists in Moscow all of whom admire Mussolini and Hitler. All dictators are very much alike. Also the natural reaction to a fascist dictatorship is a communist dictatorship. But the communist has little to hope for from a country like England.

A man called Baker came to see me. He said he was going to write some articles for the *Economist*. He had been in Moscow for about two weeks and while he was there the price of bread in the co-ops had suddenly been doubled. He asked how this bore out the claims of the authorities that there had been a good harvest. I said I thought the measure was financial—to get more roubles in in the quickest time, by taxing everyone's bread 100%.

[13] Alexander Vasilevich Kolchak, Anton Denikin and Baron Peter Wrangel were successive commanders of the White armies in the Civil War. Kolchak, having been appointed supreme ruler of Russia in 1918, was executed in 1920.

★

Baker was surprised to find trade unions in this country. I told him that since economic power and political power were both concentrated in the hands of the Government, in no country were trade unions more necessary, though in fact they could do very little to defend the interests of their members. In any case where the interests of the authorities were concerned I did not think the union would do more than enforce the orders of the Party. Baker thought that everyone was living on much the same level. I told him this was not true. There is a much greater difference than an outsider might think between the most and the least favoured worker, though it is not so great as the revolting distance between wealth and poverty in England. On the other hand we have not the brutal exclusion of a class, on political grounds, from the right to a food-card, house room, political rights etc. This differentiation in status between one man and another seems to me as repugnant as the institution of slavery.

I forget whether I recorded my two interpretations of the Soviet emblem. One is that it is an appeal to the world not to let the Soviet worker have anything more complicated than a hammer and a sickle to play with lest he should ruin it. The other is that the superposition of the hammer on the sickle means that the factory will knock hell out of the agricultural worker if the grain to feed the towns is not produced— whatever may happen to the grower.

In restoring old buildings so carefully and having fountains with coloured lights playing on them when the price of bread has been doubled and overcrowding is still appalling, the Russians are remaining true to type. I was re-reading Turgenev's *Fathers and Sons* the other day and I came on the place where Bazarov sneers at Russian 'progress'. He says: 'There's an English wash-stand in my room but you can't shut the door.'

I have just been comparing the area and population of Soviet Russia with those of England, Scotland, Wales and Northern Ireland. Soviet Russia has over ninety times our area, whereas its population is only about 3½ times as great. That is to say, every Soviet citizen has about twenty-five times as much land as a citizen of the United Kingdom. As to natural resources, the list at the disposal of the Soviet Government is enormous, and some of them are almost monopolies: e.g. timber, platinum, manganese, apatite. This shows how absurd it is to use Soviet Russia as a political example or warning for other countries.

Lady Muriel Paget went to Moscow a few days ago. I learn from Pott she returned unexpectedly to her hotel room and found a woman there using the telephone. The woman said she was the manageress and that

☆

it was her birthday and she was telephoning to a few friends. The OGPU really ought to be able to think of better excuses than that. She had of course been going through Lady Muriel's kit. She whitewashes them a good deal in England in order to keep the Relief Association in their good books, but her visits are obviously unnecessary and I suppose they are trying to find the reason why she comes. Last week she nearly fell into a trap. A man asked her to come and see some antiques and took her to a flat in which there were some very valuable pieces and offered her a priceless piece of china for a very small price in pounds. She would have taken it (and I suppose have tried to smuggle it out of the country) if Miss Daunt had not been with her. Miss Daunt recognised the man as the head of the antiques department at the Hotel Europa, and she let him see that he had been recognised. She reminded him and Lady Muriel that no foreigner could take such a piece out of the country unless it was bought at Torgsin and accompanied by a certificate to that effect. The man then proposed to put the piece in the Torgsin shop at the Hotel Europa and let Lady Muriel buy it at that price, provided she gave him so much on the quiet. I am not sure that Lady Muriel might not have consented to this, but Miss Daunt carried her off and frightened her at home.

I must look up Waldhauer today. One cause of the acuteness with which he feels his subordination to the kind of man who is now in authority is, I think, that he is not Russian, but a Balt from Riga. But even so he does not approve of the way the Germans there treated the local population. His father was once derided because he received the son of a Latvian peasant, whom he was supporting at university, in the drawing-room instead of the kitchen. The Latvians have now taken their revenge for centuries of subservience, in that they have broken up the large German estates and distributed them to the peasants.

The latest cry is the 'liquidation of cowlessness'. The Government is going to advance 35 million roubles to enable every member of a collective farm who does not possess a private cow to buy one. I read this in the newspaper on the same day that the price of bread was doubled. This suggests that the authorities have at least realised that the towns were living on the country and have begun to try to restore the balance. One can be certain that no consideration for the lives and happiness of the people will be allowed to interfere with State policy. At the same time one must not be too self-righteous. I am just reading the Webbs' *History of Trade Unionism*, which I bought here for twopence. It is the 1920 edition, and the account of the official treatment of trade unionists during the War, and of the miners just after the War, does not make

☆

pleasant reading. But wartime is perhaps exceptional.

In the days when it popularised the national guilds policy, the *New Age* was always hammering away at the slogan 'Economic power precedes political power' and trying to show that the vote is no good to a workman while the means of production and exchange are in the hands of another class.[14] It is interesting to remember this here, where economic and political power alike are concentrated in the hands of a small group of men over whom the worker has no control. His job is to do as he is told until the classless State is established and conditions suitable for pure communism are ripe: then the State will no longer be necessary and will 'wither away'. I should like to see the OGPU and Stalin withering away.

A few days ago I went to the nearest *univermag* which is supposed to sell everything. The proportion of unnecessary to necessary things is absurdly high and the prices are high too. There was an enormous section filled with bottles of scent and washes and powders but in the middle a notice in pencil: 'No soap'.

28 Aug. Yesterday I saw an American doctor named Gant who worked here from 1926 to 1929 with Pavlov, the physiologist, and translated his book into English. He is horrified at what he considers the change for the worse since he went away. No one is interested in anything but getting enough food. He visited a very well-known doctor who four years ago lived more or less like a European. Now he found the stairs filthy, the tablecloth dirty with a lump of black bread lying on it, the room neglected and shabby, though the doctor is in a better position, in theory, than he was before, as he does some work for the OGPU. The flat in which he formerly had a room was shared by four people when he moved in, it now contains twenty-five. He had left a gramophone and some records and some furniture in the care of a woman in the flat but she had been arrested and exiled for three years and all the stuff confiscated. The charge appears to have been speculating—perhaps selling some of these things. In Moscow he heard everywhere about the typhus epidemic, so he went to the Commissariat of Health and asked for some figures. They said there was not and never had been an epidemic of typhus. There was no such concealment when he was here before.

[14] *New Age* was the mouthpiece of the Guild Socialist movement, the most distinguished ornament of which was G.D.H. Cole. It propagated a mild syndicalist doctrine, that workers should own and control the industries in which they worked.

31 Aug. One of Dr Bell's jobs is Medical Officer of Health in the port.
A few days ago he was called to a vessel which had arrived from the new
canal with 150 sick prisoners. They were lying down in the two holds
suffering from typhoid, typhus, dysentery and other diseases and *all*
suffering from scurvy. They were taken out like sacks and laid on the
quay, where they remained for six or eight hours and where several of
them died. Some of them were quite young—eighteen, twenty, twenty-
two. All were *kulaks* but at that age they could only be the children of
kulaks. The boat that carried them was required urgently, and in seven
hours it was cleaned and disinfected as well as possible, and filled with a
hundred shock-workers who were being given a trip to the canal as a
reward. Dr Bell said that one of the sailors spoke to him about the
wretched sick, and said, with tears running down his face: 'We *can't*
stand this.'

2 Sept. Chamberlin reports that any foreign correspondent wishing to go
outside Moscow must now submit his itinerary to the authorities and if
allowed to go must be accompanied by some Government
representative. Chamberlin applied to visit the chief grain areas, the
Ukraine and the North Caucasus, but permission was refused. Both of
which he has visited before, but not last year when Muggeridge went in
his place and wrote the devastating articles.

Our barber was told to travel with the shipload of shock-workers who
were to visit the new canal as a reward for good work. He was away ten
or twelve days and he was kept very busy. The food was wonderful, meat
every day and plenty of fish and vegetables.

Mrs Diedrichs took me to the writers' home where she lives to give
me tea and show me her books. Her room is crowded to the point of
madness with a small grand piano in the middle. Nevertheless she
considers herself fortunate with a room to herself, looking out on some
trees. She has hundreds of books, Russian, English, French, German,
Italian and Spanish. I borrowed two of the books which the tourists on
a recent boat had given her—Stephan Zweig's *Marie Antoinette* and
Eugene O'Neill's play *Strange Interlude*—and an early novel of Charles
Morgan, *First Love.* A good haul.

3 Sept. Lady Muriel is going today and everyone is glad. She lives in a
world of make-believe. She is confident that everything that her helpers
have managed to do was done by her, and would have been done even
better if she had been on the spot. Lady Muriel decided that the onions
in the villa garden must be pulled up so that she might herself play Lady

★

Bountiful and present them to the Distressed British Subjects when they come for their monthly pensions on the 2nd. On the night of the 1st, Miss Daunt was kept up until 3 a.m. making the onions up into parcels. But Lady Muriel is impatient of any opposition and thinks all her plans are perfect. She launches her 'brilliant' ideas and leaves other people to try to carry them out. However when Lady Muriel dies I am sure that the biographical notices will say how kind and thoughtful she was.

11 Sept. An American woman, a middle-aged Jewess named Freedlander, came in today for an English visa. She spent several months here four years ago, and she has just spent two months in the country—part of the time in the south. She speaks enough Russian to get along with. She told me that the system of education has been completely changed. They now admit differences of intelligence and accept that hard work is essential. Examinations are now held, and the best schools were well laid-out and seemed to be able to give the children good food. The leading authority on Bolshevik education, Pinkévich, admitted to her that his book can now be scrapped. She has strong socialist sympathies, but she is beginning to wonder whether the people are not paying too high a price. No one who has only seen Leningrad and Moscow knows anything about the Soviet Union. She found Kharkov fairly prosperous and the people attributed this to the fact they work in the favoured heavy industries. But Kiev, which has only light industry, was in a dreadful state and the country was far worse. She found people much more afraid to talk than they were four years ago.

12 Sept. Poor Waldhauer is in a very bad way. He seems to have a heart attack every day. He felt very cold after the attack, so I gave him one of my numerous hot-water bottles and an old grey sports coat which I bought ready made several years ago. It was almost exactly like the coat he was wearing, except that his elbows were sticking through, and I thought that the change might escape notice. He was very grateful, and insisted on my accepting a book of line drawings illustrating Shakespeare plays and an earthenware pot.

From a report to HM Ambassador in Moscow, 13 Sept. There is no cause to modify the opinion I expressed nearly a year ago, that there is a general spirit of disillusion abroad in Leningrad. In this Soviet world of material rewards, this present feeling of disillusion could be dissipated, in all probability, by a slight improvement in material conditions. Only no prospect of such improvement is visible here at present. On the

☆

contrary, for the ordinary town-dweller the situation is worse than it was a year ago, even if he does not belong to that minority which tries to keep relatives in the grain areas alive by sending them bread by parcel post. Housing is on the whole no better, wages are lower, food is not less scarce, and in the matter of fruit and vegetables it is even scarcer, and the price of bread has just been raised by 70–100%.

It has long been recognised that for years Soviet industry was living to a large extent on agriculture. In this area some measures have been adopted to restore equilibrium, e.g. not only has the price of bread been raised, but the taxes in kind have in most cases been reduced. But it may well be doubted whether these measures rest on any reasoned principle, and above all, whether they have that prospect of permanence which is required if the agricultural population are to be reassured.

14 Sept. Miss Goyer and her sister went to the Caucasus some weeks ago expecting to return early in September. This evening the post brought two letters from her. The sister is very ill and the diagnosis is typhoid.

Mrs Diedrichs told me some more stories when she came for my last Russian lesson before I go on leave. One of them came from a man in the Urals and it went something like this: 'During the Civil War we were in a village in the Urals with White troops not far away. We found that in a cellar under the house of the priest there was a telephone connected with the Whites. The priest and his wife were shot at once. The court debated whether the priest's daughter should not also be shot. She was a lovely girl and I fell in love with her. She said that she was betrothed to an officer in the White Army, but that if I could save her life she would marry me. I went to my chief and begged for her life saying I would marry her and win her from the wrong views she held. But they said she also must be shot. It was the duty of my detachment to shoot her, but I was afraid that they might bungle it, so I decided to shoot her myself, and to shoot her without warning, so that she might not have the fear of death before she died. So at night I went to her in prison and said I was going to help her to escape. Now she had begun to like me, and she became mine. But the night wore on and my orders were to shoot her before daybreak. So I said we must escape, and took her out of the prison across some fields. I asked her to walk in front and then I shot her dead. And to this day, comrades, I cannot make up my mind whether I did right. Perhaps I might have turned her from the error of her ways.'

RWB was on leave in England from mid-September to mid-December.

★

17 Dec. It seems already natural to be in the office doing my daily work, but it seems wrong to have no one to talk to in the evenings and I do not feel able to settle down to steady reading. However last night I found myself dipping into history, so I suppose that my spirit is being broken in again.

Miss Goyer and her sister have returned from Tiflis, but the sister has a high fever and Mrs Bell said she must be put on a diet, kept warm and so on. I insisted on their moving into the Consulate for a few days. Mrs Finke can look after them.

Lady Muriel surpassed herself during her last visit. The villa, itself an extravagance, is to have a tennis-court. Who is to play there? Oh, sailors from British ships. The harbour is miles away and the villa is a long way from the nearest tram. Then she has engaged a permanent dentist with a nurse and an assistant nurse. The teeth of the Russian relatives of the DBSs as well as those of the Russians whom Lady Muriel has picked up are all to be seen to at the expense of the Fund.[15] A Swedish woman has been put in charge of the archives and an Englishwoman engaged to teach the British subjects English, and one of these has been engaged as bookkeeper. Yesterday a Russian girl arrived and told Miss Daunt that Lady Muriel had engaged her to arrange the library—a few score novels left behind by Metro-Vickers, which most of the DBSs can't read. Lady Muriel had a furious quarrel with Miss Daunt having discovered a note from Miss Daunt to Mrs Hay, one of her helpers, telling her to see that Lady Muriel did not waste money. Miss Daunt resigned at once, but Lady Muriel, knowing she is irreplaceable, refused to accept her resignation. The accounts appear to be in some confusion. £200 cannot be accounted for, but Lady Muriel cashes large cheques and spends right and left for herself and for the Association and forgets to keep account.

21 Dec. I knew that Cave was nearly always overdrawn, but I now find that he would have been in great difficulties while I was away had it not been for Pott. He is about £50 in debt. I have stopped him sending the maid out to the beer-shops twice a day. The beer-shops are far worse than public houses were in England half a century ago, and it is improper for our maid to have to go into them.

Miss Goyer's sister is much better and was allowed up today. She

---

[15] Lady Muriel recorded in her diary: 'The five sets of teeth that I brought out, given by the British Red Cross, are required by at least twenty-five people.' She also described an 'at-home' for the DBSs, with 'sandwiches, cake, musical chairs and Old Maid, with safety-pins for prizes'.

liked the Caucasus so much that she proposes to come out again. To this I said that I hoped she would wait until someone else was Consul!

I shall have another visitor next week. An eighteen-year-old girl, a Miss McEvoy, a daughter of the artist and a friend of Lady Chilston. She is on the Soviet ship *Smolny*. I shall be glad when she has come and gone, for I hate not having my own room. The only protection against loneliness is routine, and not to have my own room disturbs the routine.

22 Dec. Waldhauer is still ill, but he looks better, probably because he says he has given up drinking. I found him in a state of squalor, the room dirty and uncared-for. There is nothing much one can do except take him some small luxury now and then—it does not take much to give people a little pleasure here.

When I was in Moscow, Cholerton and the other journalists were full of the tale of the arrest of a large number of men in various parts of the country and also in the Army, Navy and Air Force. The authorities seemed to be trying to keep this as secret as possible, but the *Times* correspondent at Riga heard about it. The strange thing is that the offence in every case is one which is not an offence in Soviet law— homosexuality. It seems the practice has now reached such proportions as to constitute, in the opinion of the authorities, a national danger. A well-known musician is among those arrested.

Miss Goyer's visa expired while she was ill, and we had to explain this to Weinstein and ask for an extension. Weinstein must have cursed the Public Heath Department, for today a doctor came round and explained that any foreigner who was ill here had only to ring up a certain number and if necessary he would get hospital treatment. The doctor explained quite seriously that, unlike Soviet citizens, foreigners would not have to wait their turn, but would be admitted to hospital at once. Moreover, if *he* signed the prescription for any medicine, it would be supplied at once. This is naive, but interesting.

26 Dec. I went to the Waldhauers on Christmas Eve. They are Lutherans. I took them some cigarettes, a pound of tea and some chocolate for their little girl and the maid. I found him much improved. He had got over his depression and had been able to get out to the Hermitage.

The Caves gave a dinner on Christmas Eve and Mrs Cave cooked various dishes of salt cod which is indispensable to a Swedish Christmas. I gave a dinner on Christmas Day and after dinner I read aloud, with great success, an amusing little tale translated from the Russian, about a

☆

factory in which illiteracy had been liquidated in three months, and with rather less success the scene from *Bleak House* where the Jarndyce party dine with the Bayham Badgers.

On Christmas morning I took the Goyers for my usual walk. The Summer Garden looked lovely under snow. Miss Goyer had just heard that a friend of hers, an American, married to a German-American chemist named Rathmann, had been taken in to hospital. You cannot possibly live on the diet the hospitals supply even in Leningrad, so Miss Goyer produced the remains of her ration of butter and we found some white bread and a tin of sardines and the Goyers managed to bluff their way into the hospital. She was grateful for the food and still more for two or three books which I sent her.

31 Dec. I saw Mrs Kulagin last night. She looks greatly changed—much thinner. She used not to know what it meant to be hungry. She knows now. She has only a second-category food-card, and although she gets a little besides her daily bread, it is not enough to live on, as there is no dining-room at her place of work. Her pay is small, and the prices at the State shops are high. Her daughter gets a midday meal at school, which is cheap but not substantial.

Just before Solovki was cut off from the mainland for its six months' winter, Mrs Kulagin went there to see her husband. His health is bad at any time owing to a shot in the back in the Civil War, but now it is much worse. The food is dreadful in quality and insufficient in quantity. He is employed in the camp commissariat and had 500 kilos of sugar to supply 5000 prisoners 'until next time', whenever that might be. Once he was sent rotten fish which poisoned seventeen of the inmates. Kulagin himself was under arrest because the feeding arrangements were so bad. Mrs K was allowed to speak to her husband for two hours, but only in the presence of an OGPU man, who stopped them at once if they referred to his alleged offence, as, for instance, when K said: 'Tell our friends that I committed no crime.'

K is much changed in manner. He used to look confident and frank, but now he walks timorously and is always looking nervously behind him. He managed to pass a letter to her and she managed to read it and tear it up into tiny pieces and scatter them about before being searched on leaving the camp. 'How fortunate for your husband,' said more than one, 'that you have come to see him. I wonder what my wife is doing. Perhaps she has taken another husband.' That often happens, says Mrs Kulagin. Mrs K saw a man named Rappoport who had been inspecting the camp, and according to her he was indignant at two things: the

☆

wretched food, and the waste of human material. He has promised Mrs Kulagin that by the first boat from Solovki in the spring he will have her husband brought to Bear Mountain, a camp very much nearer to Leningrad and on the mainland, and therefore accessible all the year round. He could there be given responsible work to employ his mind, and she could send him parcels of food all the year round; whereas Solovki is cut off for the whole winter. She was only able to take him two kilos of butter and two of sugar, to last him until the spring. Rappoport made similar complaints about the bigger camp at Kem' on the White Sea—the one Miss Clyman gate-crashed. He spoke to five or six men whom he saw engaged on menial tasks—all men with valuable professional qualifications. He wants them employed on their own jobs as far as possible.

I have been reading Cummings' book on the Moscow trial. The Soviet Embassy refused visas to the other journalists. From the Soviet point of view C had two valuable qualities: he had never been in Russia, and as a liberal and political editor of a liberal daily he would naturally be opposed to 'interference in the internal affairs of an independent country'. In his book he has scored every possible point against HMG and gone lightly on all points tending to tell against the Soviet Government. He regrets that the Deputy Prosecutor made the remark about Thornton being used as manure for Soviet fields, and regrets that the comment, having been made, should have been omitted from the official Soviet report. But he says that this is the only important omission. There is a far more important one—Kutuzova's concluding remark: 'But there is one thing on which I do not congratulate myself, although the Public Prosecutor congratulates me on it—my confession.' Kutuzova declared that Thornton received a large sum of money from the British Consulate in Moscow. This point was the only one which we knew for certain to be untrue, and if Kutuzova had made this up the rest of her evidence was worthless. But when Thornton brought up the question the Public Prosecutor brushed it aside as improper to be dealt with there.

On two disputed points, viz. whether Vyshinsky bullied the accused and whether MacDonald looked more cast down than usual after the famous interval, he sums up against what seems to be the general opinion, and he says nothing about Roginsky's methods, which seem to have been bullying without question.[16] He deals very lightly with the

---

[16] Roginsky was deputy public prosecutor. Andrei Yanuarievich Vyshinsky (1883–1954) had shared a prison cell with Stalin in 1908. Originally a Menshevik, he joined the

two cardinal points of the trial, viz. what is a case worth which rests entirely on confessions extracted in secret, and what would be left of the 'confessions' if the accused could be cross-examined?

The worst point in Cummings' book is his treatment of the shooting of the thirty-five agricultural saboteurs.[17] Since the men were tried and shot in secret, reports about the case can only come from the OGPU. The most that a foreigner could honestly say is that Soviet officials seemed to believe that the accusations of sabotage against the thirty-five were well-founded. But C repeats the accusations as a true story and uses it to show that there is no reason why the accused in the M-V case should not be guilty. He does not see that the evidence for the sabotage is just as complete, just as neatly fitted together, as that for the espionage, and that if the former were shaken, as it could be, the whole case would collapse. MacDonald's 'confession' was a terrible blow, not merely to the British Government but to all of us who believe that British engineers of that type would not commit sabotage, and who think that for an honest man to be condemned unjustly is a dreadful thing and one to be resisted if at all possible, but it is the essence of the charge against Soviet justice that its methods can secure such confessions from honest people, even—if the pressure is great enough and the victim carefully chosen—from an Englishman.

Bolsheviks in 1920 and taught law at Moscow University between 1921 and 1928. Stalin appointed him to preside over the great show trials of the 1930s.

[17] On 12 March 1933, the OGPU chief Menzhinsky had ordered the arrest of a great many senior officials, including the vice-commissar of agriculture in charge of grain collection, on charges of complicity, sabotage and counter-revolutionary conspiracy in connection with the agrarian difficulties. They were convicted of falsifying the figures for grain collection, which had caused the Kremlin to believe that grain was being hoarded. Apart from the thirty-five officials sentenced to death, another forty were sentenced to between eight and ten years in prison.

☆

ON THE EVE OF THE TERROR

LENINGRAD, 1934

WHEN THE *Seventeenth Party Congress—officially labelled the 'Congress of the Victors'—met from 16 January to 10 February, collectivisation had been achieved but at a terrible and unacknowledged price. Meanwhile industrial targets had not been reached, and living conditions had declined steeply. Bukharin, Zinoviev and Kamenev were denounced as spies and saboteurs wanting to overthrow the regime, to split the Party and restore capitalism. They were permitted to speak and confess their errors. The subsequent election of Bukharin, Rykov and Tomsky as candidate members of the Central Committee, together with the election of the Leningrad Party leader Kirov to the Politburo, seemed to indicate that the advocates of more moderate policies had gained some ground at the Congress. Indeed, the ovation given to Kirov suggested that he was beginning to rival Stalin for popularity in the Party.*

4 Jan. I went to Cave's quarters a few nights ago. He and his wife were sitting opposite each other drinking beer. Their daily consumption is said to be eight litres and Mrs Cave is on a diet to lose weight. I must talk to him again about his finances. He buys mineral water from the Caucasus and most weeks orders Roquefort cheese from Finland. I have had to ask that his wife should discontinue washing her cat and dog in Pott's bath. The entry to their flat smells like a dogs' home.

A British subject named Theakston came here from Moscow recently because his son, unfortunately a Soviet citizen, had been arrested. The son was a student at Kiev University and all the ex-students from the Ukrainian universities have been arrested on suspicion of participation in the movement for independence. The Soviet constitution theoretically allows any portion of the Union to secede, but in fact those involved are arrested and tried for counter-revolution. The son is lucky to have been released. The father thinks that his own British nationality had some influence. The others are still in prison.

9 Jan. I had an interesting letter today from Chapman Andrews, who is Vice-Consul at Kirkuk. He writes: 'Kirkuk I like, though there is very little consular work to do. Many people here, both European and local, talk to me of you. People also speak of course of Lionel Smith.[1] It is unfortunate that some of those who stayed didn't go, and some of those who went didn't stay, for I put this country down in the list of "bad shows". As the finished product of fifteen years of British help, advice, friendship, guidance, instruction and financial generosity, Iraq is a monument to the folly of it. Nobody likes us, nobody wants us; they malign us, throw stones at us, threaten to shoot us, murder our friends, insult us. And all the time we *will* persist in keeping alive the tradition of the "Arab Bureau", "Revolt in the Desert", "the Noble Arab".'

10 Jan. Miss Daunt had to go to the bank the other day, and while she was there she saw a large number of sacks of tsarist gold coins being opened. They had all come from Torgsin and the people at the bank told her there was plenty more gold still to be got out of the peasants. The towns have been searched many times and people suspected of having gold tortured. I suppose it is less easy to search 140 million peasants.

13 Jan. The incredible hardiness of the Russians continues to surprise me. Miss Daunt was invited by a member of the OGPU to go to see some trotting races. They began at 5 p.m. Miss Daunt went at 7.00 and stayed until 9.00, and there was so much of the programme still to come that the show must have gone on until after midnight. She considered the horses were 'pulled' in every race. In one race the pulling was so gross that the crowd yelled at a jockey who was clearly having the greatest difficulty restraining his horse, and he had to give it its head, whereupon it rushed ahead and won easily. The races were in the open with a temperature well below freezing, and the spectators were in a shed open to the wind on all sides except the back. Miss Daunt stuck it out for two hours because she was sure the OGPU man had been sent to try to get some information out of her and she enjoyed seeing that he was colder

---

[1] Lionel Smith (1880–1972), fellow of Magdalen College, Oxford, adviser on education to the government of Iraq from 1923 to 1931, and headmaster of Edinburgh Academy from 1931 to 1945. He was also RWB's brother-in-law.

☆

than she was—not perhaps having thought that she would agree to go to the races, and having come without enough warm clothes. Miss Daunt warned the young Englishman, Wild, who was with her, that the OGPU man would probably try to pump him and that the first move is usually to offer to introduce the foreigner to women. A few minutes later the OGPU man got Wild on one side and offered to introduce him to 'a nice woman'. The OGPU don't waste time through squeamishness. The OGPU man asked Miss Daunt to bring in a portable gramophone for him the next time she went to Finland, and she said that if he could get permission from the Department of Foreign Trade she would be glad to bring it. Then he asked her to bring him a watch, but she said this wasn't necessary as Torgsin now sell watches very cheaply. I wish one knew what the game was. Perhaps they are always trying people on the off-chance that sooner or later they may be successful. The OGPU is a huge machine for which the raw material is political crime, real or imaginary, and the material has to be provided somehow.

The OGPU man asked questions about the Norwegian engineer, Lie. I wonder if they are trying to get up a case against him. We have often thought that he must be well in with someone very high up to be able to do all the things he has done for so long with impunity, but one never knows. A day or two after the races Mrs Lie came round to Miss Daunt and told her that there was a man in Leningrad who had brought up a lot of valuable things from the museum at Kiev and was selling them on the quiet, and suggested that she might be interested. Since Miss Daunt is known to be strictly law-abiding and not interested in antiques, it is difficult to see what Mrs Lie's object was unless it was an attempt to provoke her to break the law and get her into trouble.

14 Jan. Sunday. While Miss McEvoy was staying with me I took her to the theatre with a young American actor, Page. We saw *The Marriage of Krechinski* performed for the first time since the Revolution. Page says that Russian acting is a great contrast to English and American. Here nothing is left to the imagination of the audience, every point is underlined, and the actors often play to the audience instead of to each other. He may modify his opinion a little after seeing the First Art Theatre in Moscow perform *The Cherry Orchard* but in the main I agree with him. The audiences need to have the drama driven in in the same way as politics—with a club.

Miss McEvoy went to mass at the Catholic church nearby. She estimated that there were two thousand people in the church, and so many of them went to confession first that the mass began an hour late.

☆

She talked to the priest afterwards, and found him sad, but not at all bitter, though he described the present persecution as the worst, because the most complete, that the Church had ever had to undergo. According to him there are 36,000 Catholics in Leningrad and he is the only priest (a Frenchman).

16 Jan. The new German Consul, Sommer, has an Austrian lady as his housekeeper; it is assumed she is his mistress, but she is accepted in society—even by the rather strait-laced Mrs Platou. I went to call on him and was introduced to Frau Wedig. Sommer was in Persia for many years, and he possesses all the books in English on eastern and middle-eastern affairs that I have ever read or heard of.

Mrs Kulagin came to see Miss Daunt the other evening. Ordinarily she would have been given a good meal, but now that the Andersons are living at the flat they have dinner in the middle of the day for the sake of the children and Miss Daunt has only a snack in the evening.

A Swedish lady who came out with Lady Muriel last time is a well-known botanical artist. Professor Emmé, a Russian scientist, offered her an extremely interesting job with an expedition going to Siberia in the spring. However she refused on the ground that she would not be free at the time, but really, as she told Miss Daunt afterwards, she could not possibly work with these people.

When Lady Muriel was last here she instituted a weekly 'working-party' of all the Distressed British Subjects. There are about seventy who come, including some Russian relatives whom Lady Muriel, with her usual expansiveness and disregard of the funds, invited to come too. They come for tea and leave about 1 o'clock after being fed in sections. They have stolen Miss Daunt's watch and fountain-pen, some of the stores and the equipment to be used by the working-party. Miss Daunt found two skeins of English knitting-wool which she recognised on sale at Torgsin. She also found there a Parker Duofold fountain-pen which Lady Muriel lost the last time she was here.

The papers report a handsome present of bulbs made to the Soviet Union by a Dutch 'sympathiser'. I saw the Dutchman yesterday, who seems to have been born here. He buys large quantities of wild bulbs in Russia, chiefly tulips from Turkestan. According to him a group of about sixty persons spend two months or more in the spring collecting bulbs in the mountains. The bulbs have to be dug up from a depth of about a foot. The Soviet Government are so hard up that they are glad to get £60 for two or three hundred thousand bulbs. He offered to send me some to England. He is going to take a little girl with him to Holland called

Cattley whose English father is in a lunatic asylum in England.

17 Jan. The unfortunate Cave is now having trouble with his teeth. Today his face began to swell rapidly and his dentist wants to take out all the teeth he has left in his upper jaw and with them the bridge which is screwed to them. He should have got rid of the stumps when his teeth were knocked out by the earthquake.

Yesterday I had dinner at the Astoria with the two American engineers and their wives. We played dominoes—but it might have been worse.

21 Jan. Sunday. The comrades are looking forward to the arrival of the American diplomatic representatives, and to closer contact with Americans in general. I think the authorities should get on better with Americans than with English people. The confidence of the Russian that in the doctrine of Marx he has a complete solution for all the problems of the world is matched by the complacent readiness of the Americans to tell Buddha and Confucius where they get off.

23 Jan. A lovely frosty day today, after several days of dirt and thaw and dull sky. The Winter Palace Square was flooded to make a large ice-rink but it thawed.

Tomorrow is kept as the anniversary of the death of Lenin. We must fly our flag at half-mast. I would fly it at half-mast for Stalin too with great goodwill. Last year Lie had a big dinner the day before (it was his wedding anniversary I think). I hear the OGPU obtained a list of the guests and attributed the absence of my name to my respect for the Soviet anniversary of Lenin's death. I wasn't there because I wasn't invited. I don't like or trust either Lie or his wife. The OGPU man who has been paying too much attention to Miss Daunt lately asked her what her politics were, and she said conservative. He was a little shocked. He asked what my politics were, and Miss Daunt said she didn't know; in England you didn't trouble about people's politics or their religion. This seemed to surprise him. He said he thought I was a liberal! I remember saying to a journalist at a dinner that Bernard Shaw made fun of the English, but what Soviet Russia needed was a Soviet Bernard Shaw who would make fun of them.

Miss Goyer says she gets some satisfaction out of asking Russians why it is, since they believe that everything is conditioned by the economic environment, that they have created economic conditions in which it is impossible to be honest. There is a great shortage of electric light-bulbs,

★

for instance, and the students at the labs, rather than sit at home in darkness, will steal bulbs from the labs.

We have still not got our electric stove connected. We filled in a form and someone came and examined the stove and the wiring. We were then told to fill up another form and to pay 40 roubles for a technical inspection of the stove. I expect we shall get permission to use the stove in the end, but if we were Soviet citizens we should not. Not even the use of electric kettles and cookers is being encouraged now.

26 Jan. The Dutch bulb-merchant was refused an exit visa for the little Cattley. I went to see Weinstein, who at once said that the child was a Soviet citizen because one of the parents was a Soviet citizen. He quoted a law of 1921, but I told him that that law only applied if one of the parents was a Soviet citizen at the time the child was born, and when this child was born both parents were British and moreover living in England. Although he is supposed to deal with such questions, he seemed never to have heard of a later law (1931) which says that if one parent becomes a Soviet citizen his or her children under fourteen become Soviet citizens *if* he or she makes a declaration to that effect. The child's mother made no such declaration. I followed up my visit with a written statement of the case and today we had the satisfaction of learning that the child may go.

A well-known Russian scientist, Frenkel, has just returned after working in America. He was asked to write a series of articles about his experiences. In the first he wrote about how the students in the college where he taught earned their keep by waiting in the dining-room, but would nevertheless have a car of some kind of their own. This caused the series to come to an abrupt end.

I saw Mrs Kulagin last night at Miss Daunt's. The place where her husband expects to be employed is on the 'Byel-Balt Combine'. This is a new industrial centre which is to be created in a forest area at a place on the White Sea–Baltic Canal.

One of the young men arrested as a homosexual addict is one of the Galitzin princes. He has been sentenced to exile for five years, and though he has committed no crime known to Soviet law, he is thought to be fortunate in that his property has not been confiscated, though the only things worth confiscating are his piano and his music. He is a brilliant pianist. None of his few relatives here would do anything for him, but Mrs Diedrichs, though astonished and shocked to hear of his vices, courageously came forward and looked after his affairs. She went to Galitzin's rooms with an OGPU man to take over the property. The

☆

man wanted to seize a large Bible with pictures by Doré and a number of prayer-books, each with an inscription showing that it had been presented to one of the Galitzins on leaving the Imperial Corps of Pages. Mrs D managed to carry off the prayer-books, but had to give up the Bible.

4 Feb. Jones, the chaplain from Helsingfors, was here for two days this week. Recently the Embassy informed the Foreign Affairs Commissariat that he would also hold a service at the Consulate General in Leningrad in addition to the services in the Embassy in Moscow. The service was in my drawing-room and afterwards I gave them all tea.

An engineer named Braithwaite, British by nationality but born in Russia and speaking only Russian, came to get a new passport. He works in a pulp- and paper-factory. The whole 'Combine' is to be erected under the direction of the OGPU. They will have complete charge of labour and unlimited powers of arrest.

My new Latvian colleague, Bissineks, called on me—a nice man, speaking English very well. He was Latvian Minister in London and has an English wife, but he resigned to go into business. He wanted to know whether anything could be done to prevent the private servants of consular officers from being examined by the OGPU. He sent his maid out with letters to deliver and she was stopped and taken to the OGPU station, where she was questioned for an hour, and finally let go with terrible threats of what would happen if she told her employer. There is of course nothing to be done. Being a border state Latvia is watched more closely than we are. Mrs Kulagin is still carrying out instructions to tell anyone who asks after her husband that he is on a mission in the Bashkir Republic, but it sometimes leads to awkward situations.

When Rapp returned from leave on 1 February he found five English workmen waiting to see him. They had come to erect half a million pounds' worth of printing machinery for *Pravda* and have downed tools because they could not stand the conditions in which they were expected to live. By the way, the machinery had been lying out in the open for a year.

Miss Daunt and Miss Goyer and I were talking of the book that Miss Cicely Hamilton sent me, and in particular of the strange shapes into which women were expected to squeeze themselves twenty years ago. I said that there was perhaps this to be said for the squeezing if it tended to make the waist round: as a circle has a larger area than any ellipse with the same circumference, the pinched area at least left the maximum room for the poor organs inside. Miss Goyer, who is a mathematician,

★

had never heard the rule I based my argument on. I don't know that I ever heard it, but it is obvious, since the ellipse at the opposite extreme from the pure circle is a straight line, which has no area at all.

10 Feb. There is a man named Stanley Joseph who comes here several times a year to buy old stamps and precious stones and antiques. He has bought a lot of the jewelled watches and other precious things from the Hermitage and he does a good trade in stamps. A week ago he came in full of mystery and importance to tell me that his interpreter was an OGPU agent, assuming that this would come as a surprise to me. He has got to know this woman quite well and she has never given him away when he occasionally overstepped the line in purchasing things secretly or in bringing in black roubles from abroad. Recently she told him that she was expected by the OGPU to spy on him, and to try to win him over to serve the Soviet Government as a secret agent. Joseph was very sorry for her and gave her some of his business letters, torn up, which she could give to the OGPU as having been rescued from his wastepaper-basket.

The first time he came Joseph informed me he was 'of the Jewish persuasion' and spoke of the incapacity of the Russians: wherever he went he found a Jew doing the work. I agreed, and said that the system could not have lasted without the organising power of the Jews. Many of the OGPU examining officers are Jewish, and many of the public prosecutors who work with the OGPU, not to mention key men all over the place who are Party men. The girl said (no news to us) that some of the rooms in the Astoria Hotel where Joseph stays are fitted with microphones. She told him, evidently meaning him to pass it to me, that Luknitsky was an OGPU agent. (If so he got little reward for it, since he had to take a job in the Arctic.) She also said that the Intourist agency in London is the centre of Soviet espionage there. Joseph is going to try to get the interpreter out of the country, but I doubt very much whether the OGPU will let her leave, still more whether the Home Office will allow her to come to England.

The Italian Ambassador found a microphone behind his bed. The Embassy had reason to suspect that the comrades had some means of listening in to their calls through the telephone receivers, so when their telephones are not in use they cover the end of the mouthpiece with a little box packed with cotton-wool. A day or two after this device had been introduced the telephone exchange rang up and asked whether their telephone was in order. 'Oh, quite in order,' said the Italians.

I asked Cave to speak to Orlov-Ermak at the Department of Foreign

Affairs about getting more suitable living accommodation for our messenger, Stevens, whose only entrance to his flat was through the common bathroom. The other people in the house will no longer let him pass through the bathroom and want him to make another door from the kitchen.

Pott says that it was sad to see the Embassy when he left; the very capable Vyvyan was on leave and there was no one who knew Russian. The Ambassador and Charles, the new Counsellor, were getting their information from *Moscow News*.

11 Feb. Sunday. Dined with the Danes on the 9th and sat next to the English wife of the Latvian Consul Bissineks. She is very nervous because the OGPU are paying the Latvian Consulate too much attention. Bissineks says that two Russians had come (not together) asking whether they might escape into Latvia. He said that if the applicant could run faster than a bullet he might succeed. Why? Because both the Soviet *and* the Latvian frontier guards would fire at him. Since then no further attempt at provocation has been made. Mrs Bissineks said she wanted to see Miss Daunt but did not dare go by herself, so Pott and I took her to Miss D's in our car. There are limits to what they can do to the subjects of the bigger powers.

In a book about Old Quebec which I have just read by Willa Cather, who wrote that much better book *Death Comes for the Archbishop*, an old Catholic bishop says: 'Schools are not meant to make boys happy, but to teach them to do without happiness.' It should be: 'Schools are not meant to give boys a good time, but to teach them to be happy even when they are not having a good time.'

Went to see the Americans at the Astoria a few days ago. I don't think their room can be furnished with a microphone. They were railing against the Russians they have to work with. The real start on the work, which in any other country they would have made about a fortnight after arrival, has not yet been made—after four months.

17 Feb. The Norwegian engineer, Lie, has been ordered to leave the country in three days. No reason given. Until recently he seemed to feel free to do as he liked. He must have had some protection in high places that has now been withdrawn.

There is a very distinguished woman poet in Leningrad named Anna Akhmatova. She has never written the sort of stuff the Bolsheviks like, and for some years she has not published anything. I saw an advertisement in the December number of the *Dublin Magazine* with an article on Anna Akhmatova, and I got a copy. I thought Mrs Diedrichs would like to see the article and show it to AA who is a friend of hers. The article was not very interesting because the author had only seen four of AA's poems. I wrote and told him of a little book published in Berlin which contains thirty of her poems. I also told him that her name is stressed Akhm*a*tova and not, as he had stressed it, Akhmat*o*va. He sent me a nice reply.[2]

My gramophone has suddenly begun to make a grinding noise. The increased friction must have been great, for the tempo sagged a little at one point in each revolution. I have looked at the works, and though I have found where the friction must be, I can't see anything wrong. Shell, one of the American engineers, has promised to have a look at it. I went round to see Shell and tell him about the gramophone and I found him and his wife preparing to move. At 3 o'clock that day they had been told they had to transfer to the Hotel Europa that night as their rooms were wanted for people who would pay in foreign currency. They managed to secure a day's respite. Next day they were told there was no room in the Europa and they must stay in the Astoria until the 22nd. So they had to unpack again.

Just heard that Lie is to be allowed to stay. The Norwegian Consul says that the trouble has blown over 'for the present'.

The Estonians gave a dinner on the 15th. Mrs Varma, the Consul General's wife, had ordered turkeys and all sorts of supplies from Tallinn by the messenger, but they did not come. She rushed off to Tallinn, fourteen hours away, had one night in the train, a day's shopping, then a night returning in the train, arrived at 4.00 on the day of the party, and had an excellent dinner ready by 8.30.

A periodical published by the Moscow Bank in London contained a glowing description of a machine which had been invented by a Soviet engineer for remaking roads. According to this report, the machine ploughs up a piece of road, passes the ploughed-up material through an electric furnace, and spreads the molten mass out behind it. The Department of Trade were interested and wrote to Moscow to ask if the machine was on sale. As the machine was said to have been invented in Leningrad, the enquiry was sent on to us here. It took us over a fortnight to get the information we required, through the Foreign Affairs people.

---

[2] Anna Akhmatova, born Gorenko (1889–1966), was perhaps the greatest Russian woman poet—ostracised for long periods as 'bourgeois and alien' but twice rehabilitated (in 1940 and 1959). (See Isaiah Berlin, *Personal Impressions*, ed. Hardy H: Oxford University Press, 1982.)

☆

Orlov-Ermak, who sometimes blurts out the truth, told us that the machine is not yet constructed: the project is still on paper. He thought the account published in London was 'premature'.

Last summer I visited a farm where a British railway-guard called Freshfield, suffering from consumption, was staying. He has recently got worse and the only thing to do was to get him away to a sanatorium, but the railway sanatoria could not find room for him. He has now got a room—through Mrs Kulagin. Miss Daunt spoke to her, and she spoke to the railway boss, and the thing was done. And that is how everything is done in this country. By knowing someone. Last night Miss Daunt brought Mrs Kulagin to dinner. All went well except that owing to Mrs Kulagin they were an hour late. She has heard indirectly that her husband is ill and is distressed because he gets no letters from her though she has written fifteen times since she saw him in the autumn.

Mrs Diedrichs seemed to be better, but the other day she had a slight haemorrhage from the lungs. Life is so tiring for people here. She has the right to dine at the Writers' Restaurant, but to get to it means a long journey in a crowded tram, and I think she often goes without a proper meal rather than face the journey. Then to obtain any supplies she has to stand in long queues. We save her some fatigue by giving her butter, sugar and chocolate in exchange for our Russian lessons. Not content with her own worries, she spends considerable time taking things to the prison where Galitzin is. He has been sentenced to five years' exile but is too ill to travel. She was allowed to see him in the prison hospital. He was like a skeleton. He picked up some infection in the prison and has had to have two operations. Mrs Diedrichs considers that it is her duty to marry him. It is true that she is already married, but this husband could, she considers, get along quite well by himself if he only had more energy, and Galitzin is quite alone. The hope of marrying her has put new life into Galitzin. This does not look as though he were the abnormal creature he was accused of being, and indeed he said to her: 'Don't you believe what they say of me.'

22 Feb. A letter from Scott: 'I don't know if it will be agreed to send a Levant man to Strasbourg, but if it is, would you like to go there as soon as we can arrange for your successor at Leningrad?'

This was a difficult question to answer. After thinking about it for a few hours, I wrote to Scott and said that if, as rumour has it, Edmonds is leaving Rabat, I would rather go there. I don't want Strasbourg if Edmonds wants it. He has always wanted a post in Europe, and with a bad heart he needs a healthy post. He says that the climate of Rabat

★

during the two or three muggy months makes him 'feel like death'. I told
Scott that there was more work there than at Strasbourg, and it might
not be a good thing to go from this idle post to another, but that, failing
Rabat, I would take Strasbourg.

Mrs Darwin's comments on her nephew John Cornford, who got a
scholarship at Trinity, are worth quoting: 'How deeply thankful I am
that none of my own dear nephews have been poisoned by communism
in the way Leonard's great-nephew John Cornford has. He is at Trinity
but might just as well be anywhere else as he thinks of nothing else but
his political religion. It seems to have affected every part of his life. He
has hardly any affection for his family, his manners have deteriorated,
and he is so dirty in his person that it is a trial to his friends to have
meals with him. But in this again one sees cause and effect: "The sins of
the fathers shall be visited upon the children." His own father was a
rebel and a violent socialist when young.'

I was a rebel and a socialist when young too! Will our boys be like
John Cornford? He seems to be the stuff out of which the real
communist is made.[3]

The possibility of a move is disturbing. I feel little inclination to go
on with my Russian lessons, or to read Russian.

25 Feb. Yesterday there was a parade of many thousands of Soviet skiers.
We were invited but declined. Better stay at home than spend several
hours standing in the cold watching other people walk past—for that is
about all that happened. I daresay the sight was beautiful, for each
factory or works has a distinctive sports colour for its skiing costume
(and its swimming or other sports costume in summer) and the colours
are massed accordingly. But the young people had better have spent the
day skiing in the sun, instead of being paraded to satisfy the passion of
the authorities for doing things in the mass. But they do little real
skiing—most of them just shuffle about on the level. Even when they go
out by train to the outskirts of the town they do not reach any
considerable slopes. But the number who go out on the free day is
enormous.

It was pleasant to receive, yesterday, a nicely written letter in Russian
from the little girl Joan Cattley whom I managed to get away to Holland
a few weeks ago. She says that she is going to school 'with the sisters'. If

---

[3] John Cornford (1915–1936), poet, was the son of Charles Darwin's granddaughter
Frances Crofts Cornford. He joined the International Brigade and was killed in the
Spanish Civil War.

the OGPU read the latter, as they probably did, they must have gnashed their teeth.

I had the four Americans to dinner again this week. The men looked at the gramophone but could find nothing wrong although they even took parts out to examine more closely. However the machine does in fact run well again. The grinding noise has ceased and the turntable runs true to time.

Whenever Mrs Diedrichs goes to take food parcels to Galitzin in prison she has to wait two, three or even as much as five hours, but she says that it is so interesting to see the other callers and the prisoners that she never gets bored. Often she is called in to write petitions for people who can't understand the regulations or cannot write.

I had Dr Bell and his wife to dinner last night. Mrs Bell refused to charge a fee for attending Miss Goyer's sister when she was ill at the Consulate. I sent her some stores at Christmas that must have been very welcome. Dr Bell thinks the typhus epidemic has abated, the number of cases in all the hospitals does not exceed fifty.

I hear that Lie declares that he cannot understand what the authorities can have against him. We have always been of the opinion that in some way or other—probably by bribes in the form of deposits in banks abroad—he had some big officials in his pocket.

I am glad to read in *The Times* the text of the trade agreement under which the Soviet Government, if they do not find some loophole, will have to spend more of the money paid for the goods they sell us in Great Britain. Italy has a similar agreement, one of the results of which is that Italian lemons can sometimes be bought here for 1½ roubles (three for a day's pay). There are some Jaffa oranges in Torgsin and some fairly wretched little Soviet tangerines in the co-operatives.

4 March. Knatchbull-Hugessen's son, who is at Balliol, has just written to ask, very diffidently, whether I could put him up from 14 to 18 March. He will come here from Riga and wants to see Novgorod. I have suggested that Pott take a day off and go with him. They could go by the night train, have a full day at Novgorod and return the next night.

There have been a number of changes in the diplomatic service. Lord Tyrrell is retiring, and to the surprise of most people Sir George Clerk is to succeed him in Paris.[4] I remember him at Constantinople as a rather

---

[4] William George Tyrrell (1866–1947), British ambassador to Paris from 1928 to 1934, stood for friendship with France above all else. His successor Sir George Clerk (1874–1951) had served in Constantinople and Ankara.

☆

conceited, very smart and not outstandingly able secretary. If I went to Strasbourg he would be my chief, but I don't know that I should like that much. He is, I should think, the perfect conservative in politics and everything else. He is perfectly dressed, does all the conventional things, and probably despises people who are less rigid. However, I haven't got to Strasbourg yet.

We had a very successful dinner for twelve last night. After dinner we found the billiard table which Metro-Vickers left with us a great boon.

7 March. I received another letter from Scott. He says that Edmonds is very keen to go to Strasbourg and if he were posted there, would I like to go to Rabat? I could not bear to compete with Edmonds in this matter, though I would snatch the tempting morsel from any other colleague. He is at the top of the list of Levant consuls, I am bottom but one. He has had his heart set on a European post for years, whereas until Scott himself suggested it to me I had never thought such an appointment possible for anyone in our service. Finally his heart is groggy, whereas my health seems to be good for anything. I would much rather be there than in any other oriental consulate general that I should be likely to get, though leave from Rabat or Strasbourg would be only eight weeks a year, not eleven as here.

11 March. Today will be spoilt by a dinner which I am giving for Russians. We receive our provisions on Friday and it is convenient for any big dinner to be given soon afterwards, and moreover tomorrow is the Soviet free day (the sixth) so that Mr Weinstein will not be so keen to hurry his people away at 11.30 as he usually is. Two of the guests at least like music. The last time Weinstein and his wife came they would not budge from the gramophone. The others can play billiards.

The Relief Association hires out its Ford van to Torgsin and to the organisation which runs shops for foreigners who work for Soviet enterprises and are paid in roubles. Recently we found that the van is being used by the OGPU to collect confiscated furniture. Confiscation of property is a common penalty, in addition to death or exile, for 'counter-revolution'. That is where most of the furniture in the second-hand shops comes from. I think I must stop this, whatever it costs. HMG ought not to be identified with the activities of the OGPU. The identification cannot be avoided so long as this furniture business goes on, for the van has to wait outside the house in question while the OGPU men bring the furniture down and on the side of the van is painted 'English Benevolent Society'.

☆

Once I met a young engineer of about twenty-two, employed in a flax factory at Pskov, at the Bells. He seemed a very decent quiet fellow and the Bells had known him from childhood. Six months ago he was arrested. His wife has just managed to see him. His face was white and bloodless and his beard nearly to his waist. He told her he had been given ten years' isolation camp—for sabotage and counter-revolution. According to him the convoy—all destined for an isolation camp—consisted of 900 people of whom ninety-seven were priests.

For some time Miss Daunt has been wondering whether the real, though not the alleged, offence for which Kulagin was sent away was that he was so rash as to flirt with the wife of the head of the Leningrad OGPU, a brute who is only known by the nickname of 'Myedvyed', or the Bear. It seemed odd that several important friends of his in Moscow had not heard of his exile through the usual channels, and that suggested that his offence could not really be counter-revolution or anything of the kind. Miss Daunt knew at the time that Kulagin was carrying on with 'Mrs Bear' and warned him that it was dangerous, only he scoffed at that as at all other political dangers. According to Mrs Kulagin, the head of the enterprise she works for asked her the other day where her husband was, and when she gave the answer the OGPU told her to give, viz. that he was away on a mission in the Bashkir Republic, he said that he had not asked out of idle curiosity but because at a committee meeting he had attended recently there had been talk about the ease with which people who had committed no crime could be sent away, and the name of Kulagin had been mentioned. Mrs K then admitted that her husband was in fact in exile, and the chief said that his exile had been attributed at the committee meeting to his having paid too much attention to Myedvyed's wife. That the matter should have been mentioned among a number of people at all suggests that the Bear is perhaps falling into disfavour. Maybe someone wants his job or wants to be revenged on him for something. If he is sent to exile and Kulagin returns it will only be one of many such cases.

On the 6th I attended what I hope will be the last Soviet fur dinner I ever attend. We were invited for 5 p.m., dinner began at 5.20 and we got away at 9.00. The longest speech was translated into English, French and German. It was so boring that even Mr Weinstein, who was next to me, complained about it.

Pott and I got much pleasure out of the new opera *Lady Macbeth of the Mtsensk District*. The music is completely unconventional. I was in the front row and could see the orchestra scores. They had no key signatures and obviously there was no fixed key in any part of the music.

☆

I suppose that theoretically the piece was full of what we call disharmonies, but we did not find that either ugly or out of place. It must be a difficult piece to play and still more to sing—the intervals being so unusual. The performance was broadcast the night we were there, and the composer was present. After the first act Shostakovich came forward from the audience and bowed. He looked like a studious English undergraduate of about twenty-one.

I have seen the Americans, Shell and Umsted, again this week. Umsted's firm has sold the Soviet Government the right to make their standard searchlight and also an instrument which is a naval device for fire control. He has been here six months and nothing has been done. He and Shell have the greatest contempt for the engineers and workmen and in particular for the common practice of having big meetings about quite simple things in order to spread the responsibility over as many people as possible.

The German Consul General, with whom I dined last night, has a fine library. I borrowed a book which I saw well-reviewed: *Further Letters from a Man of No Importance*. It deals with the period 1914–29. It contains some good things. I will copy out a few . . . .

> From Cambon, French Ambassador in London before and during the War, the first time he saw jazz-dancing: '*Je n'ai jamais vu des figures si tristes, ni des derrières si gais.*'

> When (General) Castelnau's second son was killed, he received the news at a meeting of his subordinate generals, which he did not break off except to send a message to ask his chaplain to break the news to his wife. Mme de Castelnau went to mass and made her communion almost daily; on this occasion as the priest gave her the host she saw his hand tremble and she just whispered: '*Lequel?*' And he whispered back to her the name.

I have never read anything more moving than this last story. Is it only because we have sons and the possibility of war in their time is by no means ruled out? I hope it is a more generous feeling.

12 March. A very successful small dinner last night. At the last moment Buchstein, who runs the Opera, sent word that he could not come, and we were only ten but the Russians seemed to enjoy themselves.

The chief English fur-buyers here, who represent the Hudson Bay Company, report with satisfaction that they have brought off a *coup* and outmanoeuvred the German, Hollander, and the American, Bernstein. Hollander and Bernstein were ostensibly working independently but in reality exchanging information in private. The Soviets were annoyed and fell in with the Hudson Bay proposals, making a yearly contract for the supply of Persian lamb 10% below that which was realised at the auction a few hours later.

18 March. Sunday. Mrs Charles is a startling sight. I was prepared for it though even then I had a slight shock when I saw her. Platinum blonde hair done in a very stiff kink, face frightfully made up, and on top of all one of those hats in which no woman looks nice—the kind something like a soft mortar-board stuck on one side at an angle of 45 degrees. To go to the ballet she wore a similar hat with a scarlet, *semi-décolleté* blouse. Her accent is the strangest I ever heard. With all this she is very nice, clever and quite unaffected. The ballet I took them to was *Esmeralda,* based on Victor Hugo's *Notre Dame* but with an anti-religious twist.

The only thing on at the Opera the night young Hugessen was here was an opera called *Demon* by Rubinstein based on a poem by Lermontov. The most dreary thing I ever saw. However the next night we were able to take him to the Children's Theatre to see *Uncle Tom's Cabin.* The theatre was nearly full of children who behaved exactly as English children would behave, siding with the weak against the strong. This is interesting when one remembers the brutality with which the *kulaks* are treated and the ferocity inculcated into schoolchildren against priests.

There are strange rumours current that the OGPU is to be abolished and a ministry of the interior created in its place. It is not to be expected that there will be any essential change, but it will be interesting to see whether the Party try to conceal the OGPU activities under a form of administration that will look a little more constitutional. They cannot make any real change, partly because it is of the nature of the Russian and in accordance with the Marxian creed to be autocratic, partly because the country cannot be run by democratic methods.

On 7 March an interesting decree was promulgated. It makes sexual relations between men an offence punishable with 'deprivation of liberty' for a period of three to five years, to be served not in one of the show prisons in the offender's place of residence, but in a labour camp.

My *Times* began to arrive irregularly—sometimes a couple of days late—and to show obvious signs of having been read. I knew the reason: someone wanted to read the debate in the House on the Anglo-Soviet trade agreement. I had to complain to Weinstein to get the nuisance abated, and then the loudspeaker outside the Consulate began again, and for the third or fourth time I had to complain about that.

★

20 March. Mrs Diedrichs came with us to the puppet-show and we brought her back to dinner afterwards. She talked about life here just after the Revolution. She was a young girl then, of course, there was no fuel and very little food. Her mother managed to get a job as housekeeper at the Party headquarters in Smolny, formerly a school for the daughters of the nobility. She was able to steal and bring back a little food now and then. Everyone was stealing, you could hardly get food otherwise. When it was discovered that her mother had owned houses, she was dismissed. She got a little money by selling cakes in the market, which was dangerous as such trading was forbidden.

The other day the manager of the State Bank, Zhidkov, asked Miss Daunt if she would teach him to dance. She has now heard that orders have been issued to encourage modern dancing (formerly looked down upon and even forbidden), because when the Minister of War, Voroshilov, visited Turkey recently, the only form of entertainment which the Turks could offer—dancing—was no good because the Russians couldn't dance.

A few days ago Mrs Diedrichs was ordered to meet her OGPU contact at a certain street corner, but when she got there she found a new man who ordered her to write down the 'characteristics' of myself, Pott and Miss Daunt. This is a new word which Mrs D hardly understands herself, but it is clear she has got to furnish full reports on us. She will get into trouble if she does not produce something soon.

The papers have been writing a lot about a Jewish revolutionary named Sverdlov, who died fifteen years ago this month. He was exiled several times in tsarist times but always managed to escape. It was a blow to the Party when he died of influenza in 1919. The newspapers praise him greatly (a safe thing to do as Stalin once praised him as one of the two most valuable men after Lenin). None of them mention that it was he who gave the order for the slaughter of the Tsar and his wife and children at Ekaterinburg—now called 'Sverdlovsk' in his honour.

Miss Daunt had to go yesterday to a distant quarter of the city and she was beset by a crowd of homeless boys of about fourteen. One of them tried to undo the shoulder-straps on her uniform, others tried to smash the car windows. The chauffeur drove them away and hit one.

25 March. Sunday. Now that the US have renewed relations with Russia there is to be an American consulate general in Moscow with one consul general, one consul, and *five* vice-consuls. No news of the opening of an American consulate here.

The unfortunate Mrs Diedrichs has to have an operation—I don't know what for, but Miss Daunt has given her the chloroform for it, otherwise it would have had to have been done without an anaesthetic. She took Anna Akhmatova the copy of the *Dublin Magazine* containing the article on her poems. She also took as a present from me a slab of chocolate and a cake each of Pears and Lux soap.

Saw Mrs Kulagin at Miss Daunt's yesterday. She showed me a postcard which her husband had sent to a communist who lives in the same house as she does. Kulagin has received almost none of the letters his wife has written, and I suppose that he thought he might be more successful if he communicated with this communist friend of his. At the end he asks for news of his wife and daughter, but five-sixths of the card is full of references—laudatory of course—to the accounts of the Party Conference which he had read in the press.

The thaw has come early this year, and Mrs Kulagin says that the central heating in her block of flats has been turned off. She and her daughter were helped by an old friend of her husband's who was head of the military air service in Leningrad, but he has now disappeared. The three young men who were killed in the Soviet airship were from Leningrad,[5] and as he disappeared immediately afterwards Mrs Kulagin supposes that he is being treated as responsible for the catastrophe.

The communist friend who lived in the same block must be a remarkable character. He was in America for eight years and was doing well, but he came back as a sympathiser in 1922—almost the worst moment of the famine. He is as keen a communist as ever. When Mrs Kulagin reminds him that all the prophecies that things would be better by a given date have been proved wrong he only says that they will be better presently. He has a large family of children and his wife has the greatest difficulty in feeding them, but he never grumbles, and if there is only bread and water for him when he comes in he puts a little salt on the bread and eats it cheerfully. He takes everything he reads in the Soviet papers as gospel. He is much too good a man to approve the means by which the Soviet power is maintained if he knew about it. Mrs Kulagin says there are very few communists like him.

All the consuls were invited to a special performance of Ibsen's *Pillars of Society* last week. It is a very good play and the acting was as usual magnificent. Orlov-Ermak was bored and described the play roundly as

[5] The Soviet balloon *Osoaviakhim* crashed on 30 January (having ascended a record 13 miles into the stratosphere) with the loss of all the crew. It was announced that their ashes would be buried in the wall of the Kremlin, near Lenin's mausoleum (see also 7 April, below).

★

'old-fashioned', and Weinstein would have said the same thing if he had not got out of the habit of speaking plainly about anything. They seem to have lost the capacity to project their minds into surroundings so different. Yet the people enjoy the classical plays of e.g. Ostrovsky very much.

28 March. Mrs Diedrichs has been telling me about a book lent to her by a writer who lives in the room next to hers. It is by a revolutionary who was attached to the late Tsar and his family as censor. Mrs Diedrichs has never seen or heard of another copy of this book, and she supposes that after it was printed the authorities realised that it was not suitable for general distribution. The author was an 'intellectual'. At first he was dissatisfied at having to pry into other people's private affairs, but when he began work he was glad, as his position enabled him to prevent the young princesses from seeing the filthy letters which were sent to them in great numbers. They had little to do and were dull and bored, and he began to read to them. He chose first a poem by Nekrasov which related a touching story of the wife of one of the Decembrist revolutionaries who insisted on following her husband into exile. Her father, who was a high official, failed to prevent her from leaving St Petersburg, so he wrote to official friends all along the route, asking them to do their best to stop her. Each did what he could, but all failed. When she was getting near the end of the journey, the governor of the place declared that there was no transport to take her the next stage, and that the only way she could travel would be if he allowed her to be chained to a gang of convicts leaving that day. The woman got up and begged him to act on this suggestion at once: the gang might leave while she was talking. While the censor was reading he heard a slight sound, and looking round he saw the Empress at the door, with the tears streaming down her face. She had come in and heard the poem. The girls asked: 'But why didn't they *tell* us there were such things?' They could not believe that their censor was a revolutionary. Having been brought up to believe that revolutionaries were social scum they thought that the censor, being a man of education and feeling, must be a tsarist officer in disguise. I wish I could read this book.

2 April. Saturday and Sunday were lovely spring days (two or three weeks early). I went with Taylor and the Waltons to the palace of Peterhof. Albert Coates came to lunch and went with us for a walk afterwards. Mrs Walton isn't a bad little creature. She had nine months in an OGPU prison without allowing it to break her spirit. She told me that it sometimes happens in these crowded prisons that one of the prisoners will have a fit of hysteria and begin to scream, which spreads to others until perhaps hundreds are screaming uncontrollably. Walton says people who live near the OGPU place in Moscow have heard the screaming more than once, and describe it as terrifying.

Coates is conducting four operas and several concerts, including some English music—Vaughan Williams and Holst, and we want to see how the audience take it.

The first prize for piano playing at the Leningrad Conservatoire was won by a former waif—one of those hordes who roamed the country for several years. It is a mark for the Soviet authorities that such a child should have been able to become a first-class pianist. But one should not forget that their policy has created a new class of waifs and strays. I have seen plenty of them myself.

Joseph came in with his interpreter the Russian girl who is quite obviously his mistress. He told me that he had had a very tough time with the customs but his interpreter suggested to the OGPU that possibly the reason for this was because Joseph is Jewish. At this, she said, the head OGPU man (?Myedvyed), himself Jewish, 'went up in the air'. She told Joseph that the OGPU were not so very well-paid and get only 350 roubles per month, but they come first on the list for everything in the way of food, clothing, medicines, holidays etc. One of them has told the girl to produce cloth for a suit, which Joseph will have to get for her.

The interpreter said that the OGPU suspect Joseph because he was friendly with Walton, whom they regard as our chief spy. She showed Joseph a picture of a group of OGPU agents, who looked a dreadful crew. They were mostly Letts, Estonians, Armenians etc. Joseph says that sales from the Hermitage have ceased for the present. The people there have no idea of the value of what they have. On his last trip he bought two King Charles plates for £8 and sold them in London for £179. He is trying to buy three models of ships for the naval museum at Greenwich. He has offered £5000 but the people in charge won't sell— at the moment.

Joseph's interpreter told him that Mrs Kulagin had been arrested but released after one night in prison. I think this must be correct because Miss Daunt has been very subdued and quite unlike herself. Mrs Kulagin sent a message thanking us for provisions and saying that she would like to see us to thank us in person, but it would be 'inadvisable'. She had never shown any fear of meeting us before, and indeed we have always been more discreet than she has. Perhaps she got off with a caution.

☆

This dialogue took place last week between Miss Daunt and the ten-year-old son of Dr Bell. BOY: 'My cousin . . . is getting married.' MISS D: 'That's splendid.' BOY: 'Yes it is. It's a long while since she was a virgin, and we were getting very anxious.'

Miss Daunt received a peremptory message to come at once to police headquarters. While she was waiting in the corridor, a Red Army officer, hearing her speak English to Mrs Hay, said it was not fitting that she should be kept waiting and he would take her in to the police chief. The army officer wanted Miss Daunt's business to be taken first, however the policeman barked at him to speak first. He asked under what law he had been ordered to put his mother and sister into the street. The police officer could not or would not quote any law, but just said brutally that the women must go and that it was a good thing. 'Let her work!' 'Work? She is sixty-seven.' 'That's not my business.'

The next time a senior OGPU man called to see her Miss Daunt told him about the incident, saying that the army officer had wished to be discreet and not tell his business in front of a foreigner, and that the fault lay entirely with the policeman. The police have been under the OGPU for the last three years or so. Miss Daunt hopes that this officer will be suitably punished. To give anything away to foreigners is an unpardonable sin, so the man may well be sent to dig a canal for some years.

Coates told me of his plans to establish an English National Opera. He speaks about it as though it were very secret, but perhaps secrecy only applies to an attempt to get the King's support. This is to be done through Runciman, who is musical and has a very musical son. Among the supporters of the scheme are Ellerman, son of the shipowner who died last year leaving £17 million, and Lady Houston.[6] There would be opera in London for six months of the year. The loss would probably be about £30,000 on the season. Coates wants the BBC to put up this money in return for the broadcasting rights. This would be expensive for the BBC, but the Opera would be part of a national system of musical education. Then it would be the aim to keep the provinces and the Dominions supplied with visiting operatic productions. These would serve as training-grounds for musical talent which at present has little or

[6] Walter Runciman (1870–1949) was president of the Board of Trade from 1931 to 1937; John Reeves Ellerman (1909–1973) was the heir to his father's baronetcy; Lady Houston DBE (1857–1936) was a philanthropist, eccentric and patriot who had financed the Schneider trophy in 1931 and the flight over Everest in 1933. The organisation now known as the English National Opera, however, was not founded until 1974.

no chance. Coates spoke of the many good singers in England who only need an opportunity. It is interesting to hear all this 'shop'.

I saw a very amusing play last week—*Somebody Else's Child*. Except at one point it has no Marxist ideology in it, and is correspondingly popular.

Lady Muriel has finished the x-ray treatment in England, but there was another scare and she rushed over to Paris. Fortunately the decision was favourable. I am glad she is better, but I hope that it does not mean she will come out here again.

7 April. An Englishman in Moscow named Wicksteed, who lives by giving English lessons, has been trying for years to get into the Russian Communist Party. His father was well-known in English university circles, but the son has rather gone to seed. He recently came to Duranty's house when Walton was there, and said: 'I have a piece of news that will interest you both. The decree against homosexual offences is not to be applied to "people of goodwill".' This was no news to us because it is well-known that certain well-placed addicts have not been touched, and because it is the nature of the Russians to use everything for political ends. But it is interesting to have one's supposition confirmed by a man who is in touch with top circles. I suspect that in future fewer men will be exiled for counter-revolution and more for homosexual offences. In future it will be easy, if the authorities want to get rid of a possible critic, to give him three to five years in a concentration camp for sodomy. He is thus branded with a moral stigma, while the authorities evade the accusation of getting rid of their political opponents on flimsy grounds.

Coates' first concert last night. Vaughan Williams' *London Symphony* not very successful. I quite liked it but I did not think it a great piece of music—but then I never like descriptive music. It ought to be possible to indicate a day in London without having the Westminster chimes and the march of the unemployed and the cries of the flower-sellers. The concert ended with extracts from *Götterdämmerung* and *Parsifal* because it is Easter. For the same reason he is giving the opera *Khovanshchina* tonight which I saw him conduct in Moscow. There was an influenza epidemic at the time and about fifteen of the principal singers were ill. The chief part had to be taken by a very old man with a wooden leg. Coates seems to be very popular here and the audience called him out four times after the end of the concert.

The FO and the Embassy have been wondering for some time whether it is possible to rescue the relief work in Russia from the clutches of Lady Muriel. The Treasury contribute £110 a month to the fund of the British Subjects in Russia Relief Association, on the reasonable assumption that if these poor people came to England, as they are legally entitled to do, it would cost public funds much more than that to maintain them. The essential relief (even including Miss Daunt's salary) costs a good deal less than twice £110, so that in order to secure for the DBSs the difference between £110 and perhaps £180 a month, HMG have to allow Lady Muriel to run the work. She now wants to have a tennis-court built in the garden. I have written her a stiff letter and sent copies to Charles and to the head of the northern department of the FO who can repudiate me if they like. She has been badgering the man who corresponds to the keeper of the gardens at Kew to provide her with a first-class gardener who can both act as night-watchman and supervise the laying out of the garden. She seems to be under the impression that he will be happy with some seeds from England in return. What a business this is! The day I began work in Moscow I spent hours trying to unravel a mess in the accounts which had been made by Lady Muriel—a mess which compelled Keane, who was then at Leningrad, to advance large sums from his own pocket, and ever since there has been a struggle to keep her extravagance—to give it no harsher name—within bounds. The FO and the Embassy consider me a marvel in that although I have always opposed Lady Muriel, I am the only person here of whom she speaks highly. Another sign of the madness I have detected in her.

An Australian engineer, Hardwicke, was brought in, accompanied by one of the prettiest girls I ever saw. He did not introduce me, so I suspected the girl was his interpreter. I invited him to lunch next day, but he did not bring the 'little lady' (whom I had not specifically invited) as she was afraid to come for fear of the OGPU. He told me that she came of a very good family (they all do), has distinguished relatives in London, etc. Pott, who saw the girl about in Moscow, says that she is Jewish, her name is Horseradish (*Khren*) and she is well known to be an OGPU agent. A year or so ago Hardwicke induced several big firms in England, notably Imperial Chemicals, to engage him to sell their products to the Soviet Government. Now that the trade agreement compels them to spend a certain amount of money in England, his chance has come, and he is doing well. A young Russian friend of his recently returned from six months' exile in Siberia. He doesn't speak now to H when he meets him in the street, but gives a sort of wink. He doesn't know himself why he was sent away, but he was arrested just after a party given by Hardwicke. Hardwicke finds that people who were formerly friendly now say, 'Thanks very much, but we had better not: it isn't worthwhile' when he invites them to his place.

When the three Soviet airmen were killed in the airship disaster, the newspapers printed on 4 February a long letter alleged to have been written to Stalin by ten persons described as the 'fathers, mothers, brothers, sisters, wives and children' of the dead men. The letter ends as follows: 'We make no exclusive claim to the dead men. No, they belonged first of all to the Party, the working class, the country that is building socialism. They died for the work of communism. We promise you, our dear Josef Vissarionovich, to devote all our efforts to carrying on the great work for which our dead members of the Society for Aviation and Chemical Warfare strove.'

One of the most unpleasant traits in the Russian character is subservience. When the OGPU held their fifteenth anniversary the press was filled with such tributes as would be exaggerated if applied to the men who helped to abolish slavery.

A thing that has always interested me is the position of the trade unions here. So far as I could see they were simply instruments of State policy and did not exist to defend their members but to make the members do what the Party ordered. Once or twice when I have heard from Russians of bad conditions in which they had no work I have asked whether such points were not taken up by the trade unions, and each time the speaker has smiled at my ingenuousness. The situation was made pretty clear in a speech made to a trade union congress a year or two ago by Mr Molotov, President of the Council of Commissars. He said, 'Certain elements in the trade unions attempted to stultify the Party's task of transforming all proletarian organisations to correspond with the new order. It is well known how these attempts ended. Only on the basis of extended socialist construction is a real improvement in the material condition of the working class possible.' The trade unions did not want their members to be sacrificed to the plans of a Party over which they had no control, and wished more attention to be paid to the common requirements of the workers and less to gigantic schemes of industrial construction. The relative failure of the Plan and the mess that industry was in at the end of the Plan forced the Government to slacken off on big building and to speed up the production of consumer goods. This has already had the happy effect of bringing more clothing and other goods into the shops. Prices are high, but at least you can buy a jug or a pair of boots if you have the money.

Foreigners receive many black looks in Torgsin. There are sometimes queues at the counters and always queues at the pay-desk, and however

★

long they are any foreigner may go straight up and be attended to first. The consuls' wives take advantage of this privilege, and the wives of the American and other engineers, but they don't like it. In other ways too the foreigner comes first. When the guides take foreign tourists to see places of interest, Soviet citizens are shoved aside without ceremony. At the office where foreigners and Soviet citizens go for all passport formalities there was an incident the other day when a Soviet citizen emptied a box of lice over a foreigner. The passport office for foreigners is being transferred to another place, so that they will not meet Soviet citizens.

Joseph has been in again. He wants to get his interpreter out and marry her. She thinks she can get a passport to go abroad as she has a hold over the man who grants them. Joseph mentioned the name of a high-up OGPU man, Löwe. Mrs Litvinov was a Miss Löwe only she calls it Low, as did her better-known father or uncle Sidney Low. He says his interpreter told him decisions to execute people are taken very casually. Löwe, according to her, had decided that a certain man should not be shot and signed a decision to that effect, when another OGPU officer came in and argued that the accused deserved death for various things he was said to have done, and Löwe said 'Oh all right' and reversed his decision.

12 April. Coates was completely laid out after conducting *Khovanshchina*—one of the longest operas and with no opportunity for rehearsal. He hardly used the score at all. We brought him back to a supper of *borshch* with little cabbage pies, followed by Easter cake and *paskha*. He had been speaking of these Russian delicacies and wishing he might taste them again and Mrs Finke produced them for him. He enjoyed himself like a child, and ate far more than was good for him. He also drank six if not more tumblers of iced lemonade. But it revived him. We have been to another of his concerts. The piece of the evening was Scriabin's *Divine Poem*. Only you mustn't put such a name on a Soviet programme, so it had to be called such-and-such a symphony. It was wonderful. Forty minutes of superb music without a stop.

Dr Petrov, chief assistant to the physiologist Pavlov, invited Coates to visit the Institute. We went with him and watched one of the experiments in progress. We saw a dog in a lighted sound-proof chamber where he can be observed through a tiny window. A tube which acts in the same way as a dentist's drain passes through one cheek and draws off the saliva from one of the three pairs of salivary glands. At five-minute intervals a signal is given in the chamber: a metronome ticks, a light appears, a musical note is sounded. Some of these mean that food is coming, some that food is not coming. For instance, food follows the ticking of a metronome at a certain rate but not the ticking at half that rate. The dog learns when to expect food. When he thinks food is coming, the saliva necessary for its digestion begins to form; one third of it is drawn off, and the amount is shown by an instrument outside the chamber. The dog we saw was not very practised, and also, according to the observer, rather stupid. He produced some—though not much— saliva even when no food was coming. The dog seemed perfectly content, and looked quite indifferent when the tube was pulled out of the little hole in his cheek. He seemed fond of the professor and gave him a paw when asked to do so. We saw other dogs too who are used for this experiment, and they wagged their tails and seemed pleased to see the professors. The professor claimed that when they have been used for a certain time they are pensioned off and all the dogs eventually die of old age. They have a garden to themselves with a swimming-pool and other doggish delights. The dog we saw was later to have his thyroid gland removed in order to study the effect this would have on the brain. For this reason these elaborate intelligence tests had to be made first. I should like to read a simple account of the work Pavlov has done and of the results claimed for it.

Pott goes on leave on the 16th. I am glad. He has had about enough of this country. The lack of company, and the knowledge that people are afraid to make friends with us, gets on his nerves, and he begins to worry.

15 April. In my 3½ years in this country I have never once seen a reference to England that was not hostile, if not grossly unfair. Here is a typical one. The *Red Gazette* prints a picture of a large water-wheel in India—one of those primitive devices used for hundreds of years for irrigating rice-fields—in which men walk round the projecting spokes of large wooden wheels. This picture is headed: 'Under the paw of the British "civilisers".' Two countries in which communists are not even allowed to exist are never criticised—Italy and Turkey.

The new American Ambassador, Bullitt, was appointed by Roosevelt as being a friend of the Soviet Union—a dangerous position to be in. The other foreign missions are watching with *Schadenfreude* to see how long the honeymoon will last. Rapp writes from Moscow: 'Bullitt has been trying for a month to get a special rate for roubles for the Embassy and the staff—with what success you may imagine. One day they were charged $2000 to have a few cartloads of snow and rubbish removed

★

from the Embassy premises. The efforts of the Consul General, Hanson, to establish contacts with the Soviet authorities are being frustrated in the way we know so well. Sokolnikov suggested that the Consul should deal with the heads of VOKS.' VOKS, ye gods! VOKS is the propaganda organisation which, if a consul asks for a teacher of Russian, will send him someone warranted to spy on him efficiently.

On 20th March there was a railway accident near Rostov. Six persons were killed and eighteen wounded, and the damage was estimated at 82,250 roubles. A man named Bragin, who was on duty at the station, sent an express and a locomotive on its way to be cleaned on to the same line in opposite directions. He has been sentenced to be shot. The station-master has been given six years' deprivation of liberty for 'contributing to a disturbance of labour discipline, nepotism and lack of organisation at the station'. According to the penal code the death penalty can only be imposed for a transport accident if the guilty party acted with evil intent, but there is no suggestion that Bragin did anything worse than make a fatal mistake. But the law means nothing here. If it is disregarded in cases reported in the press, what of the other cases?

18 April. M is right in being taken aback by my suggestion that she should come out for a few weeks. It would be rash, financially, and the arrangements for the children would be very difficult to make. It just seemed sad that with a car—probably the only car I shall ever have— and so many things to see in an interesting place, M should not be able to come out. But we ought not to spend the money when things are so tight.

We have found an unexpected ally in our opposition to the tennis-court—the OGPU. Dr Emmé, the woman scientist who hung round Lady Muriel a lot on her last visit and makes clumsy attempts now and then to pump Miss Daunt, has sent Lady Muriel a message that the tennis-court must on no account be built: it would make the worst impression.

The other day I was ragging our hairdresser, asking whether it would be the hairdressers who would 'demand' the next loan. Two days later the newspapers contained resolutions from two large factories in Leningrad and in the Urals, demanding another loan. The 'demand' comes regularly once a year. Sometimes people are expected to contribute at home as well as at their place of work.

Coates strayed in on Sunday to ask for a couple of oranges. He wanted to make a cocktail for Alexei Tolstoy and some other Russians who were coming to dinner. We had no oranges—there have been none here for weeks, but we gave him some Kia-Ora lemon squash. He was regretting that the hotel could not produce the common Russian fish, the *sig*, but as we had two in the house (brought from Finland) we gave him one. He carried it off under his arm, wrapped up in fair imitation of a musical score. In gratitude he gave me and Mrs Finke free seats in the second row for Rimsky-Korsakov's *Tsar Sultan* the following night. He had as usual a tremendous reception.

21 April. Pott thinks that he would like to learn to play the piano, and I have encouraged him as he needs as much occupation as possible to keep him from brooding. Mrs Diedrichs could give him some lessons. The Estonian Consul General will lend us one of the several pianos belonging to an Estonian who cannot get permission to export them. I wish I had thought of this before: I might have played a bit myself.

Miss Daunt's OGPU visitors have remarked more than once on the loneliness of the life she leads. Mrs Emmé asked why the British Consulate does not invite some of the members of the Academy of Sciences to receptions. She admitted it might be dangerous for one or two of them to come alone, and they must first be invited by the consuls before they could return the invitations. I shan't do anything about this at present. My successor can inaugurate the new regime. The Germans used to have tremendous shows five or six years ago with two hundred or more Russians, but as the political control grew tighter the number fell off to such an extent that it was hardly worth while to invite Russians any more.

Mrs Emmé related some of her love-affairs to Miss Daunt, as, it is said, Russian women will with a little encouragement. She has had three husbands (I don't know what has become of them all), and now has a lover who is high up in the Party. She loves this man 'more than any of my husbands, more than my only son'. The wife of a theatrical scene-designer told Mrs Diedrichs the other day that she had two husbands: one was her love, the other her passion.

Lady Muriel has written to Miss Daunt cancelling the tennis-court. She does not refer to my letter. She alleges as grounds for giving up the project that the tenancy of the villa is so insecure. This is to save her face. The lease is for thirty years, though if Lady Muriel ceased to have anything to do with the Relief Association we should give the villa away. I fear Lady Muriel is not well. I am sorry for the poor woman; she has trouble at home too.

When Mrs Diedrichs went to visit Galitzin in prison, she found he had been sent into exile. The authorities had promised that she would be allowed to see him before he went, but naturally Bolshevik promises have little weight. Mrs D thinks that she wasn't allowed a farewell visit to punish her for not producing the right reports about me and Pott. She is worried that Galitzin had no money or food with him. He is being sent to Gorod Svobodnykh, literally the 'City of the Free'. It is in the Far East, and at the rate prisoners travel it may take a month or more to get there. It is apparently a place where prisoners are distributed to the various places of exile, so it is no good sending money there, she will have to wait until the prisoner knows where he is to be.

Torgsin now keep fashion books, and any woman who can pay in foreign currency may bring a piece of tracing-paper and copy any fashion she fancies. During 1933 the authorities have concentrated on consumer goods and the result is apparent. Boots are better and clothes a good deal better. At the Coates concerts I have seen several women wearing evening-dresses of a kind—some of them velvet. You can even buy pots and pans—at a price.

Every now and then Herr Sommer, the German Consul General, sends me the latest official Hitlerite pamphlet in English, sometimes in German too. He never speaks about these pamphlets to me, and I always feel that he is not an enthusiastic Nazi. His position is hard. He is a very able man, with long service, promoted from the ranks of the clerical archivist staff. He feels that some day he may be asked to take a rest for his health, and a supporter of Hitler put in his place. The former Vice-Consul, Pfleiderer, who was transferred to the German Foreign Office some months ago, is not happy there. He is not a Prussian, and he is a liberal. The place is run by young men who support Hitler and the position of the senior officials especially is not agreeable. Pfleiderer hoped that at least he would be asked his views on Soviet Russia, but no one has taken any notice of him.

Everybody has to subscribe to the new loan, but they are only being asked for one month's pay. Last time it was 1½ months' pay and this resulted in a lot of complaints. Perhaps public opinion has to be studied a little, even here.

23 April. The pretty green space opposite the Consulate is to be hidden for I don't know how long by a huge model of the Chelyushkin incident—the camp on the ice from which the Soviet expedition was rescued by aeroplane.[7]

---

[7] In February 1934 a Soviet vessel on the way from Murmansk to Vladivostok by the

I have been asking about the Pavlov laboratory experiments. Miss Goyer saw a dog whose nerve-centres had been completely severed so that he had no feeling at all and could not get up. There is probably no anti-vivisection legislation here, and scientists are able to do anything they like with animals. Where human life is so cheap it cannot be expected that animals should be protected.

25 April. An Englishman called Metcalfe passing through told us about three articles in the *Sunday Express* about Stalin, which report that he does himself very well and costs the country a good deal. I don't know what alternative, if any, the writer has to propose. That a dictator should be a good and not a bad man, perhaps. But a good man could not work with the people who run this country: indeed, he would never get into a high position. Metcalfe is not a man I like, because he is always flattering the Soviet authorities in public in order to ingratiate himself to get business. I agree that we should try to get business, and that the Soviet methods of government are no concern of ours, but I dislike the licking of the comrades' boots.

Mrs Finke left for a holiday in England this morning. The customs would not let her take her gold brooch and wrist-watch with her and the chauffeur had to bring them back.

I find most of the food I gave to Mrs Diedrichs in payment for my lessons went to Galitzin in prison. I asked whether it wasn't risky to give him English chocolate, but she says she scraped the word 'Cadbury' off each little square and then rubbed the slab in the chocolate dust, and when wrapped in a dirty piece of paper it looked all right.

Hanson came to see me this morning. I liked him. The Americans are already tired of the way in which the Soviet Government make them pay through the nose for everything. For one month Hanson lived on roubles bought at the swindling State Bank rate, but then he gave it up. As to the Ambassador, the friend of the Soviet Union, the more roubles he can buy illegally, the better pleased he is.

28 April. I thought it certain that I should hear something about my transfer yesterday, but there wasn't a word. It is very odd. Seven weeks

---

northern route sank near Wrangel Island, off the north-eastern coast of Siberia, after being trapped and crushed in the ice with 111 men, women and children on board. Their hazardous rescue by air, which took over two months, aroused tremendous excitement, and the order of 'Hero of the Soviet Union' was specially instituted to reward the pilots involved in the rescue.

★

have passed since the date when Scott must have received my letter.

The reduction in income tax leaves us £12 or £13 more a year. I have chafed at our inability to subscribe to 'worthy' objects: the Friends' scheme for allotments etc. and the Oxford Birth-Control Clinic.

Last year there were paeans of triumph in the press because a Soviet factory was producing pianos. Before the War there were two factories in St Petersburg turning out excellent pianos, but never mind that. The triumph was short-lived. A professor at the Conservatoire writes about a grand piano which was delivered by the 'Red October' works of the music trust. It has already lost its qualities. The sound is dead and uneven. The keys have begun to drop. The wood used will not stand a change of temperature. The intervals between the keys are unequal. The celluloid used in place of ivory is too thin and the sharp edges cut the player's fingers. Similar complaints come from other quarters in an article headed: 'Why should a piano become a hurdy-gurdy?' Other instruments, guitars, balalaikas etc. made by the music trust have earned a similar reputation.

Miss Daunt told Dr Emmé that Lady Muriel had sent instructions cancelling the plans for the tennis-court, and she expressed great relief, and admitted that the warning had been given by someone high up in the OGPU—as though we couldn't guess that. Dr Emmé said that life is hard these days. She claimed that it didn't matter, they were building socialism etc., but still, it *was* difficult.

The Times of 18 April (with news of the budget) reached me in seven days instead of four. It was clear that the paper had been opened, though this time they had tried to hide the fact.

I invited Metcalfe and his wife to dinner, and I was repaid by being taken to hear the violinist Heifetz. I had never heard a first-class violinist before, and I did not know that it was possible to get such music out of a violin.[8]

Nearly all the passengers on the Soviet boat on which Mrs Metcalfe travelled were communist delegates for the 1 May celebrations. There were meetings, speeches and films every night.

Miss Goyer's section in the acoustics lab is to be closed down for lack of money. The Gramophone Works are supposed to subsidise it but

---

[8] Jascha Heifetz (1901–1987) had settled in the USA after the Revolution. He described his Russian tour as one of the most profound emotional experiences of his life; he was able to meet his uncle Nachum who presented him with the original quarter-size violin on which his father had taught him to play, and which he took back with him to the United States.

haven't done so. Soviet gramophones and records are so bad that they only sell at all because the people cannot get any others.

The transfer of the Academy of Sciences to Moscow will make it unnecessary for me to decide whether to invite scientists to my parties or not. When Dr Emmé suggested this she cannot have known that the Academy was to be transferred. Indeed I believe that it has come as a complete surprise to the scientists. I am sorry for them. Leningrad is a handsome city with a character which seems to suit the study of science, and being some distance from Moscow it has greater freedom than the capital where there will be no escaping the Kremlin.

A recent article about building work in Leningrad says: 'We are building slowly, badly, and expensively.' This reminds me of the Latin motto suggested for the Indian Public Works Department: '*Nec pulchriter, nec celeriter, sed multo argento*.'[9]

I had been reading some German every day, but when it seemed probable that I should be going to Rabat, I stopped. I have just read Helen Waddell's wonderful *Wandering Scholars* for the third or fourth time. Among some books that Tearle left for the DBSs I found *The Little Minister*. It confirmed my opinion of Barrie. I detested him and myself for being moved at the emotional parts. Now I am reading *Victory* again. It seems to me a great book, and by far the best of Conrad's.

1 May. At last, on 28 April, I heard from Scott. He has been ill and that has delayed the decision about Rabat and Strasbourg. I always knew how much depended upon Scott, who's the only man in the FO who knows the men in the consular service.

The authorities put up a formidable parade today. It lasted for 3½ hours and it was hot sitting in the sun. I was doubly hot because I had my overcoat on: I could not take it off because I was trying to take some notes in my pocket. I arrived just too late to see what must have been the most interesting event of the day. In the square where the parade is held there is a tall column surmounted by a huge angel with a cross. Some years ago the Soviet authorities tried to remove the angel. It is said that some men lost their lives in the attempt, and the task was abandoned. Anyhow there the angel stands, and it looks particularly inappropriate in the middle of a parade in honour of an atheist government. At the parade last November they hit on the ingenious plan of covering the angel in a mass of coloured balloons. They repeated the scheme this year forgetting that it is hotter in May than November, and

[9] 'Neither beautifully nor speedily but expensively.'

★

after all the spectators had assembled, the balloons all exploded, covering everyone with sand from the square and revealing the angel with its finger pointing to heaven!

The model opposite my windows is very cleverly made. It looks just like an ice-field complete with models of the wrecked ship, an aeroplane, a boat or two, a sledge with dogs and some members of the marooned party. It looked well against the grey cathedral, but the artistic effect has been completely ruined by the 30-foot-high portrait of the inevitable Stalin. One's eye is led relentlessly to the portrait. Doubtless what was intended, but artistically disastrous.

Mrs Kulagin went to see Miss Daunt a few days ago. She said nothing about being called up by the OGPU but her nerve has gone completely. She was always cheerful and courageous, and made light of her troubles, but now her spirit seems quite broken. She wept and wept, though she gave no reason for her distress. She has got a job through the railway manager who was a friend of her husband's. She starts at 8 a.m. in a goods office and sometimes gets home at 11.00 or 12.00 at night.

3 May. Is it only because Jews are more musical that all the prominent pianists here seem to be Jewish? Do Jewish pianists not get sent into exile? Hard to say.

6 May. Sunday. Miss Daunt has been planting apple trees and raspberry canes and blackcurrant bushes in the huge garden at the villa.

Mr Boothby[10] came in for a few minutes. He wants the Soviet Government to buy Scottish herrings and had been to see Rosengoltz, head of the Foreign Trade Commissariat in Moscow. He seems an active, sensible man and I wish I had seen more of him.

A man has just returned to Leningrad after spending several years in Solovki. He brought back as a souvenir a domino from a set which he and his fellow prisoners had made out of dried bread. He said that in Solovki you get the best company in the Soviet Union, so many cultivated men have been sent there. But there is little to do, little contact with the world outside, and the monotony is dreadful.

At the Poles' National Day I had a long talk with a Mrs Radlov, an artist and the wife of a well-known caricaturist, whom I first met at the German Consulate. She has read a good deal of English literature—like all Russians, she has read too much Byron and Wilde and too little

---

[10] Robert Boothby (1900–1986), Conservative MP for East Aberdeenshire from 1924 to 1958 before being made a life peer.

☆

Keats, but it is something to talk to a woman who has read anything. I offered to lend her Ethyl Colburn Wayne's book on Byron, but she did not dare either to come for it or to let me send it to her house. I found that Mrs Radlov was the painter of the portrait of Larissa Reisner, one of the heroines of the Revolution, that I had seen reproduced in the press a few days before. The portrait is considered a remarkably good likeness considering she never saw her subject. She obtained all the photographs she could, studied the woman's character from records and people who knew her, and finally painted the picture without looking at the photos.

Mrs Diedrichs came to give me my lesson looking like death. She had been told to report to the OGPU on the 7th. To give her a bone to throw to them I told her that I should probably be leaving soon. She was very grateful for the piece of exclusive information that Weinstein doesn't know and she thought this might win her a reprieve. She said she would take with her a little packet with soap, towel and a change of clothing in case she should be detained.

According to the *Listener* of 2 May, Professor H. Levy said in a wireless debate with Sir H. Samuel,[11] 'The Soviet system is the exact opposite of the fascist state.' The motive power of the Soviet system is exactly the same as that of the fascist, viz. a self-elected dictatorship. Indeed, one always supposes that Mussolini learned the trick from Soviet Russia. The elections by the workers' and peasants' councils are a farce, and the people 'elected' are not the leaders. Only one party is allowed to exist, and it draws up the list of candidates to be elected *en bloc*. When the people chosen by a series of indirect elections get to Moscow, all they do is to approve what is put before them from Party sources. No bill has ever been amended or even subjected to criticism by the Council of Soviets, and no speech that was not obviously a set speech has ever been made. No, I am wrong. It is recorded that a member from the Crimea was once so unguarded as to say, truthfully, that his constituency was starving. The Party at once flung him out of the Council. These people can hardly be called leaders. The leaders are the top men in the Communist Party, which is a self-selected body. They are personified by Stalin, whose power is not less obvious because he calls himself Secretary of the Politburo. Stalin and the other members of

[11] Professor Hyman Levy (1889–1975), professor of mathematics at the Royal College of Science. He worked as a publicist for the Communist Party until his expulsion in 1958 after reporting unfavourably on the treatment of Jews in Russia. Herbert Louis Samuel (1870–1963), Liberal politician, was twice home secretary (1916 and 1931–32) and also high commissioner for Palestine (1920–25).

☆

the Party junta do exactly as they please. Let them, by all means: it is their country; but don't let us pretend that these leaders are elected. I notice that the tendency to praise Soviet Russia, or to avoid criticism of it, is strongest among the 'advanced' 'intellectuals'. Mr D.N. Pritt KC, who was so hostile to Germany during the Reichstag trial,[12] even thinks Soviet courts better than ours.

I have ceased to expect Jews to criticise anything done in Soviet Russia. I understand their point of view. The Russian Jew was bottom-dog before the Revolution, and now he is a member of the ruling class, with the diplomatic service, foreign trade, journalism and propaganda largely in his hands. But it is disturbing to see false statements made on so important a point by a man like Levy when he is in charge of an important series of debates for the BBC. The trade unions, perhaps because they deal with men and not with books, have openly stated that they object to dictatorships of the left as well as of the right.

I think that Russia has turned the corner now. The lowest point was just at the end of 1932, when the Five-Year Plan came to an end, and during the following few months. There was almost a panic when more than five million people died of starvation in the main grain-producing areas and the end of the Plan brought, not prosperity, but fierce cuts in piece and time rates (most people lost about a third of their pay), a decree providing that if you lost your job you also lost your food-card and your accommodation, and the new passport decree under which many thousands of people were turned out of the principal towns by the OGPU. The authorities seemed to have received a healthy scare and they are now going much more slowly. More attention has been paid to consumer goods in 1933 than in any year since the Revolution and the result is already evident. Another thing that has made life more tolerable is the obligation the Soviet are under to spend in specified foreign countries a proportion of the proceeds of sales to those countries. I don't see why the Soviet Government should not now become steadily more prosperous. This being so it becomes even more necessary than it was to realise how the success—economic success—has been obtained. G.D.H. Cole and his like seem to imply that what Soviet Russia can do England could do. This is to disregard first of all the point I have laboured above—that the country is run by a self-appointed dictatorship which is absolutely ruthless in its methods. It also disregards the fact that Russia

---

[12] D.N. Pritt (1887–1972), fellow-travelling Labour MP who was expelled from the party in 1940. The conclusions from his enquiry into the Reichstag fire—that it had been engineered by the Nazis—subsequently gained widespread support.

is a large country with a relatively small population which can expand for many years and still live on its own rich resources.

10 May. Tearle has been sent out by Metro-Vickers for a month or two. He is stationed in Moscow, but he has been here for a few days, to see over the works where the turbines are made. He finds that now that the hysterical haste of the first Plan has been abandoned, better work is being done.

Tearle says that Thornton has written a book about his life in Russia and the trial and that it is very good. He had given no hostages to fortune. The form of pressure was just to wear him out. One statement they wanted him to sign he says he wrote out in twenty-nine different forms, and even now he can't say whether the one brought up against him at the trial was the one he signed, or one pieced together from several others. Tearle fears that Thornton's book will not be published, because the firm want the matter to be forgotten, for business reasons.[13]

Mrs Diedrichs was summoned to meet her OGPU contact in a public garden near the writers' home where she lives. He was annoyed that she had not written down our 'characteristics', and said that it was a gross breach of discipline. It would be the worse for her, he said, and for those near to her. The OGPU could persecute her through Galitzin, or they could arrest her former husband or her mother. There is no limit to what they are prepared to do.

12 May. Writing from Moscow, Paton says: 'I hear that you are going to Rabat.' He doesn't say where the news came from and I still have no news other than that.

In spite of the militant atheism taught by the Government, people are very superstitious, and the bursting of the air balloons at the demonstration and the reappearance of the angel have been hailed as a 'miracle'. Two days ago a high wind arose and made it impossible to keep in place the huge portrait of Stalin that had been hung over the front of the Kazan Cathedral. The portrait was removed, and now they have taken away the model too. I am glad to see the garden again.

The head of the OGPU is dead. The reports do not mention the cause of death, as they usually do. His predecessor shot himself. Perhaps

[13] Thornton's and Monkhouse's accounts are referred to in Nikolai Petrovich Vitvitskii's book *The Moscow Trial* (ed. W.P. Coates: Anglo-Russian Parliamentary Committee, 1933), but Thornton's was never published. Allan Monkhouse's account appears in his book *Moscow 1911–1933* (Gollancz, 1933).

☆

he committed suicide like Stalin's wife, or was murdered. He deserved to be murdered.[14]

Waldhauer came to dinner on the 10th. He is as much afraid as ever that there are microphones concealed in my rooms, and he was alarmed because of the visit of an Englishwoman, a Miss Hilda Harrison, who brought a letter of introduction from Professor Beazley. She asked him all sorts of questions about living conditions here. Naturally he gave her such answers as he would not mind having attributed to him in public. Waldhauer told me his little girl of ten is being educated privately. He could never send his daughter to a Soviet school: he did not want her to be a mother at fourteen. He gave me the names of five of the leading men from the Russian Art Gallery and the Ethnographical Museum who have been exiled for ten years. All five are accused of counter-revolution. Waldhauer is in favour and his scheme for the organisation of museums, which in 1926 was considered reactionary, is now accepted in full.

Waldhauer says that Jews are no longer in such high favour as they were. Georgians and Armenians are coming to the front. Never Russians! Russians are extremely intelligent, but seem to lack will power or some such quality.

One defect of the system here is that people tend to be herded together within their professions. Clubs, rest-homes and even living-quarters are allotted by trades or professions. Mrs Diedrichs lives in a writers' home and the writers can all have their main meal at the writers' dining-room. A scheme for a rest-home for writers has now been published where they can all meet during their holidays.

Two interesting people have been in this week, a Quaker doctor named Jenkins with an ex-captain in the merchant service called Graham. Jenkins had lived with a Russian family in Riga and learnt the language. He is here with a party from Birmingham and has been looking at housing conditions and judicial procedure and so on.

At a court they visited one judge told him that if the prisoner in a case which he had just witnessed had been an ex-'White Guard', he would have got six months instead of one. Jenkins asked whether this wasn't unjust, but the judge said that it was necessary, and that anyhow it was exactly like 'justice' in capitalist countries, where there was one law for the rich and another for the poor. The rest of his party were mostly communists who hailed the most ordinary things in Russia as 'marvels', and evidently knew little about their own country. The only

[14] Vyacheslav Menzhinsky had probably been poisoned on Stalin's orders. (See Edvard Radzinsky, *Stalin*: Hodder and Stoughton, 1996.)

☆

exception was a public-schoolboy of about eighteen who interrupted the guide at the anti-religious museum to say that he found her propaganda disgusting and with her permission he would go and see something else until she had finished.

15 May. Freshfield, the British railway-guard whom Mrs Kulagin managed to arrange a place for in a sanatorium, invited Miss Daunt and me to visit the place and have dinner. The usual Russian dinner-hour is 3.00, but when we arrived we found they had expected us at 11.00. The sanatorium consists of two buildings in a huge park—a lovely place. The rules require that nearly all the inmates should be 'workers', so that you have to go by employment (and social origin) and not by need. The doctor in charge is a youngish man who earlier commanded a Red detachment during the Civil War. He is something like Gogol, and tries to emphasise the likeness by having an enormous bang of hair hanging down to the level of his left ear. His wife, formerly a village schoolteacher, seemed pleased to have foreign visitors. But neither of them showed the slightest interest in asking about England, or our families or our past lives. I should think that personally he is very good with the patients. His wife chattered away about the Crimea saying how much pleasanter it was there, although you could get very little in the shops in comparison with Leningrad. She put up a good spread of sandwiches and cakes from the hospital kitchen. The cakes were a kind of shortcake. We liked them, and she said they were very easy to make: all you need is a kilo of flour, half a kilo of butter and half a kilo of sugar. Knowing that all these ingredients are things the ordinary person cannot get, Miss Daunt and I were amused. It is right that the consumptive patients should be well-fed, but a communist woman should have more sense than to talk airily about getting 'deficit' ingredients for making cakes.

17 May. Yesterday I received a letter from Scott: 'We have now held our promotions board meeting. Edmonds is to go to Strasbourg and you are to succeed him at Rabat. I only hope that he will be so happy there that you will not regret not going there. An official despatch will reach you shortly. You are being succeeded by Gilliat-Smith from Sarajevo.' I have been trying to send a telegram to Gilliat-Smith, but the telegraph office say there is no such place, and the central telegraph office confirm their denial. I had to telephone to the director-general of telegraphs before I could get the telegram accepted.

Rabat ought to suit me pretty well, except that it is on the wrong side

☆

of the Bay of Biscay.

Now that I know I am going, I begin to be glad that I am going to say goodbye to the dishonesty, greed and hypocrisy here. These qualities exist in all countries, but this is the only country I have struck where they are shamelessly practised by the Government and no one can criticise it or check it. Miss Goyer was with some Russians talking about the factory laws here—for protecting workmen from dangerous machinery, as though it was a Soviet idea. Nothing would make them believe that we had factory inspectors who could enforce the law. Miss Goyer is going back to England in the autumn. She also says she feels relief at going for good. The unhelpfulness of her fellow workers in the labs had been a great disappointment after working in England and America and Vienna. If one of them breaks a piece of apparatus, for instance, not only will he not own up but he will try to throw the blame on someone else.

Joseph, the antiques man, is back. His girlfriend has not yet been given a passport, but she says that two OGPU men came from Moscow to see her, and to ask her to work for them if she is allowed to go abroad. She is to throw Joseph over when she reaches London and mix with Russians who have relatives here so as to find out about the latter for the information of the OGPU.

I have begun to work at Moroccan Arabic. It differs less than I had expected from the colloquial Arabic I know, but as usual it is the little, common words which are different. I must learn the fifth way of saying 'my' that I have had to learn.

Graham told me that an English boring-machine was purchased for work in construction of the Moscow underground. This was taken to pieces and an exact replica made. I passed this on to Paton. He said he had not heard about the boring-machine, but the English firm that hopes to supply the escalators for the metro is under no misapprehensions about the possibility that they will copy it, and have told the authority concerned that the price for one or twelve escalators is the same.

22 May. On 10 May, for the first time for eighteen months, figures for the population of Leningrad were published in the press: men 1,302,200; women 1,406,200. Over 200,000 less than there were last time. It is still almost impossible to get a room except by exchange.

On Sunday afternoon I suddenly received two tickets from Intourist for a concert that evening. I went with Miss Goyer. The conductor was a Greek named Mitropoulos but the star turn was a Polish woman: Eva

Bandrovska. I have never heard anything approaching her singing. The concert was a tremendous *Judenabend*. To my eyes it looked as if almost all the performers, the audience and the Intourist guides were Jewish. I think that the Jews have a monopoly of Soviet music.

Mrs Kulagin managed to get an appeal through to someone of importance in Moscow, and about ten days later she was called up by the local OGPU and told that her husband's case was to be reopened, and that he was in any case to be transferred to a place where he could work and show whether he was a shock-worker or not. He should meet that test very well, for he is a glutton for work, and capable as well. I hope the poor woman will get her husband back soon. She is very hard-up and is selling her furniture.

24 May. Edmonds writes from Rabat. He asks whether I would like to buy any of his furniture or his car. I've told him that in principle I want everything. I have no furniture except a camp-bed and a reading-stand. I am refusing the offer of a sailing-boat.

Joseph has secured a passport (by paying about £100), which will enable him to take his 'interpreter' abroad. I should much like to know what induced the OGPU to let one of their agents leave: Joseph's money, or the fact that he is a good customer for their antiques, or the fact that he is a Jew, or the hope the girl will serve them as a spy abroad.

27 May. Sunday. Lord and Lady Chilston and one of their two sons are coming here on the 2nd. Lord Chilston has to return to Moscow the following night, but the rest of the party will stay another day. It will be a scramble as Lady Chilston and her son will overlap Pott and his uncle by a few hours, and the beds and bedrooms will have to be arranged late at night.

A few days ago Miss Daunt received a circular from the transport department of the Leningrad Soviet, saying that they would need her car in good order at a given date for use by the large number of tourists expected this summer. The car is in Lady Muriel's name and the authorities had forgotten it belongs to a charitable society. I took it to Weinstein and said I supposed Miss Daunt need not comply with the order. He was annoyed that we had seen the circular I think.

Miss Harley, who was here two years ago, has just paid another visit of two months studying Georgian art. She tells me that of five hundred tourists in Moscow on 1 May who wanted to see the procession, only seventy were given seats. The only place you can see the procession is the Red Square, if you aren't there you might as well be in London. The tourists had had the May Day demonstration held out to them as one of the attractions. By sheer persistence Miss Harley and her friend secured tickets. Many who did not were sympathisers and were therefore all the more annoyed. One old Englishwoman was very distraught and said to Miss Harley: 'I never saw such a bloody country.' That evening she apologised for having let herself go and explained that she was a communist and had paid what was for her a very large sum to come to Russia, and then paid for another week to be here for 1 May. While the demonstration was on she was practically shut up in the hotel. The guide in charge collected the people on her list of seventy and marched them to the square, checking them three times on the way. At the third and last check it was found that there were seventy-one tourists. The guide was so paralysed with fear she could not even speak. The police just turned back the unfortunate man at the tail of the queue who was an American communist. Intourist in London of course are partly responsible, since they book as many people as the Soviet steamers can carry.

I had a very interesting man to lunch today, an ICS man called Ramamurty from the Indian Department of Agriculture. He was much interested in the agricultural methods here and a bit envious at the scale on which a country can work when one man in Moscow can initiate a policy for the whole country and see that it is carried out. The well-known Soviet economic botanist Vavilov has 800 experimental stations, each of about 100 acres in different parts of the country. There seems to be one original research project being carried out here, it is called 'vernalism'—making a false spring, so to say. You take wheat of a kind which doesn't fit the local season, and keep it at a temperature which makes it think the autumn has come. It then germinates and after so many days it can be sown in the ordinary way.

Some other things the Soviet people boast about—sowing in wet ground from aeroplanes—he considers pure stunts and of no practical value. He was much interested in artificial insemination. He told me that a Soviet scientist, Ivanov, now dead, had tried to fertilise a woman from a gorilla by artificial insemination, though without a positive result. Ramamurty is to see tomorrow the photographs of some Soviet sheep which are alleged to be the product of an experiment to increase the weight of the Soviet sheep by crossing it with a heavy ram from Tibet, but since the rams did not breed in captivity, the essential parts were flown in by aeroplane, and a number of sheep fertilised artificially. He was an able and a likeable man and I was sorry that he could only stay an hour or so.

☆

1 June. Just been to the hospital to see a fireman from a British vessel who has been there several days with three broken ribs. A very decent Scot, nearly sixty, almost alone in the world, was unemployed all the winter and meets with this trouble the first time he gets a job. I saw the written statement he gave the captain in which he stated that he had been assaulted by a drunken donkeyman and some firemen. All I could do was to give the man some cigarettes and chocolate and promise to try to find some newspapers for him.

A notice in the paper says that the grain crops in southern Russia are poor because of drought, so the price of bread will be raised. The same notice announces increases in pay for the lower-paid workers in certain industries to meet the increased cost of bread. How benevolent, the Soviet enthusiasts will exclaim. I would also applaud had I not seen the price of bread raised 70–100% last August without any obvious cause, without any public admission of the increase, and without any increase in pay for anybody.

A woman of about sixty came into the office this week. She was born in England of an English mother and a Russian father and speaks perfect English. She married a member of the Rimsky-Korsakov family and earns her living by teaching English and music in a small provincial town a few hours away. She wanted to know whether she could recover her British nationality, or alternatively how she could get to England or to Germany in both of which countries she has relatives. She considers herself rather well off because she gets a better ration than second category: 2 lbs of black bread a day and 1 lb of sugar a month. I gave her a 2 lb packet of lump sugar (English) and she nearly wept.

5 June. No wonder the newspapers merely said that the price of bread was to be raised, without saying by how much. From 1 June the price of all bread is *doubled*. Mrs Morton told Miss Daunt that, at a factory meeting called to approve the new decree, many refused to go, and those who did complained about the rise in the price of bread. They were scolded by the Party leaders and told that they must observe discipline. They replied that they would observe discipline when they got bread. But these insubordinate people were women, who are always more courageous than the men. There is no public sign that anyone objects to paying twice as much for bread.

Had the Chilstons here for the weekend. They had three fine days in the middle of some wet ones and they made the most of it. They were easy to please.

Scott sends the encouraging news that the days I take to get my kit

★

together in England will not be deducted from my proper leave.

Pott has returned from leave bringing with him his uncle who has been employed by Lever Bros in the Belgian Congo. It is interesting to hear his stories of business life. When I hear such tales I always feel grateful that I secured a safe job when I was young—and I am a bit anxious about the boys. I do not think it will be easier for them to get jobs when they are twenty-one than it is now, and it is difficult enough now.

I described some time ago the little room in which our excellent messenger lives with his wife and child. There will be a second child soon, and life in that room would be dreadful. I happened to hear of a man who had a big room which he was leaving because he had been given a job in Moscow. In theory he and Stevens exchange rooms. Stevens takes the big one, the other man takes the small one but gives it up on removal to Moscow. And for the advantage he gets, Stevens gives the other man a thousand roubles. We advance the money to Stevens and he repays the loan in instalments out of his salary. So money still talks.

I met a Russian named Burov at Miss Daunt's who claims to be the inventor of the Soviet machine which tears up the ground, melts the torn up material in a furnace and spreads the molten stuff behind it to form a new road surface. He says the machine has its own unit for generating a current of 7200 kilowatts of electricity. Burov is apparently a favourite because of the various bits of machinery he has designed. I saw in a newspaper that he was credited with 1300 inventions. He was introduced to Miss Daunt by Mrs Lie. She says he has papers which allow him to go where he likes, take what he likes and do what he likes, without being even questioned, much less stopped. There is a petrol shortage and neither Mrs Lie nor Miss Daunt could get any, but he got 500 litres for each of them in a moment and offered to get them any further quantity they wanted. I liked him. He is a workmanlike kind of man. He has had no proper education and has had to pick up his engineering knowledge, but his claim to be an inventor seems to be genuine.

Waldhauer came round the other day and borrowed 50 roubles to last him until he drew his small pension the next day. He rarely gets his pension or his salary at the proper time. Of the reward of 5000 roubles voted to him last autumn he has so far received only about 250 roubles. The poor old professor enjoyed showing the Scythian gold to the Chilstons. He had put on an old black morning coat in which he looked less pitiful than he does in the old sports coat I gave him. I went too and saw the Scythian gold for perhaps the eighth time.

☆

7 June. The Russian inventor was at Miss Daunt's last night before returning to Moscow. I came home at 3.15 a.m. having been taught to foxtrot! Mrs Lie came in with a sister in law, and the scientist Dr Emmé was there, and everybody danced and I was made to dance too. The foxtrot seems very easy—much easier than the old waltz, which is now in fashion again. Mrs Lie brought with her a Russian—formerly a sailor, now a playwright—and he sang songs, and Mrs Lie sang and the Russians all sang together. By 8.00 this morning I was ready to get up and not a bit tired.

From a report to HM Ambassador in Moscow, 18 June. The notes transmitted herewith are submitted rather to round off my work here, now that I am being transferred, than because there is anything fresh or interesting to report. The difficulty the foreigner experiences in coming to any conclusion about the Soviet Union is well-known. All that one can do is to catch an occasional glimpse of the reality through the smoke-screen of suppression of the truth. However, I have formed rough conclusions on several points, and although they do not differ greatly from those held by many foreign officials working in this country, they may be recorded for what they are worth.

1. Soviet Russia is a far more favourable field for the Soviet experiment than the highly industrialised State in which Marx supposed that the change would most naturally come about. Indeed, it is the most favourable field in the world, since: (a) it is in the main an agricultural country producing, even with primitive methods, a surplus of food. The capacity for agricultural production cannot be destroyed by a revolutionary upheaval. (b) Soviet Russia has unequalled natural resources, and the few things she needs to import can be obtained in exchange for foodstuffs and raw materials which other countries require urgently. Her industrial products, however poor the quality, can be disposed of in the protected home market. (c) A dictatorship requires ruthlessness in the governing class and a subservient population. These Soviet Russia possesses in perfection.

2. The industrial workers, who form an increasing proportion of the population, are on the whole a good deal better-off than before the Revolution, for if their wages buy them little more than the bare necessities, they now receive benefits in the matter of education, sport, medical services, social services and amusements. This estimate neglects such imponderables as the existence before the Revolution of a Church which at least served as the channel for the transmission of an ideal which has for centuries been a valuable corrective to the doctrine that

★

the State is always right.

3. It seems probable that nothing but an unsuccessful war could seriously disturb the Soviet regime; and even then the regime would probably recover for lack of any serious alternative. The size of the country, the variety of races, and the long subjection of the people to autocratic rulers, render the Soviet Union particularly suitable for a despotic form of government, and if it comes to a choice between dictatorships, the Bolshevik dictatorship will win, being complete in theory and highly organised. The Party is the essential skeleton of the State, and its doctrine provides answers to every problem in politics, economics, religion and morals. There is no organised opposition, nor can there be any, and such dissatisfaction as there is could be almost entirely allayed by a slight increase in material comfort. The Soviet authorities have applied with good effect the principle of Polycrates, that people appreciate a little relief after a period of repression more highly than conditions in which there is no repression.

An improvement in industry has followed the slowing-down of the State plans, and, while that may be due in part to the increasing skill of the workers, it is probably due mainly to the fact that there is not the inducement there was to declare a given job done by an impossible date and to scamp the work for the purpose. During the last six or nine months the Leningrad newspapers have said much less about failure to fulfil the Plan and about the proportion of throw-outs to sound work, and although during the first quarter of 1934 the heavy industries of Leningrad completed only 59% of the quarterly plan, there was much less fuss about this than there would have been two years ago over a 10% deficit. Provided that the quantity of goods continues to increase, the Soviet buyer will probably not complain too bitterly about the quality.

On Soviet agriculture, it seems incredible that even collectivised agriculture should not be at least as productive as the uneconomic methods in force in Russia before the Revolution. I continue to think that the worst was over when the authorities decreed that industry must no longer be a parasite on agriculture and began to make concessions to the farming population at the expense of the urban workers.

Mr Bernard Shaw has expressed admiration for the Soviet method of progress by trial and error. One might retort that, whereas the errors are committed by the Soviet Government, the trials have to be borne by the people. It must be admitted that the authorities allow nothing to prevent their changing a policy which does not work, and that during the last three or four years they have made Soviet industry more businesslike than it was. Just as by the *khozraschot* system they made

☆

industry independent financially, so that the less competent could no longer cover their deficits from the others, so the policy of 1931, which reintroduced the principle of payment by results, has put pressure upon the worker. During a period of less than two years the worker was reduced to complete dependence upon the will of his employers. His piece-work rates were cut repeatedly. He has to work hard to earn the standard wage. He has even lost the remedy he formerly had, when he could leave one factory to seek better conditions in another. Loss of work means loss of one's food-card; moreover, nearly all the living accommodation now being built seems to consist of 'tied' quarters for workers in particular factories. The last shred of independence went when the functions of the Commissariat of Labour were handed over to the trade unions. At the meeting of the Plenum of the All-Union Council of Trade Unions in 1933, speakers referred to the defeat of the right opportunists, who had tried 'to set the so-called protective functions of the trade unions against their productive tasks', i.e. to ask that the needs of the human being and not a theoretical plan should be taken as the basis of calculation. Wages are insufficient to meet the increase in the price of rationed bread.

I place first among the benefits secured by industrial workers the reduction of the hours of work. There are great masses of factory workers who really do work an eight-hour day, with an hour off for rest and a meal. The boasted holidays on full pay do not stand examination so well, since the average worker has a formidable list of free days when he has to work without pay, either on the factory farm or on some work declared to be of State or municipal importance.

Supplies of food, which were plentiful at the end of the NEP, became more and more scarce as the first Plan proceeded. Apart from the general trend, better food conditions have been created for certain classes of the population during the last two or three years. Professions formerly neglected receive privileged ration-cards and have co-operatives and dining-rooms which are very well supplied. The great extension of the communal dining-room system means that a growing proportion of the urban workers, students and school children receive at least one meal a day which is not restricted to bread and a substitute for tea. Finally, the State shops are an alleviation of conditions to many, and now seem to have become a regular part of the Soviet economy, enabling people to buy butter etc. for which they were formerly dependent on the expensive private market. For the first time for many years, oranges and lemons have been seen recently in the Leningrad shops.

The supply of consumption goods is certainly greater here than it was

☆

a year ago—still more so than in Moscow three years ago. Crockery and other articles of domestic use can be bought; many tolerably good suits and dresses can be seen; Soviet athletes manage to obtain sports clothes. But the height of triumph has been reached by the sale of wallpaper, and by the presence of toilet-soap (of a kind) in the shops.

From a report to HM Ambassador in Moscow, 3 July. The temptation for the Soviet citizen to believe the worst of conditions in other countries, and to be the more content with those in his own, is very great. He probably finds some satisfaction in conditions which our people would think intolerable. A prominent organiser of 'mass feeding'—a process which suggests burnt gruel eaten with an iron spoon—speaks of it with a look of ecstasy such as we might expect to see on the face of Mr Belloc at the prospect of drinking home-brewed beer in a non-tied house with Sussex men holding the correct views on the Distributive State. Once it is understood that to march in a tiring procession twice a year is part of your work it is at least possible to find pleasure in the military show, in the expression of chauvinistic instincts, and in the feeling of being one of a great army. The average worker knows better than to criticise or disobey the party or the GPU, but in everything else he is encouraged to think himself the salt of the earth.

To us the immense Palace of the Soviets, which it is proposed to erect in Moscow, seems to be an unnecessarily large box to keep a rubber stamp in; but the rank-and-file member of the Congress of Soviets, who has no Magna Charta or Habeas Corpus Act or Tolpuddle to look back upon, probably thinks the mass-meeting of yes-men in which he takes part useful as well as inspiring.

The Russian is full of conceit, but without pride, and the sycophancy and moral cowardice which the present regime call for require no effort on his part. The counterpart of this is the lust for power and adulation, which Stalin now appears to experience in increasing measure. 'He were no lion, were not Russians hinds.' The fading away of the State which is to herald the dawn of true communism is not so near that it need to be insured against. It would seem to be inevitable that the control by the dictatorship should become even closer. It takes a great soul to enjoy uncontrolled power without wanting to retain it. The machine of administration will become more and more complicated as industry develops and collectivisation in agriculture extends to the remoter corners of the Union, and will demand closer control. Finally the kind of mind that revolts against mental and moral tyranny must tend to disappear.

☆

If the Soviet citizen does not always act as a bundle of conditioned reflexes it is not the fault of the authorities. How far-reaching the use of the appropriate stimuli can be is revealed in Soviet propaganda, and it is particularly well illustrated by the following incident. After the spring thaw the public parks in Leningrad, which are beautiful and very popular, are kept closed for about a fortnight so that the water may drain away and the paths may harden, and by then it is usually about 1 May and the parks can be opened for Labour Day. This year the thaw was extraordinarily early and the parks were quite fit for use a fortnight earlier than usual, but they remained closed until 1 May nevertheless. The Soviet citizen, who experienced a feeling of pleasure at the prospect of the opening of the parks in the middle of April, thus received a check such as is administered to one of the dogs in Pavlov's laboratory when the saliva begins to form at the wrong signal and the door behind which the food is concealed remains closed. Another time he will, perhaps, remember to associate the opening of the parks with 1 May and not with the weather. Or will he be refractory to the elaborate mental treatment to which he is subjected? At present the odds seem to be in favour of his rulers.

I have, etc.

R.W. BULLARD

EPILOGUE

Reader Bullard left Leningrad in July 1934, to enthusiastic tributes from his colleagues and superiors. Lord Chilston described Bullard's last reports to London as 'witness to the zeal and efficiency with which he has carried out his duties as an observer of the working of the Soviet system and of the Russian manner of life.' Sir Robert Vansittart, permanent under-secretary at the Foreign Office, wrote:

> I am very sorry that your time in Russia is coming to an end (I have no doubt you are glad), for I have always been one of your regular readers and have always looked forward to this part of my reading.
>
> I hope you will enjoy your new post and have the successful career which you deserve. I think you will always be a happy man, for I feel from your writing that you must enjoy your own mind—as indeed you ought to enjoy it.

Sir Lancelot Oliphant, under-secretary at the Foreign Office, wrote to Reader Bullard to praise his despatches as 'real oases in the drab Desert of Print'; and he enclosed a despatch from the foreign secretary, Sir John Simon:

> I desire to take this opportunity to place on record my deep appreciation of Mr Bullard's reports, which have—like all his work—been of a consistently high order throughout his term of service in Russia and which I and my colleagues have never failed to read with great interest.

Bullard's method of handling such letters, as he described earlier, was to put them into a large envelope marked 'Butter' or sometimes 'Best butter'. He wondered later whether he had been wise to ask to be left out of the short-list for the post of consul general/ambassador in Iraq, on the grounds that as a former military governor of Baghdad (in 1919), his appointment 'might be made a ground of criticism if the Baghdad politicians wanted at any time to embarrass HMG.' However, he concluded that 'Jeddah should suit me better than Baghdad.'

Soon after Reader Bullard's departure, Mary Lucy Dorothea O'Neill Daunt ('Dot' to her family and friends, but evidently not to the Consul General) also left Leningrad, and shortly afterwards was operated on for appendicitis, possibly the reason for her attacks of ill-health. She moved to south-west Cork, Ireland, after inheriting Kilcascan Castle, a country house in a sad state of repair which had been in her family for six generations and which she valiantly tried to keep habitable. Her great-nephew, Sir Timothy Daunt, remembers the rows of buckets and chamber-pots to catch the drips from the roof. She died there on 1 March 1975.

In September 1934 the USSR joined the League of Nations, symbolically underlining Moscow's desire for international stability; but on 1 December 1934 Sergei Kirov was assassinated at Leningrad Party Headquarters by a young communist, Nikolayev, probably with Stalin's connivance. The murder was to be the pretext for the launching of the Great Purge, inaugurating the period of the Terror, when an estimated five million people were killed. The trials of Zinoviev, Kamenev, Radek, Pyatakov, Bukharin, Rykov, Krestinsky and Yagoda followed close on each other, and in most cases confession was followed by execution.

Miss Daunt's admirer, Pyotr Andreyevich Kulagin, who had been born in 1898 in Rostov-on-Don, was sentenced to death on 14 October 1937 by the three-man commission who were then running the NKVD in the Leningrad district, on a charge of counter-revolutionary activity. He was posthumously rehabilitated on 4 August 1989.

On 11 January 1938 the British ambassador in Moscow was told that Leningrad was to be a naval port and that the British consulate and the Paget Mission must close. K.G. Rokowsky, Soviet ambassador in London from 1924 to 1925, denounced Lady Muriel as a spy, a charge rebutted in Parliament by Neville Chamberlain. Lord Halifax recommended her for the CBE for services to British interests in Russia: but on 16 July, before the honour could be conveyed, Lady Muriel died. A memorial service for her was held in Westminster Abbey.

After two years as Consul General in Rabat, Bullard was posted as minister in Jeddah and given a knighthood. In 1939 he was appointed ambassador to Tehran where it fell to him to make the arrangements for the historic 1943 Tehran conference between Churchill, Roosevelt and Stalin. At a dinner in the ambassador's residence to celebrate Churchill's sixty-ninth birthday, Bullard found himself seated between Molotov and Marshal Voroshilov and opposite Stalin. 'I was particularly pleased to see Stalin at close quarters,' Bullard recorded. 'He looks like a benevolent church-warden, and talks in a slow, soft voice.'

Afterwards Churchill suggested erecting a silver plaque to mark the occasion, and the following inscription was chosen: 'To the fulfilment of this purpose they here pledged themselves anew to devote their unceasing efforts, trusting for success to the toil, endurance and valour of the Allied peoples: CRESCIT SUB PONDERE VIRTUS.'[1] Churchill also told Bullard that he intended to put his name before the King for a KCB, to which Bullard replied: 'Oh, you want to stick a plaque on me as well as in the dining-room!'

Reader Bullard met Stalin on one subsequent occasion. While accompanying the British foreign secretary Ernest Bevin to a conference in Moscow in December 1945, he was greeted by Stalin with a smile and the words '*Stariy drug*' ('Old friend'). He would have been seriously worried if he had thought Stalin meant this as a compliment. A more accurate pronouncement was made later by Winston Churchill, when he described his ambassador as 'a tough Briton, . . . with no illusions.'[2]

Sir Reader Bullard retired in 1946, and died in Oxford on 24 May 1976 at the age of ninety.

---

[1] 'Virtue grows under every weight' was the motto of the Earls of Denbigh.
[2] Winston Churchill, *The Second World War, vol. IV, The Hinge of Fate*: Cassell, 1951.

☆

GLOSSARY

AMO: Moscow Motor Company (renamed after Stalin in 1934)

ARCOS: Organisation for the Promotion of Anglo–Soviet Trade

bezprizorny: homeless child, stray

brak: defective product, reject

BS: British Subject

Burobin: Service Bureau for Foreigners (later UPDK)

Centrosoyuz: Central Trades Union Organisation

chistka: purge

CID: Criminal Investigation Department

CIE: Companion, Order of the Indian Empire

CMG: Companion, Order of St Michael and St George

Comintern: Communist International

Comsomoltsy/Komsomoltsy: Young Communist League members

dacha: cottage or villa in a rural area usually just outside a town

DBS: Distressed British Subject

DoT: Department of Trade

Drusag: German government agricultural concession operating in the North Caucasus in early 1930s. Closed in 1933 as a result of foreign workers there sending reports abroad on the famine

dvornik: caretaker, janitor

Exportlyes: Timber Export Organisation

FO: Foreign Office

Gigant: State farm used as a showplace for western visitors

GPU: *see* OGPU

HMG: His Majesty's Government

ICS: Indian Civil Service

Karelyes/Severlyes: Karelia Timber/ Northern Timber

kasha: buckwheat porridge

KC: King's Counsel

KCB: Knight Commander of the Bath

khozraschot: self-financing economic unit

kolkhoz: collective farm

kommandirovka: business trip

kopek: coin, one-hundredth of a rouble

kulak: 'rich peasant proprietor exploiting the labour of others' (official contemporary definition)

kvass: slightly alcoholic drink made from fermented bread

LCC: London County Council

lishentsy: disenfranchised person

MOPR: International Organisation for Aid to Fighters of the Revolution

Mostorg: Moscow Trading Organisation

nagruzka: load

Narkom: People's Commissar, i.e.

minister

Narkomindel: People's Commissariat for Foreign Affairs, i.e. the Soviet Foreign Ministry

NEP: New Economic Policy

NKVD: People's Commissariat for Internal Affairs

OGPU: United State Political Directorate (i.e. secret police) from 1922 to 1934; formerly the Cheka (1918–1922), and later known as the NKVD (1934–1946) and the KGB (from 1953)

paskha: sweet cream-cheese dish eaten at Easter

physkultur: physical culture, PT

PP: Public Prosecutor

proryv: hitch, breakdown, hold-up

Rabfak: Workers' Faculty

RWB: Reader William Bullard

Sovnarkom: Council of People's Commissars (the executive and administrative branch of the Soviet government)

Sovtorgflot: Soviet Merchant Marine

Spartakiad: athletic contest

ssylka: exile

Ssylkigorod: suburb of Murmansk where exiles were sent

TASS: Telegraph Agency of the Soviet Union

tekhnik: technician

tovarishchi (*tovs*): comrades

Torgsin: All-Union Association for Trade with Foreigners

TSIK: Central Executive Committee

Univermag: department store

valuta: foreign currency

verst: measurement of 1.06 kilometres

VOKS: All Union Society for Cultural Relations with Foreign Countries

vozmozhnost: possibility

Vsoaviakhim: Society for Co-Operation in Defence and in Aviation and Chemical Development of USSR. Created 1927 to supervise military training of civilians

Zhakht/Zhilotdyel: housing department of local council.

☆

DIPLOMATIC AND CONSULAR STAFF

HM Embassy, Moscow

OVEY, SIR ESMOND (1879–1963): ambassador until 1933. He had previously served in Tehran, Rome and Mexico, and later became ambassador to Belgium and Argentina. Lady Ovey was his second wife.

CHILSTON, VISCOUNT (1876–1947): ambassador from 1933 to 1938.

STRANG, WILLIAM (1893–1978): head of Chancery and political counsellor. He served in the Foreign Office 1933–1950, retiring as permanent under-secretary of state for foreign affairs. He was given a peerage in 1954. (See his *Home and Abroad*: Andre Deutsch, 1956.)

CHARLES, N.H.H. (1892–1975): acting counsellor from 1933. After postings in Brussels, Lisbon, Rio and Rome, he was appointed ambassador to Ankara.

PATON, G.P.: commercial secretary. His final post was as consul general, Istanbul.

WALKER, E.A.: first secretary until 1933; served later in Athens, Stockholm, Ankara and at the Foreign Office.

COOTE, E.O.: first secretary from 1933; served later in Rio and Sofia.

GREENWAY, J.D.: second secretary; served later in Bucharest, China, Budapest and Tehran.

VYVYAN, J.M.K. (1907–1992): third secretary (from 1932). After serving at the Foreign Office and in Washington, he resigned in 1938 in protest against HMG's appeasement of Stalin. He was elected a fellow of Trinity College, Cambridge.

SIMMONDS, S.: commercial secretary; later consul in Hamburg, Tehran, Moscow, Athens and Rome, before becoming consul general in Copenhagen.

POTT, L.: vice-consul and acting consul general. After consular posts in Ankara, Piraeus, Athens, Baghdad, Alexandria and Tabriz, he became deputy high commissioner in Bombay and finally consul general in

☆

Istanbul and Marseilles.

RAPP, T.C.: consul from 1933; later became consul general in Zagreb, Tabriz and Salonica, then finally minister and head of mission in Mexico.

BOSTOCK, H.V.: pro-consul from 1933; later held consular posts in Budapest, Algiers and Dusseldorf.

WALTON, W.G.: press reader. His appointment was terminated in 1934.

TAYLOR, M.E.: archivist.

VINCENT, G.W.: archivist.

BERGSON, MISS: Russian clerk.

BENNETT, ——— : Chancery servant.

SURKOV, ——— : messenger and second chauffeur.

HM Consulate General, Leningrad

KEANE, D.W.: consul in Leningrad until 1930. Transferred to Moscow, and later held various special appointments.

CAVE, A.J.: vice-consul, having previously served in Siberia (1918), Vladivostok (1919), Leningrad (1924) and Riga (1927). His appointment was terminated in 1934.

TODD, G.F.: probationary vice-consul; served later in consular posts in Damascus, Aleppo, Bushire, Ahwaz, Casablanca, Moscow and Wilmington. His final posting was as assistant to the press counsellor in Washington throughout the Second World War.

STEVENS, ——— : messenger.

Other diplomats

KNATCHBULL-HUGESSEN, SIR HUGHE (1886–1971): minister to the Baltic States; later minister in Tehran, and ambassador to Peking, Ankara and Brussels.

HODGSON, SIR ROBERT (1874–1976): chargé d'affaires in Moscow (1924). After being withdrawn on the suspension of relations with the USSR in June 1927, he became minister, consul general and head of mission in Durazzo (1928), retiring in 1936.

☆

INDEX

★

☆

★

☆

★

☆

☆

☆

★

☆

☆

☆

★

☆

☆

☆

☆

☆